This volume is part of the
AMERICAN CLASSICS
series

THE AMERICAN COLONIES
1492-1750

AMERICAN CLASSICS

THE
AMERICAN
COLONIES
1492-1750

*A Study of Their Political, Economic
and Social Development*

MARCUS WILSON JERNEGAN

With Maps

FREDERICK UNGAR PUBLISHING CO.
NEW YORK

First published 1929

Republished 1959

Printed in the United States of America

Library of Congress Catalog Card No. 58-59875

"No man is fit to be entrusted with the control of the *Present*, who is ignorant of the *Past*, and no *People*, who are indifferent to their *Past*, need hope to make their future great."

AUTHOR'S PREFACE

In recent years several single volume histories of the American Colonies have been published, but nearly all of them carry the story through the revolutionary period. This has tended to cut down the space given to the period before 1750.

Nevertheless historians of the American Revolution are now studying the earlier period, especially that from 1689 to 1763, with much more care than formerly. For it is now realized that the issues involved in the Revolution lie deep in the colonial thought and institutions of this period. At that time the colonists commenced to diverge rapidly from English thought and institutions. In this period, too, arose those forces which eventually led to the feeling of isolation and aloofness from the mother country; to the conception of the English government as something outside of, and even hostile to, the interests of the colonists; to a sense of, or desire for, self-sufficiency; and even in the case of a few leaders to a wish for a much larger measure of independence if not for complete separation — political, economic, and religious.

One main purpose of this book is to set forth those factors, forces, and events that produced a new colonial society, different from that of England; so different, by 1750, that the probability of agreement upon the extent of English political and economic control was much diminished. In developing this thought it has been necessary to omit many picturesque and interesting events often included in accounts of the colonies, especially details of political, military, and local history.

ix

On the other hand, much more space than usual has been given to economic changes and tendencies affecting the relations of the colonies to the Empire, to England, and to each other.

Besides the chapters describing the European background, conditions of English colonization, and the origin and political development of each colony, separate chapters discuss the economic and social development of each of the three sections previous to 1689. Five chapters on the significant period from 1689 to 1750 not only describe problems of internal development — land and labor systems, industries and occupations, trade and commerce, but also treat of the political and commercial policy of England towards the colonies; their political and constitutional development; the growth of population and immigration; and the French-English wars, with particular attention to frontier policies, westward expansion and sectionalism.

In the last chapter an analysis is made of the structure of colonial society, of religious and moral tendencies, and particularly of the intellectual development of the colonies, the transfer of English and European ideas; education, reading and cultural progress. Some of these topics are closely related to the growth of antagonism towards England and later to the Revolution and Independence.

The choice of topics and the emphasis upon them must be more or less a matter of personal interest. In comparison with other volumes on this period, much less space has been given to Spanish and French colonization, to the region west of the Alleghenies, to Canada and the outlying British possessions to the north and in the West Indies. This has been necessary in order to gain space for a more extended treatment than usual of the internal economic and social development of the colonies. The references to Chapters I, II, XIII and XIV give opportunity for adequate reading on these topics. In order that the reader may gain a knowledge of the varied interpretations of men and events, as set forth by writers on this period, the references to secondary and original sources for each chapter are more extensive than in any volume of similar scope yet published. This is particularly true of biography and original sources.

Acknowledgment is here made to those who have most aided the author in the preparation of this book. Professor Albert Bushnell Hart has given unfailing encouragement and valuable help throughout the preparation of the Volume. I am greatly indebted to Professor Charles M. Andrews for reading Chapters X and XI and for placing at my disposal his unrivalled knowledge of these topics. Others who have given aid on one or more chapters are: Dr. Conyers Read of Philadelphia, Professor Frederick C. Dietz of the University of Illinois, and my colleagues, Professors A. C. McLaughlin, A. O. Craven, A. P. Scott, Godfrey Davies, D. S. Whittlesey, H. C. Hill, and particularly Professor William T. Hutchinson, who has read the whole manuscript and made many helpful suggestions. My wife has helped in the preparation of the bibliographies, and in many other ways assisted in my work on this volume.

MARCUS WILSON JERNEGAN

SUGGESTIONS FOR TEACHERS, READERS AND STUDENTS

In a book of limited size and scope many interesting topics must be omitted and others greatly condensed. Other books are likely to present a different point of view from that given in this volume and perhaps will contain contrary conclusions. For both of these reasons, it is indispensable that teachers and students should indulge in extensive collateral readings. This practice gives the opportunity to weigh conflicting evidence for the purpose of arriving at the truth, one of the chief values to be obtained from the study of history.

Information on most of the important topics not treated in this volume may be obtained from the list of books given in Channing, Hart and Turner's *Guide* (title No. 7 of the " Brief List," below). An excellent single volume for parallel reading, including the bibliographies, is that by Evarts B. Greene, *Foundations of American Nationality* (title No. 11). This may be followed by Channing's first two volumes of his *History of the United States* (title No. 6) or by the first seven volumes of the *American Nation Series* (title No. 12). A comprehensive general account of the economic and social aspects of the period may be found in the *History of American Life Series* (title No. 15).

For interest and charm of style the best books are those in *The Chronicles of America Series* (title No. 27), and the various volumes by John Fiske (title No. 25), and those by Francis Parkman (title No. 30). **The** same comment applies to Charles A. and Mary Beard's *Rise of American Civilization* (title No. 20).

Advanced students may use the essays in Winsor's *Narrative and Critical History of America* (title No. 48); the seven volumes by Osgood (title No. 43); and the sectional histories by Bruce (title No. 21), Weeden (title No. 35), and Adams (title No. 18). Some of the books on special topics are of great importance, such as those on England's political and commercial policy by G. L. Beer (title No. 37), J. R. Seeley (title No. 45), and C. M. Andrews (title No. 19); and those on manufactures (titles 22, 33), and literature (titles 34, 44, 46). For illustrative and source material it is very desirable that access be had to maps (title 10), documents, and pictures (titles 4, 13, 14, 23, 29, 39, and 42).

Nowadays much emphasis is placed upon a study of original as well as secondary historical sources. For this reason effort has been made to indicate many of the former, not only in the library lists but in the references preceding each chapter, especially under "Contemporary Accounts." For the benefit of those students who may wish to undertake some original research, the following additional guides are listed. All bibliographies are limited by their closing date of publication. (1) In American history this defect is supplied by Grace Griffin (Ed.), *Writings on American History,* published *annually* from 1906. Each volume includes books, articles, and printed sources on all phases of American history. (2) The original and secondary material found in the proceedings and collections of historical societies is of great value. This will be found listed in A.P.C. Griffin (Ed.), "Bibliography of American Historical Societies," in *American Historical Association Report,* 1905, vol. II. This guide lists the contents of the important magazines, proceedings, and collections of historical societies from 1792 to 1905, and has an extensive subject index. It is continued by Grace Griffin (Ed.), *Writings on American History.* Consult also Channing, Hart and Turner's *Guide,* § 45 (title No. 7 of " Brief List " below). (3) Printed official documents (laws, colonial records, etc.) are listed for each colony in A. R. Hasse, " Materials for a Bibliography of the Archives of the Thirteen Original Colonies to 1789 " in *American Historical Association Report,* 1906, vol. II. (4) The important General Index to Papers in Annual Reports of the American Historical Association, 1884–1914, is printed in *American Historical Association Report,* 1914, vol. II. (5) The general indexes (3 vols.) to the *American Historical Review* (1895–1925) are also of great value. For other indexes see *Guide* §§ 21–25. (6) Many of the contemporary accounts written by explorers, travelers and others are listed in the *Guide,* § 38, and under " Sources " in each numbered topical section in the *Guide.* Consult also Milton Waldman, *Americana, the Literature of American History,* which gives an interesting description of the accounts of voyages, explorers and contemporary authors. (7) A guide to the extracts from a wide variety of sources appears in New England History Teachers' Association, *Historical Sources in Schools* (1902). It indicates in which of the various source books extracts are printed, e.g., Nos. 14, 29, 42 below, and others. (8) J. N. Larned, *Literature of American History* (1903), contains classified lists of standard books on American History. (9) *A Guide to Historical Literature* (in press, The Macmillan Company) contains a section on American history (edited by M. W. Jernegan).

It gives evaluated lists of books in each major field, chronological and topical. (10) For religious history the best guide is Peter Mode, *Source Book and Bibliographi-*

cal Guide for American Church History. (11) For state and county histories the best guide is T. L. Bradford and S. V. Henkels, *Bibliographers' Manual* (5 vols.). Consult also *Guide*, § 43.

At the beginning of each chapter of this volume, under "References," the best procedure for finding additional material for reading or for purposes of research is usually as follows: (1) Use Channing, Hart and Turner *Guide;* (2) J. N. Larned, *Literature of American History;* (3) bibliographies in the volumes of the *American Nation Series* and *History of American Life Series;* (4) Grace Griffin (Ed.), *Writings on American History*, 1906 to date; (5) References given in the other titles listed under " Bibliographies " and " Contemporary Accounts," and numbers 2, 3, 4, 5, 10 and 11 in the preceding paragraph.

Brief List of Authorities

The following, is a short list of the most desirable books covering all or a considerable portion of the period under consideration. Access to these books is necessary if the student wishes to obtain a reasonably comprehensive and well-rounded knowledge of this period of colonial history. Many of these volumes contain bibliographies which list other titles than those mentioned in the text.

1. CHARLES MCLEAN ANDREWS, *The Colonial Period*. (New York, Henry Holt & Company, Home University Library, No. 47, 1912.) — This is a brief summary by an eminent authority. [50 cents]

2. CARL LOTUS BECKER, *Beginnings of the American People*. (Boston, Houghton Mifflin Company, 1915.) — Places emphasis on the European background and relationships. [$2.00]

3. GEORGE LOUIS BEER, *Commercial Policy of England Toward the American Colonies.* (Columbia University Studies in History, III., No. 2, 1894.) — This is the best brief outline of the commercial aspect of English control of the colonies. [$1.25]

4. ERNEST LUDLOW BOGART and CHARLES MANFRED THOMPSON (Editors), *Readings in the Economic History of the United States.* (New York, Longmans, Green and Co., 1916.) — Contains interesting extracts from contemporary sources: Ch. I, Exploration and Colonization; Ch. II, Agriculture, Industry and Trade; Ch. III, Labor, Exchange and Population; Ch. IV, English Colonial Theory and Policy; Chs. I–IV cover period 1607–1763. [$3.20]

5. HERBERT EUGENE BOLTON and THOMAS MAITLAND MARSHALL, *Colonization of North America, 1492–1783.* (New York, The Macmillan Company, 1920.) — The best outline of the international background of colonization and the colonial systems of European powers in America. [$4.25]

6. EDWARD CHANNING, *History of the United States,* Vols. I–II to 1760. (New York, The Macmillan Company, 1905, 1908.) — Standard work; best comprehensive account of the period in 2 vols., fair-minded and scholarly. [$4.00 each]

7. EDWARD CHANNING, ALBERT BUSHNELL HART, and FREDERICK JACKSON TURNER, *Guide to the Study and Reading of American History.* (Boston, Ginn and Company, rev. ed., 1912.) — Classified list of books and bibliographies; indispensable for the study of the period. [$3.50]

8. FREDERICK CHARLES DIETZ, *Political and Social History of England.* (New York, The Macmillan Company, 1926.) — An excellent one-volume history of England, desirable for parallel reading. [$4.00]

9. HAROLD UNDERWOOD FAULKNER, *American Economic History*. (New York, Harper & Brothers, 1924.) — Historical approach with topical arrangement; excellent chapters on colonial agriculture, industries and commerce. [$3.50]

10. DIXON RYAN FOX (Editor), *An Atlas of American History*. (New York, Harper & Brothers, 1920.) — Excellent maps selected from American Nation Series, with map studies. [$2.75]

11. EVARTS BOUTELL GREENE, *The Foundations of American Nationality*. (New York, American Book Company, 1922.) — The best of the larger single-volume studies of the colonial and revolutionary period. [$2.60]

12. ALBERT BUSHNELL HART (Editor), *The American Nation, etc.*, 28 vols. (New York, Harper & Brothers, 1904–1908.) — Vol. I, Edward Potts Cheyney, *European Background of American History, 1300–1600;* II, Livingstone Farrand, *Basis of American History, 1500–1900;* III, Edward Gaylord Bourne, *Spain in America,* 1450–1580; IV, Lyon Gardiner Tyler, *England in America,* 1580–1652; V, Charles McLean Andrews, *Colonial Self-Government,* 1652–1689; VI, Evarts Boutell Greene, *Provincial America,* 1690–1740; VII, Reuben Gold Thwaites, *France in America,* 1497–1763. — The best comprehensive coöperative history written by specialists; a standard work; very valuable for collateral reading; mainly political and constitutional with some attention to economic and social history; contains notes, maps, and extensive bibliographies. [$2.25 each]

13. ALBERT BUSHNELL HART (Editor), *American History told by Contemporaries*. (New York, The Macmillan Company, 5 vols., 1897–1926.) — Vols. I and II cover the period to 1783. Most comprehensive collec-

tion of source extracts, covering all phases of colonial life. [$2.00 each]

14. WILLIAM MACDONALD (Editor), *Select Charters and other Documents illustrative of American History, 1606–1775.* (New York, The Macmillan Company, 1904.) — Standard work giving text of important documents for each colony. [$2.00]

15. ARTHUR MEIER SCHLESINGER and DIXON RYAN FOX (Editors), *A History of American Life,* in 12 volumes. (New York, The Macmillan Company, 1927.) — Vol. I by Herbert Ingram Priestly, *The Coming of the White Men, 1492–1819;* Vol. II by Thomas Jefferson Wertenbaker, *The First Americans,* 1607–1690; Vol. III by James Truslow Adams, *Provincial Society,* 1690–1763. — In these volumes the emphasis is placed on economic and social conditions; the most comprehensive outline of these topics, with bibliographies listing most recent books. [$3.50]

16. ARTHUR MEIER SCHLESINGER, *New Viewpoints in American History.* (New York, The Macmillan Company, 1922.)— Gives new interpretations of important topics based on recent studies. [$2.40]

17. ELLEN CHURCHILL SEMPLE, *American History and its Geographic Conditions.* (Boston, Houghton Mifflin Company, 1903.) — Relationship of American History to physical environment. [$2.75]

Small Reference Library

Most of the following works are more specialized than those given in the brief list and treat of geographic sections or special phases of the colonial period. Combined with the brief list above this would make a good collection for the study of the period.

18. JAMES TRUSLOW ADAMS, *Founding of New Eng-*

land and *Revolutionary New England*. (Boston, Atlantic Monthly Press, 1921 and 1923.) — These give a connected account of New England in the light of modern research, treating the political, economic and social development. The attitude towards the Puritans is critical and somewhat unfavorable. [$5.00 each]

19. CHARLES McLEAN ANDREWS, *Colonial Background of the American Revolution*. (New Haven, Yale University Press, 1924.) — This excellent volume traces the relation of the colonies to England and considers them as a world problem in British colonial policy. [$2.50]

20. CHARLES AUSTIN and MARY R. BEARD, *Rise of American Civilization*. (New York, The Macmillan Company, 2 vols., 1926.) — Brilliant interpretation. [$12.00]

21. PHILIP ALEXANDER BRUCE, *Economic History of Virginia in the Seventeenth Century*, etc., 2 vols., *Institutional History of Virginia in the Seventeenth Century*, 2 vols., *Social History of Virginia in the Seventeenth Century*. (New York, The Macmillan Company, 1895–1907.) — Though these volumes are on Virginia, they illustrate the history of the South in the seventeenth century, with respect to land, labor, crops, religion, education, and other topics. [$5.00 and $6.00]

22. VICTOR SELDEN CLARK, *History of Manufactures in the United States, 1607–1860*. (Washington, Carnegie Institution, 1916.) — A comprehensive work, devoting the first nine chapters to the colonial period. [$6.00]

23. JOHN ROGERS COMMONS (Editor), *Documentary History of American Industrial Society*. (Cleveland, Arthur H. Clark Company, 10 vols., 1913.) — Vols. I and II Ed. by U. B. Phillips, are entitled " Plantation and Frontier Documents," 1649–1863; very useful and important. [$10.00]

24. DAVIS RICH DEWEY, *Financial History of the United States*. (New York, Longmans, Green & Co., 1928.) — This work traces the evolution of various topics from the early colonial period, such as money, taxation, banking, etc. [$2.50]

25. JOHN FISKE, *Discovery of America,* etc., 2 vols. *Old Virginia and her Neighbors,* 2 vols., *Beginnings of New England; Dutch and Quaker Colonies,* 2 vols., *New France and New England.* (Boston, Houghton, Mifflin Company, 1892–1902.) — These volumes are written with great charm of style and with much emphasis on picturesque incidents and striking personalities. [$2.50]

26. CARLTON JOSEPH HUNTLEY HAYES, *Political and Social History of Modern Europe,* 2 vols. (New York, The Macmillan Company, 1916–1924.) — Covers the period 1500–1924. Excellent chapters on European colonial expansion and social development. [Vol. I, $4.00; Vol. II, $3.75]

27. ALLEN JOHNSON (Editor), *Chronicles of America Series,* 50 vols. (New Haven, Yale University Press, 1918–1919.) — Vol. I, Ellsworth Huntington, *Red Men's Continent;* Vol. II, Irving Berdine Richman, *Spanish Conquerors;* Vol. III, William Wood, *Elizabethan Sea-Dogs, etc.;* Vol. IV, William Bennett Munro, *Crusaders of New France;* Vol. V, Mary Johnston, *Pioneers of the Old South;* Vol. VI, Charles McLean Andrews, *Fathers of New England;* Vol. VII, Maud Wilder Goodman, *Dutch and English on the Hudson;* Vol. VIII, Sydney George Fisher, *Quaker Colonies;* Vol. IX, Charles McLean Andrews, *Colonial Folkways, etc.* — These volumes are for the most part scholarly and at the same time written in an unusually interesting " story-telling " manner. [Cloth edition, 50 vols. $97.50]

28. EMORY RICHARD JOHNSON and others, *History of Domestic and Foreign Commerce of the United States.* (Washington, Carnegie Institution, 2 vols., 1922.) — Describes the development of colonial and later commerce. [$3.00]

29. OLD SOUTH LEAFLETS. (Old South Association, 8 vols., Boston, 1883–1928.) — These leaflets are reprints of important original sources. [$1.50 per vol. or 5 cents per number]

30. FRANCIS PARKMAN, *France and England in North America,* etc., 9 vols. (Boston, Little, Brown & Company, Centenary Ed., 1922.) — Important for this study are, *Pioneers of France in the New World; Old Régime in Canada, Count Frontenac and New France under Louis XIV;* and *A Half Century of Conflict.* — Authoritative and brilliantly written history of the struggle of England and France for North America. [$2.00 each]

31. ULRICH BONNELL PHILLIPS, *American Negro Slavery.* (New York, D. Appleton & Company, 1923.) — The best work on the important aspects of slavery as an institution and on the slave trade. [$3.50]

32. FREDERICK JACKSON TURNER, *Frontier in American History.* (New York, Henry Holt & Company, 1923.) — The first two chapters on the influence of the frontier on American history and on the "Old West" are of great importance for a study of this period. [$3.00]

33. ROLLA MILTON TRYON, *Household Manufactures in the United States, 1640–1860, etc.* — The best work on the subject. [$2.00]

34. MOSES COIT TYLER, *History of American Literature During the Colonial Time.* (N. Y., G. P. Putnam's Sons, rev. ed., 2 vols., 1897.) — A survey of colonial literature; written in a scholarly and interesting manner. [Out of print]

35. WILLIAM BABCOCK WEEDEN, *Economic and Social History of New England*. (Boston, Houghton Mifflin Company, 2 vols., 2nd ed., 1896.) — These volumes picture the life of the people, and discuss such topics as manners, morals, prices, travel, agriculture, fisheries, slave trade, etc. [Out of print]

Larger Reference Library

The following volumes with the two lists previously given will provide material for a comprehensive study of the period.

36. WILBUR CORTEZ ABBOTT, *Expansion of Europe*. (N. Y., Henry Holt & Company, rev. ed., 2 vols. in one, 1924.) — A history of European colonization and expansion, 1415–1789. [$5.00]

37. GEORGE LOUIS BEER, *Origins of the British Colonial System, 1578–1660*. (N. Y., The Macmillan Company, 1908.) Continued by his *Old Colonial System 1660–1688,* (2 vols.) 1912, and No. 3 above — These volumes are scholarly and present a thorough study of the subject, the best in the field. [$3.00]

38. HUGH EDWARD EGERTON, *Short History of British Colonial Policy*. (London, Methuen & Co., 1897.) [$2.50]

39. RALPH HENRY GABRIEL and others (Editors), *Pageant of America, a Pictorial History of the United States*, 15 vols. (New Haven, Yale University Press, 1926.) — Various editors; volumes cover exploration, settlement, political, economic, social development; thousands of illustrations, facsimiles, maps, etc., with text; very valuable and conprehensive picture of American life. [$5.00 each]

40. OLIVER MORTON DICKERSON, *American Colonial*

Government, 1696–1765. (Cleveland, Arthur H. Clarke Co., 1912.) — Treats of the workings of the Board of Trade. [$4.00]

41. JOHN ANDREW DOYLE, *English Colonies in America.* Vol. I, *Virginia, Maryland and the Carolinas;* Vols. II and III, *The Puritan Colonies;* Vol. IV, *The Middle Colonies;* Vol. V, *The Colonies under the House of Hanover.* (N. Y., Henry Holt & Company, 1882–1907.) — These volumes are written by an Englishman and are scholarly and useful. [$3.50]

42. JOHN FRANKLIN JAMESON and others (Editors), *Original Narratives of Early American History.* (N.Y., Charles Scribner's Sons, 1906–17.) *Northmen, Columbus and Cabot,* ed. by J. E. Olson and E. G. Bourne; *The Spanish Explorers in the Southern United States,* ed. by F. W. Hodge and T. H. Lewis; *Early English and French Voyages,* ed. by H. S. Burrage; *The Voyages of Champlain,* ed. by W. L. Grant; *Narratives of Early Virginia,* ed. by L. G. Tyler; *Bradford's History of Plymouth Plantations,* ed. by W. T. Davis; *Governor John Winthrop's Journal,* etc., 2 vols., ed. by J. K. Hosmer; *Narratives of New Netherland* and *Johnson's Wonder Working Providence,* ed. by J. F. Jameson; *Narratives of Early Maryland,* ed. by C. C. Hall; *Narratives of Early Carolina,* ed. by A. S. Salley, Jr.; *Narratives of Early Pennsylvania, West Jersey and Delaware,* ed. by A. C. Myers; *Journal of Jasper Danckaerts,* ed. by B. B. James and J. F. Jameson; *Narratives of the Indian Wars,* ed. by C. H. Lincoln; *Narrative of Witchcraft Cases,* ed. by G. L. Burr; *Narratives of the Insurrections,* ed. by C. M. Andrews; *Spanish Explorations in the Southwest,* ed. by H. E. Bolton; *Early Narratives of the Northwest,* ed. by L. P. Kellogg. A most valuable and interesting collection of original accounts of colonization and development. [$4.00 each]

43. HERBERT LEVI OSGOOD, *American Colonies in the Seventeenth Century,* 3 vols. (N. Y., The Macmillan Company, 1904–1907.) [$3.50 each] *American Colonies in the Eighteenth Century,* 4 vols. (N. Y., Columbia University Press, 1924–1925.) — These volumes treat in a comprehensive manner mainly the legal, institutional and administrative aspects of colonial history to 1763, with some attention to economic and social development, e.g., land systems and religion. They are thoroughly scientific and accurate. [$5.50 each]

44. VERNON LOUIS PARRINGTON, *Main Currents of American Thought.* (N. Y., Harcourt, Brace & Company, 3 vols., 1927.) — Volume I is on the Colonial Mind, 1620–1800. The method is biographical. [$4.00 each]

45. JOHN RICHARD SEELEY, *Expansion of England.* (N. Y., The Macmillan Company, 1911.) — Traces the territorial expansion of England in the eighteenth century. [$1.40]

46. WILLIAM PETERFIELD TRENT and others, *Cambridge History of American Literature.* (N. Y., G. P. Putnam's Sons, 4 vols., 1917–21.) — Volume I covers the colonial period, with valuable bibliographies. [$5.00 each]

47. JUSTIN WINSOR, *The Mississippi Basin.* (Boston, Houghton Mifflin Company, 1895.) — A description of the struggle in America between England and France 1697–1763, etc. [$3.00]

48. JUSTIN WINSOR (Editor), *Narrative and Critical History of America,* 8 vols.: I, Aboriginal America; II, Spanish Explorations and Settlements in America, etc.; III, English Explorations and Settlements, etc., 1497–1689; IV, French Explorations and Settlements in North America and those of the Portuguese, Dutch, and Swedes, 1500–1700; V, English and French in

North America, 1689–1763. (Houghton Mifflin Company, Boston, 1884–1887.) — These volumes contain exhaustive critical essays on various topics with a mass of valuable bibliographical information. [Out of print]

CONTENTS

———◆———

CHAPTER I

EUROPEAN BACKGROUND

CHAPTER II

AMERICAN CONDITIONS OF ENGLISH COLONIZATION

CHAPTER III

COLONIZATION AND DEVELOPMENT OF THE SOUTHERN COLONIES TO 1689

CHAPTER IV

ECONOMIC AND SOCIAL DEVELOPMENT OF THE SOUTHERN COLONIES TO 1689

CHAPTER V

COLONIZATION AND DEVELOPMENT OF NEW ENGLAND TO 1643

CHAPTER VI

NEW ENGLAND (1643–1689)

CHAPTER VII

ECONOMIC AND SOCIAL DEVELOPMENT OF NEW ENGLAND
TO 1689

CHAPTER VIII

COLONIZATION AND DEVELOPMENT OF THE MIDDLE COLONIES TO 1689

CHAPTER IX

ECONOMIC AND SOCIAL DEVELOPMENT OF THE MIDDLE COLONIES TO 1689

CHAPTER X

POLITICAL AND COMMERCIAL POLICY OF ENGLAND TOWARD THE COLONIES (1689–1750)

CHAPTER XI

CONSTITUTIONAL AND POLITICAL DEVELOPMENT OF THE COLONIES (1689–1750)

CHAPTER XII

POPULATION AND IMMIGRATION PROBLEMS (1689–1750)

CHAPTER XIII

THE FRENCH-ENGLISH WARS, FRONTIER POLICIES AND WESTWARD EXPANSION (1689–1750)

CHAPTER XIV

ECONOMIC DEVELOPMENT (1689–1750)

CHAPTER XV

SOCIAL DEVELOPMENT (1689–1750)

LIST OF MAPS

THE AMERICAN COLONIES

1492-1750

CHAPTER I

EUROPEAN BACKGROUND

1. References

Bibliographies. — H. E. Bolton and T. M. Marshall, *Coloniza. of North Am.*, 11–12, 50–51, 111; E. G. Bourne, *Spain in Am.*, 320–337; Channing, Hart and Turner, *Guide*, §§ 97, 100–106, 111–113; E. P. Cheyney, *European Background of Am. Hist.*, 316–331; F. C. Dietz, *Polit. and Social Hist. of Engl.*, 110–111, 134–135, 181, 202–203; H. U. Faulkner, *Am. Econom. Hist.*; 53–55; E. B. Greene, *Foundations of Am. Nationality*, 19, Grace Griffin, *Writ. on Am. Hist.*, 1906–1923; C. J. H. Hayes, *A Polit. and Social Hist. of Mod. Europe*, I, 69–73; J. N. Larned, *Lit. of Am. Hist.*, 50–68; H. J. Priestly, *The Coming of the White Men, 1492–1819* (*Hist. Am. Life*, I, ch. xiii); R. G. Thwaites, *France in Am.*, 296–305; Justin Winsor, *Nar. and Crit. Hist. of Am.*, I–III, (crit. essays on authorities).

Historical Maps. — H. E. Bolton and T. M. Marshall, *Coloniza. of North Am.*, 6, 9, 15, 18, 30, 35, 43, 57, 63, 83; Channing, Hart and Turner, *Guide*, §§ 32–34, 96–97 (bibliography); D. R. Fox, *Atlas of Am. Hist.*, 1–5; E. B. Greene, *Foundations, etc.*, 13, 28–29; C. J. H. Hayes, *Polit. and Social Hist. of Mod. Europe*, I, 3, 49; Justin Winsor, *Nar. and Crit. Hist. of Am.*, maps in, IV, 33–47; 81–103.

General Accounts. — (a) EXPANSION OF EUROPE AND ENGLAND. W. C. Abbott, *Expansion of Europe*, I, 34–42, chs. ix-x, xii-xvi; Carl Becker, *Begin. of the Am. People*, chs. i-ii; E. P. Cheyney, *European Background of Am. Hist.*, chs. i-vii, ix-xi; C. J. H. Hayes, *A Polit. and Social Hist. of Mod. Europe*, I, chs. i-ii; C. P. Lucas, *The Begin. of Engl. Overseas Expan.*; J. R. Seeley, *Expan. of Engl.*; J. A. Williamson, *Short Hist. of Brit. Expan.*; W. H. Woodward, *A Short Hist. of the Expansion of the Brit. Empire*, chs. i-iii. (b) DISCOVERY AND EXPLORATION. C. R. Beazley, *The Dawn of Modern Geog.*; H. E. Bolton and T. M. Marshall, *Coloniza. of North Am.*, chs. i-v; E. G. Bourne, *Spain in Am.;* Edward Channing, *Hist. of U. S.*, I, chs. i-vi; J. A. Doyle, *Engl. Colonies in Am.*, I, chs. iv-v; John Fiske, *Discov. of Am.;* Joseph Jacobs, *Story of Geographical Discovery;* H. E. Osgood, *Am. Cols. in the 17th Cent.*, I, ch. i; R. G. Thwaites, *France in Am.*, ch. i; L. G. Tyler, *Engl. in Am.*, chs. i-ii; Justin Winsor, *Nar. and Crit. Hist. of Am.*, I, chs. i-ii; II, chs. i-iv, vi-vii; III, chs. i-iv; IV, chs. i-ii, v.

Special Accounts. — ENGLISH BACKGROUND. See chs. iii, v. vii, x; W. J. Ashley, *Int. to Engl. Econom. Hist. and Theory*, I; Frank Aydelotte, *Engl. Rogues and Vagabonds;* Chas. and Mary Beard, *Rise of Am. Civilization*, I, ch. i; G. L. Beer, *Origins of the British Colonial System, 1578–1660;* D. Harriet Bradley, "The Enclosures of Open Fields in England," in *Columb. Studies*, LXXX; E. P. Cheyney, *Soc. Changes in Engl. in the 16th Cent.*, and *Hist. of Engl., etc.* (1588–1603), I, 309–459; J. S. Corbett, *Drake and the Tudor Navy* and *Sir Francis Drake;* William Cunningham, *Growth of Engl. Industry and Commerce in Mod. Times*, I, 214–279; F. C. Dietz, *Polit. and Social Hist. of Engl.*, chs. vi, ix, 188–202, x–xi; Edward Eggleston, *Beginners of a Nation*, bk. I, ch. i; E. B. Greene, *Foundations, etc.*, chs. i-ii; R. H. Gretton, *The Engl. Mid. Class;* M. A. S. Hume, *Sir Walter Raleigh;* A. H. Lybyer, Influ. of Otto. Turks upon Orien. Tr. Routes in *Am. Hist. Asso. Rpt.*, 1914, I, ¹127–133. H. D. Traill, *Social Engl.*, IV–V; A. P. Usher, *Intd. to the Indust. and Soc. Hist. of Engl.;* William Wood, *Elizabethan Sea Dogs.*

Contemporary Accounts. — Channing, Hart and Turner, *Guide*, §§ 97, 100–104, and *Hist. Sources in Schools*, §§ 55, 65–69 (bibliog.); E. P. Cheyney (ed.), *Readings in Engl. Hist.*, ch. xii, xiii; Ralph Gabriel (ed.), *Pageant of America*, I, chs. i-viii; A. B. Hart (ed.), *Am. Hist. told by Contemps.*, I, ch. ii-v, esp. §§ 29–44 (Harrison's description of Engl., § 44; and extracts from Hakluyt's voyages, §§ 28, 40); R. Hakluyt, "A Discourse Concerning Western Planting" in *Maine Hist. Soc. Colls.* II; J. F. Jameson (ed.), *Original Narratives of Early Am. Hist.* (*The Northmen, Columbus and Cabots; The Spanish Explorers in the Southern U. S.; Early Engl. and French Voyages*); Milton Waldman, *Americana, etc.*, ch. i (bibliography); E. J. Payne (ed.), *Voyages of Elizabethan Seamen to America;* G. W. Prothero (ed.), *Select Statutes and Other Constitutional Documents, etc.* (Sir Thos. Smith, on classes of people, 176–181).

2. Expansion of Europe

THE establishment of the thirteen English colonies was part of a larger movement commonly known as the "Expansion of Europe." From the beginning of the fifteenth century to the present day there ·has been ceaseless activity in discovery, exploration, conquest, settlement and development of the vast regions of North, Central and South America, Asia, Africa, Australia, and the islands of the Atlantic, Pacific, and Indian Oceans. This phenomenon was, in its origin, a manifestation of the spirit of the Renaissance, an effort to extend the bounds of human knowledge. Unlike its literary and artistic phases, the geographical aspect had an important economic motive, namely, the acquisition of overseas territories, and the founding of colonies by states, companies, and private adventurers. As a result many a nobleman and merchant, pirate and buccaneer, manufacturer and artisan, farmer and field laborer, pauper, vagabond, and even thief, profited by the wealth of the new world — land, timber, furs, and fish in the North, and gold and silver in the South.

Relation of Colonies to European Civilization

As colonies multiplied, the mother country extended its language, law, political, economic, religious, and social ideals and institutions into the new world. Colonization was based on a theory defended on economic and religious grounds, of conquest, subordination, enslavement, or annihilation of the infidel native inhabitants and the acquisition of their lands, by Christian white men. The economic defense of this policy was the failure of the Indians to utilize the natural resources of America for the advance of civilization. The religious defense was based on the belief that Christianity was superior to all other religious faiths and that it was the duty of Christian nations to carry the gospel to heathen lands.

The awakening of Europe to overseas expansion was one of the results of the Crusades (1095–1291). These epoch-making events brought western Europeans into closer contact with the costly products of the Orient. European civilization at the opening of the twelfth century was on a much cruder and coarser basis than one can easily realize now, with respect to such things as food, clothing, house furnishings, articles of personal adornment, and objects made of gold and silver. Contact with the civilization of the more luxurious East brought a realization of these facts to western Europeans.

The Crusades and Expansion of Europe

The first crusaders, partly through the plunder of cities, towns and villages, brought back to western Europe samples of oriental products that for quality, design, and expert workmanship were far superior to European wares. Such articles as tapestries, brocades, damasks, silks, " cloths of silk and gold," rugs, cottons, glassware, swords, porcelains, precious stones — diamonds, sapphires, and pearls — ornaments, and inlaid work, came by caravan or by water route from Arabia, India, Persia, Japan, and China, and other eastern states. From these regions and from the islands of the Indian and Pacific Oceans came also tropical products, such as spices — pepper, ginger, and cloves — sugar, tea, dried fruits, nuts, camphor, balsam, alum, and hundreds of other products not native to Europe.

The wealth and luxury of the East had whetted the appetites of Europeans for nearly two hundred years, when in 1298 Marco Polo, then in jail in Genoa, dictated his account of the fabulous wealth of the Far East. After a residence of twenty years at the court of the Great Khan in China,

The Occident and the Orient

he gave to his contemporaries such a detailed description of hoards of gold and silver, and wonderful objects of luxury and art, as to astonish them beyond measure. The tale of Marco Polo fired the imagination of his readers and turned their attention to the Far East; to the lands of spices, silks, precious metals, and gems.

Following the overthrow of the Kingdom of Jerusalem in 1291, Europeans were gradually confronted with two serious problems. First, their taste for oriental goods tempted them to buy more than they could pay for. The few articles they had for exchange, such as woolen cloth, tin, linen, furs, lead, and soap, were of so little relative value, that Europe was confronted both with a rise in the standard of living and, eventually, an adverse balance of trade together with a drain of its precious metals. Secondly, Arab traders, to reach the West, had to make a long journey overland by caravan or by water. Thus oriental goods were expensive. Arab and Italian merchants controlled the larger part of this trade at the terminal ports on the Black Sea, and the eastern ports of the Mediterranean. Trebizond, Constantinople, Acre, Jaffa, and Alexandria, and the inland cities of Antioch and Damascus, were the trading points. The Italian merchants re-exported these goods westward, some passing overland from Italy to German merchants. Others were carried in great fleets, the " Flanders Fleet," from Venice to Lisbon, Southampton, Bruges, and Antwerp. In the fourteenth century additional information concerning the Far East came through the activities of Catholic missionaries. Other motives induced the great explorers and their backers to seek new lands and trade routes. The Renaissance, in its geographical aspect, bred the spirit of new discovery, adventure and conquest. Hence arose thoughts of exploration through or around Africa, if there existed such a passage. The religious motive also operated — the desire to convert the heathen to Christianity.

3. A Century of Discovery and Exploration
(1492–1592)

The idea of the sphericity of the earth and the possibility of reaching the Indies by water had been held by
Geographical Ideas in the Fifteenth Century some men from a very early date. The first had been asserted by Aristotle in the fourth century B.C., and the second by Eratosthenes, librarian at Alexandria, in the third century B.C., in a most remarkable geographical prophecy, or guess, as follows: " If the extent of the Atlantic Ocean were not an obstacle, we might easily sail from Iberia (Spain) to India, on the same parallel . . . it is quite possible that within the same temperate zone there may be two or even more inhabited earths."

How far the ideas of the Greek thinkers influenced those of the early fourteenth century is problematical. But after Marco Polo had journeyed by water from China to the head of the Persian Gulf, and his description of China had become better known, and after his statement that eastern Asia was washed by the waters of the " Ocean Sea " was confirmed by other merchants who had journeyed to China and returned, it seems reasonable to suppose that the idea of sailing into the Indian Ocean by circling Africa and thence to India and China was in the minds of some geographers and mariners.

At any rate it appears that two men did actually start out on a voyage to India around Africa before 1300, and that a map, or sailing chart, was made in 1351, the Laurentian *Portolano*, showing the union of the two oceans at the southern point of Africa; then thought to be much farther north than was actually the case. It is worth noting, too, that the Norse seamen had knowledge of Greenland and Labrador from the eleventh century on. However, there seems to be no direct evidence that the geographers and explorers of the fifteenth century were aware of these voyages. If it could be positively shown that Columbus had heard of the story of Leif Ericsson and his discovery of " Vinland," in the year 1000, then the influence of the Norse voyages on the discovery of America by Columbus would be of great significance.

Every age has its adventurous spirits, who, not content with things as they are, dream of unexplored realms
The Age of of achievement and with courage and dar-
Adventure ing push out into the unknown and try to translate their dreams into realities. It was in the fifteenth century that a host of these restless and adventurous spirits of western Europe turned their minds to the problem of exploring unknown and forbidding seas and lands. In their little ships they pushed down the coast of Africa until finally they reached the Cape of Good Hope (1487) and found the long-sought all-water route to the Far East and its treasures.

The first of the western nations to produce a group of these great spirits was Portugal, and the second
Prince Henry was Spain. Though the latter's size and
of Portugal position and advance to national unity were favorable factors — especially the union of Aragon and Castile and the conquest of Granada in 1492 — yet it was Portugal that laid the foundation for geographical exploration. This tiny nation was fortunate in the possession of a great man, Prince Henry the Navigator, the son of King John, who as early as 1412, and during the next forty years and more, interested himself in geographical discovery and in opening up

trade routes along the western coast of Africa. He established at Sagres, on Cape St. Vincent, a school of navigation and an observatory, where he gathered many of the known accounts of travels and discoveries, together with maps and charts, for the purpose of training navigators for their work. He set in motion expeditions that led to the exploration of the western and southwestern African coast and finally to the rounding of the Cape of Good Hope by Bartholomew Diaz in 1487. Diaz was accompanied by Bartholomew Columbus, the younger brother of the great discoverer.

Christopher Columbus was a Genoese map maker who resided in Portugal from about 1473 to 1484. When Christopher Columbus King John of Portugal rejected his plan for reaching India or possibly new lands by sailing directly west, he turned to Spain and finally in 1492 secured a commission from Ferdinand and Isabella, which appointed him admiral in those "islands and mainland in the ocean" which he might discover. It was Columbus who, with a vision of a shorter route to the Far East, brushed aside the superstitions of the ages, and sailed towards the setting sun. His first landfall, October 12, 1492, was probably Watling's Island, one of the Bahamas in the West Indies. This historic event opened up a realm of undreamed-of wealth and opportunity. Though his discovery was a by-product of the attempt to solve the age-old problems of the relations of Orient and Occident, it was of greater consequence than the final discovery of the all water route to India across the Indian Ocean finally completed by Vasco da Gama in 1498. For now Europe gradually awakened, geographically, from a long sleep and with feverish activity commenced to play the great and fascinating game of acquiring colonial empires. Men and nations had now a new outlet for their energies and power. Prince Henry, Diaz, and Columbus gave Portugal and Spain, the former mainly in the Far East and the latter in the West, the greatest opportunity for conquest in a thousand years.

The news of the discovery of Columbus and its advantage to Spain troubled King John of Portugal, because the Pope had been asked by Ferdinand and Isabella to confirm Spain in the possession of lands discovered by Columbus. To prevent a quarrel over land claims, Pope Alexander VI issued a papal bull (1493) which established an imaginary "Line of Demarcation" drawn from pole to pole, 100 leagues west of Cape Verde Islands, and then in 1494, by another treaty between Spain and Portugal, was placed 370 leagues west of Cape Verde Islands. The lands discovered to the east were to belong to Portugal and those to the west to Spain. Each was to have exclusive rights to explore, trade, and colonize in such lands as were not occupied by Christian princes.

Spain and the Division of the New World

The Pope seems to have had in mind a plan to promote world peace by a fair division of territory. On the other hand it will be noted that France, England, Holland, and other European countries, were ignored in this remarkable division of known and unknown lands. As a result Spain in theory obtained a monopoly of all North America and most of South America. Brazil, however, fell to Portugal. One of the Portuguese voyagers, Cabral, touched the coast of Brazil in 1500. Amerigo Vespucci, an Italian navigator, explored the coast to the south in 1501. The name "America" was at first applied to South America, and later to all the mainland, including North America.

Spain's new empire embraced all South America (except Brazil); all of Central America, Mexico, the

southern and southwestern portions of what is now
the United States and a large part of the West Indies.

Spanish Ex- A few of the notable discoverers, explorers,
plorers and and conquerors who carried the banners of
Conquerors   Spain far and wide are Juan Ponce de Leon
in Florida; Balboa, who crossed Panama to the Pacific
in 1513; Magellan, who sailed around Cape Horn in
1520, one of whose ships circled the globe in 1522;
Cortez in Mexico, 1519–20; Pizarro in Peru, 1532–
1538; De Soto in the Mississippi region, 1540–1543,
and Coronado in the lower Mississippi and southwestern portions of the United States, 1540–42. Thus up to
the latter part of the sixteenth century, Spain's occupation lay mainly south of the Rio Grande. It was only in
the Florida region and the West Indies, in this period,
that Spain came into contact with the French and
English on the seaboard.

It was between 1492 and 1550 that Spain laid the
foundations of a great colonial empire. It has been
estimated that by 1574 there were 200 Spanish settlements with a population of some 150,000 white inhabitants. The wealth of the ancient Indian civilizations of the West Indies and North and South America
poured into the coffers of Spain, while France, England,
and Holland looked on with envy and a growing desire
to share in the spoils of the new world.

France was so occupied with religious wars and plans
of Italian conquest that her interest in the new world
First Efforts of developed considerably later than that of
France   Portugal and Spain, though French fishermen were off the coast of Newfoundland in the first
years of the sixteenth century. It was not till 1524 that
Verrazano, a Florentine navigator, made a voyage under
the auspices of Francis I in which he seems to have
cruised along much of the Atlantic coast. In 1534

Cartier explored the Gulf of St. Lawrence and the next year entered the river and proceeded as far as the site of Montreal. Between 1562 and 1565 further French attempts were made to found colonies in Florida but without permanent success.

The effects of the discoveries of Portugal, Spain, and France were epoch making in their economic aspects. Commercial Revolution Particularly, the discovery of a water route around Africa to India caused a shift in the great world trade routes. This meant first, that the monopoly of the western Mediterranean trade, so long enjoyed by the Arab and Italian traders, was broken; second, that the long overland and water routes from the Far East were superseded by an all water route; third, that eastern goods could be obtained more quickly and more cheaply, and hence could be more generally used; fourth, that the towns and merchants of western Europe — Lisbon, Cadiz, and Antwerp — obtained a large share of the trade, partly at the expense of Genoa and Venice. Other effects were: an increase in the size and strength of ocean-going ships suitable for long voyages; new methods and agencies for carrying on trade, especially through chartered companies; an increase in Europe's specie supply, and a consequent rise in prices, through the plunder of Mexico and Peru and the returns from their gold and silver mines; the rise of the African slave trade; a great increase in the wealth of the commercial classes — manufacturers, merchants, and traders — the bourgeoisie; and finally the ushering in of the international rivalries of Portugal, Spain, France, Holland, and England, each struggling for a monopoly of the trade and commerce of its own colonies; and also for maritime supremacy, additional territory and the opportunity to exploit the wealth of the new lands.

4. Economic Background of the Expansion of England

That portion of English history falling within the period 1485–1603 is significant for many reasons. Under the Tudor sovereigns England gradually emerged as one of the great national states of Europe, in which the crown virtually established an absolute monarchy and thus superseded the warring feudal lords fighting each other for supremacy. The Tudor kings were interested in making the nation powerful and wealthy through the enlargement of trade opportunities for the English, in competition with foreign merchants and traders. Henry the Seventh commissioned John Cabot to seek new lands in 1497 and his successful landing on the coast of North America gave England her original claim to territory on this continent. Henry also negotiated political and commercial treaties with continental states. As early as the beginning of the sixteenth century, more than 2000 English merchants were engaged in foreign trade in the Baltic and near coast regions. Henry the Eighth supplemented the work of his father by establishing a navy board and a training school for pilots.

Policies of the Tudor Sovereigns

But it was Queen Elizabeth who contributed most to the expansion of England, because of the encouragement given to the great trading companies acting under national charters, which gave them the monopoly of English trade within specified areas. Elizabeth also connived at the simpler method of enriching the nation by allowing freebooters and buccaneers to plunder the Spanish fleet and colonies in time of peace. The prosperity and enrichment of the bourgeoisie, or middle class — the manufacturer, merchant, and trader — may be said to be the keynote of the English commercial policy. As the volume of trade grew customs duties yielded more and national power increased. The royal treasury would profit, and thus the state on the one hand could defend itself in case of attack, and on the other protect its overseas colonies, merchant ships, trade, and commerce.

In the sixteenth century England passed through great economic, political, religious, and social changes, all Economic of which tended to turn the attention of Changes in the crown and many of her citizens towards the Sixteenth Century the " new world " of America. So great was the industrial and commercial expansion that by the opening of the seventeenth century England's foreign policy centered more and more on the increase of trade and commerce. For example, the manufacture of cloth increased, and the merchant adventurers sought new markets, especially in the Netherlands. Increased demand for woolen cloths stimulated sheep raising. This was one reason for the enclosure movement, the fencing in of open fields for grazing. There resulted a decline in the emphasis on agriculture, and in consequence a surplus of unemployed agricultural laborers, an important element in the plans for English colonization. Some were set free to labor in the rising industrial towns or, after the discovery of America, to find new homes in the lands beyond the sea.

The sale of England's products abroad stimulated shipbuilding, the development of a merchant marine Foreign Trade and gradually the building of a navy for and Trading the protection of commerce. At the re-Companies quest of merchants the crown granted national charters, conveying a monopoly of trade within certain limits, to the exclusion of other Englishmen. The associations or companies thus formed by merchants, promoted trade and commerce more than any other single agency. In 1553 two or three hundred London merchants formed a company and subscribed £25 each for the purpose of finding a passage to China and the East Indies, and to trade with nations on the way. The company was generally known as the Russian or Muscovy Company. It sent out fleets each year, exporting such products as cloth and paper, and importing rope, cordage, tallow, hides, and whale oil. Similarly trade developed in the Baltic; and by 1588 more than a hundred English ships were trading in this region. The Eastland, or Baltic, Company, and the Turkey, or Levant, Company, for trading in the Baltic and Mediterranean respectively, were chartered in 1579 and 1581, and the great East India Company in 1600. Under the old system of production western Europe and England could hardly supply their own needs. To produce a surplus a new order was demanded in the economic and political world.

It was believed by 1576 that there was little or no hope of reaching the Orient by the northeast route The North around Russia as planned by the Muscovy West Passage Company. Attention was therefore turned toward finding a possible northwest passage. The first known contact of England with the new world since John Cabot's voyage in 1497, except through English fishermen off Newfoundland, and possibly by buccaneers like Sir John Hawkins, was through the voyages of Martin Frobisher and his explorations along the coast of Labrador and farther north, 1576 to 1578. These expeditions were financed by such men as Sir Francis Walsingham and Lord Burghley, ministers of the Queen, and even Elizabeth herself ventured £1000. Though these voyages did not lead to the discovery of the northwest passage or the development of trade, they gave the English some claim to this region and familiarized them with the coast and the difficulties of overseas expansion.

The interest of England in America was stimulated by the voyages of Frobisher and also by English fishermen who had for many years visited the Newfoundland fisheries for cod, mackerel, haddock, and halibut. They were also probably more or less familiar with inlets and harbors on the coast farther south. By 1578 fifty English vessels sailed regularly to the "Grand Banks" off Newfoundland.

The New-foundland Fisheries

5. The First English Colonies (1574–1587)

The idea of colonization was in the minds of several prominent men as early as 1574, especially Sir Humphrey Gilbert. He is believed to have written an essay, entitled "*Discourse of a New Passage to Cathaia,*" in which he proposed settlements in America. In 1578 Gilbert secured letters patent for discovery and settlement in America, but his fleet of ten ships was scattered by a storm. In the period 1582–1585 important men were interested in colonization, such as Sir Francis Walsingham, one of Elizabeth's chief ministers, Sir George Peckham, one of the subscribers to Gilbert's expedition, Sir Walter Raleigh, who had commanded one of Gilbert's ships, and Sir Richard Grenville. Richard Hakluyt, the noted editor of voyages of discovery, secured information (1578) about Newfoundland and places suited to settlement from an English Newfoundland fisherman. Gilbert's second expedition of five ships left Plymouth in 1583. Arriving at St. John's, Newfoundland, Gilbert took possession of the land in the name of the Queen, but on the return trip he lost his life in a storm off the Azores.

Gilbert, Raleigh, and Other Leaders in the Colonization Movement

Next of the founders of America was the famous Sir Walter Raleigh, who secured a charter March 25, 1584, with power to discover, settle, and govern new lands. Under this charter one expedition in 1584 and one in 1585, the first under Amadas and Barlow, and the second under Sir Richard Grenville with seven vessels, reached Roanoke Island, North Carolina, but failed to establish a permanent colony. Thomas Hariot, a mathematician, was on this last voyage and after he returned to London published in 1588 the first description of this portion of America. The third Raleigh expedition to the coast of North America resulted in the famous " lost colony." It was led by John White in 1587 and consisted of one hundred men, seventeen women, and several children. Their complete disappearance has long remained a mystery. Whether they were massacred by the Indians, or absorbed by them, is uncertain.

Raleigh financed these ventures largely out of his own pocket, at a cost of £40,000, the equivalent of much over a million dollars today. Their failure convinced the English that colonization was a difficult problem, and needed more careful planning, greater capital, equipment, and supplies; that it was not a " one man " affair. Though unsuccessful these expeditions, like those of Frobisher, familiarized the English with the coast and possible sites for settlement.

6. Rivalry of England and Spain (1580–1598)

It was during the latter part of the reign of Elizabeth that a few English statesmen began to consider
Colonies and Commerce the possible outcome of the development of a vigorous nationalism, competition for colonies, trade and commerce, and the struggle for racial supremacy among European powers. Spain's hos-

tility to England and her economic prosperity bred national rivalry with the probability of war as the outcome. But success by war required great resources, a well filled treasury, a highly centralized and powerful government, with authority to regulate commerce for national and imperial reasons. A few observers saw also that England should become as self-sufficing as possible. These ideas were in part the foundation for the later theories of English economists respecting the place of colonies in the empire. Instead of obtaining naval stores, lumber and cordage from the Baltic regions, fish from Holland, sugar from the Mediterranean states, and tropical products from the colonies of rival powers, why not develop an empire that would produce all these things within its own area? This is the essence of the later doctrine of mercantilism — primarily a state building policy. Moreover, England's rivals were disposed to restrict her markets with tariffs and tolls and Spain had shut England out entirely from direct trade with her colonies.

By the latter part of the sixteenth century it was known in England that America was a source of supply for fish and naval stores; that tropical products could be obtained in the West Indies, and that there was still a possibility that a northwest passage might be found to the Far East. Unoccupied regions in America might produce gold and silver; and those already occupied might be obtained by conquest. Before all these visions could be realized, one important condition would have to be fulfilled — mastery of the sea. This meant a navy, a merchant marine, and the overthrow of the sea power of England's great rival, Spain. Colonization was an overseas proposition, measured not by hundreds but by thousands of miles; and the ocean highways of trade and commerce were the weakest links in the chain which bound an empire together. England's great expansion of trade through the chartering of the Muscovy, Baltic, Levant, and other companies, and her attempts to get a foothold on the coast through the expeditions of Frobisher, Gilbert, and Raleigh had shown her the dangers of overseas expansion without control of the sea.

Spain's rapid increase in wealth and power, arising from the mines of Mexico and Peru, and her hostility to the English reformation, led King Philip II of Spain to seek greater political and religious power. Failing in his effort to reach an accord with Elizabeth, he had decided by 1580 that England must be conquered. In this year Portugal and her colonies in Africa and the East Indies became a possession of Spain and from 1580 to 1640 the Portuguese and Spanish crowns were united. Elizabeth had good reason to fear Spain, for England's national security and religion were threatened, as well as her personal stake in the throne. For Philip appeared to favor making Mary, Queen of Scots, a Catholic, Queen of England. In addition to the ambitions of Philip to extend his power in Europe he had other motives for crossing swords with England; because of the activities of her so-called "freebooters" and "sea dogs."

Antagonism of Spain and England

These high handed pirates attacked Spanish treasure ships laden with gold and silver obtained from her possessions in the new world. Sir John Hawkins commenced his activities as a slave trader in 1562, and was among the first to acquaint England with the possibility of a great expansion of trade in the new world. Sir Francis Drake, who had accompanied Hawkins on one of his voyages, conceived a plan in 1573 to plunder Spanish ships and colonies on the Pacific coast. Not

Freebooters and "Sea Dogs"

only individuals, but joint-stock companies, were formed for carrying on the slave trade and for privateering, with the main purpose of seizing and destroying Spanish ships wherever found, and the confiscation of their cargoes. Stockholders included Elizabeth and other high personages at court.

Ships were built or purchased, fitted for service, and manned by officers and crews who were to receive a share of the booty. Sir Francis Drake's famous expedition of 1577–1580, organized to plunder Spanish colonies and perhaps to force Philip into war, was authorized by the Queen and approved by her minister Sir Francis Walsingham. Drake sailed in November 1577, with four vessels and 150 men, at a capital cost of £5000, of which Elizabeth subscribed 1000 crowns. He brought back booty valued at £1,500,000 sterling; Hakluyt reported twenty-six tons of silver and eighty pounds of gold besides other booty. Shareholders are said to have received 4700 per cent on their investment and Elizabeth is believed to have received a million dollars or more as her share. Drake had well earned the knighthood she conferred.

In 1588 Philip II of Spain organized a great fleet of about 120 ships. It was originally intended that they should sail to the Netherlands and convoy soldiers thence for the invasion of England. Though the English royal navy was small, consisting of only twenty-nine ships in 1588, it was efficient and up to date. There were also some sixty privateers commanded by such men as Hawkins, Drake, Frobisher, and Grenville. As the Spanish fleet was passing through the English Channel it was attacked by the English fleet and later by the Dutch. A great storm completed the destruction of the Armada. Spain was weakened by costly wars in France and the Netherlands and the death of Philip in 1598. In the next few years three hundred Spanish ships were taken, so that Spanish sea power declined rapidly.

7. Influence of English Political, Religious, and Social Conditions on Colonization

The chief political tendency during the reign of the Tudor sovereigns was more and more in the direction of enlightened absolutism. The Tudor ideal was a personal or paternal government assisted by the Privy Council, and obedience of Parliament and people. During Elizabeth's reign Parliament sat infrequently and in short sessions. Thus the actual government was in the hands of Elizabeth and the Privy Council. The success of the Tudor policy and the popularity of Elizabeth led Englishmen to acquiesce in her personal government so long as the danger of foreign invasion lasted. When this passed away Parliament demanded an increasing share in directing the national policy.

James I (1603–1625), handicapped by his lack of popularity, as compared with the Tudor sovereigns, attempted to emphasize the royal power. But he found Parliament restive, the middle class dissatisfied, and much talk of Magna Carta and the rights of Englishmen. The reason for the tendency to oppose the growth of absolute power may perhaps be better appreciated by a quotation from a speech of James I to Parliament in 1610: " Kings are not only God's lieutenants upon earth, and sit upon God's throne, but even by God himself are they called gods, . . . that as to dispute what God may do is blasphemy . . . so it is seditious in subjects to dispute what a king may do in the height of his power." Arbitrary government then undoubtedly turned the thoughts of many towards America.

Growing dissatisfaction with the ecclesiastical policy of the crown produced a similar result. The separation of the church in England from the author-

The Anglican
Church and
the Dissenters

ity of the Pope, begun in 1534, was followed by the rise of the national or Anglican Church with the King at its head. Henry VIII and Edward VI dissolved most of the monasteries and other church institutions and confiscated and disposed of their lands and other property. Some was bestowed on friends, and some was given to the parishes to endow schools to take the place of the old church schools. The sixteenth century witnessed such a tremendous increase of interest in religion by large numbers of people, that many varying and opposing views arose with respect to church government, creeds, and ceremonies. Many followed the views of Luther, Calvin, John Knox, and other great religious leaders. The Anglican church did not wholly satisfy the numerous groups known as dissenters or non-conformists; the Separatists, Puritans, and Presbyterians for example. The determination of the early Stuarts to make these dissenters conform to the doctrines of the established church and the desire to avoid such conformity was a second principal motive for colonization.

The important elements in the old order of society, the feudal lords and powerful churchmen — abbots and archbishops — were supplanted during the

Social Classes
Noblemen and
Gentlemen

sixteenth century by a new landed nobility who owed their position largely to the crown. Many benefited as a result of the confiscation of the estates of the church by Henry VIII. The King created a new nobility by conferring on favorites not only the title of Earl, Viscount, Baron, and Knight, but by granting to these men huge landed estates. Said Sir Thomas Smith, in his *Commonwealth of Eng-*

land (1589), "Who can live idly and without manual labour, he shall be called master, and be taken as a gentleman."

The changing economic conditions increased the number of those who became wealthy by commerce and trade. It was the townsmen — the manufacturer, merchant, and trader — who profited especially through foreign trade. Immense wealth came to some noblemen and merchants as a result of privateering, piratical exploits, and freebooting, mainly at the expense of Spain and in the African slave trade. The stockholders in the great trading companies, the Muscovy, Baltic, Levant, East India, African, and others, belonged principally to this group — the so-called bourgeoisie.

Manufacturer, Merchant and Trader

Sir Thomas Smith has well described another class as follows: "Those whom we call yeomen, next unto the nobility, knights, and squires, have the greatest charge and doings in the commonwealth. . . This sort of people confess themselves to be no gentlemen, and yet they have a certain pre-eminence and more estimation than labourers and artificers and commonly live wealthily. . . These be, for the most part, farmers unto gentlemen, and by these means do come to such wealth that they are able daily to buy the lands of unthrifty gentlemen."

Independent Landowner or Yeoman

In comparison with the landed aristocracy the rich merchant or the yeoman, the great bulk of the rest of the population, the poor tenant farmer and husbandman, the common laborers and artisans, were poor men. The tenant farmer suffered because of high rents which tended to lower his standard of living. The policy of enclosing the common lands to promote sheep raising was disastrous to the agricultural classes. It reduced the number of tenants and

Poor Man

threw many farm laborers out of work. Again some of these lands had been available for grazing land to the poor people with a few cattle or sheep. Evictions now became common. Many of the master craftsmen made a good living, but the day laborers, the journeymen, and apprentices were struggling for the bare necessities of life. Of these Sir Thomas Smith says: " The class of day laborers, poor husbandmen, yea, merchants or retailers which have no free land, copyholders and all artificers . . . these have no voice nor authority in our commonwealth, and no account is made of them, but only to be ruled."

Unemployment, rise in prices, and wage-fixing caused a large increase in the number of poor persons and Beggarman criminals. The justices of the peace fixed and Thief the maximum wages of farm laborers, rarely more than a shilling a day. At the same time from 1500 to 1600 wheat rose in price nearly fourfold. Thus a man worked forty weeks in 1600 for as much food as he received in 1500 by working ten weeks. The Statute of Apprentices (1563) forbade anyone below the rank of a yeoman to withdraw from agricultural pursuits to be apprenticed to a trade. Moreover, a series of poor laws provided that paupers must not pass from one parish to another, and provided penalties, such as whipping, for vagrancy.

Thus the farm laborer had no chance to better himself. Vagrancy and unemployment increased and riots and even rebellions broke out. Sir Thomas More, in his *Utopia,* complains that sheep from being meek and tame now " consume devour and destroy whole fields, houses, and cities," that the husbandmen were forced out of their homes, or compelled to sell all for almost nothing and to " depart away, poor innocent wretches, goods, men, women, husbands, wives, fatherless children, widows, woeful mothers, and their young babes . . . out of their known and accustomed houses, finding no place to rest in. And when they have wandered abroad . . . what can they else do but steal, . . . or go about begging. And then also they be cast in prison as vagabonds, because they go about and work not, whom no man will set to work."

These men were a terror to the countryside and were estimated in number as high as ten thousand. As early as 1574 Sir Humphrey Gilbert declared: "We might inhabit some part of those Countreyes (America) and settle there these needy people of our country which now trouble the commonwealth and through want here at home are enforced to commit outrageous offences whereby they are dayly consumed with the gallows." So Velasco, the Spanish minister to England, wrote in 1611: "Their principal reason for colonizing these parts is to give an outlet to so many idle, wretched people as they have in England, and thus prevent the dangers that might be feared of them." These classes of society were all represented, and to some extent reproduced, in the American colonies. Younger sons of the new nobility became planters and "gentlemen." Merchants became shipowners and shopkeepers; the tenant farmers became the small farmers; and the artisans, farm and day laborers, vagabonds and convicts often became the indentured servants. Thus the motives for colonization were many; to check the power of Spain; to gain wealth by seizing lands and by developing agriculture, commerce, and trade; to escape arbitrary government and religious persecution; to convert the heathen; and to relieve England of a portion of her most undesirable classes. Economic factors were of primary importance in southern colonization, while the religious motive was strongest among those who settled in the northern colonies.

Colonial institutions and ideals are the product of two great forces, inheritance and environment. Where English institutions, traditions, and ideals were not in conflict with the new environment there was a natural tendency to reproduce them. Thus the "rights of Englishmen," the administration of justice, trial by jury, many legal, educational, and religious ideals and practices and the general structure of society were transplanted to America. On the other hand, a titled nobility, bishops, and many habits and customs that could exist only in a settled civilization, were either greatly modified or abandoned. In their place the colonists substituted some entirely new institutions, practices, and ideals.

The English Inheritance of the Colonies

CHAPTER II

AMERICAN CONDITIONS OF ENGLISH COLONIZATION

8. References

Bibliographies. — H. E. Bolton and T. M. Marshall, *Coloniza. of North Am.*, 102–103; E. G. Bourne, *Spain in Am.*, 320–337; Channing, Hart and Turner, *Guide*, §§ 33–34, 37, 42–43, 45, 97–99, 104–108, 111, 113–114, 122, 127; Livingstone Farrand, *Basis of Am. Hist.*, 272–289; E. B. Greene, *Foundations of Am. Nationality*, 224–225; Grace Griffin, *Writings on Am. Hist.*, 1906–1923; Ellsworth Huntington, *Red Man's Continent*, 173–175; J. N. Larned, *Lit. of Am. Hist.*, 50–68; H. J. Priestly, *The Coming of the White Men, 1492–1819* (ch. xiii); R. G. Thwaites, *France in Am.*, 296–305; L. G. Tyler, *Engl. in Am.*, 328–339; Justin Winsor, *Nar. and Crit. Hist. of Am.*, I–III (crit. essays on authorities).

Historical Maps. — J. T. Adams, *Founding of New England*, 40; H. E. Bolton and T. M. Marshall, *Coloniza. of North Am.*, 83, 89, 95; Channing, Hart and Turner, *Guide*, §§ 32–34, 96–97 (bibliography); see number 1 in this volume; D. R. Fox, *Atlas of Am. Hist.*, 3–6, 8, 11; E. B. Greene, *Foundations, etc.*, 37, 44, 164; Justin Winsor, *Nar. and Crit. Hist. of Am.* (maps in vols. III, IV).

General Accounts. — W. C. Abbott, *Expan. of Europe*, I, chs. xvii–xviii; Carl Becker, *Begin. of Am. People*, 17–57; H. E. Bolton and T. M. Marshall, *Coloniza. of North Am.*, chs. iii, xiii; E. G. Bourne, *Spain in Am.*, chs. xii–xiii; Edward Channing, *Hist. of the U. S.*, I, ch. iv; J. A. Doyle, *Engl. Col. in Am.*, I, chs. ii–iii; Edward Eggleston, *Beginners of a Nation*, bk. II, ch. i; E. B. Greene, *Foundations, etc.*, ch. ii; J. G. Palfrey, *Hist. of New Engl.*, I, ch. ii; Francis Parkman, *Pioneers of France in the New World;* R. G. Thwaites, *France in Am.*, chs. iii–iv; L. G. Tyler, *Engl. in Am.*, chs. iii, ix, xii, xiv–xv; Justin Winsor, *Nar. and Crit. Hist. of Am.*, II, ch. v; IV, chs. vi–vii, and *Cartier to Frontenac*, 1–47; G. M. Wrong, *The Rise and Fall of New France.*

Special Accounts. — (a) RIVALS IN COLONIZATION. J. T. Adams, *Founding of New Engl.*, ch. ii; J. P. Baxter, *Pioneers of France in New England*, and "Sir Ferdinando Gorges and his Prov. of Maine," in *Prince Soc. Publs.;* H. P. Biggar, *Trading Com-*

panies of New France; H. E. Bolton and T. M. Marshall, *Coloniza. of North Am.*, ch. iv; Alexander Brown, *Genesis of the U. S.*, and *The First Republic in Am.;* H. S. Burrage, *Begin. of Colonial Maine;* James Douglas, *New Engl. and New France;* P. Edgar, *Struggle for a Continent,* (selections from Parkman); John Fiske, *New France and New Engl.;* C. H. Levermore, *Forerunners and Competitors of Pilgrims and Puritans;* W. B. Munro, *Crusaders of New France;* H. O. Thayer, *The Sagadahoc Colony,* (Pubs. of *Gorges Soc.*); T. A. Wright, "Spanish Policy Towards Va.," in *Am. Hist. Rev.* (April 1920). (b) LAND TITLES AND INDIANS. Edward Channing, (*Hist. of the U. S.*, I, 336–338, 354; Chas. Deane, "Roger Williams and the Mass. Charter," in *Mass. Hist. Soc. Proc.* (1871–1873), XII, 341–358; G. E. Ellis, *The Red Man and the White Man in Am.;* Livingstone Farrand, *Basis of Am. Hist.;* B. A. Hinsdale, "The Right of Discovery," in *Ohio Arch. Soc. Qr.* II, 349–379; Ellsworth Huntington, *Red Man's Continent;* W. B. Scarfe, "Devel. of International Law as to Newly Discov. Territory" in *Am. Hist. Assoc. Papers,* IV; Justin Winsor, *Nar. and Crit. Hist. of Am.,* I, (Aborigines) and "The Rival Claimants for North America" in *Am. Ant. Soc. Proc.* 1894, 415–17.

    Contemporary Accounts. — J. P. Baxter, *Sir Ferdinando Gorges, etc.,* (contains Gorges' *Brief Relation, Briefe Narrative, etc.*); "Relation of a Voyage to Sagadahoc," in *Mass. Hist. Soc. Proc.,* (1880–1881) XVIII; *Cal. of State Papers, Colonial and W. I.;* Channing, Hart and Turner, *Guide,* §§ 105–108, 113–114, and *Hist. Sources in Schools,* §§ 65–69, and Milton Waldman, *Americana,* chs. ii–v (bibliography); Ralph Gabriel, *Pageant of America,* I, chs. i, vii, xvii–xxviii; A. B. Hart, (ed.), *Am. Hist. told by Contemporaries,* I, chs. v, ix, xxii, esp. §§ 34–43, 60, 64, 91; J. F. Jameson, (ed.), *Original Narratives of Early Am. Hist. (Early Engl. and French Voyages; Voyages of Champlain; Narratives of New Netherland*); *Old South Leaflets,* nos. 69, 94; G. P. Winship (ed.), *Sailors' Narratives of Voyages Along the New Engl. Coast, 1524–1624.*

9. Conflicting Titles to Land and Territory

THE occupation of the Atlantic Seaboard by England calls for some explanation of her right and title to this
Old World   immense area, in view of the conflicting
Land Titles   claims of other European nations and those of the native inhabitants. The old European idea of

title to land was based on conquest, confirmed by possession and treaties. War and conquest being lawful, the ultimate protection of title to land would depend on the presence of a military force to hold it.

The discovery of the new world, however, led to the development of another principle, in order to safeguard the discoveries of particular nations and to justify the seizure of lands from the native inhabitants. When Columbus reported his discoveries to Ferdinand and Isabella in 1493, they asked Pope Alexander VI to confirm Spain in the possession of the lands discovered. After hearing from King John of Portugal, the Pope issued the famous bull of partition of 1493, which divided the unknown world between Spain and Portugal, as previously narrated (ch. I, p. 9).

The Pope and the New Discoveries

The Pope asserted that God had conferred on him the power to distribute unoccupied lands. The bull of partition reads, " By authority of God omnipotent granted by him to blessed Peter, hence to Alexander VI . . . we grant lands discovered or to be discovered as an eternal possession." The church at this time not only claimed power over Christians, but also over pagans and infidels. The Pope granted only certain lands, for the bull reads, " except such lands and islands as may have been in possession of some Christian prince on the Christmas preceding," viz., Dec. 25, 1492.

Though England was a Catholic nation at this time, she refused to be bound by the Pope's decree. When John Cabot applied to Henry VII for a commission to discover new lands, the king not only ignored the papal bull, but stated that he might seek such new lands " that may belong to heathens and infidels." And nearly one hundred years later, in 1584, the charter given to Sir Walter Raleigh

Attitude of England

gave him power to discover and take possession of "heathen and barbarian lands not actually possessed by any Christian Prince nor inhabited by Christian people." Thus England denied Spain's claim to the Atlantic Seaboard, whether based on the Pope's donation or the fact that Spanish explorers had later touched on the shores at various points not explored by Cabot.

The right of discovery raised many points of difficulty and produced conflicts of authority and wars for the possession of the new lands in America and the West Indies. Did John Cabot's landfall give England title to the whole continent of North America? Spain in fact modified her claims to North America and agreed that actual possession and use were factors in establishing a valid title. England did not dispute the claims of France to the St. Lawrence basin, as based on the explorations of Cartier and later Champlain, notwithstanding Cabot's prior discovery. De Soto, a Spaniard, first discovered the Mississippi River, but Spain allowed France to take possession of much of the Mississippi Valley in the seventeenth century without serious protest.

Problems Relating to Discovery

Moreover, France maintained that the discovery of the mouth of a river gave title to all the territory that it drained. This led to a dispute with England at a later date over the title to the Ohio Valley. Spain also usually maintained that discovery and possession of the coast gave her the right to lay claim to territory far into the interior, viz., as far as the sources of those rivers, with their branches, that emptied into the coast discovered. When two nations occupied regions at some distance from each other, the middle distance was sometimes taken as the boundary between them.

Thus a number of different principles underlay

claims to territory in America, and the disputes and wars that followed. The chief claims were based on discovery, papal sanction or donation, exploration, possession and use, and river drainage. Of course conquest by war was always an available source of title to land. These principles have reference to the claims of European nations as they affected each other. Their bearing on land which native inhabitants claimed is another question.

10. The Native Races

When the European and English colonists reached the Atlantic Seaboard they found it occupied by native Distribution races. Columbus supposed them to be na-
and Character tives of India and so called them "Indians." Perhaps there were 200,000 living east of the Mississippi, divided into nations, tribes, and clans. The Algonquin group occupied the seaboard from Nova Scotia to North Carolina. The Iroquois were in the central New York region; and the Muskhogeans, including the Chickasaws, Choctaws, Creeks, etc., occupied the South Carolina-Florida region and the interior to the southwest. The seaboard Indians were a woodland people, settled in villages rather than nomadic, depending on wild foods, hunting, fishing, and simple agriculture for their sustenance. Indian maize, or corn, was the most important cultivated food product. They lived in small temporary villages, the large areas between being practically unoccupied, though used for hunting and fishing.

The stage of civilization attained by the seaboard Indians was little above that of the true savage. They Stage of had no written language, were without
Civilization domesticated animals other than dogs, and had advanced little in the mechanical arts. They were

in the stone age so far as tools and weapons were concerned, and lived for the most part in flimsy huts or wigwams, made of poles, bark, and bushes, covered with matting or skins. They were often dirty and covered with vermin. The Indians clothed themselves in skins in winter, but went almost naked in summer. They had a slight knowledge of weaving, making mats and baskets, knew something of clay modeling, and were expert in making canoes and boats. Land was held in common by tribal and clan ownership, the individual having the right of use only. Their agriculture, fishing, and hunting were based on a more or less communistic system. The division of labor between the sexes provided that the male should hunt, fish, and fight, fashion the rude weapons, and build the wigwams and canoes. The squaws, for their part, were the farmers, though sometimes aided by the old men and boys. They prepared the soil, planted, cultivated, and harvested the corn and other vegetables — pumpkins, beans, etc., and cooked them. In addition they wove baskets and mats, taught and cared for the children and in general performed domestic duties.

These characteristics of the Indians affected the colonists both to their advantage and disadvantage. The Indian was physically fit, able to endure fatigue and hardships on an incredibly small amount of food. Indian runners were known to have covered eighty miles in a single day. They were brave, cunning, patient, and endured pain and torture with stolidity. They were, however, extremely indolent, lacked forethought, and often starved in the midst of plenty, particularly after their habits were modified by contact with and dependence on the white traders. While the Indians were treacherous, and little dependence could be placed on their word or

Character-
istics

treaties — a trait often equally true of the whites —
yet they were often generous and hospitable to the
colonists, giving them food and helping them in an
emergency; instructing them in their arts — their
methods of agriculture, fishing, hunting, woodcraft, and
warfare.

Their religious ideas were very crude, the "manitou"
of the Algonquin tribes being a power or force to be
found in physical objects, mountains, and animals.
Priests were in charge of religious rites, and the work
of the "powwow" or "medicine man" was to propi-
tiate or obtain aid from the gods or forces, by magic,
incantations, and charms. Under these conditions it is
clear that the gap between the Indian and white civilization was tremendous. This is the reason why the races
found so much difficulty in understanding each other's
political, social, and religious ideas. In economic intercourse they were nearer on a par; but even here the
Indian was at a great disadvantage, because of lack of
organization, self-control, and knowledge of the value
of his goods to the white man.

11. The Indian Problem

Long before the English made their first permanent
settlement on the Atlantic Seaboard, Spain and France
had been in close contact with the Indians. Spain had
occupied the Florida-Georgia region, where she followed a ruthless policy of exploiting the native inhabitants. France had tried to occupy the same region, and
had even entered into an alliance with some of the
tribes against Spain. Their settlements, however, were
destroyed by the latter (1563–1565). Farther north,
Cartier (1534–1535), and Champlain (1604–1609),
learned the conditions of colonization as affected by the
Indians. The various English expeditions from 1584 to

1607 — Raleigh's in the South (1584–1589), and those of Gosnold, Pring, Weymouth, and Capt. John Smith (1602–1620), along the New England coast — acquainted the English with the nature of the Indian problem through printed accounts of these expeditions. Some Indians were kidnapped and taken to England. The famous Squanto, later closely connected with the fortunes of the Pilgrims, was one of these Indians.

The first contacts of the two races gave rise to a number of pressing problems. Some of them arose out Four Major of alleged rights of the Indians — particu-Problems larly resistance to cession of their lands by conquest or purchase. Another problem was the development and regulation of trade, especially the fur trade; a third difficulty was the assertion of a right of "protection" by the whites through treaties of amity and alliances; a fourth arose out of the system of Christianizing the Indians, which was undertaken not only from a religious standpoint, but as a means of making them less dangerous, more docile, and more easily managed. All of these problems encountered by the Spaniards were known to the French, and more or less realized by the English before the last established permanent colonies.

During the early period of exploration and settlement of the Atlantic Seaboard down to 1607, Spain, Reasons for France, and England experimented with Attitude the Indians, while endeavoring to colonize Toward Indians and profit from the natural resources of America. In general each nation dealt with the native inhabitants according to its own needs. Since the French and English were the two great antagonists an examination of their policies toward the Indians will be of interest.

The French policy was that of occupying territory at distant points and the establishment of military French posts and trading stations. They wanted Policy the Indians near at hand and therefore believed that joint occupation was both feasible and desirable. Hence they were spared one of the most important causes of friction between the English and Indians. To use the Indian to exploit the great natural resource of his region, furs, and at the same time to Christianize him, were the main features of the French Indian policy. Some attention however was given to agriculture by the French seigneuries along the St. Lawrence. French character differed from the Anglo-Saxon in one important respect. The French saw no serious objections to a policy of fraternization and even intermarriage with the Indians, and in general a willingness to live on terms of intimacy with them in a manner that the English found impossible. This fact was of great advantage to the French in their long conflict with England for the possession of the interior of the continent.

The Englishman, like the Frenchman and the Spaniard, denied to the Indian most of the privileges and rights he English claimed. All were more or less interested Policy in his religious welfare. The Englishman's main motive for colonization, however, was occupation of the land for agricultural purposes, which prevented any easy solution of the land problem. Joint occupancy was impossible, and eventually the Indian had to leave his hunting grounds to the sole possession of his enemy, because the land was needed for farms. It is to be noted that the Raleigh patent and the charter granted to the Virginia Company ignored Indian titles to the land granted. However the English " purchased " lands for hatchets, blankets, or smaller articles, though the Indians often understood this to mean no more than joint occupation. The English also adopted the policy of Christianizing the Indians, for much the same reasons that motivated Spain and France.

Hence from the first arose an irrepressible conflict between the English and Indians, due to incompatibility of temper, differences in legal and social systems, the hiatus between the two civilizations, and the land problem. Several square miles of land were needed to support an Indian family in the hunting and fishing stage. Since the economic policy of the French and English caused a great expansion of the fur trade, the game supply was rapidly reduced, thus forcing the Indians to leave their lands situated near the coast, because of scarcity of game and food.

The Irrepressible Conflict

The various English colonies were affected by special influences peculiar to the Indians of each section. In the extreme South, on the Florida-Georgia frontier, Spain and England were rivals for territory and for the Indian fur trade. It was the policy of the Spaniards, from an early date, to incite and inflame the Indians against the English. Indeed it is probable that they incited the Indians to carry out the Virginia massacre of 1622 (p. 59).

Sectional Aspects of the Indian Problem

The Dutch, and later the English, were much aided in their contest with the French by the hostility of the Iroquois to the French, the reason for which will be explained later. Possessing the Mohawk Valley, they were enabled to deflect a part of the fur traffic of the Northwest which would otherwise have flowed through the St. Lawrence, to Albany; in consequence, New Netherland, New York, and New England profited at the expense of the French. The Delaware tribes of Pennsylvania had been conquered by the Iroquois and in fact paid tribute to them. Thus Pennsylvania was fortunate in having comparatively weak eastern tribes to contend with.

The Indians of New England were not only a weak branch of the Algonquins, pushed to the coast in earlier times by the fiercer Iroquois, but a terrible pestilence raged from northern Maine to Connecticut, between 1613 and 1618, which almost exterminated important tribes, particularly in the Plymouth-Boston region. Some estimates suggest that two thirds of the fighting men were destroyed by this scourge. It appears therefore that the New Englanders, like the Pennsylvanians, were fortunate in the region chosen for settlement.

The policy of both Spain and France was to incite the Indians to attack the English settlements, in order
Ultimate International Aspects
to weaken them and prevent expansion of their territory. This danger was one of the important reasons for the support and aid England received from her colonies, in the long struggle between the French and English for the possession of the interior and a share in the fur trade. The first contacts of Champlain with the Indians in 1609 led him to make an alliance with the Hurons, one of the Algonquin tribes, a tribe closely related to the Iroquois. This, with other factors, led the Iroquois to support the Dutch and English rather than the French, a most fortunate advantage for the English.

English agricultural policy forced the Indians to fight, or retreat to the frontier, where they became a ready tool of the French in the long struggle that followed. The Anglo-Saxon was unable to use Indians to much advantage because of his " superiority complex; " his unwillingness to mingle or intermarry with them, or make his standards conform to those of the

Indians. The French on the other hand lived in comparative amity with the Indians and intermarried with them. The English were interested in the fur trade but traders often angered the Indians by sharp practices. Thus England entered the contest for Indian trade and lands at a great disadvantage. In the matter of religion also, the English, Dutch, and Quakers were at a disadvantage on the frontier, since the western and southern Indians were already partly under the influence of the Catholic priests of Spain and France.

12. Early Rivalries and Conflicts of Spain, France, and England on the Atlantic Seaboard

When the English founded their first permanent colony in the new world (Virginia, 1607) the Spaniards had been struggling for nearly a hundred years to colonize the Atlantic Seaboard. From 1521 they extended their settlements along the Atlantic coast into what is now Florida, Georgia, South Carolina, and on the Gulf of Mexico in the Alabama region. Menendez, sent by Spain to Florida, founded St. Augustine in 1565, the oldest European settlement within the present United States. Menendez destroyed the French settlement at Port Royal on the St. John's River, and in the next two years several small Spanish posts and missions were established between Florida and North Carolina. Jesuit missionaries founded a mission as far north as Virginia in 1570, but this outpost failed also because of Indian attacks. It is thus clear that Spain and France both claimed the right to occupy the lands on the seaboard in the same general region which Raleigh attempted to occupy from 1584 to 1589.

When Spain heard of Raleigh's first attempt at colonization there was alarm. Spain disputed the right

of England to colonize in a region where for sixty years
and more she had tried to found colonies. Drake, how-
Spain and   ever, sacked and burned St. Augustine in
England   1586. When the Spanish ambassador to
England learned of Raleigh's second project to found
a colony, he wrote his sovereign, " Such a bad project
should be uprooted now, while it can be done so easily."
In 1609 the commander of the garrison at St. Augustine led an expedition to Virginia to eject the English;
and later another to incite the Indians to attack them.
Spain so extended her holdings along the coast in the
period from 1590 to 1634 that she had forty-four
missions in the Florida-Georgia-South Carolina region.
Much of this area continued in dispute between Spain
and England for the next century with resulting border
warfare and rivalry for territory and trade.

France and England were in conflict on the northern
border from the opening of the sixteenth century. The
France and   voyage of Cabot opened the way to the
England   fisheries of Newfoundland; and by 1550
fishing fleets were sailing from England to Newfound-
land every spring and autumn. French, Spanish, and
Portuguese fishing vessels also shared in the fisheries.
France occupied Sable Island and landed cattle there
as early as 1518. Later (1535) Cartier settled at Quebec.
From 1603 France and England were rivals in the
Maine region. In fact a charter was issued by the
French king to the Sieur de Monts, 1603, granting territory from the 40th to the 46th degree of latitude.
Later (1606) the grant to the Plymouth branch of
the Virginia Company covered much of the same
territory (see p. 51). Both de Monts and Champlain
were active in attempts to settle this region in the
next few years; and in 1604 a colony was established on
St. Croix Island. Three years later the English estab-

lished the ill-fated Popham colony at the mouth of the Kennebec, within the grant made to de Monts. The French asserted that the English were usurpers and claimed lands to which France had prior title because of earlier discovery and occupation. In the year 1611 a Frenchman, Biencourt, visited the site of the Popham colony at the mouth of the Kennebec and set up a cross with the arms of France, thus asserting claim to the territory.

These claims and activities of the French startled the Virginia Company. So in July 1612 Capt. Samuel Argall of Virginia received orders to drive out foreigners. In 1613 and 1614 he broke up the French settlements at Mt. Desert, Port Royal, and St. Croix; burned the houses, killed the cattle, tore down the French cross, and erected an English cross in its place. England having already chartered the Newfoundland Company in 1610, and another company to seek the northwest passage in 1612, was determined to dispute the claims of the French to this region.

As on the Atlantic Seaboard, so in the West Indies, the European nations and England came into bitter conflict. John Hawkins engaged in the slave trade until stopped by the Spaniards who almost destroyed his fleet in 1568. Drake was preying on Spanish commerce from 1572, and, in 1585, with twenty-five vessels captured Santo Domingo, one of the Spanish West Indies. Spain had failed to lay claim to the lesser West Indian islands, and from the opening of the seventeenth century England and France were active in taking possession of these unoccupied islands. Bermuda was occupied in 1609 and a charter was granted the " Somers Islands Company " in 1614, most of the stockholders being members of the Virginia Company. Between 1614 and 1635 England occupied

Spain, France, and England in the West Indies

other islands — St. Christopher, Barbados, Nevis, Tortuga, Antigua, and Providence Island. Within the same period France and Holland extended their control over a number of small islands. Thus Spain, England, France, and Holland were rivals in the Caribbean Sea as on the mainland. The importance of the West Indies in relation to the trade of the colonies, both legal and illegal, will appear later.

13. Influence of European Colonial Systems on England

European colonial systems and ideas respecting colonies could hardly fail to influence, to some extent,

Spanish
Colonial
System

English ideas before permanent colonization was effected. Some examination of general Spanish and French policies is therefore desirable. We have already considered Spanish ideas of discovery, title to land, and treatment of the Indians, all of which probably influenced English practice. The Spanish policy was to center government in Spain, laws being issued by the king through a body called " The Council of the Indies," organized in 1524. This body had supreme legislative, executive, and judicial power, assisted by officials in the colonies — viceroys and governors. Trade was also regulated by a Spanish body subordinate to the council, called the *Casa de Contractacion*. It had a manager, treasurer, auditor, and other officers with supreme authority 'over trade and commerce. It supervised the export and import of goods, provided fleets, and organized expeditions in Spanish America. The king exercised authority through a viceroy (1574) with arbitrary power, who represented the king and had under him minor officers.

Spanish policy was arbitrary, paternalistic, and monopolistic. Neither the Spanish government nor its representatives within the colonies felt interest in the Anglo-Saxon idea of self-government or representa-

Nature of
Government

tive government. Spain did recognize a duty or obligation to Christianize the natives, and the Jesuits and Franciscans were active in the establishment of posts, missions, and colonies. The land in theory was a possession of the king to be granted as he saw fit. The weakness of the system was the lack of emphasis on agriculture, as a basis for the building up of colonies. The eagerness of Spain to profit from mines and from trade and commerce resulted in policies and restrictions that hampered the development of successful agricultural colonies.

In order to gain the largest profits and to protect Spanish fleets from European enemies, buccaneers, and

Regulation
of Trade

pirates, Spain enacted that goods were to be carried to and from America only in Spanish ships by Spaniards, sailing from and to specified ports in Spain and America. The fleets were convoyed by naval vessels and private ships were generally prohibited from sailing singly. The plan was for fleets twice a year to leave Spain and to return with the treasures of the mines and land. Hawkins, Drake, and other freebooters reaped rich profits by attacking the Spanish treasure ships on these voyages.

The French colonial system was just beginning to develop when the English established their first perma-

French
Colonial
System

nent colony. Between 1607 and 1640 their main objects were exploration and exploitation of the region, especially the development of the fur trade. They aimed to remain friendly to the Indians, to use them as allies wherever possible, and to secure joint occupation of the land. The disposition of such territory was based on the principle of large grants as a source of individual profit.

" The Seigniors," who were the recipients of the grants, adopted the feudal idea of subinfeudation for a small perpetual rental fee, with other practices of the feudal régime. Trade was hampered by monopolies and restrictions.

Most of the French population in the early seventeenth century was engaged in the fur trade. This was practically a government monopoly, farmed out to commercial companies or favorites of the king. The colonial system thus not only tended to prevent the rapid growth of population, but also to scatter it over a broad area, to stifle individual enterprise, to minimize the development of agriculture, and to prevent the growth of a large body of free landowners — men possessed of the individual initiative of the home seeker. The government was absolute in form and paternalistic in character, the governor, with minor officials, being appointed by the crown. There was little attempt, in comparison with the English policy, to give the settlers a voice in the government or to allow them local self-government.

The French pushed inland along the Great Lakes and rivers and gradually obtained control of the interior and much of the fur trade. This advance was accomplished by an alliance of fur traders and Jesuit missionaries, for the twofold purpose of commercial advancement and of converting the Indians to Catholicism.

Champlain is the great figure in early French history, Governor of Quebec in 1608, and explorer as far west as the tributaries of the Mississippi; his discoveries being the basis of the French claim to the great valley. His ambition was to found a great French empire protected by a far-flung system of military forts and trading posts, placed at strategic points. A great weakness of the French colonial system was the difficulty of protecting and holding such a wide territory, and the failure to develop self-sustaining agricultural colonies, based on free, independent, and patriotic citizens.

When the English made their first permanent settlement (1607) it cannot be said that English statesmen had thought out any well-defined colonial policy. However, the knowledge and experiences gained in the early expeditions, and the information set forth in printed accounts, acquainted the English with the work of Spain and France, with the Indian problem, and with the general problem of colonization. Many accounts of the work of the Spanish and French in the new world were early printed. Richard Hakluyt, after spending four or five years in France (1584-1588) returned to England and commenced writing accounts of voyages. In 1600 he published his famous *Collection of Voyages* (1600), containing over two hundred narratives of voyages to the new world. Samuel Purchas supplemented this collection by publishing (1613–1614) his *Pilgrimage,* which gave accounts of twelve hundred more voyages. From the experience of Spain and France and from her own experience, England became acquainted with a variety of plans and principles of colonial policy.

She saw how Spain forced the Indians to give up their lands, and noted the policy of the king in granting title to lands; in monopolizing trade for the mother country; in furthering plans for Christianizing the Indians; in granting lands to a company on which was placed the responsibility of colonizing, and to which were given large economic powers. From the Spaniards also were learned the value of the commercial slave trade and the use of African negroes as slaves for the exploitation of natural resources.

England watched France develop the fur trade and

English Policy (marginal note)

gradually realized its relation to the penetration and occupation of the West. She also observed the tendency to confer opportunities for exploiting new regions on favorites of the crown, and the policy of granting immense tracts of land to a few individuals. How far Spanish and French policies directly influenced English statesmen in this respect is difficult to say.

England's own experience previous to 1607 had emphasized the necessity of using the chartered company as one of the agencies of colonization. The character of the Atlantic Seaboard was known through the voyages of Raleigh and those of Gosnold, Weymouth, and Pring. (See p. 33). The opportunity of exploiting its agricultural possibilities, and of utilizing its natural resources was early appreciated. The English also knew something of the Indian problem. The relation of colonization and internal problems was set forth by Hakluyt in his *Discourse* and by others; particularly with respect to the pressing problem of unemployment.

What English statesmen had not thought out was the proper relation of crown or Parliament to colonies planted by private initiative. For, unlike Spain, the English plan for colonization did not provide for direct governmental stimulation, support, and control. On the contrary, England depended rather on private adventurers, groups and companies, who were given patents or grants of land, with little governmental control and in some cases practically none. In fact, considerable time elapsed before the statesmen of England grasped the importance of the colonies from an imperial standpoint. The start the colonists obtained in managing their own affairs was thus in great contrast to the Spanish and French development. This fact together with the agricultural economy of the English colonies marks the greatest difference in the policy of the three nations who first contended for supremacy in America.

CHAPTER III

COLONIZATION AND DEVELOPMENT OF THE SOUTHERN COLONIES TO 1689

14. References

Bibliographies. — C. M. Andrews, *Colonial Self-Govt.*, 337–354; H. E. Bolton and T. M. Marshall, *Coloniza. of North Am.*, 134, 195; Channing, Hart and Turner, *Guide*, §§ 31–34, 36–39, 42–43, 45, 48, 96–97, 99, 113–120, 149, 163, 164; Godfrey Davies (ed.), *Bibl. of British Hist., 1603-1714.*, E. B. Greene, *Prov. Am.*, 351–354, and *Foundations of Am. Nationality*, 65–66, 85–86; Grace Griffin, *Writ. on Am. Hist.*, 1906–1923; J. N. Larned, *Lit. of Am. Hist.*, 69–70, 100–106, 375–383; E. G. Swem, *Bibliog. of Colo. Va.*; L. G. Tyler, *Engl. in Am.*, 328–334; T. J. Wertenbaker, *First Americans*, 320–321; Justin Winsor, *Nar. and Crit. Hist. of Am.*, III, 121–127, 153–167.

Historical Maps. — Nos. 1 and 2 of this vol.; H. E. Bolton and T. M. Marshall, *Coloniza. of North Am.*, 115, 126, 161, 209; Channing, Hart and Turner, *Guide*, §§ 33–34, 96–97 (bibliography); D. R. Fox, *Atlas of Am. Hist.*, 1–4; E. B. Greene, *Foundations, etc.*, 37, 44, 164, 188; Ralph Harlow, *Growth of U. S.*, 62, (colonies in 1655); Justin Winsor, *Nar. and Crit. Hist. of Am.*, III, 166.

General Accounts. — For Engl. background see refs. in chs. i and v, "Special Accounts"; ch. vi, "Rela. of New Engl. with Brit. Emp.;" ch. vii, "Gen. Accounts," and ch. x; W. C. Abbott, *Expan. of Europe*, II, chs. xxiii–xxvii; C. M. Andrews, *Colonial Period*, chs. i-ii, and *Colonial Self-Govt.*, chs. ix-x, xiii-xv; Chas. and Mary Beard, *Rise of Am. Civiliza.*, I, ch. ii; G. L. Beer, *Origins of the British Colo. System 1578-1660*, 78–175; and *Old Colonial System;* and "Com. Policy of Engl. Towards the Am. Colonies" in *Columb. Studies*, III; H. E. Bolton and T. M. Marshall, *Coloniza. of North Am.*, chs. vi, viii, ix-xi; Edward Channing, *Hist. of the U. S.*, I, chs. vii-ix; II, ch. i; F. C. Dietz, *Polit. and Social Hist. of Engl.*, chs. xi-xiii; J. A. Doyle, *Engl. Col. in Am.*, I, chs. vi-xii; H. E. Egerton, *Short Hist. of British Colonial Policy*, 66–80; Edward Eggleston, *Beginners of a Nation*, bk. I, chs. i-iii; bk. III, ch. i; John Fiske, *Old Va. and her Neighbors*, I and II; J. E. Gillespie, "Influ.

of Overseas Expan. on Engl. to 1700," in *Columb. Studies*, XCI;
E. B. Greene, *Foundations, etc.*, chs. iii-iv; H. L. Osgood, *Am.
Col. in the 17th Cent.*, I, chs. ii-iv; II, chs. i-iv, ix-x; III, chs.
ii, iv, viii-ix, xvi; Gustav Schmoller, *The Mercantile System,
etc.;* J. R. Seeley, *Growth of Brit. Policy*, I; L. G. Tyler, *Engl. in
Am.*, chs. iii-viii; Justin Winsor, *Nar. and Crit. Hist. of Am.*,
III, ch. v; V, chs. iv-v.

Special Accounts. — J. S. Bassett, "Constitutional Begins. of
N. C." (1663–1729), in *J. H. Studies*, ser. XII; W. H. Browne,
Md. a Palatinate, and *George and Cecilius Calvert;* P. A. Bruce,
Econom. Hist. of Va. in 17th Cent.; George Chalmers, *Political
Annals of the Am. Cols.* (vol. I, to 1688); Edward Channing,
"Town and County Govt. in the American Colonies of North
Am.," in *J. H. Stud., in Hist.*, ser. X, and "The Navigation
Acts" in *Am. Antq. Soc. Proc.* n. s. VI, 160–179; E. P.
Cheyney, "Some Engl. Conditions Surrounding the Settlement
of Va.," in *Am. Hist. Rev.* XII, 507–528; J. H. Claiborne,
William Claiborne of Va.; P. S. Flippin, "Royal Govt. in Va.,
1624–1775," in *Columb. Studies in Hist.*, LXXXIV; Mary
Johnston, *Pioneers of the Old South;* Edward McCrady, *Hist.
of S. Carolina under the Proprietary Govt., 1670–1719;* N. D.
Mereness, *Md. as a Proprietary Prov.;* C. L. Raper, *North
Carolina, a study in Engl. Colonial Govt.;* E. C. Semple, *Am. Hist.
and its Geographic Conditions;* L. D. Scisco, "Plantation Type of
Colony," in *Am. Hist. Rev.*, VIII, 260; W. R. Scott, *Constitu-
tions and Finance of English, Scottish, and Irish Joint-Stock Com-
panies to 1720*, II, 246–289; J. H. Shea, *Cath. Ch. in Colonial
Days*, I; B. C. Steiner, "Begin. of Md.," in *J. H. Stud.*, ser.
XXI; T. S. Wertenbaker, *Va. Under the Stuarts*, and *Planters of
Colonial Va.;* E. L. Whitney, "Govt. of the Col. of S. C.," in
J. H. Stud., ser. XII.

Contemporary Accounts. — J. T. Adams, *Prov. Society*, 326–
328; E. Arber and A. G. Bradley (eds.), Capt. John Smith,
Travels and Works; E. L. Bogart and C. M. Thompson, (eds.),
Readings, etc., ch. i; Alexander Brown, *Genesis of the U. S.*, and
*First Republic in America; Cal. of State Papers, Colonial and
W. I.*, 1607–1689; B. R. Carroll, *Hist. Colls. of South Carolina*
(2 vols.); *S. C. Hist. Colls.*, V, (Shaftesbury Papers); Channing,
Hart and Turner, *Guide*, §§ 37, 113–120, and *Hist. Sources in
Schools*, §§ 55–57, 69–70, and Milton Waldman, *Americana, etc.*,
ch. vi, and Hasse, "Materials for a Bibliography" *etc.*, in *Am.
Hist. Assoc. Rpt.*, 1906, II, and W. P. Trent (ed.), *Cambr.
Hist. of Am. Lit.*, I, 365–382 (J. Smith) (bibliography); Peter
Force, *Tracts and Other Papers, etc.*, (4 vols.); Ralph Gabriel,

Pageant of America, I, ch. ix, xiii-xiv; A. B. Hart (ed.), *Contemporaries*, I, chs. ix-xii, esp. §§ 53–54, 59, 61, 63–81, 84, 93, 94; J. F. Jameson (ed.), *Orig. Narratives of Early Am. Hist.*, (*Nars. of Early Va., Nars. of Early Md., Nars. of Early Carolina, Nars. of the Insurrections*); Susan Kingsbury, *Records of the Va. Co.;* William MacDonald (ed.), *Select Charters, etc.*, nos. 1–3, 6, 12, 22, 23, 25, 26, 28, 32, 33, 34 (last five, nav. acts); Peter Mode, *Source Book and Bibliographical Guide for Am. Church Hist.;* W. P. Palmer (ed.), *Cal. of Va. State. Paps.*, I, *1652–1781;* L. F. Stock (ed.), *Proceed. and Debates of the British Parl. respect. North Am.;* F. N. Thorpe, *Federal and State Constitutions, Colonial Charters, etc.*, (7 vols.); colonial records are in *Archives of Maryland*, 41 vols., *Colonial Recs. of North Carolina*, 10 vols.; W. W. Hening, *Statutes at Large of Va.*, 13 vols.

15. The Physical Environment

THE region which was the scene of England's first attempt at successful colonization had certain physical characteristics which should be understood; for there existed a relationship on the one hand between plans of colonization, the policies of England and the acts and thoughts of the colonists themselves, and on the other hand between the colonists and the physical environment.

Importance of Physical Environment

First in importance was the position of the region chosen for colonization in relation to English control. Its great distance from England made ease of control difficult. Sailing vessels seldom crossed the ocean in less than six weeks to two months and often the voyage took three months or failed entirely. Unenforced laws encouraged the colonists to evade or break them. Thus a feeling of self-sufficiency developed which, in the end, stimulated a desire for independence. No doubt from the time of the first settlements, geographical distance led to the questioning of the authority of crown and Parliament. Edmund Burke once remarked, "Three thousand miles of

Geographical Position

ocean lie between you and them. No contrivance can prevent the effect of this distance in weakening government." It was this geographical isolation that laid the foundation for the early principles of American foreign policy; the belief in a policy of political isolation, neutrality, freedom of the seas for neutral nations, and the Monroe Doctrine. Isolation also favored variation in manners, customs, and speech to an extent not possible had America's position been much nearer England. Thus were Englishmen made Americans.

The general formation of the land area in the southern region is that of a narrow coastal plain, Coastal Plain bordered by the Appalachian Mountain system. It is divided into two distinct areas — eastern and western. That extending from the coast to the falls of the rivers, known as the tidewater region, though narrow north of New York, gradually widens to a distance of about one hundred and fifty miles in South Carolina and Georgia. Near the coast the plain is low and level with many swamps and marshes. The soil in the river valleys is relatively rich, with a favorable climate and rainfall and good transportation facilities by ocean and river. With a long hot summer the conditions favored agriculture, trade and commerce, extraction of raw materials, and the plantation system, thus making possible an extensive system of agriculture based on the growing of staple crops for export, particularly tobacco. (See also p. 89.)

In the interior upland area the conditions were favorable for raising live stock. The immense forests were a source of naval stores — tar, pitch, turpentine, masts, spars, etc. The forests were also a source of food supplies — game, which also furnished furs and skins.

Next to the character of the soil and natural resources
the river system of the South was of greatest impor-
Rivers and   tance in directing settlement. The rivers
Climate   were longer, with a slower current, and
navigable to a greater distance than most of those in
the North. They flowed from northwest to southeast
in nearly parallel lines, were relatively near each other
and thus furnished direct and easy means of transportation to the coast for a large area. On the other
hand the climate near the coast was debilitating. Mos-
quito swamps and impure water, which the colonists
were forced to drink, were among the causes which led
to illness and many deaths among the early immigrants.
Dense forests reached nearly to the water's edge of
river and coast, making the problem of clearing the
land for agricultural purposes one of great physical
labor.

16. Conditions Favoring Colonization

The first attempts by Gilbert and Raleigh to found
English colonies in America having failed, English
Methods and   adventurers waited fifteen years before re-
Agencies of   newing their efforts. Within that period
Colonization   occurred the great victory over Spain —
the destruction of the Armada in 1588, which gave
England virtual control of the seas, a condition favorable for the establishment of permanent colonies. It
was evident that lone adventurers could not provide
sufficient resources to finance a colony, a costly under-
taking involving ships, supplies, and resources to meet
unexpected losses or disasters. The age of adventure,
in which such gentlemen as Gilbert and Raleigh hoped
for great dominions and personal power and profit, was
bound to give way to a more utilitarian age with
new plans for pooling capital, minimizing losses, and

dividing power and profits among a larger number, a form of effort described by the term "joint-stock company."

The English were accustomed to such companies organized to trade overseas at distant points under national charters. Though private corporations they were subject to national regulation and were dependent on the crown for rights, privileges, and protection. The most common of the privileges granted was a monopoly of trade in given regions with a restriction, such as that requiring (1566) that all goods must be carried solely in English ships, manned for the most part with English sailors. The system of authorizing companies to elect their governors and make laws was tried out. For example, a charter granted by Edward IV, to merchants resident in the Netherlands, provided that the king should appoint a governor while the merchants were to elect twelve men to sit with him as a court, but with the understanding that laws made must be approved by the royal governor. This is the principle later developed in the government of the royal colonies.

Early Joint-Stock Trading Companies

The patent granted to Sir Humphrey Gilbert in 1578 not only gave him permission to discover, occupy, and trade in new lands, but to establish a colony with full proprietary rights, such as the power to make laws and ordinances "as near as conveniently might be to the laws of the realm," an important step in the development of colonial government. Gilbert associated with him a group of twenty merchants, to whom he promised land in proportion to subscriptions, as well as to settlers. Raleigh's patent was similar and, like Gilbert, he promised to grant land to his associates. Thus it is clear that for nearly a generation before permanent colonization

Early Proprietary Grants of Land and Government

was effected plans were conceived for proprietary colonies founded by private individuals under government patronage, with colonists governed by a landed gentry. Hence the promoters of permanent colonies could draw on the experience of trading companies and their charters, and also on the patents of Gilbert and Raleigh, for ideas respecting trade, land grants, colonization, and government.

17. The Virginia Company Charter and Colony (1606–1608)

A patent, or charter, was granted to the Virginia Company April 10, 1606. It provided for two subordinate companies known as the London and Plymouth Companies or Colonies. To the former was granted land from north latitude 34° to 41°, and to the latter from 38° to 45° inclusive, the overlapping area from 38° to 41° being open to settlement by either company, though neither could settle within 100 miles of territory occupied by the other. These grants covered the Atlantic Coast from Cape Fear to Halifax. The first settlement or colony of the London Company was limited to 100 miles along the coast. An important clause of the charter granted the company the right to "have, take and lead out colonists." Another clause provided that the colonists "shall have and enjoy all liberties, franchises and immunities . . . as if they had been abiding and born within this our realm of England." Thus by inference was extended to the settlers the protection of the common law of England, trial by jury, etc.

James I had no wish to establish a self-governing colony which might question his power; hence he did not grant powers of government to the proprietors. He acted through a royal council which he appointed, with

power to govern all the colonies established. Two additional and separate councils, resident in England,

Form of   were created, one for each subordinate
Government   company — the London and Plymouth
branches. A local council resident in each colony was
also appointed.

The king issued " Articles and Instructions " providing for the details of government and settlement in
Virginia. Large legislative, executive, and judicial power
was given to a resident council in Virginia. Thus self-
government was not granted to the colonists themselves,
but to representatives or agents of the king. Provision
was made for the maintenance of the Church of England, for a penal code and for trial by jury. Laws made
by the resident council must be ratified by the council
in England or by the crown, and be " consonant to the
laws of England."

The economic aspect of the company merits particular attention. The instructions given by King James

The Trade   provided for a joint-stock system of trade,
Aspect of the   land holding, and industry, by means of
Company   " magazines " or storehouses, located in
England and in the colony, and " factors " or managers,
the one in Virginia being called the " Cape Merchant."
All goods sent to the colony or produced by it were to
be brought to the " magazines." From them all necessities were to be supplied, and in them were stored the
food and products to be exported. On the patentees
fell the burden of providing ships, supplies, colonists,
and their maintenance and protection. The resident
council in the colony undertook the task of directing
the government, of exploration, building, managing,
and directing the work of the colonists.

It is misleading to speak of the " colonists " of Virginia. Many of those who migrated in the first few

years of settlement were servants and laborers, under a form of contract with the company; in reality inden-
The Col-
onists
tured servants, a status which will be described later. They received neither land nor wages, had few personal or civil rights and worked in gangs under harsh overseers. The " colonists " furnished the labor power necessary for the establishment of a settlement, clearing the land of trees, planting and harvesting crops, building houses, forts, and magazines, exploring the region and guarding the colony from attacks by the Indians.

The most these early settlers could hope for was transportation to Virginia, food, clothing, shelter, and protection for a period of years with a vague promise of a share of land, and of the profits if any, a number of years later. This system of colonization was a temporary plan, thought to be the best means of financing, peopling, defending, and making permanent a colony while at the same time providing a method of returning to the original investors their capital and interest in the form of dividends on their investment.

December 20, 1606, three small vessels, the *Sarah Constant,* the *Discovery,* and the *Goodspeed,* carrying
The Settle-
ment of
Virginia
about 120 persons, all men, set sail under Captain Christopher Newport for some point in Virginia; and nearly four months later entered the Chesapeake Bay, May 6, 1607. A peninsula in the James River was chosen for settlement, principally because it was easy to defend. One of the instructions read, "Neither must you plant in a low or moist place because it will prove unhealthful." Nevertheless this bit of marshy land was both unhealthy and infested with mosquitoes. In fact, hardly a worse choice could have been made in this respect.

The process of opening up a new settlement is well described by Capt. John Smith in his *General Historie of Virginia:* " Now falleth every man to worke, the Councell contrive the Fort, the rest cut downe trees to make place to pitch their tents; some provide clapboards to relade the ships, some make gardens, some nets, etc."

The council was composed of Edward Wingfield as president and six others, including Capt. Bartholomew Gosnold and Capt. John Smith. With no settled plan of action, quarrels, mismanagement, and plots were inevitable. Wingfield was deposed and imprisoned on the charge of misappropriating funds, food, and of making an unfair division of the supplies. As Smith says, he seized for his private use, " Oatmeale . . . beef, eggs, or what not." By the summer of 1609, through death or return to England of the others, Capt. Smith found himself the sole councillor, in fact governor and, as it turned out, saviour of the colony. His energy and rigid enforcement of discipline saved the colony. He obtained food from the Indians, forced lazy men to work and instilled courage into the weary and sick. " Scarce ten amongst us could either goe or well stand, such extreame weakness and sickness oppressed us."

Other difficulties developed which hindered the immediate success of the colonists. A number who classed themselves as " gentlemen," were quite unfit for hard physical labor. Incentive to work was lacking for they had neither houses nor land of their own and were fed, clothed, and protected by the company whether they worked hard or not. The Indians made it dangerous to work in the cornfields, while food supplies brought over spoiled and famine threatened. Capt. George Percy thus described the misery of the first summer: " There were never Englishmen left in a foreign country in such miserie as we were in this new discovered Virginia. Wee watched every three nights, lying on the bare ground, what weather soever came — which brought our men to bee most feeble wretches. . . If there were conscience in men, it would make their hearts bleed to heare the pitiful murmurings and outcries of our sick men without reliefe, every night and day for the space of sixe weekes; in the morning their bodies being trailed out of their cabines like Dogges, to be buried." By January 1608 only 38 colonists were alive out of the 120 who had sailed for Virginia.

18. Progress of Virginia (1609–1624)

In view of the complaints and reports of deposed councillors who returned to England, a new charter

The Charter of 1609 and the Second Expedition

was obtained in 1609, which created a corporation to which was granted the direct management of its affairs. Sir Thomas Smith was made treasurer and a council was provided for in England, composed of members originally appointed by the king. Vacancies were to be filled by vote of the whole company. This council had legislative power and the right to appoint officials. A new plan of government was drawn up which abolished the old council in Virginia and provided for a powerful one man government — a governor who had almost the power of a despot. The charter of 1609 was modified in 1612 by a third document providing for general meetings of the stockholders four times a year. The new boundaries of 1609 gave to the colony an extent of four hundred miles along the coast; — 200 north and 200 south of Old Point Comfort — and into the interior "West and Northwest" to the Pacific Ocean; a description which later gave rise to serious and long contested boundary controversies.

Shares of stock were sold at twelve pounds and ten shillings each. Planters or emigrants above ten years of age were entitled to one share and were promised transportation, food, clothing, a house, orchard, garden, and one hundred acres of land at the end of the joint-stock period. Nine vessels sailed June 2, 1609 with five hundred emigrants, including one hundred women and children. Their character left much to be desired. A contemporary declared that parents rid themselves of "lascivious sons, masters of bad servants, wives of ill husbands."

Governor Gates, who arrived in May 1610, gave a dismal picture of the colony at that date showing how
Condition of the Colony 1610–13 difficult was the problem of successful colonization. He complained of idleness, embezzlement of provisions, killing of hogs, illegal trading with the Indians, failure to store food for the winter, allowing fourteen fishing nets, all they had, to "rot and spoile," and so "fishing perished." He described Jamestown as a town that appeared rather like the ruin of some "auntient fortification than that any people living might now inhabit it," — the palisades down, gates off their hinges, church in ruins, and only food enough in the storehouse to last sixteen days at the rate of "two cakes" (corn meal) a day for each colonist. Gates decided to abandon the settlement, but just as he was leaving with all the colonists, Governor Delaware arrived with supplies and the discouraged colonists were obliged to return.

Two obstacles retarded the success of the colony for the next few years, namely sickness and the Indians. Many colonists who embarked for Virginia never arrived, because of the terrible conditions on shipboard. The small vessels were crowded, unhealthful, and foul beyond description. The London plague, yellow fever, scurvy, and various forms of tropical fevers caused great loss of life. On one vessel one hundred and thirty out of one hundred and eighty-five died. These diseases were spread after landing and to them were added malaria, pneumonia, and dysentery. By the end of 1610 hardly 60 colonists were alive out of the 700 or 800 that had started. Those who survived became acclimated, but of every fresh ship-load of colonists perhaps half were taken ill, most of whom soon died.

Indians were responsible for the loss of many settlers. About 5000 of them lived within sixty miles of Jamestown. They were resentful and plotted continually for the destruction of the colony. They made it unsafe to hunt in the woods, fish in the river, or work in the fields. When corn was planted, they often cut it down. These facts account in part for the complaints of idleness of the colonists, for they were compelled to seek the protection of the fort. Individuals and small parties were likely to be killed by the Indians if they ventured into the woods, or even into the tall grass surrounding the settlement. The Indians plotted continually against the whites, and this culminated in the great massacre of 1622, when three hundred and fifty-seven colonists were killed. By that time only eleven hundred were alive out of some five thousand who had migrated from England since 1607.

From 1610 to 1619 Virginia was under a succession of governors, Gates, Delaware, Dale, and Argall, each of whom ruled with an iron hand. Governor Delaware was instructed to "rule, punish, pardon, and governe according to such directions" as were given him by the London Company; or, in matters not covered by his instruc-

Character of the Government from 1610 to 1619

tions, to "rule and governe by his owne discretion or by such lawes" as he saw fit. Delaware organized the colony on a military basis in the belief that the failure so far was due to lack of discipline. Sir Thomas Dale, however, a stern soldier and "High Marshall of Virginia" from 1611 to 1616 attempted to make the colonist a soldier "who laid down his gun to take up the hoe" and regulated his life by the drum beat. Dale was a terror to the lazy man because a believer in hard work and a strong government. Under the code of laws that bears his name, twenty crimes were made punishable with death, and minor offenses were punished by whipping, such as failure to attend Sunday service, speaking against the King's majesty, trading with the Indians and failure to work diligently. Some severe penalties were imposed; one man at least, for conspiracy, was broken on a wheel. Another law breaker "had a bodkin thrust through his tongue and was chained to a tree till he perished." It must be remembered, however, that the criminal codes of Europe and England were very severe and that in Massachusetts cruel punishments were often inflicted.

Dale brought order out of chaos and put the colony on a better economic basis by granting land to individuals for their own use. By his energy were established new settlements, one (1611) the "City of Henricus" fifty miles up the river. He made the colonists work and thus raised corn in sufficient quantities to supply pressing needs. The growing of tobacco now commenced with increasing exports to England (p. 89).

An element of the English stockholders in the Virginia Company was dissatisfied with the government The First and the slow economic progress of the Assembly colony. Sir Edwin Sandys, who represented this group, was liberal minded and was also treasurer of the company. He succeeded in having Sir George

Yeardley appointed governor in 1618. Yeardley's instructions, with the ordinances drawn up in 1621, practically gave Virginia a new constitution. The company
not only granted a more liberal government but also
made plans for a more rapid economic development.
Land was granted to settlers and to those who were of
service to the colony. Trade and tobacco were organized for the benefit of the company or its members.
Governor Yeardley was given the power to summon
a representative assembly. Hence twenty-two " burgesses," from eleven settlements met in the church at
Jamestown, July 30, 1619, the first representative assembly in America. Here was born the institution of
self-government in the English colonies. Laws were
passed against idleness, gaming, and drunkenness; and
the clergy were given power to warn persons guilty of
" enormous sin " and to excommunicate them if necessary. The assembly levied taxes to pay for the cost
of government and also sat as a court.

The Virginia Company was nearing its downfall. This
was hastened by factional disputes within the company,
Revocation of numerous complaints made by its enemies,
the Charter   Spanish intrigues for its overthrow, the
Indian massacre of 1622, sickness, and a dispute with
the king because of his attempt to levy an import tax
on tobacco for revenue. Joined to these troubles, was
the king's dislike of the important leaders of the company, who opposed him in Parliament. Finally commissioners were appointed in 1623, with instructions to
investigate the company; and when they reported ad-
versely, the charter was revoked (1624). Virginia thus
became a royal colony, or as Charles I said in his
proclamation, " The Government of the Collonie of
Virginia shall immediately depend upon our selfe, and
not be committed to anie Company or corporation."

19. Political Development of Virginia
(1624–1689)

The plan for the new royal government involved in part a return to that of 1606, where the power rested almost wholly with the king who appointed a royal governor. The representative assembly was allowed to remain, however, and the king governed through written instructions to the governor who had the power of vetoing acts of the assembly. Two councils aided, one in England and one in Virginia, members of both being appointed by the king.

Plan and Workings of the Royal Government

The history of the first period from 1624 to 1641 is one of a long struggle between despotic governors, the planters, and the assembly. John Harvey, who arrived in 1630, was accused of usurping powers, issuing proclamations to enforce his will on the people, repealing statutes, imposing illegal taxes and ignoring the courts. Finally the planters and assembly petitioned for redress of grievances. Deserted by his council, Harvey was forced to return to England in 1635. Upheld by Charles I, he returned in 1637, created a new council, made himself master of the courts and introduced a system of arbitrary government involving confiscation of property, unjust fines, and cruel punishments. Finally he was replaced by the famous Sir William Berkeley, twice governor of Virginia, 1641–1653 and 1658–1677.

Berkeley's commission and instructions gave him power to order all affairs of peace and war; to maintain the established church, to convoke a general assembly yearly, to retain the veto power, appoint officials and, with the council, to act as a court of justice; to see that all tobacco

Sir William Berkeley, 1641–53

was shipped to England and that no foreign vessels were regularly to trade in Virginia, thus anticipating a principle of the navigation acts.

The first administration of this picturesque and energetic governor was, on the whole, advantageous to Virginia. Berkeley was an ardent royalist, but he protected the judiciary, signed a number of good laws, one of which allowed appeals from the quarter courts to the assembly, and another prohibiting the levying of taxes by the governor and council without the consent of the assembly. A third limited excessive fees by officials. He personally led troops to attack the Indians after a second massacre in 1644, when 500 people lost their lives; and brought them to terms by a treaty favorable to the settlers. When the civil war broke out in England (1642) it divided the people in Virginia as it did in England. Most of the larger land owners were supporters of the king, while the small farmers were in sympathy with Parliament.

During the Commonwealth Period (1652–1660) Virginia was almost a republic. Berkeley refused to Virginia acknowledge the Commonwealth, but was During the forced to submit to parliamentary comCommon-wealth missioners (March 12, 1652) sent for the purpose. This commission, among other things, agreed that Virginia should be free from taxes and customs unless the assembly assented. A Puritan governor, Richard Bennett, elected by the House of Burgesses, acknowledged this assembly as the chief ruling body, with power to elect and remove the governor and specify his powers and duties. The burgesses also elected the council and appointed officials. When Governor Matthews dissolved the assembly in 1657, that body refused to obey and declared the act illegal. With the approaching Restoration in England the assembly appointed (1659) Sir William Berkeley governor of Virginia.

Berkeley's rule now became arbitrary, despotic, and inefficient. No new election of burgesses was allowed for

Misgovern-
ment Under
Berkeley,
1660–1676

some fourteen years in order to prevent the choice of members adverse to the governor. Berkeley had such thorough control of the House of Burgesses that he practically dictated the whole legislation of this period. Local government, administered by the commissioners appointed by Berkeley, imposed heavy taxes which bore heavily on the poor farmer. The people were deprived of the right to elect their own vestries, and poll taxes rather than land taxes were levied for public, county, and parish purposes, thus adding to the burdens of the poor and favoring the wealthy. Taxes collected were wasted and expenditures were extravagant, the excessive cost of forts being one example. The members of the council, appointed by Berkeley, were given practically all the important, desirable, and lucrative offices.

With the Restoration completed, Charles II commenced to think of ways and means to raise more rev-

The Naviga-
tion Acts

enue. Important features of this plan were regulations of the trade of the colonies for England's benefit through navigation acts; the beginning of the " Mercantile System," (See p. 257), with increased duties on tobacco coming into England from the colonies, for revenue purposes. The first English navigation act had been passed in 1651; an important clause provided that exports of the colonies must be carried to England in English ships. This law, designed to break the Dutch monopoly of the carrying trade, was now reënacted (1660) in more detail. It provided that goods should be carried in ships of Great Britain or the plantations, with masters and three-fourths of the crew English. A clause was added providing that various "enumerated" products, including tobacco, sugar, and some other products should be exported only to the mother country. This was another step in the development of mercantilism; that colonies should be sources of raw materials. Another act of 1663, for the encouragement of trade, provided that European manufactured goods destined for the plantations must first be carried to England, and hence they could be purchased only in the English market. This would prevent the colonies from developing a direct import trade of their own, and compel them to receive goods from England in exchange for their raw materials — another step in the development of mercantilism. The general object of these acts was to keep the colonies "in a firmer dependence upon" England, following the usage of other nations by keeping "their plantations to themselves." In other words international competition compelled each state to adopt a national policy, which gradually developed as the "mercantile system." (See p. 257.) The immediate effect of these acts was to cause (1) a rise in freight rates, because the Dutch carried goods more cheaply than the English ships; (2) the market for tobacco was restricted and the price fell rapidly; (3) the price of manufactured goods increased in the colonies; (4) the king gained revenue through the duties on tobacco brought into England; (5) most important was the principle that Virginia and other colonies must be governed so that the mother country might become wealthy and powerful.

Arbitrary and corrupt government, economic distress, caused in part by the navigation acts, overproduction Bacon's and fall in the price of tobacco, and heavy Rebellion taxes were the chief causes of Bacon's Rebellion. Other grievances were: the grant of Virginia

(1672) for 31 years, to two of the king's favorites, Culpeper and Arlington, and its erection into a proprietary province; the capture by Dutch men-of-war (1667) of eighteen vessels loaded with Virginia tobacco; the epidemic which caused the loss of fifty thousand cattle (1672–1673); poor harvests for several years in succession, so that acts were passed forbidding the exportation of corn and wheat; and, finally, an outbreak of Indian warfare and the failure of Governor Berkeley to protect the settlers. Nathaniel Bacon, an energetic member of the council, had a plantation on the frontier, and had suffered greatly from Indian attacks (1676). Bacon was placed in command of a body of armed troops by men of Charles City County and marched against the Indians. Berkeley, however, called out troops against Bacon and declared him a rebel and a traitor.

A new assembly met in May 1676, the first to be hostile to the governor since his appointment. Laws were passed, thereafter known as Bacon's laws. Their purpose was to restrict the power of the governor and increase that of the House of Burgesses. The laws provided that sheriffs should have one term only and hold only one office at a time; that vestries be elected triennially by the freemen; that the power of the county courts be restricted; that the people elect representatives to act with the justices in levying assessments; that councillors be subject to taxation; and that the franchise be extended to all freemen. This was distinctly a democratic program.

During the summer and fall of 1676 Bacon and Berkeley were fighting for the control of the government, but Bacon was taken ill and died October 26, 1676. Berkeley later executed fourteen of Bacon's followers. This ended the rebellion. While the new laws were disallowed by the king, some of them were later reënacted. The general effect was to pave the way for the House of Burgesses to dispute more successfully the power of arbitrary governors, and gradually to encroach on their power. The rebellion also aroused among the poorer planters and farmers a feeling of class consciousness which stimulated democratic ideas.

After Berkeley's return to England in 1676 great confusion prevailed for a few years, followed by a series

Quarrels Between Burgesses and Governors, 1680-1689

of quarrels with Governors Culpeper and Howard (1680–1689). The political history of this period consists mainly of the struggle of the Burgesses to resist arbitrary government. With the news of the success of the great revolution in England, the attacks on the constitutional rights of the people of Virginia were for the time being ended. Governor Howard was not allowed to continue as resident governor, and Francis Nicholson was appointed lieutenant-governor of Virginia in 1691.

20. Maryland (1632–1660)

Virginia was planted mainly because of economic motives: conquest, international rivalry with Spain and

Origin of Maryland

France, hope of gain — gold and silver, lands, and profits of trade. One motive for founding Maryland was the desire to have a buffer state between Virginia and the Dutch in New Netherland. A powerful religious motive was present however. Roman Catholics were discontented with religious conditions in England. In fact intolerance was a greater grievance for Catholics than for Pilgrims or Puritans.

Maryland owes its charter and establishment to the interest in colonization of Sir George Calvert, Lord Baltimore, a Catholic, a secretary of state under James I, and a member of the East India Company, the

Virginia Company, and the Council for New England.
He first received a grant of territory in Newfoundland
Lord and attempted, unsuccessfully, to found a
Baltimore colony there in 1623. In April 1632 he received from the crown a grant of land extending from
the Potomac northward to the fortieth parallel; owing
to his death, the charter was given to his son, Cecilius
Calvert, who planted but never visited his colony. The
father was influenced largely by economic motives, the
founding of a great landed estate, while the son was
chiefly interested in a colony which would be an asylum
for persecuted English Catholics.

The charter granted to Lord Baltimore conveyed not
only a great proprietary grant of land, but in addition
The Charter extensive political rights and privileges.
The proprietor was made almost inde-
pendent of the crown, both with respect to land and
government. Land granted to settlers was held of the
proprietor and not of the king as in royal colonies.
Baltimore was given the right to erect manors with
separate courts, and manorial privileges, and to impose
quit rents. He could inflict punishments, even the death
penalty, appoint all officials, and in general was made
the sole source of military, executive, and judicial
authority.

On the other hand the charter contained limiting
clauses. The proprietor could enact laws only with the
advice, assent, and approbation of the freemen or their
representatives. He could make ordinances which would
have the force of law, but laws must be reasonable, and
not contrary to those of England. The settlers were also
to have "all the privileges, franchises, and liberties
which other English subjects enjoyed." No provision
was made for the submission of the laws to the king or
for appeals to the English courts and the king re-

nounced his right to levy taxes on any persons or goods in the province. The colonists thus were given the means to resist arbitrary government. The religious clause was vague but under it religious toleration was made possible, since there was neither prohibition of Catholics nor of non-conformists.

In November 1633 two ships, the *Ark* and the *Dove*, sailed with about 200 emigrants, including several Jesuit priests. Perhaps half the emigrants were Catholics. The instructions to Governor Leonard Calvert, brother of the proprietor, provided for religious toleration. The first settlement was made at St. Mary's in February 1634, near the mouth of the Potomac. The immigrants were independent colonists and of much better caliber than those who originally went to Virginia. They also escaped many of the adverse conditions of that colony because of better management and because they chose a better site. They made peace with the Indians and purchased land from them. Father White, a priest, wrote, " We bought from the King (of the Indians) thirty miles of that land, delivering in exchange axes, hatchets, rakes, and several yards of cloth." They raised so much corn the first season that they were able to export some to New England to be exchanged for salt codfish. The first report declared, " Nothing was wanting which might serve for commerce or pleasure." Lord Baltimore bore nearly all the expenses, and is said to have expended some £40,000 in two years, the greater part of his fortune.

The Lord proprietor, a far seeing man of upright character, appointed the governor, as he did all other important officials; thus all were dependent on him. The governor was military and naval head of the colony. In the commission of Leonard Calvert, April 15, 1637, he was called " Lieu-

(The First Maryland Expedition)

(The Governor and other officials)

tenant-General, Admiral, Chief, Captain, and Commander, as well by sea as land." As chancellor the governor issued all land patents and writs for elections. He was the chief justice of the province, and had the important power of vetoing acts of the legislature. Other officials were the members of the council, secretary, surveyor, judges, attorney general, sheriffs, naval officers, and other minor officials.

The first assemblies of 1634 and 1636 seem to have been made up of the more important freemen, but the governor and secretary held enough proxies at one time to out-vote the rest of the assembly. It was not until 1650 that it became regularly the custom to elect delegates from each hundred, a small political subdivision. In this year also the two houses sat separately; the upper, with members appointed by the proprietor, standing for his rights, and the lower for those of the people. No law could be made or repealed without the consent of both houses, the governor and lord proprietor. The purpose of the proprietor was to control the proceedings of the assembly in his own interest, through instructions to the governor and council, through his veto and through the power of initiating legislation.

This power to initiate laws was the first important question in dispute. However, the proprietor was in 1638 forced by the assembly, a majority of whom were Catholics, to concede this important power. He instructed the governor to assent to such laws as should be "concerted with and approved of by the freemen or their deputies," to be later ratified by the proprietor himself. The legislative history of the province shows that the proprietor sought to secure legislation to support him in his proprietary rights, in the land surveys, rents, etc., and in his political power; while the assembly favored laws to aid the people.

Part of the energies of the colony were absorbed in a dispute with Virginia over territorial jurisdiction, Virginia and involving the claim to Kent Island in the Maryland Chesapeake Bay. William Claiborne, secretary of the province of Virginia, a man of energy with an indomitable will, had purchased the island from the Indians, established a trading post there, and fought for his claims and those of Virginia. The Virginian occupants returned a representative to that colony in 1631. A contest followed which lasted for several years, and resulted in the carrying of the case to England and a long legal battle. Finally Baltimore was confirmed in his claim to the " Isle of Kent." The case illustrates the recklessness with which overlapping land grants were made, regardless of claims of settlers or earlier grants.

The great civil war in England, begun in 1642, split the people of Maryland into parties, supporting the Maryland king on the one hand and Parliament on in the the other. One reason was the fact that Civil War Puritan settlers, many coming from Virginia, increased rapidly. Another reason was the attitude of certain Jesuit priests who were accused of disregarding the acts of the assembly and of Parliament. Baltimore was forced to interfere, and appointed William Stone, a Protestant, as governor (1647), with a council in which there were only two Catholics. In order to prevent further religious dissensions, the governor took oath that he would not molest any persons on the ground of their religion. The outcome of this controversy was the famous toleration act of 1649, described later.

The commissioners sent over by the English commonwealth government proceeded to Maryland in

March 1652, after remodelling the new government in
Virginia. It was agreed that the authority of the Com-

Maryland
during the
Common-
wealth monwealth should be accepted. When
England came under the rule of Lord
Protector Cromwell (1654) Governor
Stone issued a proclamation acknowledging that Maryland was subordinate to and dependent on the government of the Commonwealth; nevertheless he sided with
the proprietor against the Puritans. The commissioners
therefore deposed Stone, took possession of the government, and disfranchised the Roman Catholics. Acts were
passed which allowed a settler to occupy land without
declaring loyalty to the proprietor, or compelling him
to take the oath of allegiance. The proprietary party resisted these encroachments and in 1655 a civil war broke
out between " Papists " and Puritans, in which the
latter were successful. Virginia plotted to overthrow
the proprietary rights of Baltimore and to join Maryland and Virginia under one colony. But Baltimore
pleaded his case with skill and finally an agreement
was reached between him and the commissioners which
gave Baltimore most of his original rights.

21. Development of Maryland (1660–1715)

The Restoration of 1660 brought little change from a
constitutional standpoint; but the plan of King Charles

Disputes
with the
Proprietors II to bring all of the colonies under a more
unified control affected Maryland. The as-
sembly in 1671 laid a tax of two shillings
a hogshead on exported tobacco, half for the support
of the government and half to the proprietor. Baltimore was accused of interfering with the king's tax
collector and in 1681 an order in council commanded
him to make good £2500, lost to the crown in taxes,
and intimated that if he did not obey his charter would
be imperilled.

From 1660 on, friction between the colonists and the proprietors increased rapidly. Among the many grievances was the practice of the proprietor in disallowing laws, often passed years before, to which the governor had given his assent. Another cause of friction was the tendency to bestow all the important offices on members of the Calvert family — governor, judges, land and military officials, tax collector, sheriffs, and even local officers being largely under control of the Calvert family. The colonists had no part in appointing or removing these officials. The Catholic office holders were out of proportion to the population at large. An attempt was made also to manipulate the system of representation, so that the proprietor could control the assembly.

The English revolution of 1688–89, was followed by a similar one in Maryland. The Protestants organized Maryland forces with John Coode at their head, and the Revolution in an "Association in Arms for the Deof 1688 fence of the Protestant religion, and for asserting the right of King William and Queen Mary to the Province of Maryland and all the English dominions." In July, 1689, they took up arms, seized the government at St. Mary's and were successful in securing control of the local government in every county but one. A convention was elected which extended the existing laws of the province for three years. Two sets of petitions were sent to England: the one pleading for the abolition of the proprietor's rights; the other seeking to have the colony made a royal colony. King William finally deprived Lord Baltimore of his political power, but left him all of his proprietary rights including the revenue from the quit rents, payable in tobacco at two pence per pound and some other revenue. The king then appointed as governor, Lionel Copley, who opened the first assembly April 9, 1692. For a period of twenty-five years Maryland was administered as a royal colony; until in 1715 it was restored to the proprietorship of the fourth Lord Baltimore, and remained under the control of that family till the Revolution.

It is clear that the development of Maryland was similar to that of Virginia in one respect; namely, the tendency of the assembly to resist, and encroach on, the power of the proprietor and governor. The general character of the people, their economic and social development, particularly their religious problems, are treated elsewhere.

22. The Carolinas (1663–1689)

In 1629 a grant of the territory to the south of Virginia was made to Sir Robert Heath. Later his patent
Early History was declared forfeited on the ground that no settlements had been made under it. By 1650 settlers from Virginia were entering the northern portion of the Carolina region, on the Albemarle River, seeking rich lands and range for stock. Meanwhile very favorable reports were made by explorers. Thus Edward Bland in 1650 declared that there was a rich soil for tobacco south of Virginia, and that two crops of Indian corn could be grown in one season.

The founding of the Carolina colonies illustrates the general colonial policy of the Restoration period.
The Origin of the Carolinas The king and his followers were poor and proceeded to exploit the colonies as a means of increasing revenue. To this end were passed the navigation acts and the import duties on tobacco already cited. The enormous proprietary grants in the middle colonies made to the Duke of

York, and those in the southern region to the proprietors of the Carolinas are further illustrations of this policy.

The men who assisted Charles II to recover his throne were those most generously rewarded. Among them were the Earl of Clarendon, Lord Chancellor; Anthony Ashley Cooper, later the Earl of Shaftesbury; General George Monk, the Duke of Albemarle, who had aided in bringing about the Restoration; Lord John Berkeley, brother of Sir William Berkeley; Lord Craven; Sir George Carteret, soon to receive also a grant of New Jersey; Sir John Colleton, a planter of the Barbados; and Sir William Berkeley, governor of Virginia. These eight men were made the lords proprietors of a vast tract of land south of Virginia in March 1663. This new plan of joint-proprietorship in land and government was distinctly in the interest of trade rather than of religion or government. The purpose was to export from the colony materials which would otherwise be purchased only from England's rivals.

The first charter, granted April 3, 1663, and amended by one in 1665, extending the original boundaries, made a grant of land between the southern frontier of Virginia and Spanish Florida. The proprietors were given absolute sovereignty over this territory, defined as stretching along the coast from the 29th parallel to 36° 30′ and westward from "sea to sea." They were to have power to appoint all officials, erect counties, establish courts, collect customs, grant titles of honor, put down and punish rebellion, and wage war. The laws were to be made "by and with the advice, assent, and approbation of the freemen, . . . their delegates or deputies;" and to be "consonant to reason" and in harmony with the laws of England. Colonists were, as in Virginia and Maryland,

The Charters of 1663 and 1665

to enjoy all " liberties, franchises, and privileges " of
subjects resident in England. No customs were to be
laid upon their goods except such as were " reasonably
assessed . . . by and with the consent of the free
people, or the greater part of them." Appeals were allowed to the crown, and liberty of conscience was
granted.

The aim of the proprietors, as in Maryland, was to advance their financial interests; and, as John Locke

The Funda-
mental Con-
stitutions

explained, to " avoid erecting a numerous
democracy." Accordingly this famous English philosopher, secretary to Lord Ashley
and clerk of the Carolina Proprietors, drew up in 1669
a new organic law known as " The Fundamental Constitutions of Carolina," which was amended several
times but never fully put into effect. This document outlined a form of government, feudal in character, with
high sounding titles for each of the proprietors and a
division of the territory into counties, seigniories, baronies, and colonies, providing for a colonial nobility,
a landed aristocracy, a peasantry, and a form of government based on a grand council and a parliament, in
which the great landed proprietors would exercise the
political power. On the other hand, the right of trial
by jury and religious toleration were provided for.

While these theoretical plans were being devised,
actual government was slowly developing and settle-

Early De-
velopment
of North
and South
Carolina

ments were being made. In 1664 William
Drummond was sent as governor to rule
over the settlements already established
by Virginians on the Albemarle River, with
power to grant lands and collect quitrents. Power was
also given to appoint a council which could, with the
governor, appoint officials; with the freeholders or their
representatives they were to form a general assembly,

which met in 1665, with power to make "good and wholesome laws."

Settlements were planned for the southern portion of Carolina, on the Cape Fear River and at Charles Town, by planters from Barbados. In 1663 an expedition started from Barbados to explore the region and another under Sir John Yeamans in 1665, which made a settlement at the mouth of the Charles River. The proprietors then financed an expedition which sailed from England for the Barbados in 1669. The fleet with upwards of a hundred colonists started for Carolina in November and after shipwrecks and adventures, finally arrived and settled Charles Town, April 1670. This was the beginning of the colony which later became South Carolina. By 1672 about 400 settlers were established in this region and by 1685 about 2500, among them some French Huguenots.

As the plan of government developed in North Carolina, the proprietors selected the governor and other important officers, including the council. Proprietors, Governors, and Assemblies of North and South Carolina The freemen chose twelve representatives to sit with the governor and council, with power to make laws subject to his veto and that of the proprietors. The assembly created the courts but the governor appointed the judges. His salary was paid by the proprietors out of the quit rents.

The Carolinas passed through much the same experience as Virginia and Maryland in the struggle for good government. Complaints were made of the distribution of lands, of the burden of quit rents, of the depredations by the Indians, of taxes, and of the navigation acts. As a result, the period is full of discontent, tumult, and rebellion. The governors were weak, ambitious, covetous, and unscrupulous. The governor of North Carolina from 1683 to 1689 was Seth Sothell one of the proprietors. He has been characterized as one of the " dirtiest knaves that ever held office in America." He was corrupt, tyrannical, a thief, accepted bribes from criminals, appropriated private property for his own use — a plantation, or slave, or cow, as fancy dictated, and if the owner complained he was imprisoned.

South Carolina was not separated politically from North Carolina until 1729, and several of the governors were common to both settled areas. Troubles arose between the governors, proprietors, and the assembly of South Carolina, as in the case of North Carolina. The people refused to submit to the fundamental constitutions or to the collection of quit rents. After the union of the two colonies under Governor Philip Ludwell in 1691, a division was made into two houses, 1692. The upper house was made up of the governor and a council of seven chosen by the proprietors, while the lower house was chosen by the people. The power to propose laws was won by the lower house in 1693, and a more liberal quit rent law was enacted in 1696. A conflict also arose over the judiciary, the governor and council at first having the judicial power. From a constitutional standpoint the development in Virginia, Maryland, and the Carolinas is a long struggle on the part of the people, acting through the lower house to resist arbitrary government by the king, proprietors, and governors on the one hand, and to enlarge their privileges and power on the other. This process was continued throughout the colonial period.

23. Local Government

The system of local government in the southern colonies was based principally on the county and county court, a system patterned after the old English shire. In 1634 the Virginia Assembly created eight counties and by 1680 there were twenty. They were divided into parishes, ecclesiastical units, precincts for the con-

The County and County Court

stables, and walks for the surveyors of highways; the last two were under the jurisdiction of the county court. This body was made up of the justices of the peace, who also filled all vacancies which might occur from time to time. They were chosen from "the most able, honest, and judicious" citizens. In practice those chosen were men of wealth, respected by the community, and recognized as capable. On court days a crowd of people of all classes assembled at the county courthouse, not only to transact court business, but to settle debts, transfer property, and for general social purposes.

The justices heard civil and criminal cases, not involving loss of life or limb, provided for highways and

The Officers and Duties

licensed taverns. One of their number was appointed sheriff by the governor. It was the duty of the sheriff to collect quit rents, the public and county levies, and usually the parish levy. He also summoned juries. The county court appointed constables, who collected fines, whipped criminals, arrested violators of the laws, and looked after the recovery of runaway servants or slaves. There was also a lieutenant, chief of the militia, who was also a member of the council.

The county was divided into parishes governed by a vestry, a body of twelve men, originally appointed by

The Parish

the governor. It had civil as well as ecclesiastical duties. The vestry made levies and assessments for the salary of the rector, repairing churches, care of the poor, etc. The vestrymen were chosen from the foremost men of the parish who were Anglicans, those of wealth, intelligence, and social position. Many of them were also members of the county court, house of burgesses, or the executive council.

It should be noted that unlike the New England town, the officers were not elected by the people but appointed by the governor or by the county court; that the people did not vote their own taxes but that sums were levied upon them by appointed officials. The dominant idea was the gradation of power from the governor downward, not upward from the people. Under this system it was easy for a relatively few families in each county to monopolize many of the most important offices. Nevertheless, the county court system was fairly well adapted to the conditions and needs of the people of the southern colonies. It had the great advantage of bringing to the front the ablest, most intelligent, and effective leaders.

Disadvantages and Advantages

CHAPTER IV

ECONOMIC AND SOCIAL DEVELOPMENT OF THE SOUTHERN COLONIES TO 1689

24. References

Bibliographies. — (See references under bibliographies to chs. iii, x, xii, xiv, xv); J. T. Adams, *Prov. Society*, 324–340; C. M. Andrews, *Colonial Self-Govt.*, 339–340, 342–344; Channing, Hart and Turner, *Guide*, §§ 30–39, 42–43, 45, 96–97; H. U. Faulkner, *Am. Economic Hist.*, 53–56, 76–77; E. B. Greene, *Prov. Am.*, 324–340; Grace Griffin, *Writ. on Am. Hist.*, 1906–1923; J. N. Larned, *Lit. of Am. Hist.*, 69–70, 100–106, 375–383; L. B. Schmidt, *Top. Stud. and Ref. on the Econom. Hist. of Am. Agricult.*; T. J. Wertenbaker, *The First Americans*, 317–338.

Historical Maps. — See refs. to ch. iii.

General Accounts. — For Engl. background see refs. under "General" and "Special" Accounts in chs. i, iii, v; ch. vi, under "Rela. of New Engl. with Brit. Emp.;" ch. vii, under "General Accts."; and ch. x; W. C. Abbott, *Expan. of Europe*, I, ch. xx; C. M. Andrews, *Colonial Self-Govt.*, chs. i, xviii–xix, and *Colonial Folkways*; Chas. and Mary Beard, *Rise of Am. Civiliza.*, I, chs. ii–iii; H. E. Bolton and T. M. Marshall, *Coloniza. of North Am.*; P. A. Bruce, *Econom. Hist. of Va. in 17th Cent.*, I, chs. i–iii; J. A. Doyle, *Engl. Cols. in Am.*, I, ch. xiii; H. U. Faulkner, *Am. Economic Hist.*, chs. i–v; H. L. Osgood, *Am. Col. in 17th Cent.*, II, ch. ii; III, ch. vii; L. G. Tyler, *Engl. in Am.*, ch. vi; T. J. Wertenbaker, *First Americans*.

Special Accounts. — (I) GENERAL ECONOMIC BY TOPICS: (see refs. to chs. iii, x, xii, xiv); (a) Land and Labor: Beverly Bond, *Quit Rent System in Am. Colonies*; J. D. Butler, "British Convicts Shipped to Am. Col." in *Am. Hist. Rev.*, II; Lyman Carrier, *Begin. of Am. Agricult.*; W. E. B. Du Bois, "Suppression of the African Slave Trade," (*Harv. Stud.* I); A. W. Lauber, "Indian Slavery in Colo. Times," in *Columb. Studies in Hist.*, LIV; M. G. McDougall, *Fugitive Slaves*(1619–1865); U. B. Phillips, *Am. Negro Slavery.* (b) Trade and Commerce: R. G. Albion, "Forests and Sea Power," 1652–1882, (*Harvard Stud.*, XXIX); C. M. Andrews, "Brit. Coms. of Tr. and Planta.

1622–1675" in *J. H. Stud.*, ser. XXVI; and "Colo. Commerce," in *Am. Hist. Rev.*, XX, 20–64; Edward Channing, "The Navigation Acts" in *Am. Ant. Soc. Proc.* n. s., VI, (1889); A. A. Geisecke, *Am. Commercial Legisla. before 1789;* E. R. Johnson, *Hist. of Dom. and For. Commerce of U. S.*, I; W. S. McClellan, *Smuggling in the Am. Colonies;* D. O. McGovney, "Navigation Acts as Applied to European Trade" in *Am. Hist. Rev.*, IX, 725–734. (c) Manufactures and Finance: W. R. Bagnall, *The Textile Industries of U. S.*, I, (1639–1810); J. L. Bishop, *Hist. of Am. Manufacts.*, 1608–1860; V. S. Clark, *Hist. of Manufacts. in U. S., 1607–1860;* D. R. Dewey, *Financial Hist. of the U. S.;* R. M. Tryon, *Hist. of Household Manufactures in U. S.* (II) SPECIAL ECONOMIC, SOUTHERN COLONIES: (see under "Special Accts." ch. iii and refs. to chs. x, xii, xiv); J. C. Ballagh, *Hist. of Slav. in Va.*, and "White Servitude in the Col. of Va." in *J. H. Studies*, ser. XIII; and "Introduc. to Southern Economic Hist. — The Land System," in *Am. Hist. Assoc. Rpt.*, 1897, 101–129; J. S. Bassett, "The Relation Between the Va. Planter and the London Merchant," in *Am. Hist. Assoc. Rpt.*, 1901, I, 557–573; P. A. Bruce, *Econom. Hist. of Va. in 17th Cent.;* A. O. Craven, "Soil Exhaustion as a Factor in the Agricult. Hist. of Va. and Md.," (*Univ. of Ill. Studies*, XIII); P. S. Flippin, "Finan. Admin. of Va." in *J. H. Studies*, ser. XXIII; Meyer Jacobstein, "Tobacco Indust. in the U. S." (*Columb. Stud.*, XXVI); U. B. Phillips, *Introduction to Plantation and Frontier Documents*, I; W. Z. Ripley, "Finan. Hist. of Va." in *Columb. Stud.*, IV; St. G. L. Sioussat, "Va. and the Engl. Com. System," in *Am. Hist. Assoc. Rpt.* 1905, I, 71–97; T. J. Wertenbaker, *Planters of Colonial Va.* (III) GENERAL SOCIAL BY TOPICS: (see refs. to chs. x, xii, xv); (a) Social Conditions: A. W. Calhoun, *Social Hist. of the Am. Family*, I; Alice Morse Earle, *Child Life in Colonial Days; Stage Coach and Tavern Days* and *Home Life in Colonial Days; Two Centuries of Costume in Am.*, Edward Eggleston, *Beginners of a Nation*, and *Transit of Civilization;* Edward Field, *Colonial Tavern;* Elsie Lathrop, *Early Am. Inns and Taverns;* Elizabeth McClellan, *Hist. of Dress in Am.*, 1607–1800; E. E. Proper, "Colonial Immigration Laws," in *Columb. Studies*, XII. (b) Literature and Education: E. G. Dexter, *Hist. of Education in U. S.;* Colyer Meriwether, *Our Colonial Curriculum;* Vernon Parrington, *Main Currents of Am. Thought*, I; W. P. Trent, (ed.) *Cambridge Hist. of Am. Lit.*, I; M. C. Tyler, *Hist. of Am. Lit. dur. Colo. Time.* (c) Religion: *Am. Church Hist. Series* (13 vols.); L. W. Bacon, *Am. Christianity;* F. S. Child,

Colonial Parson and Colonial Parish; S. H. Cobb, *Rise of Relig. Lib. in U.S.;* W. H. Perry, *Hist. of Am. Epis. Church,* I. (d) Legal: C. M. Andrews *et al., Select Essays in Anglo-Am. Legal History;* A. E. McKinley, *Suffrage Franchise in Am. Colonies;* P. S. Reinsch, "Engl. Com. Law in Am. Cols.," in *Univ. of Wis. Bull. No. 31.* (IV) SPECIAL SOCIAL, SOUTHERN COLONIES: P. A. Bruce, *Institutional Hist. of Va. in 17th Cent.,* and *Social Hist. of Va. in 17th Cent.* (2d ed. rev. 1927); O. P. Chitwood, "Justice in Colonial Va.," *J. H. Stud.,* ser. XXIII; E. L. Goodwin, *Colonial Churches in Va.;* C. J. Heatwold, *A Hist. of Education in Va.;* M. W. Jernegan, "Slavery and Conversion in the Am. Colonies" in *Am. Hist. Rev.,* XXXI, 504–528; George Petrie, "Church and State in Md.," in *J. H. Stud.,* ser. X; St. G. L. Sioussat, "Engl. Statutes in Md." in *J. H. Stud.,* ser. XXI; Mary N. Stannard, *Colonial Va., its People and Customs;* L. G. Tyler, "Colonial Education in Va.," in *Wm. and Mary College Qr.,* V–VII; S. B. Weeks, "Religious Devel. in the Prov. of N. Carolina" in *J. H. Stud.,* ser. X; G. F. Wells, *Parish Education in Colonial Va.*

Contemporary Accounts. — Channing, Hart and Turner, *Guide,* §§ 37, 113–120; and "Contemporary Accounts" in chs. iii, xii, xiv; (bibliography); see lists of printed sources in J. T. Adams, *Prov. Society,* 326–328; and C. M. Andrews, *Colonial Self-Govt.,* 338–339, 340–342; and T. J. Wertenbaker, *First Americans,* 321–322; E. L. Bogart and C. M. Thompson, (eds.), *Readings, etc.,* chs. i-iv; B. R. Carroll, *Hist. Collections of S. Carolina* (2 vols.); Elsie Clews, *Educational Legislation and Administration of the Colonial Govts.;* Peter Force, *Tracts, etc.,* II, no. 8; III, no. 12, 14, *etc.* (many reprints of contemporary accounts); Ralph Gabriel (ed.), *Pageant of America,* I; A. B. Hart (ed.), *Contemporaries,* I, chs. ix, xiii, esp. §§ 61, 82–88; F. L. Hawks, *Contribu. to Ecclesiastical Hist. of U. S.* (2 vols.); J. F. Jameson, *Privateers and Piracy in the Am. Colonies;* A. C. McLaughlin and others, *Source Problems in U. S. Hist.* (section iv, *Relig. Toleration and Freedom in Va., 1689–1786,* by M. W. Jernegan); Thomas Mun, *English Treasure by Forraign Trade* (1664), ed. N. Y., 1910; W. H. Perry, *Hist. Collecs. Relat. to Am. Colo. Ch.* (Va.); U. B. Phillips, *Plantation and Frontier Documents* (2 vols.); Hester Richardson, *Side Lights on Md. Hist.* (2 vols.); L. B. Schmidt and E. B. Ross, (eds.), *Readings in Economic Hist. of Am. Agricult.;* E. S. Stedman and E. W. Hutchinson, *Library of Am. Literature,* I–II.

25. Population

THE South increased in population during the seventeenth century slowly, because of the scarcity of
Number and   women and children in the early migra-
Character   tions, and partly because of disease. It has
been estimated that during the first thirty years of the
settlement of Virginia nearly five out of six immigrants
died from sickness. The white population of the southern colonies in 1665 was about 50,000; and even in
1689 there were hardly 115,000. At this time Virginia
and Maryland probably contained about nine-tenths of
the people in the southern group. Included in the white
population were about 12,000 indentured white
servants. There were also some 5000 negro slaves.

Contrary to common belief, before 1700 comparatively few planters owned estates of several thousand
acres of land, with numerous servants and slaves. A
group of great planters existed such as William Byrd,
William Fitzhugh, and Robert Beverley, but there were
a much larger number of lesser planters. Among them
was John Washington, who came from England in 1657
and founded the family from whom George Washington
sprang.

These two groups increased rapidly in the eighteenth
century because of the expansion of the plantation system
and the large importation of negro slaves. A report from
Virginia as late as 1703, however, minimizes the great
planters. It states that on each of the four great rivers
of Virginia there resided from "ten to thirty men who
by trade and industry had gotten very competent
estates." As late as 1716, out of 200 slave owners in
Lancaster county, 165 owned only from one to four
negroes; and only four held 20 or more. In spite
of the fact that the planters were few in number

they exerted great influence in the political, economic, and social life of the colony.

Nevertheless generally speaking Virginia and the other southern colonies were, in the seventeenth century, communities in large part composed of small land-holders, but without either slaves or servants, each hold-ing a few hundred acres or less. In 1704, in Virginia, at least 6000 men owned land, and it was this group that was the backbone of the colony. These freeholders came from those who immigrated as freemen, and from the freed servants, plus the descendants of these two groups. Plantations and farms were mainly in the tide-water region, almost all within fifty miles of the coast scattered along the river valleys. The whites were almost pure English and largely from the middle and south-eastern counties of England.

26. Land Problems

The original title to land in the colonies was in the crown, based on discoveries by Cabot, Raleigh, and Land others. In 1624 the undistributed land, Problems originally granted to the Virginia Com-pany, again became a possession of the crown. Pro-prietary grants of land were made to Lord Baltimore and the lords proprietors of the Carolinas. The pro-prietors in turn granted lands directly to individuals, but reserved a large portion for themselves. Their great wish was to secure revenue, especially from a rental fee known as a quit rent, amounting to about one shilling annually for every fifty acres. This fee was one of the serious causes of discontent in the later colonial period, and payment by both the rich and poor settlers was evaded as far as possible. In Virginia, after 1624, the crown disposed of lands and collected quit rents through the royal government.

In the southern colonies the soil and climate favored the production of staple crops, particularly tobacco; and a system of agriculture prevailed based on cheap, plentiful, and unskilled labor — such as the indentured servant and the negro slave. It was natural therefore to dispose of the land in a manner to stimulate the immigration of settlers and laborers, the more so because in the South the religious motive for settlement was weak. Thus arose the " head-right " system described below. Because of the great amount of land available, the general practice was to place no limit on the amount an individual might acquire. The planters, knowing that there was plenty of rich virgin soil to be had at low cost, made little or no effort to conserve their holdings by careful cultivation or by the use of fertilizers. As soon as a few crops had been grown, they preferred to allow the land to go to waste and secure other rich tracts.

Distribution of Land and Effects

The inevitable result was rapid depletion of the soil, and consequently a scarcity of available, fertile, virgin lands. The tendency in the latter portion of this period was to develop large plantations of thousands of acres with only a small proportion under cultivation at any one time. That portion uncultivated consisted of worn-out and abandoned land, of forests, and areas held in reserve for later cultivation or for speculation. This system also produced a scattered population with but few towns and villages, mostly located near the coast. The great planters loaded much of their produce for export on boats and ships at their own wharves, at the river banks. Another tendency was a rise in the value of the better lands. Immigrants, principally poor people, were thus forced to take up the less fertile lands, first back from the river valleys, then in the interior counties, and later west to the mountains. Here we find one of the early causes of the westward movement of population. Because of the rapid exhaustion of the soil there were decreasing returns from the land and resort to poorer land, even by the great planters.

The principal land problem was to prepare wild regions for cultivation. First came the laborious process Headright of removing from the land the great vir-System gin forests that reached to the river banks and the coast; or that of merely girdling the trees and then planting between them. The first method called for the expenditure of prodigious physical labor by a large number of laborers, with primitive implements; such as the axe, spade, and hoe, and perhaps a wooden plough. Laborers were relatively scarce because few immigrants had the money to pay for their cost of transportation, amounting to ten or twelve pounds.

This difficulty led to an economic and social invention — the headright system. Land, to the amount of from 50 to 150 acres, was granted as a free gift to anyone who would import a laborer into a southern colony, or to one who migrated at his own charge. If the immigrant was unable to pay the cost of his transportation, he might sign an indenture or contract, with a shipowner, a planter or his agent. That is, in return for his transportation, food, clothing, and shelter, he promised to work for the planter four or five years and in some cases seven or more. Many emigrants were willing to make such agreements, because at the end of their term of service they became free men. They also generally received a tract of 50 acres of land free, as provided by the laws of the southern colonies. With the cost of transporting a laborer around £8, land would cost from two shillings per acre up. This was the only method of securing either laborers or land in large quantities except through the purchase of negro slaves. Perhaps around 1500 servants a year came to Virginia alone during the seventeenth century.

In Maryland tracts of land of 1000 acres or more were granted to settlers who would transport serv-

Land Policy in Maryland and the Carolinas

ants in large numbers. The "Lord of the Manor" exercised court privileges somewhat similar to the practice under the old manorial system. Some sixty manors were established before 1676. Lord Baltimore also reserved for himself two manors of 6000 acres each in each county. In the Carolinas the original plan for the distribution of land provided for enormous reservations for the proprietors and others, as set forth in the Fundamental Constitutions of 1669. Each of the eight proprietors was entitled to 12,000 acres of land in each county, or about a fifth of all the land to those eight men. However, this scheme was not actually put into effect. Instead, the headright system was introduced, and the assembly limited the size of the grant to 600 acres with a requirement of speedy settlement. The purpose was to encourage settlement by small farmers. Land in Maryland and the Carolinas was subject to a quit rent of one shilling annually for every 50 acres.

27. Labor Problems

The indentured white servant was practically a semi-slave for a term of years. Generally speaking the planter

The Indentured Servant

was under few restrictions with respect to the amount and severity of the labor he could exact, or the nature of the shelter, food, and clothing he might supply, or the punishments he might inflict. The servant often tried to escape his hard lot by running away but the penalty, upon capture, was time added to his service, perhaps a year or more.

Theoretically the indenture and the laws protected the servant, calling for good treatment and care in case of illness. But few of those unjustly or cruelly treated could bring their cases into court and gain redress. One chief advantage of the system to the planter was the reasonable certainty of labor supply. By the end of the century, however, pressure for economy led to the introduction of more negro slaves. They were cheaper and their term of service, for life, much longer. The opportunity to purchase land for money (1705) and the tendency towards large-scale production, both influenced the planters to substitute the negro slave for the indentured servant. This process is one indication of the change from the seventeenth to the eighteenth century agricultural economy.

The introduction of the negro slave into the southern colonies was due to several reasons. The precedent was set by the Spaniards in the West Indies, Mexico, Central, and South America. Climatic conditions, the character of the soil, and other factors, were favorable to the profitable use of slave labor in the South. Thus when, in 1619, the first negroes were brought into Virginia by a Dutch ship they were welcomed by the planters. From this date slaves were introduced into other colonies, by the Dutch and English, into New Netherland and New York, and as early as 1638 in Massachusetts, where later the slave trade became an important industry. Negro slaves, however, were not as numerous or important in the seventeenth century as the indentured servants. Indeed it is estimated that in 1683 there were about 12,000 indentured servants in Virginia, and only 3000 negro slaves.

Negro Slaves

The first negroes imported were not legally slaves but servants. The southern colonies, however, passed laws defining the status of the negro. In general he was eventually deprived of most of those political, economic, and social privileges often accorded to free citizens. The significant feature of the negro slave labor system was absolute control by the master; such as power to buy and sell, punish, work, and otherwise use or abuse his slave for his own profit, with little or no legal restriction. Negro slaves increased not only by importation, but because the laws provided that the child of a female slave became a slave, whether the father was bond or free.

28. The Plantation System

A southern plantation was based primarily on three great factors: a plentiful supply of cheap land, abundance of cheap labor, and the production of staple crops. Compared with a farm, the plantation was much larger and made use of slave or semi-slave labor. Thus a tract of land, of one thousand acres, worked by ten or more slaves might be called a plantation rather than a farm. William Fitzhugh of Virginia stated that, to start a plantation properly, two hundred pounds would be needed for land, two hundred for slaves, and additional sums for provisions and implements. Another difference between a farm and a plantation was the fact that the latter alone was organized to produce a surplus for export. In most cases the purpose of a farm was to supply the needs of the family, and a small surplus for sale or exchange in the immediate neighborhood. Usually also the farm was worked by the owner and his family, with perhaps one or two " hired hands." In the seventeenth century the principal crop of the southern colonies was tobacco and the plantations developed in Maryland and Virginia concentrated on this product.

Plantations varied in size and character. Colonel William Fitzhugh of Virginia had a large plantation of one thousand acres, consisting of various tracts of land not contiguous to each other. It was divided into three " quarters " so called, each " well furnished with all necessary houses, grounds, and fencing, together with a choice crew of negroes at each plantation." There were " stocks of cattle and hogs at each quarter." A large plantation was similar to a small village of several hundred inhabitants. Besides the large house of the owner, numerous buildings were erected, such as tobacco houses, smoke houses, store houses, tanhouse, cooper shop, barns, dairy, slave quarters, coach house, poultry houses, etc. Agricultural implements included ploughs, hoes, axes, shovels, and tools for carpenters, coopers, and blacksmiths. Boats and mills were also necessities. Slaves were trained not only as agricultural laborers, but as carpenters, coopers, blacksmiths, and boatmen. For very few purposes were free artisans available; and each large plantation tended to become self-sufficing in this respect.

Plantation Equipment

From a modern standpoint the system of agriculture was unscientific. Practically no use was made of fertilizers, rotation of crops, deep ploughing, or similar methods designed to enrich or conserve the soil. Negro slave labor was costly from two standpoints; because of the effort to evade work and the lack of intelligence of newly imported negroes.

The Tobacco Problem

As early as 1612 Captain John Rolfe planted and cured a crop of tobacco. The enormous demand in England soon led to concentration on this crop, so that exports leaped to the figure of half a million pounds by 1627. Throughout the seventeenth century it was the chief crop of Maryland and Virginia. This one crop plan greatly influenced the type of economic life — the land and labor systems and the nature of the exports. The serious consequences of concentrating on one crop became apparent in the late seventeenth century, when over-production, a fall in price, and a decrease in the yield per acre (in Maryland from 4000 pounds to 2000 pounds per acre) caused many planters to produce tobacco at a loss.

England gradually increased the import tax on tobacco, while at the same time the price fell to a half-penny per pound. Virginia complained (1665) of the uncertain and low price of tobacco and glutted markets, so that " great quantities are yearly left in the country and that which is sent out at so mean and inconsiderable rate as neither merchant nor planter can well subsist by." To the middle of the seventeenth century the planter might reckon on the production of four hogs-heads of tobacco per slave. From this time on the returns from the exhausted and poorer soils resulted in a decrease so that by the middle of the eighteenth century the return was only one hogshead of tobacco per slave.

A Perfect Description of Virginia published in London in 1649 gives a very favorable picture of Virginia Virginia at that date. There is nothing wanting "to in 1649 and make people happy." The land " produceth 1700 with very great increase, whatsoever is committed to the bowels of it. . . A fat rich soil every-where watered with many fine Springs, small rivulets and wholesome waters. . . Men are provided with all necessaries, have plenty of victual, bread, and good beer . . . all which the Englishman loves full dearly. . . Of Kine, Oxen, Bulls, and Calves there are 20,000 large and good and there is plenty of good butter and cheese. There are 200 horses, 50 asses, 3000 sheep with good wool, 5000 goats, and swine and poultry innumerable."

A description of Virginia about 1700 is not so favorable as that of 1649. It was asserted that forests covered most of the land, that swamps were not drained, that soil wastage was everywhere evident and barren fields that would not grow crops profitably. Labor was inefficient, hard worked in summer and idle in winter. The hoe was used in place of the plow and tree stumps were left in the ground. There were no towns, no markets, and little money, a great hindrance to the speedy sale of commodities. Of course there were exceptions. The favored plantations, with the best management and labor, might prove profitable; but most of the medium or poor plantations were not prospering because of the adverse factors described. One of the effects of these conditions was the famous Bacon's rebellion, previously described.

29. Industries and Occupations

While agriculture was the main support of the southern colonies, many other industries were carried Types of   on either for profit or because of necessity. Manufactures These industries included first those having for their primary purpose production in large quantities for export. In this class belong the naval stores, lumber products and provisioning, based principally on the forests, and the raising of live stock. Home manufactures supplied necessary immediate needs not sufficiently provided for by trade with England. In the interior or back country regions local manufactures were even more necessary because of the high cost of imported articles and the lack of good roads.

Manufactures were of slow growth because of lack

of capital, skilled artisans, and machinery, oppositon of Great Britain, high cost and particularly the attractive power of free land. For artisans would not work for a daily wage when there was the opportunity to obtain one hundred acres of land at small expense. Many industries calling for partial or complete transformation of raw material into finished products were encouraged or regulated both by Great Britain and the assemblies of the southern colonies. In fact the colonial policy of England was two-sided. One aim was to restrict the colonists mainly to agriculture; a second was to stimulate certain non-agricultural industries, when beneficial to England. The individual colonies also found it to their advantage to do likewise, sometimes in direct opposition to the English law, sometimes in harmony with it, at other times to encourage industries neither forbidden nor encouraged by England.

The British restrictive system, especially the early navigation acts, (1651–1660) while designed to stimu-

British Policy and Non-agricultural Industries

late agriculture and prevent manufactures in the colonies, in fact tended to encourage manufactures. Thus the act of 1651 to prevent rival powers, especially Holland, from carrying goods to the colonies, actually encouraged colonial shipbuilding and other allied industries, such as cordage. The act of 1663 preventing direct trade with the continent tended to make goods so high priced that the colonists were stimulated to supply themselves with certain products of their own manufactures, as in the case of woolen cloth. England was not opposed to the colonial development of the livestock industry, the packing of beef and pork and the preparing of grain and flour for export purposes; nor to the development of other industries, provided they did not compete with her own.

Some attempt at rough plantation manufactures began very early. A striking account of the work on one Manufactures plantation is available for 1649. A Captain in Virginia Samuel Mathews, a member of the Council, and Maryland sowed "annually Hemp and Flax, and causes it to be spun; he keeps weavers, and hath a tanhouse, causes Leather to be dressed, hath eight Shoemakers employed in their trade, hath forty negroe servants, brings them up to Trades in his house." Several Virginia Acts (1662 to 1693) offered bounties for the production of linen and woolen cloth, one granting five shillings for every square yard. Maryland prohibited the export of wool in 1672, in order to encourage spinning and "making cloth for ourselves." Both Virginia and Maryland, in the last quarter of the seventeenth century, were exporting pipe staves, barrel staves, oak knees, oars, and sawed plank. Other industries started in Virginia before 1689 include brick making, iron work, salt manufacturing, and distilling. It must be said, however, that manufactures were relatively weak and of small value when compared with agricultural products and raw materials.

30. Trade and Commerce

Trade and commerce were important to the southern colonies. Indeed the plantation system was based on the principle of a large exportable surplus; and in the minds of the great planters foreign was of greater consequence than domestic commerce. This was particularly true of Maryland and Virginia because of their one large staple crop — tobacco. Normally most of their trade must have been with England, but the colonists desired more and more to sell and buy their products in the most advantageous markets.

The machinery of trade was complicated, and was so arranged and carried on that hostility on the part of Machinery of Trade the planters to the British commercial system, and particularly to the English merchants, was almost sure to develop. Most of the tobacco crop was sold on the commission plan; it was consigned to an agent in London, a merchant perhaps, and the planter did not know for months at what price it was sold. Nevertheless he sent an order for goods at the same time — really purchasing on credit. Numerous charges and deductions were made before the planter knew the final net amount due him for a shipload of tobacco. Commissions for handling the tobacco, petty charges, such as cooperage, porterage, wharfage, cartage, warehouse rent, and brokerage, amounted to about 10% of the gross receipts. In addition must be deducted from the gross receipts, insurance, and freight charges. Besides, import duties, levied by the British government and one of its important sources of revenue, were as high as sixty per cent. In 1676 Virginia paid £150,000 to the royal revenue — import duty on tobacco.

The total overseas exports and imports of the southern colonies to 1700 are unknown, because of lack Exports of complete records, and the practice of smuggling. Up to 1700 the great bulk of the exports were shipped to England; principally tobacco from Maryland and Virginia, and naval stores from the Carolinas. North Carolina exported, before 1700, small quantities of beef, pork, tallow, hides, deerskins, furs, wheat, corn, and peas, besides naval stores. South Carolina was more closely linked with the West Indies than the other colonies, and her products were mostly sent there before 1700 — corn, cattle, pork, in exchange for sugar, molasses, rum, and slaves.

Since the price for tobacco was set by the merchants, some of them made a practice of setting their buying price to be paid to the planter, below the market. The merchant then resold the tobacco at an advance. The merchant often sold goods to the planters at a huge advance over London prices, 25% profit being considered fair. Sometimes this "rake off" was as high as 50%. In addition the goods were often of inferior quality. Of course the merchant took risks and perhaps sold goods to planters already heavily in debt to him. He perhaps purchased these goods before he knew his own profit on his tobacco. Nevertheless the advantage was with the merchant and the planter was more or less helpless in protecting his rights and legitimate profits.

The planter might sell his tobacco to an agent who would come to his plantation and purchase the crop; but the price in this case was usually very low, say a penny a pound. While tobacco planting was profitable to about 1660, during the latter part of the seventeenth century the planter was very fortunate if he received thirty per cent of the total gross receipts for a shipload of tobacco; viz., after all charges had been paid. Under this system the natural tendency for the tobacco planters was to fall in debt, particularly because of their desire for luxuries, and the high cost of goods purchased in England, leaving out the possibility of being deliberately cheated by the merchant. With the tendency to overproduction of tobacco and very low prices, only a prudent and efficient planter could make his plantation pay and keep out of debt.

31. Social Conditions

The members of the land-holding class consisted of various social elements, as follows. Some were younger sons of the great noble families, others came from the lesser nobility; and still others came from the English middle class. There were also the "yeomen," or independent small farmers, the tenant farmers, and the freed servants. Many such persons were entitled to land because they had transported laborers or emigrated themselves. From these various sources came the men who established most of the plantations and farms, large and small. They represented the upper and middle classes of southern society.

Composition of the Population. Planters and Farmers

The laboring class, those who emigrated as servants, laborers or artisans, were generally from a lower stratum of English society as described in Chapter I above. An observer in the middle of the century says: "The people that are sent to inhabit the Colonie are the most of them the very scum and offscouring of our nation, Vagrants or condemned persons, or such others as by the looseness and viciousness of their lives have disabled themselves to subsist any longer in their nation; and when they come thither either know not how, or will not betake themselves to any sober, industrious course of living." Convicts and felons, indentured as servants, were forced on Maryland and Virginia in such numbers that the Virginia House of Burgesses passed an act in 1670 to forbid their further shipment. The act, though vetoed by the king, speaks of "the great number of felons and other desperate villains sent hither from the several prisons of England"; and adds that through such imports "we are believed to be a place only fit to receive such base and lewd persons." On the other hand it must be remembered that those called criminals were often only poor people who through stress of circumstances had committed some minor offense, such as stealing a sheep.

Labor Classes

Others were political offenders. There is no good evidence that most of the servants were criminally inclined; rather they were poor folks, with no crime record. A number even became planters and founders of families of considerable consequence.

Southern society was an outgrowth of the English political, economic and social system, inherited and
Structure
of Society
transplanted to the new world, but modified by the efforts of the colonists to adjust themselves to their new environment. Among the prevailing ideals was the belief that a wealthy minority should control the government and hold this power by restricting the political opportunities of the majority. Another guiding principle was partiality to large landed estates, devoted to agriculture and worked by cheap labor. Again the inherited class distinctions were stimulated by the presence of the indentured servant and negro slave. Social prestige of one class of freemen as compared with another class was based on family, official position, and wealth.

It was natural that an aristocratic type of government should arise. Minority government fostered an undemocratic system of suffrage, representation and office holding in colony, county, and parish. This was, however, largely the case in the northern colonies in the seventeenth century. Thus was stimulated the theory and practice of social superiority and inferiority. Those of high rank, wealth, or office demanded respect and reverence and generally received them from the less fortunate. It might even be said that the upper class claimed the social as well as the political rights of the English upper class.

Four principal classes of society developed in the southern colonies; the great planters, the small farmers, the indentured white servants, and the negro slaves, the two latter already described. By 1689 some of the great planters lived in spacious houses, were provided with the best foods, drank the finest liquors and wore expensive imported clothes. They were hostile to social legislation in the interest of the people as a whole; such legislation as Jefferson was later to struggle for — manhood suffrage, equality of representation, religious liberty, public education, and abolition of the system of primogeniture and entail. An interesting sidelight on the theory of minority rule was that set forth by John Locke, in explanation of the "Fundamental Constitutions" which he drew up for the government of the Carolinas in 1669, at the instance of the proprietors. He explained that their purpose was to found a government agreeable to the monarchy, "and that we may avoid a numerous democracy." The social position of the upper class was made known through the titles, "Mr." for a gentleman, "Esq." for a member of the council, and "Hon." if the occupant of a high office; by the wearing of fine cloths, of velvet, silk, and lace, by powder and periwigs, and especially through the display of coats of arms on coaches and tombstones. In the counties of Essex, Lancaster, and Middlesex, Virginia, forty-seven families made use of such coats of arms before 1700.

The more prosperous lesser planter and small farmer were independent but without great influence. The poor farmers were in a wretched condition in the latter half of the century, because of the low price of tobacco. Nathaniel Bacon, the leader of the famous rebellion of 1676, stated that the small farmers were so deeply in debt that it was "not in the power of labor or industry" to extricate them. During the government of Sir William Berkeley

(1660–1676), they had been heavily taxed, deprived of political rights, and had sunk lower in the social scale.

The poor whites, many of whom were formerly indentured servants, the white servants and negro slaves constituted perhaps three-fourths of the total population in 1700. These three groups received little benefit from those forces and agencies that make for social progress. On them acted only slightly a weak public sentiment that demanded a high standard of morals, organized religious and secular instruction through churches and schools — the clergyman and schoolmaster. The planter aristocracy was either hostile or indifferent to such progress: first, because of the fear that social progress for the servant and slave would lessen profits; and second, because religious toleration and free education would weaken their power in church and state. A famous saying of Governor Sir William Berkeley in 1671 is in point here. He thanked God that there were "no free schools nor printing" in Virginia because both were foes to good government. It should be noted, however, that small planters, farmers, and even freed servants might pass into the class of great planters, if they had the ability and industry.

Basis of Social Classes

32. Religion and Morals

The Anglican Church was organized in Virginia on the principle of the union of church and state, and intolerance of other religious sects. In the South as in England, existed privileged classes who had formed a church establishment in part because they feared that religious toleration and freedom would undermine and weaken their political power. The same principle was active in Massa-

Religious Organization of Virginia

chusetts during the seventeenth century. The union of church and state was a plan to make the civil and religious powers support each other for their mutual interest.

The early assemblies of Virginia passed acts (1619–1664) providing for church services according to the laws and orders of the Church of England. Ministers must conform to its canons and Nonconformists were ordered out of the colony. Counties were divided into ecclesiastical divisions called parishes. In each parish twelve persons elected by a majority of the parishioners constituted a vestry, which had power to make levies and assessments and lay tithes for the building of churches and chapels, purchasing glebes, paying the salaries of the clergy, and for the care of the poor. The vestry, during the rule of Governor Berkeley (1660–1676), had the power to fill its own vacancies. Each vestryman had to subscribe to the doctrines and discipline of the Church of England.

Church attendance was made compulsory for all, under penalty for neglect, modified only in 1699 as a result of the English toleration act of 1689. Up to this time the law required a man to help support and attend a church in which he might not believe. A legal marriage could be performed only by a clergyman of the established church. In practice the church in Virginia was hardly more than a collection of independent vestries without effective central control. The Bishop of London, who, after 1685, was nominally the head of the Anglican Church in the colonies, was three thousand miles away. He sent The Reverend James Blair to Virginia in 1690 as his "commissary" or agent. Blair and his successors had little power; and the governor was in a fight with the vestries almost from the first over the question of induction of the clergy to office. The vestries successfully insisted on choosing their clergy, for such periods as they wished.

The clergy had to be ordained in England, and many of them were second rate men, in intellectual, religious, and moral qualifications. It was a com-
The Clergy mon complaint that many of the Virginia clergy, in the seventeenth century, were incompetent. Nicholas Moreay, rector of St. Peter's Parish, wrote the Bishop of London, 1696, " Several ministers have caused such high scandals of late and have raised such prejudices amongst the people against the clergy, that hardly can they be persuaded to take a clergyman into their parish."

Clergymen found conditions not to their liking in Virginia in the seventeenth century; and so few were available that rather than be without religious leaders, incompetent rectors were often continued in office. In 1661 hardly a fifth of the parishes were supplied with clergy. When William Black became rector of Accomack parish in 1709 it had been destitute of a minister for fifteen years. In 1702 there were twenty-nine counties and forty-five parishes in Virginia, of which thirty-four only had ministers.

The distribution of population and the layout of plantations and parishes were not conducive to religious
Reasons for progress. The great plantations along the
Weak Re-
ligious In- river banks were often separated from each
stinct other by many miles. The parishes were laid out on both sides of the rivers, and were two to five miles wide and thirty or even fifty miles in length. Consequently it was difficult to locate a church without causing many to travel long distances to attend service. A writer (1661) says, " The families of such parishes being . . . at such distances from each other, many of them were very remote from the House of God, though

placed in the middest of them . . . and divers of the more remote Families being discouraged by the length or tediousness of the way, through extremities of heat in Summer, frost and snow in Winter, and tempestuous weather in both, do very seldome repair thither."

Neglect to attend church caused loss of interest in religion. Many clergymen refused to locate in Virginia because of the isolated life they would have to lead, and others tried it out for a short time and then left the colony to return to England. The isolation of the planters also deprived them of town-life, often a great stimulus to religious life. The fact is that there were relatively few Virginians in this period who regularly attended church and many not at all; about one in twenty was a communicant. The Anglican clergy did not reach the lower orders of society. Neither the easy-going planter aristocracy, nor the poor whites, nor the indentured servants, nor the negro slaves were, generally speaking, vitally interested in religion. Not until the Great Awakening of the eighteenth century, with its new type of sermon, its great revivals and its evangelistic and democratic clergy, did religion reach the lower orders of society in this section.

As might be expected the standard of morals among many of the servants and most of the negro slaves, was Standard very low. Some of the servants came from of Morals the lowest classes, even the criminal classes, " jail birds," men on whom the penalty of transportation to the colonies had been imposed. In the seventeenth century race intermixture was not uncommon between white servants and negro slaves and between some immoral masters and their slaves. Both Maryland and Virginia passed acts to prevent intermarriage between whites and blacks. The latter colony (1691) imposed a penalty of banishment and a heavy penalty on white women servants and free white women to whom were born mulatto children. Since the laws declared that children must follow the status of their mother, the children of female slaves must remain slaves, and thus race intermixture and immorality would be likely to be encouraged by some slave owners because of a strong economic motive. Mulattoes, for example, had greater immediate and prospective value than the pure blacks. The plantation system, the thinness of population and the absence of villages and towns prevented the crystallization of a public sentiment against such practices. Moreover, the tendency towards crime was accentuated by the presence of convict servants and negro slaves having low standards of conduct and morals.

Cecilius Calvert, Lord Baltimore, was a Catholic and looked on his proprietary grant as a refuge for the persecuted of his faith. Three Jesuit priests and a considerable number of the two hundred or more first colonists were Catholics. Those of other faiths, however, for example the Puritans, were encouraged to settle, so that Maryland offered substantial religious toleration. Nevertheless the Catholics demanded special privileges of Lord Baltimore, notably that their adherents should not be amenable to civil laws in temporal affairs. This controversy led to the appointment of a Protestant governor in 1648. An invitation from Governor Stone was extended to the persecuted Puritans of Virginia to settle in Maryland and a toleration act was enacted in 1649. The principal clause provided that those "professing to believe in Jesus Christ shall not from henceforth be anyways troubled, molested, or discountenanced for, or in respect of, his or her religion, nor in the free exercise thereof within this province . . . nor in any way compelled to the belief or exercise of any other religion against his or her consent."

Immigration into Maryland was mainly non-Catholic, Puritan, and Presbyterian, so that in the generation following the first settlements intolerance towards the Catholics was the tendency. It was expressed in hostility towards the third Lord Baltimore, Charles Calvert, a Roman Catholic feudal proprietor. After the revolution of 1688 in England, and the deposing of King James the Second, the anti-Catholic feeling gained ground. The accession of William and Mary encouraged the Protestants in Maryland, who then constituted nine-tenths of the population, to overthrow the proprietary government. The English toleration act of 1689 was followed by the appointment of a new governor, Sir Lionel Copley, a member of the established church. Maryland became a royal province in 1692, but later the proprietorship was restored (1715).

In 1692 the Church of England was established in Maryland, and an annual tax of forty pounds of tobacco was imposed on every planter, his male children, white men servants, and negro slaves, male and female, over sixteen years of age. The tax was intended for the building of Anglican churches and the support of Anglican clergy; though out of the population of 25,000 at this time about one twelfth were Catholics, one tenth Quakers and the rest of other Protestant denominations. In 1700 five Catholic priests and two lay brothers, two Quaker preachers and sixteen Anglican rectors were enumerated in Maryland. Fifteen parishes of the Church of England were vacant, and the character of the Anglican clergy left much to be desired, as in the case of Virginia.

North Carolina developed very slowly on the religious

side. In fact William Edmundson, a Quaker missionary from England, claimed the honor of being the first Christian minister to preach in North Carolina (1672). Later in the same year George Fox, the founder of Quakerism, was the second. Quarterly meetings of Friends began in 1689.

Religious Conditions in Carolina

Governor Walker wrote the Bishop of London (1703) as follows: "We have been settled near this fifty years in this place, and I may justly say most part of twenty-one years, on my knowledge without priest or altar, and before that time, according to all that appears to me, much worse." With reference to the Quaker missionaries he says they sent in men to "exhort their wicked principles; and here was none to dispute nor to oppose them in carrying on their pernicious principles for many years." It was not until 1700 that the first Anglican missionary was sent to North Carolina, and not until 1702 that the first church was built. The Anglican Church was not established in South Carolina until 1704.

33. Education and Intellectual Life

The conditions of settlement and the organization of society affected the problem of education in a manner similar to that of religion. The educational theory of the southern colonies was based on the principle that education was rather a private than a public matter. Virginia and Maryland, it is true, enacted a few laws designed to further the education of the poor through the apprenticeship system, and to give some aid to secondary or higher education. But no laws were passed similar to those in New England, requiring the local organ of government to establish schools, or to make legal their support by taxation. An example of

Theory of Education

education through the apprenticeship system is seen in the binding out of a poor boy by the Surrey County Court, Virginia, June 15, 1681, "his master to teach him his trade of blacksmith, and to read and write."

Through private initiative various types of private schools were set up in the seventeenth century. In Virginia money was left by Benjamin Symes (1635), to found an endowed free school; and in 1649 a writer declares " I may not forget to tell you we have a Free schoole, with two hundred acres of Land, a fine house upon it, forty milch Kine, and other accommodations to it . . . other petty schools we have." A writer in 1661 bewails " their almost general want of schooles, for the education of their children (as) another consequent of their scattered planting."

Types of Schools in Virginia

However, Beverley, the historian of Virginia, said in 1705, " There are large tracts of land, houses and other things granted to free schools, for the education of children in many parts of the country, and some of these are so large that of themselves they are a handsome maintenance to a master; but the additional allowance which gentlemen give with their sons render them a comfortable subsistence. These schools have been founded by the legacies of well-inclined gentlemen, and the management of them hath commonly been left to the Direction of the County Court, or to the vestry of the prospective parishes. In all other places, where such endowments have not already been made, the people join and build schools for their children where they may learn on very easie terms." The number of schools of all sorts, in proportion to the population, was very small and hardly half a dozen of the so-called endowed free schools were in operation at any one time in the seventeenth century.

For the landed gentry the system of education under private tutors was the most prevalent and popular

The Private Tutor

method in use. John Carter directed in his will, 1669, that his son Robert should have a servant bought for him "to teach him his books in English or Latin." It may be noted that George Washington was taught in this manner about 1740 (reading, writing, and accounts) by a servant whose time his father purchased. Sir John Randolph was taught by a Protestant clergyman who came over among the French refugees. A few planters sent their sons abroad for their education; to Oxford and Cambridge; or to the Inns of Court for a legal education. Indeed in the records of the Virginia Company (Oct. 31, 1621) it was agreed that a public free school was greatly needed in Virginia because planters "through want whereof they have been hitherto constrained to their great coste, to send their children from thence (Virginia) hither (England) to be taught."

Several attempts were made in the seventeenth century to found a college in Virginia. Ten thousand acres

William and Mary College

of land were set aside by the Virginia Company in 1618, and money was collected in England for a "University" for the education of the infidels, viz., the Indians. Nothing came of the project. Again in 1660–1661 the assembly passed an act to provide for a college. Subscriptions were made in money and tobacco, but this project also failed. Subscriptions were again made to the amount of £2500 in 1688–1689. Finally the assembly (1691) sent The Rev. James Blair to England to solicit a charter from the Crown which was granted in 1693. This was the foundation of the College of William and Mary. It developed very slowly and was hardly more advanced than a secondary school for many years. The purpose was similar to that for the founding of Harvard College nearly sixty years earlier; "that the church of Virginia may be furnished with a seminary of ministers of the Gospel, and that the youth may be piously educated in good letters and manners and that the Christian faith may be propagated amongst the Western Indians to the glory of almighty God."

The educational conditions in Maryland were similar to those in Virginia; dependence on private initiative. A free school act was passed in 1696, outlining an elaborate secondary school with provision for state support; but the school was not put into operation during the seventeenth century. Farther south, in the Carolinas, practically nothing was done before 1700 in the way of establishing schools.

Education in Maryland and the Carolinas

It is clear that the conditions for general social progress were unfavorable in the southern colonies with respect to the encouragement of religion and education. The same can be said with respect to other agencies for the advancement of culture. There were no newspapers in the southern colonies before 1700, nor was there at that date any printing establishment of any kind. Few collections of books could be dignified by the name of "library," and most of them were of a private character. Learned men and literary productions by native southern authors were few in number. The fine arts, music, painting, architecture, etc., were in their infancy. But a faint glimmer of science and scientific thought can be discerned, though The Reverend John Banister and The Reverend John Clayton, contributed scientific articles to the Royal Society of London of which the latter was a member. The South to 1700 was essentially a frontier, and life was on a coarser basis, for the great majority,

Literature Printing Libraries and Learned Men

than one can now easily imagine. The prevalence of ignorance and superstition may be better realized when it is known that about one-half of the adult free male population was illiterate and perhaps three-fourths or more of the adult females.

CHAPTER V

COLONIZATION AND DEVELOPMENT OF NEW ENGLAND TO 1643

34. References

Bibliographies. — (See references under bibliographies, chs. vi, vii, xii, xiv, xv); J. T. Adams, *Founding of New England* (footnotes); C. M. Andrews, *Fathers of New England*, 201–204, and *Colonial Self-Govt.*, 337–340, 344–347; H. E. Bolton and T. M. Marshall, *Coloniza. of North Am.*, 151; Channing, Hart and Turner, *Guide*, §§ 31–34, 36–39, 42–43, 45, 48, 96–97, 99, 114, 127–141, 163–164; H. M. Dexter, *Congregationalism as Seen in its Literature;* Edward Field, *State of R. I.*, III, 653–681; C. A. Flagg, *A Guide to Mass. Local Hist.*, and *Ref. List on Conn. Local Hist.;* E. B. Greene, *Provincial Am.*, 325–340, and *Foundations of Am. Nationality*, 110–111, 129; Grace Griffin, *Writings on Am. Hist.*, 1906–1923; A. B. Hart, (ed.), *Commonwealth Hist. of Mass.*, I (bibliographies following each chapter); J. N. Larned, *Lit. of Am. Hist.*, 64–76, 76–92, 358–365; L. G. Tyler, *Engl. in Am.*, 334–336; Justin Winsor, *Nar. and Crit. Hist. of Am.*, III, chs. vii–ix (crit. essays on authorities); and *Memo. Hist. of Boston*, I, 299, 352.

Historical Maps. — Nos. 1 and 2 of this vol.; J. T. Adams, *Founding of New England*, frontispiece, New Engl. in 1640; 120 ("stream of immigration, 1620–1642"); H. E. Bolton and T. M. Marshall, *Coloniza. of North Am.*, 144, 154, 219; Channing, Hart and Turner, *Guide*, §§ 33–34, 96–97; (bibliography); D. R. Fox, *Atlas of Am. Hist.*, 8; E. B. Greene, *Foundations, etc.*, 37, 44, 164, 188; J. G. Palfrey, *History of New Engl.*, I, 94, 360, 466; Justin Winsor, *Nar. and Crit. Hist. of Am.*, maps in III, 380–385.

General Accounts. — (See refs. in ch. vii); J. T. Adams, *Founding of New Engl.*, chs. v–vii, xiv; C. M. Andrews, *Colonial Self-Govt.*, chs. i–iv, xv–xvii, and *Fathers of New Engl.*, chs. i–viii; Chas. and Mary Beard, *Rise of Am. Civilization*, I, ch. ii; Carl Becker, *Begin. of Am. People*, 80–100; G. L. Beer, "Commer. Policy of Engl. Towards the Am. Col.," in *Columb. Studies*, III; H. E. Bolton and T. M. Marshall, *Coloniza. of North Am.*, vii–viii, x; Edward Channing, *Hist. of the U. S.*,

I, chs. x-xiv; E. P. Cheyney, "Some Conditions Surrounding the Settlement of Va.," in *Amer. Hist. Rev.*, XII, 507–528; W. M. Davis, *The Physical Geog. of Southern New Engl.*, F. C. Dietz, *Polit. and Social Hist. of Engl.*, chs. ix, 239–244; X, 250–261; J. A. Doyle, *Engl. Col. in Am.*, II, pt. I, chs. i-viii; Edward Eggleston, *Beginners of a Nation*, bk. II, chs. i-iv; bk. III, chs. ii-iii; John Fiske, *Begin. of N. Engl.*, chs. ii-iii; E. B. Greene, *Foundations, etc.*, chs. v-vii; A. P. Newton, *Colonizing Activ. of the Engl. Puritans;* H. L. Osgood, *Am. Col. in 17th Cent.*, I, pt. I, ch. v; pt. II, chs. i-iv, vi-ix; J. G. Palfrey, *Hist. of New Engl.*, I, chs. i, iii, iv-xiv; J. R. Seeley, *Growth of Brit. Policy*, I; G. M. Trevelyan, *England under the Stuarts;* L. G. Tyler, *Engl. in Am.*, chs. ix-xv; Justin Winsor, *Nar. and Crit. Hist. of Am.*, III, chs. vii-ix.

Special Accounts. — (a) ENGLISH BACKGROUND: (see "General Accts.," chs. i, vii); E. P. Cheyney, *Social Changes in Engl. in the 16th Century;* J. N. Figgis, *Theory of the Divine Right of Kings;* G. P. Gooch, *English Democratic Ideas in the 17th Century;* W. A. S. Hewins, *English Trade and Finance, Chiefly in the 17th Century;* A. B. Hinds, *The England of Elizabeth;* H. D. Trail, *Social Engl.*, IV, ch. xii; G. M. Trevelyan, *England under the Stuarts.* (b) ECCLESIASTICAL: Champlin Burrage, *The Early Engl. Dissenters, etc., 1550–1641;* W. H. Frere, *Hist. of the Engl. Ch. in the Reigns of Elizabeth and James;* W. H. Hutton, *The English Church, 1625–1714;* A. J. Klein, *Intolerance in the Age of Elizabeth, etc.;* G. B. Tatham, *The Puritans in Power;* Eleanor Trotter, *17th Cent. Life in a Country Parish;* R. G. Usher, *The Reconstruction of the Engl. Ch.;* S. L. Ware, "The English Parish," *etc.*, in *J. H. Studies*, ser. XXVI. (c) PILGRIMS, PURITANS AND MASS.: C. F. Adams, *Mass., Her Historians and Hist.*, and *Three Episodes of Mass. Hist.*, I, 1–208; J. T. Adams, *Founding of New Engl.*, ch. iv; John Brown, *The Pilgrim Fathers of New Engl. and their Puritan Successors;* E. H. Byington, *The Puritan as a Colonist and Reformer;* E. P. Cheyney, *European Background of Am. Hist.*, ch. xii; H. M. Dexter, *The Engl. and Holland of the Pilgrims;* G. E. Ellis, *The Puritan Age and Rule in Mass.;* Errett Gates, *Relig. Lib. in Mass.;* John A. Goodman, *The Pilgrim Republic;* W. E. Griffis, *The Pilgrims in Their Three Homes;* Elizabeth Hanscom, *The Heart of the Puritans;* A. B. Hart (ed.), *Commonwealth Hist. of Mass.*, I; G. B. Haynes, "Rep. and Suf. in Mass.," *1620–1691*, in *J. H. Studies*, ser. XII; C. J. Hilkey, "Legal Devel. in Colo. Mass.," 1630–1686, in *Colum. Stud.*, XXXVII; J. F. Jameson, Introduction to Johnson's *Wonder Working Providence*, (*Orig.*

Nar. of Am. Hist.); P. E. Lauer, "Church and State in New Engl.," in *J. H. Stud.*, ser. X; Arthur Lord, "Mayflower Compact," in *Am. Ant. Soc. Pro.*, 1921; T. M. Merriam, *Pilgrims, Puritans and Roger Williams;* Peter Oliver, *The Puritan Commonwealth;* H. L. Osgood, "Polit. Ideas of the Puritans," in *Polit. Sci. Quart.*, VI; J. G. Palfrey, *Hist. of New Engl.*, I, ch. vii, xiv; F. J. Powicke, "John Robinson and the Beginnings of the Pilgrim Movement," *Harvard Theol. Rev.*, July 1920; R. G. Usher, *The Pilgrims and Their History;* G. L. Walker, *Some Aspects of Religious Life of N. Engl.*, chs. i-ii; Emory Washburn, *Judicial Hist. of Mass.;* Justin Winsor, *Memo. Hist. of Boston*, I–II. (d) R. I., CONN., NEW HAMP., MAINE: C. M. Andrews, *Connecticut's Place in Colonial Hist.*, and "River Towns of Conn.," in *J. H. Studies*, ser. VII; H. S. Burrage, *Begin. of Colonial Maine;* W. E. Foster, "Town Govt. in R. I.," in *J. H. Studies*, ser. IV; W. H. Fry, "New Hampshire as a Royal Province," in *Columb. Stud.*, XXIX; M. L. Greene, *Devel. of Relig. Lib. in Conn.;* C. H. Levermore, "Republic of New Haven," in *J. H. Studies*, extra vol. I; W. De L. Love, *Colonial Hist. of Hartford;* J. B. Richman, *Rhode Island, its Making and Meaning;* Benjamin Trumbull, *Hist. of Conn.* (2 vols., ed. 1898).

Biographies. — Bibl. in W. P. Trent (ed.) *Camb. Hist. Am. Lit.*, I, 389–398; C. H. Bell, *John Wheelwright*, in *Prince. Soc. Pubs.*, IX, 1876; J. W. Bicknell, *Story of Dr. John Clarke;* W. H. Burgess, *John Robinson, Pastor of the Pilgrim Fathers;* Jeremiah Chaplin, *Life of Henry Dunster;* A. S. Dearborn, *Sketch of Life of Apostle John Eliot;* F. B. Dexter, "John Davenport," in *New Haven Hist. Soc. Papers*, II, 205; A. M. Earle, *Margaret Winthrop;* G. E. Ellis, *Life of Mrs. Anne Hutchinson, etc.;* Chas. M. Endicott, *Memoir of John Endicott;* Adelos Gorton, *Life and Times of Samuel Gorton;* T. W. Higginson, *Francis Higginson;* J. K. Hosmer, *Life of Young Sir Henry Vane;* G. L. Kittredge, "Dr. Robert Child, the Remonstrant," in *Colonial Society of Mass. Pubs.*, XXI, 1–146; Cotton Mather, *Magnalia Christi Americana or Ecclesiastical Hist. of New Engl.* (1702), ed. 1853; (biogs. of leaders); Henry C. Shelley, *John Harvard and His Times;* J. L. Sibley, *Biog'l. Sketches of Harvard Graduates*, 1642–1689 (3 vols.); Ashbel Steele, *Elder Brewster;* O. S. Straus, *Roger Williams: The Pioneer of Religious Liberty;* J. M. Taylor, *Roger Ludlow;* C. W. Tuttle, "Captain John Mason, The Founder of New Hampshire" in *Prince. Soc. Pubs.* XVII, 1887; J. H. Twichell, *John Winthrop;* G. L. Walker, *Thos. Hooker;* W. Walker, *John Calvin, the Organizer of Reformed Protestantism:*

and *Ten New England Leaders;* R. C. Winthrop, *Life and Letters of John Winthrop.*

Contemporary Accounts. — (a) BIBLIOGRAPHY: See list of published recs. in Adams, *Prov. Soc.*, 326–328, and C. M. Andrews, *Colonial Self-Govt.*, 344–347; Channing, Hart and Turner, *Guide*, §§ 42–43, 114, 127–140; *Hist. Sources in Schools*, §§ 55–66, 71; A. R. Hasse, *Materials for a Bibliog., etc.;* Peter Mode, *Source Book and Bibliographical Guide for Am. Church Hist.;* W. P. Trent (ed.), *Camb. Hist. Am. Lit.*, I, 365–380; 382–398; Milton Waldman, *Americana, etc.*, ch. vii. (b) RECORDS AND COLLECTIONS: Edward Arber, (ed.), *Story of the Pilgrim Fathers,* and *Engl. Scholars' Library; Cal. of State Papers, Colonial and W. I. to 1689;* Peter Force, *Tracts and Other Papers, etc.* (4 vols.); Ralph Gabriel, *Pageant of America*, I, ch. x; A. B. Hart, (ed.), *Contemporaries*, I, chs. xiv–xx; Thomas Hutchinson, *Collection of Papers, in Prince. Soc. Publications,* II–III; J. F. Jameson, (ed.), *Orig. Narratives of Early Am. Hist.;* (Bradford's *Hist. of Plymouth Plantation,* Johnson's *Wonder Working Providence,* Winthrop's *Journal, etc.*); William MacDonald, (ed.), *Select Documents,* nos. 5, 7, 8, 10, 11, 13–18; *Prince. Society Publications,* contain "Antinomianism in Colony of Mass. Bay," XXI; Wm. Wood, *New England's Prospect* (1634), I, and Thos. Morton, *New English Canaan* (1632), XIV; "Records of Council for N. Engl." are in *Am. Ant. Soc. Proc.*, 1867, 59–131; L. F. Stock (ed.), *Proceed. and Debates of Brit. Parl. etc.;* Williston Walker, *Creeds and Platforms of Congregationalism;* Alex. Young, *Chronicles of the Pilgrim Fathers and Chronicles of Mass. Bay;* many documents and reprints of original accounts are in *Mass. Hist. Soc. Coll.,* series I to VII; for list see *Am. Hist. Assn. Rpt.* for 1905; vol. II; collections of official docs. are in *Pub. Rec. of Col. of Conn.*, 1636–1776, 15 vols.; *Maine Hist. Soc. Colls.; Recs. of the Gov. and Co. of Mass. Bay*, 5 vols., 1628–1686; *New Hamp. Prov. and State Pa.*, 1623–1800, 31 vols.; *Recs. of Col. of New Haven*, 2 vols.; 1638–1665; *Recs. of Plymouth Col.* 12 vols.; and *Recs. of the Col. of R. I.*, 10 vols., 1676–92. (c) PERSONAL PAPERS: Farnham Papers, 1603–1688, in *Doc. Hist. of State of Maine,* VII; T. Lechford, "Plaine Dealing," is in *Mass. Hist. Soc. Collect.*, ser. III, vol. III; Roger Williams, "Writings," in *Narragansett Club Publications* (6 vols.).

35. Physical Environment

GEOGRAPHICALLY speaking, there were certain limits within which colonists to New England would be forced to act; for it had a small area, scarcity of fertile soil and climatic conditions that limited the expansion of agriculture and the number of different crops. These factors also made it desirable for the colonists to engage in certain non-agricultural occupations.

Relation of New England History to Natural Environment

The physiography of New England is due largely to the grinding of the great ice cap or sheet, perhaps a thousand feet or more in thickness, which formerly covered this region. It wore down the mountains of northern New England, and formed the hills and lower areas in the southern portion. Valleys were formed and soils laid down, composed of various sorts of rock fragments; and lakes, ponds, and swamps were fashioned. The glacial drift was composed of a great mass of boulders, rocks, and stones, part of which can still be seen; the larger boulders where they were originally deposited, and some of the smaller rocks and stones in the stone walls now dotting New England pastures and waste lands. The extremely rocky character of the land surface was a great hindrance to the early agricultural development. Indeed it has been estimated that at least thirty days of labor were necessary on every acre, after removal of the forests, to put the land into arable condition. In general the soil was poor, thin, and sandy, though there were some fertile areas in the river valleys. Thus when New England was settled from one-half to two-thirds of the territory was either sterile or had a very poor soil. Included in this area were some ten thousand square miles or more of swamp lands.

Physical Characteristics

Some advantages were, however, connected with this rather inhospitable environment. Extensive areas known as "marsh meadows," where "salt hay" was cut, were an important basis for stock raising. Some degree of isolation gave protection from the more powerful Indian tribes located in the West; while the poor and stubborn soil tended to limit the number and strength of the coast Indians. Poor soil also forced the people to seek other occupations than agriculture. Fishing was encouraged because of easy access northward to the "Grand Banks." Shipbuilding was encouraged by large forests near the coast. Trade and commerce were promoted by numerous bays, sounds, and harbors. Manufactures were stimulated by numerous waterfalls, giving cheap water power. The surface features, hill and valley, in connection with varied industries promoted settlement in compact communities — the town and village. This was favorable to social progress, especially the development of the church and school.

Because of her natural boundaries and barriers the population of New England was confined to a comparatively small area. This helped produce unity of thought and purpose, and a section with a peculiar culture of its own. The mental, moral, and religious characteristics associated with New Englanders, made familiar by such phrases as "Puritanism," "New England conscience," "town meeting," "free public school," etc., were in part an outgrowth of their environment.

Environment and Mental Characteristics

From an economic standpoint colonies formed out of such an area were less valuable to England than those in the South. For they necessarily became to some extent economic competitors, both in production and in trade with other regions. The development of shipbuilding and

New England and Old England

the growth of trade and commerce, with the favorable geographic conditions, gave opportunity to violate the acts of trade — to smuggle. Thus conditions and practices growing in part out of the physical environment were the source of unending trouble and conflict and became an influence in the movement for independence.

36. Early Attempts to Explore and Settle New England

Bartholomew Gosnold was the first known Englishman to visit the New England coast. His voyage in 1602 re-

Voyages of Gosnold, Pring, Weymouth

sulted in a landing on Cuttyhunk, the easternmost of the Elizabeth Islands northwest of Martha's Vineyard Island, where he attempted to establish a trading station. He built a house and took back to England a load of sassafras, the first of the exports of goods from this region. He was followed (1603) by Martin Pring, who entered Plymouth Harbor, and George Weymouth, who in 1605 explored the Maine coast. Contemporary narratives of these voyages were published and had much to do with arousing the interest of Ferdinando Gorges and his associates in this region. Three kidnapped Indians came into the possession of Gorges who said that this event was " the means of putting life into all our plantations."

Gorges and Chief Justice John Popham were the backers of an ill-fated attempt to establish a colony at

Settlement of Maine

the mouth of the Sagadahoc, or Kennebec River, Maine, in 1607, under the auspices of the Plymouth branch of the Virginia Company. Many of the colonists died the first winter because of sickness and attacks by the Indians; so that, as Gorges said, our " hopes were frozen to death " and the colony was pursued with " the malice of the Divell."

Between 1608 and 1620 numerous exploring and trading expeditions were sent out to New England, financed

Exploration of New England

largely by Gorges, Sir Francis Popham and the Earl of Southampton, patron of Shakespeare. Captain John Smith (1614) made a careful examination of the region, named it New England, traded with the Indians, made a map, wrote a description of the country, and took back a cargo of fish and furs valued at £1500. None of these ventures resulted in permanent settlement. The French and Dutch were both on the New England Coast before 1610, as narrated in Chapter II. Thus France, England, and Holland were all claiming part of this region from 1603 to 1620.

37. English Separatism and the Plymouth Colony

From 1602 to 1620 the motives for New England colonization were almost exclusively economic. Large

New Motive for Colonization

sums of money were spent in the endeavor to gain a foothold and to exploit the region; but neither colony nor profits were as yet forthcoming. Within this same period, however, other considerations were occupying the minds of many Englishmen, especially religious problems. The next efforts to colonize New England, as well as much of its later history, are intimately connected with religious motives.

Opposition to certain ceremonies, and parts of the creed, of the English church appeared as early as 1550.

Rise of Separatism

One aspect of this movement was that known as " Separatism," well stated by certain ministers as early as 1567. " Seeing they could not have the word freely preached, and the Sacraments administered without idolatrous gear . . . concluded to break off from the public churches, and separate in private houses." About 1580 Robert Browne, a clergyman, commenced to declaim against the discipline and ceremonies of the church and to urge the people to separate; that is, set up independent congregations. Some clergymen who followed these teachings were persecuted, imprisoned, and even hanged. These events stimulated emigration to Holland, in order to secure greater freedom of worship. Less radical than the Separatists were other Nonconformists, some of whom were called Puritans. Such were willing to remain within the Church if it would purge itself of certain doctrines and practices.

A group known as Separatists, " Brownists," and later, Pilgrims, decided to migrate to Holland. The little
Migration of Pilgrims to Holland
congregation at Scrooby in Nottinghamshire, under the lead of their pastor, John Robinson, thus fled to Holland and settled in Leyden in 1609. Here, with others who followed, they lived for twelve years, laboring hard, but secure in their freedom of conscience. But they wanted to remain Englishmen, to remove their children from the temptations of a foreign land, to secure greater economic independence, and to dwell where their religious ideas would be more easily perpetuated. This congregation seems to have numbered about two hundred and was made up of Separatists who had come from various congregations in England.

The plan for emigration to some point within the bounds of the Virginia Company slowly matured. At
Plan of Emigration to New England
last, a patent was secured June 9, 1619, from the Virginia Company for a private plantation. Money was subscribed to the amount of £7000 by a group of seventy London merchants, Thomas Weston being a leader. The partnership or agreement between merchants and colonists provided that each share should be ten pounds value, and an

emigrant over sixteen was entitled to one share, or two shares if he fitted himself out or paid his transportation. The joint-stock enterprise thus planned was to run seven years, when the company would be dissolved and the stock divided: that is, the accumulated houses, lands, "goods and chattels." The profits to the merchants were to come from the labor of the colonists, "trade, traffic, trucking, working, fishing, or any other means," the products to be put into a common storehouse, as in Virginia. In the meantime the colonists were to be provided with food, clothing, and other necessaries from the common stock.

38. The Settlement of Plymouth (1620–1628)

The Pilgrims embarked at Delft Haven for Southampton, England, and after an unsuccessful start, the Mayflower finally sailed from Plymouth in the month of September, 1620, with 102 passengers. Nine weeks later they arrived off Cape Cod, November 12, at Provincetown, some 200 miles north of the limit of their patent. John Carver, agent in obtaining the patent, William Bradford, William Brewster, Edward Winslow and Captain Myles Standish, a soldier who loved a fight, were the ablest leaders of the company. Only about one-third of the emigrants were from Leyden, that is from John Robinson's congregation, and not more than a dozen or so were members of the original Scrooby congregation. Not all were Puritans or members of the congregation, notably Captain Myles Standish. A few were servants sent out by the merchants to labor in their behalf.

The Pilgrims, unlike the colonists to Virginia, Maryland, and the Carolinas, were without a charter. It was necessary that some form of government should be set up; therefore the company drew up a document on board ship, November 11, 1620, known as the "May-

Mayflower Compact

flower Compact" or "Civill body politick," signed by forty-one men, seventeen of whom were from Leyden. The essential feature of the agreement was this: all who signed it agreed to submit to "such just and equal laws" thought best for the general good of the colony. Conformity to the laws of England and the method of making laws were not mentioned. John Carver was chosen governor, and on his death in April 1621, William Bradford succeeded him, though his duties as governor were not defined. The whole body of the free male settlers met and enacted the laws — the first pure democracy in America.

After some exploration out from Provincetown, part of the company landed at Plymouth in a small boat

Conditions of Settlement

December 11th, old style, or December 21st, new style. The Mayflower finally arrived in Plymouth harbor five days later. The plan of common labor made possible the erection of a common storehouse about twenty feet square, with a thatched roof, and later a fort; though each man was allowed to build his own house. The first winter was a hard one, with scant supplies, sickness, hostile Indians and wolves. By April 44 persons, or nearly one-half of the whole company, had perished. Of 18 married women, only four survived. No supply ship arrived until the next autumn. Fortunately a treaty of peace and friendship was made with the Indian chief Massasoit which lasted for fifty years. From two Indians who lived with them, one of whom was the famous Squanto, the Pilgrims were taught how to plant corn, where and how to fish for herring or "alewives," how to use them for food and fertilizer, and how to find their way through the woods.

From the time the Pilgrims took possession of Plymouth they were "squatters" with no legal right to the

The Council for New England and Patent of 1621

land. In 1620 the survivors of the old Plymouth Company, led by Gorges, petitioned for a charter and were granted land from the 40th to the 48th parallel, from "sea to sea" with the title *Council Established at Plymouth in the County of Devon for the Planting, Ruling and Governing of New England in America.* It was to this body that the adventurers, or financial backers of the Pilgrims, applied for a patent November 9, 1621, which was granted.

Governor Bradford wrote (1623) that "sometimes two or three months together, they neither had bread

Economic Aspect of Settlement

nor any kind of corn . . . they were divided into several companies, six or seven to a gang or company, and so went out with a net they had brought, to take bass and such like fish . . . neither did they return till they had caught something, though it were five or six days before, for they knew there was nothing at home, and to go home empty would be a great discouragement to the rest."

In the summer of 1623 the common labor and land system broke down. The older men disliked working in a common gang, while the younger were dissatisfied because their labor was no better rewarded than that of the old and infirm. Husbands disliked having their wives act as public servants and having them wash and cook for any member of the community. So an individual allotment of land was made, extended in 1624 to one acre each. Soon all became industrious and much more corn was planted. Women went into the fields to set corn "whom to have compelled would have been thought tyranny and oppression."

In 1627 the partnership was dissolved by agreement,

whereby the London merchants were to receive £1800 in annual instalments of £200, plus £600 for current debts, and the monopoly of the trade of the colony was vested for six years in Bradford, Winslow, Standish, Brewster, Bruce, Alden, Howland, and Allerton, who made themselves responsible for payment of the debt. One annual payment by each colonist of three bushels of corn or six pounds of tobacco was provided for. The economic development was advanced by a further division of lands (1627) in tracts of 20 acres each and a distribution of the company's live stock — a cow and two goats to every twelve persons.

The Plymouth colony is remarkable in two respects. By 1628, almost unaided, the Pilgrims had established a

The Plymouth Experiment
colony, defended themselves from the Indians, and by their own industry become self-supporting and accumulated in a few years by hard work and skilful trading enough to pay off their debt; in other words to purchase the share of the land and goods of the partners in England. They developed a free and independent political and economic unit. Their government first consisted of the body of freemen, and then, as new towns developed, a representative assembly was organized. Their economic system gave each individual an opportunity to work out his economic freedom, while submitting himself to strict religious and moral control.

39. Politics and Religion in England (1603–1630)

The founding of the Massachusetts Bay Colony was a consequence of a great movement in England in which

Political Views of James I and Charles I
politics and religion were associated in an intimate alliance. Among the purposes of James I were these: opposition to the advance of popular government, acting through the House

of Commons, and the establishment of arbitrary government dependent largely on the will of the king. Charles I extended the extra-legal methods of raising revenue used by James I, such as forced loans. He squandered large sums in futile wars with France and Spain and announced through his court chaplain that "The King is not bound to observe the laws of the realm concerning the subject's rights and liberties, but that his royal will and command in imposing loans and taxes without common consent of Parliament doth oblige the subject's conscience upon pain of eternal damnation." The Commons replied with the famous "Petition of Right" in 1628, denying the power of the king to levy a tax or loan without action by Parliament and calling for a cessation of acts contrary to the "rights and liberties of the subject."

In his speech to his first Parliament (1604) James declared that the "Puritans and Novelists" were a sect
The Religious   "unable to be suffered in any well-governed
Conflict   commonwealth." While the Puritans were at first willing and anxious to remain within the fold of the established or Anglican church, yet as time passed they advanced towards the Separatist point of view. This was hastened by the determination of James and his advisers to force strict conformity. A close relation existed between the political and religious aims of James and Charles. The Reformation in its early stages was based not solely on the overthrow of the ecclesiastical power of the Pope, but also on the transfer of that power to kings as heads of secular states. But kings used their religious authority to bolster up their political power, so that in matters of religious freedom the English dissenters were hardly better off than before. Nonconformity, in the view of James I, and many of the most prominent and wisest Englishmen, was dan-

gerous to the state. In 1603 James I was presented with a petition drawn up by Puritans asking for changes in the form of church service, such as the omission of the cross in baptism, the ring in marriage, the wearing of the cap and surplice, abolition of "popish opinion," modification of the church songs and music, better observance of the Sabbath, improvement of the character of the clergy and other reforms. The reply of James was made known at the famous Hampton Court Conference in 1604, when he declared that he would make them conform or "harry them out of the land, or else do worse."

Under Charles I religious persecution increased, particularly under Laud, Bishop of London, then Archbishop of Canterbury. He undertook to stem the tide of Puritanism and to suppress all unorthodox preaching by severe penalties. A practice which greatly disturbed Laud was that of using the funds of the established church to support a Puritan clergyman. The king issued instructions, formulated by Laud, which imposed fines on ministers preaching Nonconformist doctrines.

Conditions Under Charles I

The political and religious theories of James I and Charles I conflicted with one of the central features of Puritanism. The political aspect of Puritanism involved a political doctrine, a denial of the arbitrary power of the king in religious matters. There followed the formation of a Puritan party to resist the king. Under such conditions some of the Puritans commenced to discuss plans for colonization, as a means of escaping the evils of arbitrary government and religious persecution, as well as for their economic betterment.

Puritanism was not, however, concerned solely with dissent from the prevailing doctrines and ceremonies of the Anglican church and opposition to the political theories and practices of James and Charles. The Puri-

Meaning of Puritanism tans were dissatisfied with many other things; for example, the low moral standards of the time, the character of the stage, and the irreverent observance of Sunday. They wished to re-model, in important respects, the social system.

40. The Beginnings of the Massachusetts Bay Colony
(1623–1630)

Between 1607 and 1640 thousands of English subjects migrated to the new world. Bermuda and Barba-

Nature and Causes of the Migration dos were settled in 1612 and 1625. By 1630 the former had upward of 3000 and the latter 2000 settlers, while Virginia and Maryland together counted no more than 5000. Along the New England coast were a number of independent plantations, besides the Plymouth colony. The population in what is now Maine and New Hampshire was perhaps 900. By 1640 it is estimated that 65,000 had left England for America and the West Indies, of whom 20,000 more or less had migrated to the so-called Puritan colonies, while the remainder had gone to settlements " where religion did not partake of the New England way." Indeed, of the 20,000 who migrated to New England, a large number had little or no interest in Puritan theology or ideals of life. The greatest magnet which drew so many Englishmen to the new world was economic rather than religious; the hope of acquiring lands and fortune. Moreover, in the region where Puritanism was strongest a decline in the cloth business, an increase of unemployment, and an actual dearth of food led to thoughts of migration. In Lincolnshire one writer reported " for there are many thousands in these parts who have soulde all they have even to theyr bedd straw, and cann not get worke to earne any munny. Dogg's flesh is a dainty dish."

Among the scattered plantations north of Plymouth was one sponsored by a group of merchants known Dorchester   as the "Dorchester Adventurers," who had Adventurers in 1623 founded a fishing station at Cape Ann. A few of these Dorchester Adventurers, among them The Rev. John White, a man with Puritan leanings and rector of Trinity Church at Dorchester, England, secured help from capitalists. They then obtained a patent, in March 1628, from the *Council for New England,* granting a tract of land extending three miles north of the Merrimac to three miles south of the Charles River and from "sea to sea." This was the foundation of Massachusetts. John Endicott, a stern and uncompromising Puritan, was sent out as governor to prepare the way for a larger migration and to govern the settlers on the tract now under the control of a private trading company called "The Company of Adventurers for New England in America." Endicott arrived in September 1628, and set up his authority over some fifty or sixty people, increased by 300 the next year.

This private company, designed primarily for fishing and trading, was without corporate powers or proper Massachu-   authority to govern a large settlement. setts Bay   Accordingly more persons were admitted to Company
Charter   the company and application was made for a royal charter. This was obtained in March 1628–29 under the title "The Governor and Company of the Massachusetts Bay in New England." The grant of land made by the *Council for New England* was confirmed by the king and a system of government outlined. The charter provided for a general court of the "freemen" of the company to meet four times a year, with power

to elect annually from their own number a governor, deputy governor, and eighteen assistants. These officers, with the freemen, were to make laws not contrary to those of England. Power was given the company to transport settlers, but nothing was said of religious liberty and no supervising royal council in England was provided for, as in the case of the Virginia Company.

Leaders in the movement such as John Winthrop and Thomas Dudley, induced the company (Aug. 29, 1629)

The Transfer of the Charter

to vote that the charter should be legally transferred to those who should inhabit the plantation. This was a most important move, for thereby a trading company or commercial corporation managed by stockholders resident in England was transformed into an almost independent self-governing commonwealth. That is, the governing body of the company was removed to the colony, and became independent of absentee stockholders and to a large extent independent of the crown. The reason for this move was that the leaders designed a self-governing, religious commonwealth, and it would have been inconvenient to submit to the government of a commercial corporation whose sympathies and aims might be antagonistic to the designs of the religious leaders.

When the company voted that the government should be under the control of those that emigrated to Massachusetts, the old officers by agreement resigned and in October 1629 John Winthrop was elected governor. A deputy governor and eighteen assistants were chosen, most of whom were expecting to emigrate. They were ambitious, intelligent, middle-class Englishmen, most of them having property and some political experience, while a few had a liberal education.

John Winthrop and Associates

John Winthrop was a man of high principles, with some training in the law, a Suffolk landholder belonging to the country gentry, with property bringing in an annual income of £600 to £700, equivalent now to $15,000 to $20,000 a year. He was a man who would probably have reached a high position in England had he chosen to remain there. Among the assistants were large landholders, wealthy men. Theophilus Eaton was an eminent London merchant. Simon Bradstreet was a Suffolk gentleman of fine estate and had studied at Emmanuel College, Cambridge, where so many Puritan leaders were educated.

Winthrop and about 840 emigrants, with 240 cows and 60 horses, embarked on eleven ships and sailed in three detachments from Plymouth, Yarmouth, and Southampton. They arrived off the coast of Massachusetts in May, June, and July, 1630. This was the greatest effort yet made in English colonization. In spite of the fact that the expedition was well equipped, there was scarcity of food, not corn enough to last two weeks after landing, and the settlers were compelled to eat acorns, mussels, and clams to eke out their scanty supplies. To escape the expense of maintenance, 180 servants, most of whom had been brought over during the two years before, were freed. Two hundred of the faint-hearted emigrants returned to England. Sickness spread rapidly, and by December about two hundred had died. Some lived through the winter in tents, their only shelter from the rigorous blasts of a New England winter. The necessity of cultivating as rich a soil as possible led to a dispersion of the settlers from Salem, and this was the occasion for the founding of settlements at Charlestown, where a few persons already resided, Boston, and Newtowne (Cambridge). Within a year there were eight separate settlements, the beginnings of future towns.

41. Workings of the Massachusetts Bay Government (1630–1634)

The government was centered in a general court or meeting of the freemen. Very few freemen had mi-

Organiza-
tion of the
Government

grated except the governor, deputy governor, and five or six assistants. The assistants, at their meeting on September 28, 1630, levied a rate of £50 for military maintenance, distributed among seven towns. It is noteworthy that non-freemen were taxed without legal warrant. These proceedings induced 118 persons, October 19, to apply to the first great and general court of admission as freemen of the corporation. For the moment this request was ignored, and on October 30, it was voted, outside of any authority in the charter, to transfer the power to enact laws and to appoint officers from the court of freemen to the governor, deputy governor, and assistants. Thus an oligarchy of seven or eight men, holding office during good behavior, obtained the power to govern more than a thousand settlers. This was not only contrary to the charter, but in conflict with the inherited idea that laws should be made and taxes should be levied in an assembly of representatives of the people, chosen at suitable intervals.

The reasons for this procedure were doubtless as follows. The leaders had in mind a peculiar and special type of colony; first, a Bible Commonwealth, in which the lives of individuals should be regulated in harmony with the will of God as interpreted by those appointed as rulers, and best qualified for the purpose; second, a desire for unanimity of opinion; for the allowance of different views of government and religion might wreck the plans of the leaders and endanger the success of the colony. It was necessary, then, so the leaders argued, that there should be restrictions of political privileges, free speech, and religious toleration. Religious toleration then was not considered desirable for Massachusetts.

Fearing that the 118 who had applied for admission as freemen might migrate to New Hampshire, Maine, or Plymouth, it was decided May 10, 1631, that they should be admitted as freemen of the company. But at this same meeting the rights of the freemen were limited to the election of assistants, when vacancies occurred, another violation of the charter. Still another act provided that in the future no person should be admitted as a freeman of the company who was not a member of one of the churches within the colony. It is evident that these proceedings must stir up resentment and cause a demand for a limitation of the power of the governor and his assistants, and a restoration of the power of the freemen as set forth in the charter.

For the purpose of fortifying the town of Newtown Feb. 3, 1632, a tax of £60 was levied on each of the

Rise of Representative Government

twelve then existing towns, by order of the governor and assistants. As a result of this, we find the famous protest of Watertown, May 9, 1632, objecting to taxation on the ground that this power was vested in the freemen meeting in general court; that " it was not safe to pay moneys after that sort, for fear of bringing themselves and their posterity into bondage." At the next general court in May, the freemen recovered their power to choose the governor, deputy governor, and assistants, and ordered the choice of " two of every plantation to confer with the court about raising a public stock."

Finally in April 1634, when the colony contained three or four thousand inhabitants, distributed in sixteen towns, a reform of great importance was secured.

It was inconvenient and dangerous for all the freemen to leave their homes at once. Hence on May 14, twenty-four delegates from the towns appeared in Boston and demanded a view of the charter and informed Governor Winthrop " that all their laws be made at the general court." This move led to the introduction of a representative assembly. From this time on no taxes were laid without a consent of the representatives. Though this procedure was not provided for in the charter, nevertheless the general court, made up of the governor, deputy governor, assistants, and the representatives from the towns was now the lawmaking body. This was the third example of the development of the representative system in the British Colonies, the first in Virginia 1619, the second that of Bermuda, 1621, and the third in Massachusetts, 1634. In spite of winning a representative assembly the relatively few persons who could vote for deputies, made the government of Massachusetts a theocratic rather than a democratic state.

42. Dissensions and Persecutions

Roger Williams was pastor of the church at Salem in 1631, and according to Bradford was " a man godly and zealous having many precious gifts, but very unsettled in judgment." For example, he asserted that the civil government had power only over men's bodies, goods, and outward estates; that it had not power over a man's conscience or religious belief, and could pass no law on religious matters. In other words, he believed in a complete separation of state and church, in direct opposition to the views of Winthrop and his associates, who maintained the right of the state to regulate men's religious beliefs, as established by law, and to punish them for infractions of the law.

Roger
Williams

Williams also opposed meetings or associations of the clergy because it was contrary to the congregational or democratic system of church government, wherein each church was its own master. He advised his own church at Salem to renounce all communication with other churches. He also denied the legal basis of the Massachusetts charter with respect to the power of the king to grant land, because he believed that the Indians alone had the legal title to land and were the true owners of the soil. Therefore the only valid title could be obtained through purchase of the land from the Indians. Finally Williams was cited to appear before the general court to answer for his opinions. On his refusal to recede from his position, the following decree of banishment was made in the autumn of 1635:

" Whereas Mr. Roger Williams, one of the elders of the Church of Salem, has broached and divulged diverse new and dangerous opinions against the authority of magistrates, as also writ a letter of defamation both of the magistrates and churches here, and that before any conviction, and yet maintaineth the same without retraction, ordered that he be banished."

Following the expulsion of Roger Williams from Massachusetts, there arose the so-called antinomian controversy, in which Mrs. Anne Hutchinson, Wheelwright and Anne Hutchinson her brother-in-law, The Reverend John Wheelwright, The Reverend John Cotton, for a brief period, and Sir Henry Vane, elected governor of Massachusetts in the spring of 1636, were on the one side, while Governor Winthrop and The Reverend John Wilson, pastor of the Boston Church, with the magistrates and clergy, were on the other side. The dispute, which was at first concerned with theological doctrines, developed into a major political issue that split the colony into two parties.

Mrs. Hutchinson was a brilliant, restless, and radical-minded woman of a "haughty and fierce carriage, of a nimble wit and active spirit, and a very voluble tongue." She took upon herself, for the benefit of women particularly, to expound, comment on, criticize, and add to the Sunday sermons preached at Boston. A hundred, more or less, attended these meetings. Mrs. Hutchinson came to the conclusion that Wheelwright and Cotton alone of all the clergy preached a " Covenant of Grace," meaning thereby that they had a direct revelation in their souls of God's grace and love. The rest of the clergy preached a "Covenant of Works," that is, a religion founded on a system of established doctrines and laws, officially interpreted by the clergy, which must be unquestioningly obeyed. The doctrines of Mrs. Hutchinson, like those of Roger Williams, were thought to be dangerous to the church and state, since the acts of those in authority, magistrates and clergy, might be questioned, or resisted, because of direct revelation or " self-illumination."

Wheelwright and Mrs. Hutchinson were summoned before the general court. The former was accused of uttering words that led to sedition, and was accordingly banished. The latter was accused of "traducing the ministers," and was banished as "a woman not fit for our society." She was also excommunicated from the church, in words pronounced by The Reverend John Wilson of the Boston Church as follows: "I do not only pronounce you worthy to be cast out, but I do cast you out and in the name of Christ I do deliver you up to Satan, that you may learn no more to blaspheme, to seduce, and to lie, and I do account you from this time forth to be a Heathen and a Publican."

Williams, Wheelwright, and Anne Hutchinson were not the last persons banished from Massachusetts because of their demand for liberty of conscience. Notwithstanding the fact that the Protestant Reformation and the controlling motives for migration were based in part on the principle of freedom of conscience, at least for the Puritans themselves, the Puritan leaders of Massachusetts built up a political and religious system based on intolerance. They desired unity and strength and hence sacrificed, for these ideals, religious freedom and democracy. Nathaniel Ward remarked, " All Familists, Anabaptists, and other Enthusiasts shall have free liberty to keepe away from us."

The Puritan Argument for Conformity

The policy of intolerance in religious and civil matters, and the suppression of free speech and inquiry undoubtedly saved for the Puritans their own peculiar ideas of church and state, but it tended to produce a narrow provincial attitude towards life and it hindered the introduction of new blood and new ideas in religion and government. It was nearly three quarters of a century later before the more liberal and democratic elements succeeded in overcoming, to any considerable extent, the practice of intolerance.

43. Rhode Island (1635–1647)

The settlement of Rhode Island, and to a great extent that of New Hampshire and Connecticut, arose out of the conflict and clash of religious and political ideas in Massachusetts, already described. The general court enacted a series of laws against heresy, criticism of the magistrates or clergy, free speech and inquiry, and immigration of unorthodox persons. The right to vote for deputies was restricted to church members, about one-fifth only of the male citizens; while church attendance and taxation for the support of the Congregational church were made compulsory for all citizens. It was under such cir-

Pressure for Additional Colonies in New England

cumstances that some of the advocates of democracy and religious liberty were banished, while others voluntarily sought refuge on the frontiers, the unoccupied regions to the south, north, and west of Massachusetts.

Roger Williams, as a result of the decree of banishment, with five or six associates, proceeded to Narragansett Bay and founded Providence. He took care to purchase the title of the Indians to the land. His government was a simple democracy, founded on a compact somewhat similar to that of the Mayflower, in which the settlers promised obedience "to all such orders and agreements as shall be made for public good of the body in an orderly way, by the major consent of the present inhabitants, masters of families, incorporated together in a town fellowship, and others whom they shall admit unto them only in civil things." The government established did not rest on the authority of the king. It was a free, independent commonwealth, as was Plymouth. Williams yielded to the wishes of his associates and shared his title to the land purchased from the Indians with twelve other settlers, retaining an equal share for himself. The settlement thus became a proprietary association with power to admit other settlers.

Roger Williams and the Founding of Providence

Following the settlement of Williams at Providence, William Coddington, from Massachusetts, with a group of eighteen friends settled an island in Narragansett Bay, called Aquidneck (1638). Their settlement was named Portsmouth. The Indians were paid twenty-three coats and thirteen hoes for the land. This group also formed themselves into a "body politick" by signing a document agreeing to submit to the laws contained in the Bible, thus forming a "Bible Commonwealth" with Coddington as

Settlement of Portsmouth, Newport, and Warwick

judge. The next year, a new compact was drawn up in which the settlers acknowledged themselves as subjects of King Charles, " and in his name doe hereby binde ourselves into a civill body, politicke, unto his lawes accord'g to matters of justice."

Meantime, soon after her banishment, Mrs. Hutchinson with her husband joined the settlers at Portsmouth, accompanied by Samuel Gorton, an agitator or " a proud and pestilent Seducer," as the Puritans called him. This group seems to have overthrown Coddington, who with seven associates went to Newport, and in the summer of 1639 formed a new commonwealth. The members signed a compact, in which they agreed to bear proportional charges and to abide by the decisions made by a majority vote. The judge, Coddington, had a double vote, and the settlers acknowledged themselves " natural subjects to their sovereign lord King Charles, and subject to his laws."

Still a fourth settlement was founded at Warwick, January 1643, by individuals from Portsmouth and Providence, led by Gorton. Thus by 1643 there were four independent towns, which were scarcely less than little independent states.

The Rhode Island settlements were surrounded by ambitious neighbors, Massachusetts, Plymouth, and Connecticut; so for mutual protection they decided to seek a patent for their lands. Roger Williams went to England in 1643 for this purpose and succeeded in securing a patent from commissioners of the Long Parliament, who in theory acted in the name of the king. It gave authority to the people of the three towns of Providence, Portsmouth, and Newport in Rhode Island, to rule themselves and others within their limits by such form of civil government as the greater part should find suitable. Not until 1647

Patent of 1643

did these three towns meet to act under its provisions
and admit Warwick to a share of their rights.

Rhode Island was thus started without a church
establishment, or taxes for the support of religion or
Character of   compulsory church attendance. There were
Settlements   no religious tests for the right to vote or
hold office, no disciplining of individuals or churches for
their views and no trouble or wars with the Indians.
Rhode Island was founded not as a result of conscien-
tious planning, but by bands of fugitives, exiles, and
individuals seeking escape from religious intolerance and
arbitrary government, settling at different places, at different times and for a time without coöperation or relation to each other. The spirit of individualism was
strong, but outside influences forced these independent
settlements to join their forces to form the colony of
Rhode Island.

44. New Hampshire and Maine (1607–1652)

New Hampshire and Maine had their origin in the
period following the collapse of the colony attempted
Beginnings   on the Kennebec (1607–1608) by the Plym-
of New   outh Company. Fishing and trading ex-
Hampshire   peditions were undertaken and plantations
and stations, more or less permanent, were in existence
through the period to 1620. The Council for New England granted several patents of land in this region. That
obtained by Ferdinando Gorges and Captain John
Mason, Nov. 3, 1631, led to an attempt at colonization.
A party of fifty men were sent over to engage in farming, fishing, etc. This settlement on the Piscataqua had
a precarious existence. Mason died in 1635 and left his
grandsons the title to the territory, but the plantation
fell into disorder. Two years later, Wheelwright, who had
been expelled from Boston, with thirty-five companions,

began a settlement at Exeter, at the falls of the Piscataqua. The customary document was drawn up, establishing a church and a "body politicke." The laws were to be enacted by the whole body of freemen and executed by a governor and two assistants chosen annually.

Massachusetts by an unwarrantable construction of her charter now laid claim to all the land of New Hampshire and Maine lying east of the most northerly source of the Merrimac. Having secured the patent rights to the Dover lands, and taking advantage of a church quarrel (1641), she annexed the town of Dover as well as Portsmouth, and two years later allowed the election of deputies to the general court although they were not church members. Soon Exeter was claimed and absorbed, and New Hampshire for the next forty years was a part of Massachusetts.

Very few English inhabitants settled east of the Piscataqua River till 1640. There were only a few trading and fishing posts. This region from the Piscataqua to Kennebec was claimed by Ferdinando Gorges, the result of a division of the territory of Maine between himself and Mason. It was almost a wilderness, with a few scattered, isolated settlements and plantations. On April 3, 1639, Gorges secured a charter from the king making him "Lord Proprietary of the Province of Maine," with large powers of legislation and government. This colony, however, failed; and after ten years, by a process similar to that in New Hampshire, Maine was absorbed by Massachusetts in 1652.

Beginnings of Maine

45. Connecticut and New Haven (1635–1643)

The Plymouth colonists, being invited by Uncas, chief of the Mohicans, hostile to the Pequots, had dispatched trading and exploring expeditions to Connecticut in

1633, although the Dutch already had a fort and trading post on the site of Hartford. The Plymouth people

Rivalry for Connecticut

purchased lands of the Indians near what is now Windsor. Massachusetts men also made a trading voyage to Connecticut this same summer. Still another claimant to part of this territory was Lord Warwick, President of the Council for New England, who in 1631 granted a tract of land 120 miles in length in southern Connecticut, to a company of twelve, very vaguely described, but to extend along the coast and westward from " sea to sea " viz., to the Pacific Ocean. Thus four parties claimed portions of Connecticut: Lord Brooke and associates, the Dutch, Plymouth, and Massachusetts.

In the year 1633 a ship arrived in Boston from England bringing Rev. Thomas Hooker, who became pastor

The Connecticut Colony

of the church at Newtowne, later Cambridge. Pressure for fresh fertile soil, the ambition of Hooker, and opposition to the narrow religious and political views of the Massachusetts leaders, caused dissatisfaction. Winthrop in a letter to Hooker, defending limited suffrage, said: " The best part is always the least, and of that best part the wiser part is always the lesser." Hooker replied that " in matters that concern the common good, a general councel, chosen by all, to transact business which concerns all, I conceive most suitable to rule and most safe for the relief of the whole people."

Hooker's congregation next applied to the general court for permission to remove to Connecticut. This petition was refused, the magistrates being against the petition and the deputies for it. The next year, 1635, permission was given to remove if those emigrating would continue subordinate to the government of Massachusetts. By the summer of 1636 settlers were passing almost daily to the Connecticut river. By the end of the year some 800 settlers were distributed in the new territory in three townships, Hartford, Windsor, and Wethersfield. They were without a charter or patent and hence were in reality " squatters " until the time of the grant of a charter in 1662.

For a short time the temporary government was subordinated to that of Massachusetts. In January, 1638–39, however, the three towns declared themselves a commonwealth and adopted a frame of government called the " Fundamental Orders." Hooker preached a sermon in which he declared that " the foundation of authority is laid in the free consent of the people and that the choice of public magistrates belongs to the people by God's own allowance." The legislature was composed of a governor and six assistants, elected annually by the freemen, and four deputies or representatives from each of the three towns. Only the governor was required to be a church member, and he was not allowed to serve two years in succession. All persons who took an oath of fidelity and had been admitted by a majority of any township had the right to vote for officers, make and repeal laws, and dispose of lands. Taxes were to be levied only by the whole legislature. This was the first form of government in the new world, other than the Mayflower Compact, enacted by the body of the people; and the first constitution drawn up by a convention of delegates.

The emigration to Connecticut brought on a serious war with the Pequot Indians, who occupied the eastern

Pequot War　　portion of the colony. They were accused of killing some of the English and naturally felt obliged to resist the seizure of their lands. Attacked by the whites in 1637, they were driven towards the South and West and finally almost exterminated. This success made settlement in this region possible on a large scale and greatly reduced the danger from Indian attacks.

The settlement of the tract granted to Lord Brooke and associates was entrusted to John Winthrop, Jr., as The New agent, who had for a time settled in what Haven is now Ipswich, but later had returned to Colony England. He was commissioned governor of the proposed colony, and instructed to build a fort at the mouth of the Connecticut. A fort was built at Saybrook, but it was only a military post and did not develop into a colony. The Reverend John Davenport, graduate of Oxford, and Theophilus Eaton with a group of settlers mostly from London, arrived in this region in the summer of 1637, with ambitious schemes for trade and a colony. They were without a charter or patent to the land and did not even purchase lands from the Indians. They founded New Haven in 1638. Other towns were organized, such as Milford and Guilford in 1639, and Stamford in 1640. A plantation covenant was drawn up for their temporary government, in which the settlers agreed to accept the rule of the Scriptures, not only as a religious system but also as a civil code. In June 1639, the settlers came together for the purpose of framing a constitution. Davenport preached a sermon to show that the Scriptures were a sufficient rule for the conduct of civil affairs.

As a result a " Bible Commonwealth " was established. An agreement was reached that the franchise should be restricted to church members. Seven men were finally chosen by an indirect method to be the first church members and freemen. They were given the power to select other church members and freemen, appoint magistrates among themselves, and make and repeal laws. Later it was voted that " the worde of God shall be the only rule to be attended unto in ordering the affayres of Government in this plantation," thus ignoring the common and statute law of England. In 1643 the four towns were united into the republic of New Haven.

Thus by 1643 New England boasted isolated plantations, fishing stations, and settlements in Maine, independent towns in New Hampshire and Rhode Island, a military fort at Saybrook, and fully organized colonies in Plymouth, Massachusetts, Connecticut, and New Haven. These large and small colonies and petty, independent settlements were practically beyond the control of England and had no political relation to each other. Plymouth, Rhode Island, Connecticut, and New Haven were without charters and the citizens of the last two were "squatters" and without legal title to the land. They were subject to dangers from French and Indians, to dissensions and disagreements with each other, and to possible arbitrary control from England. Owing to conditions in England the New England colonies for the next twenty years developed with practically no interference from the mother country, and thus were free to work out their own ideas for protection, relations with the Indians, and their political, economic, social, and religious institutions.

CHAPTER VI

NEW ENGLAND (1643–1689)

46. References

Bibliographies. — See refs. under bibliographies in chs. v, vii, xii, xiv, xv; Channing, Hart and Turner, *Guide*, §§ 36–39, 42–43, 45, 131, 135, 137, 138–141, 143–145; Grace Griffin, *Writ. on Am. Hist.*, 1906–1923; J. N. Larned, *Lit. of Am. Hist.*, 76–92.

Historical Maps. — See refs. in ch. v.

General Accounts. — See refs. under "General Accounts" and books listed under separate colonies in ch. v; J. T. Adams, *Founding of New Engl.*, chs. ix-xi, xii-xiv, xvi; C. M. Andrews, *Fathers of N. Engl.*, chs. iv-vi, and *Colonial Self-Govt.*, chs. i-iv, xvi-xvii; Carl Becker, *Begin. of Am. People*, 80–124; J. A. Doyle, *Engl. Col. in Am.*, II, pt. I, chs. viii-ix; III, chs. i-v; John Fiske, *Begin. of New Engl.*, chs. iv-vi; E. B. Greene, *Foundations of Am. Nationality*, chs. v-vii; A. B. Hart (ed.), *Commonwl. Hist. Mass.*, I, chs. iii, v-ix, xix; H. L. Osgood, *Am. Col. in the 17th Cent.*, I, chs. x, xii-xiv; III, chs. iii, vi, x-xi, xiii; J. G. Palfrey, *Hist. of New Engl.*, I, ch. xv; II, 112–140, 154–160, 448–453; chs. v-vi, viii-x, xiii-xv; III, ii-v, vii-x, xii-xiv; L. G. Tyler, *England in Am.*, chs. xvi-xviii; Justin Winsor, *Narr. and Crit. Hist. of Am.*, III, ch. ix.

Special Accounts. — (For English background see refs. under "General and Special Accts.," "Pilgrims" and "Puritans," ch. v); (a) RELATIONS WITH BRITISH EMPIRE: (bibliography in C. M. Andrews, *Colonial Self-Govt.*, 339–340; see also refs. to chs. iii, x, xiv.) J. T. Adams, *Founding of New Engl.*, chs. xii-xiii; C. M. Andrews in *Cambridge Hist. of British Empire*, volume I, and *British Committees etc.*, *of Trade and Plantation*, in *J. H. Stud.*, ser. XXVI; G. L. Beer, *Origins of British Colonial System*, and *Old Colonial System;* and "Com. Policy of Engl. Towards the Am. Colonies," in *Columb. Studies*, III, and "Cromwell's Policy in its Econom. Aspects," in *Political Sci. Quart.*, XVI, 611; G. G. Edmundson, *Anglo-Dutch Rivalry;* H. E. Egerton, *Origin and Growth of Brit. Dominion;* Ralph Harlow, *Growth of U. S.*, ch. vii; J. W. Horrocks, *Short Hist. of Mercantilism;* P. L. Kaye, *Engl. Colo. Admin. under Clarendon;* W. T. Root, "Lords of Trade and Plantation, 1675–1696," in

Am. Hist. Rev., XXIII, 20–41; Gustav Schmoller, *The Mercantile System, etc.* (b) NEW ENGLAND PROBLEMS: Brooks Adams, *Emancipation of Mass.;* Charles Borgeaud, *Rise of Modern Democracy in Old and New Engl.;* R. P. Hallowell, *Quaker Invasion of Mass.;* Rufus Jones, *Quakers in the Am. Colonies;* L. K. Matthews, *Expansion of New Engl.;* H. M. Sylvester, *Indian Wars of New Engl.* (3 vols.). (c) NEW ENGLAND CONFEDERATION. John Fiske, *Begin. of New Engl.*, ch. iv; Richard Frothingham, *Rise of the Repub. of the U. S.*, 33–100; A. B. Hart, (ed.), *Commonwealth Hist. of Mass.*, I, ch. ix; Justin Winsor, *Memo. Hist. of Boston*, I, ch. vii. (d) LOSS OF CHARTER: J. T. Adams, *Founding of New Engl.*, ch. xv; Violet Barnes, *Dominion of New Engl.*, also in *Commonwealth Hist. of Mass.*, ch. xxi; G. L. Beer, *Old Colonial System*, II, chs. xi-xii; K. B. Murdock, *Increase Mather*, chs. xii-xiv; H. E. Osgood, *Am. Col. in 17th Cent.*, III, pt. iv, chs. vi-vii, x, xiii-xiv; W. H. Whitmore, "Andros Tracts," in *Prince. Soc. Publs.* (Introduction); Justin Winsor, *Memo. Hist. of Boston*, II, ch. i.

Biographies. — See list in ch. v; and bibliog. in W. P. Trent (ed.) *Cambr. Hist. of Am. Lit.*, I, 406, 424–425, 432; W. H. Chamberlain, *Samuel Sewall and the World he Lived in;* Everett Kimball, *Public Life of Joseph Dudley;* G. L. Kittredge, "Doctor Robert Child the Remonstrant," in *Publs. of Colo. Soc. of Mass.*, XXI; A. P. Merwin, *Life and Times of Cotton Mather;* K. B. Murdock, *Increase Mather;* R. N. Toppan, "Memoir of Edward Randolph," in *Prince. Soc. Publs.*, XXIV–XXV; Barrett Wendell, *Cotton Mather the Puritan Priest.*

Contemporary Accounts. — (a) BIBLIOGRAPHY: See bibliogs. in ch. v, under "Contemporary Accounts"; Channing, Hart and Turner, *Guide*, §§ 42–43, 140–146; W. P. Trent (ed.) *Cambr. Hist. of Am. Lit.*, I, 365–380; 382–398. (b) NARRATIVES: J. F. Jameson, (ed.), *Orig. Narratives of Early Am. Hist.;* C. M. Andrews, *Nars. of the Insurrections* and C. H. Lincoln, *Nars. of the Indian Wars;* George Bishop, *New Engl. Judged, etc.* (1703); Peter Force, *Tracts, etc.*, esp. Byfield's "Account of Late Revolution" in IV, no. 10; Samuel Maverick, "Description of New Engl. Towns" (1660), in *New Engl. Hist. and Gen. Reg.*, XXXIX, 33–48; *Prince. Society Publications* (esp., W. H. Whitmore (ed.), V–VII, "Andros Tracts"); see also accounts of the revolution in New Engl., John Dunton's *Letters from New Engl.* (IV), Edmund Randolph's *Letters and Official Papers*, 7 vols. (1676–1703) and Thomas Hutchinson, *Collection of Papers, etc.;* E. C. Stedman and E. M. Hutchinson, *Library of Am. Lit.*, I–II. (c) DOCUMENTS AND RECORDS: "Andros

Records," are in *Am. Antq. Soc. Proc.*, 1900, n. s., XIII, 239–268, 463–99; Ralph Gabriel (ed.), *Pageant of Am.;* W. L. Grant (ed.), *Acts of the Privy Council of Engl. Colonial Ser.;* A. B. Hart (ed.), *Contemporaries*, I, chs. xiv–xx; "Mass. Charter of 1691 and Mass. Royal Commissions," 1681–1774, are in *Colonial Soc. of Mass. Publs.*, II; Recs. of Commissioners of New Engl. Confed., in *Plymouth Col. Records*, IX, X; "Records of Council Meetings under Dudley," in *Mass. Hist. Soc. Proc.*, 2nd ser. XII, 226–286; Williston Walker, *Creeds and Platforms of Congregationalism*.

47. The New England Confederation (1637–1684)

By 1643 the New England colonies were acting almost as if they were sovereign and independent states. They formed governments acknowledging no superior, took up unoccupied lands without a patent, treated with the Indians, French, and Dutch, all without asking leave of England, which was then engaged in civil war. Massachusetts had been aggressive in encroaching on lands within New Hampshire, Rhode Island, and Connecticut. By an unwarranted interpretation of her charter she alleged that such territory was included within her grant.

Character of New England Colonies

Jealousy and fear, on the part of the weaker states, were factors which led to plans for a colonial confederation. Another influence was the Pequot Indian War of 1637, conducted by Connecticut. This tended to increase the fear of attacks by the Indians on the frontier. Moreover, as New England expanded to the North and West she came closer to the French and Dutch. Hence there was a suggestion of union as early as 1637.

Confederation

Six years later, without authority from England, commissioners from Connecticut, New Haven, and Plymouth met a committee of the general court of Massachusetts (1643) to frame articles of union. Maine and

Rhode Island were not represented. Massachusetts claimed the former was within her grant and annexed it ten years later. Besides, as Winthrop said, "they ran a different course from us both in their ministry and civil administration." The bitterness over the Rhode Islanders was expressed in the statement: There was no desire to converse with them "further than necessity or humanity may require."

The commissioners agreed upon eleven articles as the Constitution of the *United Colonies of New England*. In general the union was a loosely organized league rather than a federated state. It was called "A firme and perpetual league of friendship and amity for offence and defence, mutual advice and succor." The only governing body set up was the Board of Eight Commissioners, chosen annually, two from each colony. They were given power to determine questions relating to Indians, war, peace, leagues, charges, numbers of men, and divisions of spoils, in case of war. They were to judge disputes between the colonies, and see that escaped servants, prisoners, and fugitives from justice were returned. Any disputed question which lacked six affirmative votes must be referred back to the colonies. No colony was to engage in either an offensive or defensive war without the consent of at least six of the eight commissioners. The plan provided that each colony should supply money and soldiers for war in proportion to the number of male inhabitants between sixteen and sixty.

Though the commissioners lacked power to enforce their own decrees, they formed a center of organization and resistance for holding in check the Indians, French, and Dutch, for promoting religion, for stimulating the collection of funds for Harvard College, and for Christianizing and

Influence of the Confederation

educating the Indians. The desirability of union was brought home to the colonies who became accustomed to act together. Massachusetts was the dissatisfied member; for by the articles she was obliged to furnish about two thirds of the soldiers and money in case of a war, perhaps declared without her wish, as she had only two votes. She refused to be bound by the votes of the other six commissioners for a war against the Dutch in 1652. Dissensions and the revocation of the Massachusetts charter in 1684 practically ended the history of the Confederation. It left a deep impress on the thought of the period, and helped to develop several principles; such as the equality of each colony, the principle of nullification, the exercise of undelegated sovereignty, and the germ of national federation and union.

48. Internal Problems of New England (1643–1675)

The history of the New England Colonies from 1643 to 1689 is concerned first with certain outstanding domestic problems and policies, and second, particularly after 1660, with their relation to the new plans of Charles II for more effective imperial control. In the first group are such questions as the continued efforts of Massachusetts to expand her territory by an aggressive policy of annexation at the expense of her neighbors, and the internal struggle for a more liberal form of government and for greater religious liberty. In Rhode Island there is the effort to form a central government and to acquire a new charter. For Connecticut and New Haven there is the union of the two colonies and the new charter of 1662, and the continued struggle with the Indians in all the colonies. Considered from the standpoint of the empire the colonies stubbornly resisted the attempt at stricter control, both political and economic.

After annexing New Hampshire, Massachusetts (1642) arbitrarily fixed the boundary between herself and Connecticut. By an unwarranted interpretation of the charter, the general court declared that the northern boundary was a line passing through a point three miles north of the source of the Merrimac and thence east and west from "sea to sea." Commissioners from Massachusetts (1653) required the submission of the inhabitants of Kittery, Maine, and later several other towns as far as Casco Bay. Thus was added to her possessions a large part of Maine, about 40,000 square miles. Massachusetts also set up claims to a portion of Rhode Island and was only headed off in this direction by the good fortune of Roger Williams in securing the patent of 1643, though as late as 1659 the larger colony was attempting to get control of part of the Narragansett region.

Expansion of Massachusetts

The lower house, established in Massachusetts in 1634, was continually in opposition to the governor and assistants, who, for example, claimed and maintained "the negative voice" — the right to veto acts of the deputies. The house gained one point when, in 1644, it won the right to sit as a separate house, and thus could more easily speak for the more liberal and democratic groups in the towns. An attempt was made to increase the civil liberties of non-church members, by Robert Child, Samuel Maverick, and others who presented a petition (1646) complaining that there were thousands in the colony who paid taxes, but had no part in the government. This effort failed and some of the petitioners were heavily fined and imprisoned. The reason for the failure was the fear on the part of the Congregational clergy that the plan involved an attempt to introduce Presbyterianism into the

Struggle for a more Liberal Government

colony, and thus weaken the power of the Congregational clergy as organized into independent churches.

The patent obtained by Roger Williams in 1643 was not taken advantage of for four years, because of the Rhode strong individualistic tendencies of the Island towns. Finally, however, the majority of and her Government the voters of three towns — Providence, Newport, and Portsmouth — came together (May 1647) and drew up a constitution, a code of laws, and voted to admit Warwick to the confederation of towns.

The Rhode Island constitution provided for a president and four assistants and other officers, to be chosen annually by the general assembly, made up of all the free inhabitants. Important laws, however, were to be initiated by the towns rather than the assembly, and such laws as the latter proposed had to be submitted to the four towns, at their town meetings for approval. The first assembly amended the constitution, so that a lawful general court was placed on a representative basis, six deputies from each town. Thus Rhode Island was the sixth colony to adopt the representative system, and the first to suggest a modified system of initiative and referendum for enactment of laws. The charter obtained in 1663 was similar to that of Connecticut, described below.

John Winthrop, Jr., Governor of Connecticut, went to England in 1661, for the purpose of securing a royal Charters of charter and to present an address of the Connecticut colonists to " his sacred majesty " in order and Rhode Island to acknowledge " their loyalty and allegiance to his highness." He secured a very liberal charter (1662) with respect to territory and government. The bounds were from Narragansett Bay to the " South Sea," thus taking in most of Rhode Island, a part of New Netherland, (Long Island), and all of the territory of the New Haven Colony. The form of government provided that there should be a governor, deputy governor, twelve assistants, and a house of deputies, two members from each town or city, elected annually by the freemen. No laws contrary to those of England were to be made, but no provision was made for transmitting laws to England for examination, as in all the other colonies except Maryland and Rhode Island. This remarkable charter granted almost complete independence to Connecticut, quite contrary to what might have been expected. After resisting union for two years New Haven Colony, fearing annexation to New York, submitted to Connecticut.

The overlapping territorial claims of Rhode Island and Connecticut led John Clarke of Rhode Island, who was in England, to petition the king for a new charter. It was granted in 1663. One clause provided that no person in the colony should be " molested, punished, disquieted, or called in question, for any differences in opinion in matters of religion, but freely and fully have and enjoy his and their own judgments and consciences in matters of religious concernments." The charter was received with great joy and was put into effect March 1, 1664, with a governor, deputy governor, ten assistants, and eighteen deputies. The Connecticut and Rhode Island charters were unique in that they gave legal sanction to the most popular form of government that had, up to that time, been instituted in the colonies.

49. King Philip's War (1675–1677)

The Indian War of 1675–1676, known as King Philip's War, is illustrative of the irrepressible con-

Indian War of 1675–76

flict between the whites and the Indians, and, like the Pequot War of 1637, was a desperate effort on their part to preserve their hunting grounds and resist the attempt of the English to impose upon them the white civilization — its laws, religion, and institutions. They had many grievances. For example, they were often forced to cede valuable lands for a song. Indeed Roger Williams declared that land was " one of the Gods of New England." They were subjected to fines, imprisonment, and forced labor for petty infractions of the law. In Connecticut the Pequots were not allowed to hunt or fish or even carry firewood, on Sunday. If caught drunk an Indian had to give twelve days' labor, one half to the accuser. The cattle of the settlers trod down and consumed the Indians' cornfields. Another grievance was the demand that the Indians surrender their firearms on the slightest suspicion of hostility, thus depriving them of their means of livelihood.

On the other hand, they attacked individual settlers, and there were also well-founded rumors of a plot to massacre the whites. The latter carried on the war by attacks on the Indian settlements, and the Indians retaliated by a series of border raids on unprotected villages, with the usual burnings and massacre of the inhabitants. The whites attacked (December 1675) the stronghold of the Narragansetts near what is now Kingston, Rhode Island, where some three or four thousand had taken refuge on an island in the middle of a large swamp. The torch was applied to four hundred wigwams and from four hundred to a thousand Indians were killed or roasted alive.

Deerfield was attacked by the Indians and most of the houses burned; and again a second time when a force of sixty men sent to relieve the town was ambushed and almost every man killed. The Indians were, however, gradually driven back while they suffered severely for want of corn. They were hunted down and scattered, the captives held as servants, and some sold into slavery to the West Indies.

The New England colonies also suffered severely. Five hundred white men were captured or killed, and nearly forty towns damaged. Sixteen in Massachusetts and four in New Hampshire were destroyed or abandoned. The cost in money was half a million dollars, equivalent to several millions today. This war finally removed the danger from the Indians. It occurred, fortunately for New England, just before the outbreak of the first French and Indian War in 1689.

50. Relation of New England to the British Empire (1643–1689)

The exact relations of New England to the British Empire, the relations both to the king and to Parliament, were an unsolved problem. Great difficulties thus arose in making political and economic control more effective, because of disputes over the extent of British control.

Place of New England in the Empire

These factors made the central government appear to the New England colonies as an external agency quite different from the way it appeared to the people in England. Moreover, the effect of the frontier was the same in New England as elsewhere. It bred the spirit of liberty, freedom from restraint, and notions of self-government. From the standpoint of England, any colony that resisted control was trying to secure all the advantages of the empire, i.e. protection and markets, but without sacrifices on its part. England thought the colonists centered their attention too much on local government and not enough on the greater problem of a self-contained and prosperous empire.

Unfortunately for England and fortunately for the colonies, the restoration of the Stuarts led to an enlargement of the spirit of independence rather than one of coöperation. The policy of Clarendon, the Lord Chancellor, was to extend and consolidate the colonies. How the Carolinas were added to the Empire we have seen. In 1664 the Dutch were forced to give up their hold in the middle region and New Netherland; and their area, which included also the former Swedish territory, was added to the possessions of England. This act had an important effect; better means of protecting the colonies from the French, for it made a continuous belt of English colonies along the Atlantic Seaboard. New agencies were therefore necessary to unify and control the economic and political life of this vast area.

The relations of Massachusetts with the mother country involved a long series of disputes and continual resistance to royal control. The original transfer of the charter was effected in order to escape English control and set up an independent government. This stiff-necked colony refused appeals to the English courts, took military measures to resist by force the authority of England, made treaties with foreign powers, and established a mint. By 1644 Massachusetts was asserting that " our allegiance binds us not to the laws of England any longer than while we live in England, for the laws of the Parliament of England reach no further "; and in 1661 Massachusetts again denied the sovereign rights of the English government over dependencies.

Early Relation of Massachusetts to England

During the English civil war and protectorate (1641–1660) New England greatly developed her trade, commerce, and wealth, while at the same time little or no attention was paid to the trade acts. Moreover, the aggressive policy of annexation of territory by Massachusetts occasioned many complaints. Protests and petitions were set up by the heirs of Mason and Gorges against the seizure of New Hampshire and Maine. Samuel Maverick, who was in England in 1660 and had long been hostile to the political and religious course of Massachusetts, advised the strengthening of royal control. Massachusetts sent agents to England to forestall adverse criticism, to make her peace with Charles II, and to prevent if possible the extension of power over her territory.

The agency for the management of the colonies to 1643 had been in the hands of the king, acting through

English Agencies of Control

the Privy Council and various committees or commissions whom he appointed. These were followed during the civil war and protectorate by committees of Parliament. In 1660 a committee for foreign plantations was appointed. Two subordinate advisory councils, one for trade and one for plantations, were created to formulate plans to bring " the several colonies and plantations, within themselves, into a more certain civill and uniforme waie of government and for the better ordering and distributing of publique justice among them." (See p. 247.) Owing to the chaotic state of the New England colonies, Charles II determined to inquire carefully into the alleged abuses and the general problem of political and economic control, and therefore appointed a Royal Commission in 1664, to go to New England and report on the state of affairs.

One problem of this commission was to determine the rights of the king and the royal government, with re-

The Royal Commission

spect to political and economic control; to inquire whether Massachusetts might pass any laws she chose and ignore any of Parliament; might decide cases of law involving English citizens in her own courts, without granting the right of appeal and in short, whether Massachusetts was, or was not, a part of the British Empire. How could she claim the military and commercial advantages of the Empire and at the same time assume the attitude of an independent state? The members of the commission, which included Col. Richard Nicholls and Samuel Maverick, were given instructions to consider how the Dutch New Netherland might be secured for England; to investigate the condition of the Indians and public education; to see that the navigation acts were observed, and to observe how far the free exercise of religion was allowed according to the laws of England. They were also to examine the charters and laws passed by the New England colonies, hear complaints and appeals, and take measures for settling the peace of the country.

The commissioners arrived in Boston in July 1664, but proceeded first to settle affairs in the New Netherland and the disputes between Connecticut and Rhode Island. In 1665, the commissioners listened to the answer of the general court to the accusations against Massachusetts. In general this body denied abuses in the government. The court of inquiry was a failure, because the magistrates gave orders to all persons to refrain from attending. The commissioners warned Massachusetts, however, that the charter might have to be forfeited and advised that they clear themselves " of these many injustices, oppressions, violences, and blood for which you are complained against, to which complaints you have refused to answer." The result of the work of the commission is seen in a circular letter of the king in 1666, expressing satisfaction except in the case of Massachusetts. This colony was ordered to send commissioners to answer the charges against her, which request Massachusetts refused to obey. This ended the first attempt to tighten the control over the New England colonies.

51.   Plans for Consolidation (1674–1684)

After this failure of the Royal Commission to bring
Massachusetts to terms, an important event occurred
in 1674, when colonial affairs were placed
under the control of a new committee of the
Privy Council consisting of twenty-four
members, henceforth known as the "Lords of Trade."
The need of revenue, the desire to regulate trade more
carefully, stimulated by pressure from the merchant
class, and the determination to bring about a greater
degree of political unity and more effective political control over the colonies — all these led to a renewal of the
attempt to bring the New England colonies into relation
with these new plans.

Charles II and New England

Accordingly Edward Randolph was selected to go to
New England, the beginning of fourteen years' residence there. He was instructed to report in detail on
New England affairs, with particular reference to the
encroachment of Massachusetts on New Hampshire
and Maine, the problem of illegal trade, laws contrary
to those of England, and the condition of religion — all
long-standing matters in controversy. After a month's
study Randolph returned to England and presented his
report to the Privy Council. He accused Massachusetts
of denying appeals to England, of refusing the oath of
allegiance, of religious intolerance, and particularly of
violation of the navigation acts. In 1676 English merchants also testified as to illegal trade, and complained
that in their trade between Europe and America they
were undersold by the New Englanders by as much as
twenty per cent. Randolph was appointed (1677) to the
office of collector, surveyor, and searcher of customs
for the New England colonies.

The Privy Council denied the claims of Massachusetts

to New Hampshire and Maine, objected to some of their capital laws; demanded that the navigation acts be observed; insisted that laws contrary to those of England be repealed, that a royal revenue officer be received, and that the religious test for the franchise be changed. In answer to the demand that laws contrary to those of England be repealed, Massachusetts declared that the laws of England did not "reach America," that since the colonies were not represented in Parliament, they were not subject to the navigation acts. In order, nevertheless, to avoid this particular difficulty, the navigation acts were reënacted by the colony, so that they might have validity in Massachusetts.

Demands of the King

The agents sent to England by Massachusetts to state her side of the case returned in 1679 with a letter from the king, who expressed his dissatisfaction with the purchase of Maine for £1250 from the Gorges heirs, and demanded the surrender of the title deeds. The king also insisted on greater religious toleration, and a property, instead of a religious, qualification for the franchise. The right of governing New Hampshire was also claimed by the king. Massachusetts refused even to consider most of these demands. Indeed Charles II wrote in 1681 that he would be obliged to "take such further resolutions as are necessary to preserve our authority from being neglected," unless Massachusetts obeyed the king's instructions. From the point of view of Massachusetts, the king was encroaching on charter rights and self-government: viz., denying freedom for the legal majority to pass whatever laws they wished for their own good as they saw it. To agree to a property rather than a religious qualification for the franchise was to agree to their own self-destruction, as they saw it.

When Randolph again took up his duties as collector of customs for New England (1680), he was obstructed in every way. He again sailed for England with another batch of complaints against Massachusetts. Finally the king decided on the drastic policy of voiding the charter. Plans for a more general consolidation of colonial government were under consideration as early as 1678, when Sir Edmund Andros appeared before the Privy Council and urged this procedure. As early as 1680, when Massachusetts relinquished her authority over New Hampshire, the king appointed a president and council in New Hampshire, and allowed a popular assembly. Later he sent out Edward Cranfield, as Governor of New Hampshire, one of the worst examples of a royal governor in the history of the colonies. He proceeded to enrich himself by all kinds of extortion and plunder; for example, he sold pardons, confiscated lands, and tried to collect illegal taxes. Finally his commission was revoked in 1684.

Early Plans for Consolidation

52. Loss of the Charter and Revolution in New England (1684–1692)

In October 1684, Massachusetts was deprived of her charter, and in 1685 James II determined on a temporary government over a large area. He appointed Joseph Dudley governor of Massachusetts, including Maine, New Hampshire, and the " King's Province," a region in western Rhode Island. His commission provided for a council of seven to assist him with large executive and judicial powers. Dudley was also vice-admiral, while Randolph became collector of customs. While the new government had no power to make changes in the laws, it included no popular assembly to make laws and levy taxes. This temporary government lasted only seven months, when the king's plans were made known for a still greater consolidation of territory under one governor.

In December 1686, Sir Edmund Andros, former governor of New York, arrived in Boston as governor, with a commission covering the region over which Dudley had governed and also Plymouth colony. Soon after, Connecticut and Rhode Island surrendered to the authority of Andros, and later (1688) New York and New Jersey were added to the domain over which he presided.

Sir Edmund Andros and the Dominion of New England

Thus within the space of two years, eight jurisdictions were brought under the control of one royal governor, responsible only to the king, with no charter to safeguard the rights of the people. In addition Andros was given control over Indian affairs. His commission made no provision for a popular assembly; but with the aid of a council of twenty-seven members he was to exercise executive, judicical, and legislative powers. Moreover, his instructions gave him power to distribute all lands "yet indisposed of," and to collect a quit rent of not less than two shillings and six pence on every hundred acres. This would strike a blow at the easy acquirement of land, one of the greatest factors in promoting democracy. It cancelled the traditional opportunity for free land and small holdings on the frontier, a dangerous policy for England. Not only were the unallotted lands involved, but other matters " for which our Royal Confirmation may be wanting." Few persons could show a title conformable to these requirements. Most titles indeed were based only on town grants or Indian purchases.

The government of Andros for the next three years involved many problems. He was accused of attacks on land titles; efforts to introduce the Church of England; levy of taxes without the consent of the people;

prohibition of town meetings except one each year; abolition of their power of taxation; suspension of the

writ of habeas corpus; censorship of the press; concentration of all public records of the various colonies at Boston, where all deeds and wills were to be registered; the collection of quit rents; and the abolition of the general court. Some of these accusations were exaggerated.

The news of the revolution against King James II in England arrived at Boston, April 4, 1689, and on the 18th the militia mobilized and the drumbeat was heard on Boston Common. A town meeting was held and Andros was told that he must surrender. He was later arrested, as were Dudley and Randolph, and all three were imprisoned. A provisional government was instituted and William and Mary who had assumed royal power in England were proclaimed as sovereigns. The final effects of the revolution were far-reaching. First it resulted in the overthrow of the Puritan theocracy; for in the new charter of 1691 the religious qualification for the franchise was changed to a property qualification, and Plymouth was united with Massachusetts. Massachusetts was also obliged to accept a royal governor appointed by the crown with veto power, and judges appointed by the governor with the consent of the council. Her laws were also subject to disallowance by the king. Hence she was unable to act as independently of England as before. Within the colony the democratic elements — political, religious, and economic — now had a chance more fully to express their views, and gradually to prepare the way for resistance to arbitrary or undemocratic government, whether it arose within the colony or was imposed by England.

CHAPTER VII

ECONOMIC AND SOCIAL DEVELOPMENT OF NEW ENGLAND TO 1689

53. References

Bibliographies. — See refs. under "bibliographies," chs. v, xii, xiv, xv; J. T. Adams, *Prov. Society*, 324–356, and *Founders of New Eng.*, (footnotes to chs. vi, viii); C. M. Andrews, *Fathers of New Eng.*, 201–204, and *Colonial Self-Govt.*, 337–340, 344–347; Channing, Hart and Turner, *Guide*, §§ 36–39, 42–43, 45, 48, 96–97, 99, 127–146, 149, 161, 163–165; H. U. Faulkner, *Am. Ec. Hist.*, 76–77, 100–101, 115–116; E. B. Greene, *Prov. Am.*, 325–340; Grace Griffin, *Writings on Am. History*, 1906–1923; A. B. Hart, (ed.), *Commonwealth Hist. of Mass.*, (bibliogs. chs. x-xiv); J. N. Larned, *Lit. of Am. Hist.*, 294–301; L. B. Schmidt, *Top. Stud. and Refs. on the Econom. Hist. of Am. Agricult.*; W. P. Trent, (ed.), *Camb. Hist. of Am. Lit.*, I, (bibliogs.); L. G. Tyler, *Engl. in Am.*, 334–336; W. B. Weeden, *Econom. and Soc. Hist. of New Engl.* (footnotes); T. J. Wertenbaker, *First Americans*, 317–338; Justin Winsor, in *Am. Antiq. Soc. Pro.*, n. s. X, 351–373 (witchcraft); T. G. Wright, *Literary Culture in Early New Engl.*, (bibliogs.).

Historical Maps. — See refs. in ch. v.

General Accounts. — For Engl. background see refs. in ch. i; and "Special Accounts," chs. v and vi; and "Relations with Brit. Emp.," ch. vi; and ch. x; C. M. Andrews, *Colonial Folkways* and *Fathers of New Engl.*, chs. i, iv, and *Colonial Self-Govt.*, chs. xviii-xix; J. A. Doyle, *Engl. Col. in Am.*, II, chs. i-ii; H. U. Faulkner, *Am. Econom. Hist.*, chs. ii-v; H. L. Osgood, *Am. Col. in the 17th Cent.*, I, chs. ii-v, xi; III, ch. vii, esp., 218–241, 406–411; J. G. Palfrey, *Hist. of New Engl.*, II, chs. i, iv, xii; III, 35–68, 546–547; IV, ch. iv, 96 ff.; L. G. Tyler, *Engl. in Am.*, chs. xiii, xix; T. J. Wertenbaker, *First Americans*, chs. ii-x; Justin Winsor, *Narr. and Crit. Hist. of Am.*, III, chs. vii-viii.

Special Accounts. — (a) ENGLISH BACKGROUND: (see also under "General Accounts" above); F. E. Baldwin, "Sumptuary Legislation and Personal Regulation in Engl.," in *J. H. Stud.*, ser. XLIV; Harriet Bradley, "Enclosure of Open Fields in Engl.," in *Columb. Stud.*, LXXX; R. M. Bradley, *The English Housewife in the 17th and 18th Cent.;* R. E. Prothero, *English Farming, Past and Present;* R. H. Tawney, *The Agrarian Prob. in the 16th Cent.;* H. D. Trail (ed.), *Social Engl.*, IV–V; Eleanor Trotter, *17th Cent. Life in the Country Parish;* George Unwin, *Industrial Organization in the 16th and 17th Cents.* (b) GENERAL ECONOMIC BY TOPICS: (see refs. under "Special Accts." in ch. iv); Edith Abbott, *Women in Industry;* W. J. Abbott, *Am. Ships and Sailors;* R. G. Albion, "Forests and Sea Power," 1652–1862, (*Harvard Studies*, XXIX); P. W. Bidwell and J. S. Falconer, *Hist. of Agricult. in Northern U. S. before 1860;* Edward Channing, "Town and County Govt. in Engl. Col.," in *J. H. Stud.*, ser. X; H. M. Chittenden, *Am. Fur Trade;* Elizabeth Dexter, *Colonial Women of Affairs;* W. L. Marvin, *The Am. Merchant Marine;* W. B. Weeden, *Econom. and Soc. Hist. of New Engl.*, I. (c) SPECIAL ECONOMIC: (1) New Engl., Anne McClear, "Early New Engl. Towns," in *Columb. Stud.*, XXIX; H. L. Osgood, "New Engl. Colonial Finance in the 17th Cent.," in *Polit. Sci. Quart.*, XIX; W. B. Weeden, "Indian Money in N. Engl.," in *J. H. Studies*, ser. II. (2) Mass., Conn. and R. I., C. M. Andrews, "River Towns of Conn.," in *J. H. Stud.*, ser. VII; C. H. J. Douglass, "Financial Hist. of Mass.," in *Columb. Stud.*, I; W. E. Foster, "Town Govt. in Rhode Island," *Ibid.* ser. IV; A. B. Hart, (ed.), *Commonwealth Hist. of Mass.*, I, ch. xv; F. R. Jones, "Hist. of Taxation in Conn." (1636–1676), in *J. H. Stud.*, ser. XIV; Curtis Nettels, "The Beginnings of Money in Connecticut," in *Trans. Wiscon. Acad. of Sci. etc.*, XXIII. (d) GENERAL SOCIAL BY TOPICS: See refs. in ch. iv under "General Social by Topics," books having chapters on New Engl. (e) SPECIAL SOCIAL: (1) New Engl., see refs. in ch. v under "Pilgrims," "Puritans," "Special Accounts," and "Separate Colonies," and refs. for ch. xv; J. H. Benton, *Warning Out in New Engl.* (1656–1817); M. C. Crawford, *Soc. Life in Old New Engl.;* G. F. Dow, *Domestic Life in New Engl. in the 17th Cent.;* A. M. Earle, *Customs and Fashions in Old New Engl.*, and *Sabbath in Puritan New Engl.;* J. B. Felt, *Customs of New Engl.* (2) Mass., Conn. and R. I., E. N. Capen, "Poor-Laws of Conn.," in *Columb. Stud.*, XXII; W. H. Chamberlain, *Samuel Sewall and the World he Lived In;* John Cummings, "Poor-Laws of Mass. and N. Y.," in *Am. Ec. Asso. Pub.*, X; A. B. Hart (ed.), *Commonwealth Hist. of Mass.*, I, chs. x–xiv; R. W. Kelso, *Public Poor Relief in Mass.* (1620–1920); Gertrude Kimball, *Providence in Colonial*

Times; W. B. Weeden, *Early Rhode Island, A Social Hist. of the People.* (f) LAND PROBLEMS. (See "Separate Colonies" in ch. v, and "Land and Labor," ch. xiv); R. H. Akagi, *Town Proprietors of the New Engl. Colonies;* Edward Channing, "The Narragansett Planters," in *J. H. Studies,* ser. IV; Melville Egleston, "Land System of New Engl. Colonies," in *J. H. Stud.,* ser. IV; L. K. Matthews, *Expan. of New Engl.;* H. E. Osgood, *Am. Col. in the 17th Cent.,* I, ch. xi; W. B. Weeden, *Econ. and Soc. Hist. of New Engl.,* I, 53–68. (g) LABOR PROBLEMS: W. D. Johnston, "Hist. of Slavery in Rhode Island," *R. I. Hist. Soc. Proc.,* II, 113–164; M. S. Locke, *Antislavery in America before 1808;* G. H. Moore, *Notes on the Hist. of Slavery in Mass.;* R. F. Seyboldt, *Apprenticeship in Colonial N. Y. and New Engl.;* B. C. Steiner, "Hist. of Slavery in Conn.," *J. H. Stud.,* ser. XI. (h) INDUSTRIES AND OCCUPATIONS. (See refs. in ch. iv, esp. under Clark, Bishop, and Tryon, and ch. xii, xiv, and "General Economic by Topics" above, Abbott and Dexter); Raymond McFarland, *Hist. of New Engl. Fisheries;* J. R. Spear, *Hist. of New Engl. Whalers;* W. S. Tower, *Hist. of the Am. Whale Fishery;* W. B. Weeden, *Econom. and Soc. Hist. of New Engl.,* I, 165–205, 293–303; C. J. H. Woodbury, *Textile Education among the Puritans.* (i) TRADE AND COMMERCE. (See refs. under "General Economic" in ch. iv and chs. x, xiv); G. L. Beer, *Old Col. System,* chs. xi-xii; A. H. Buffington, "New Engl. and Western Fur Trade," in *Colonial Soc. of Mass. Pub.,* XVIII, 160–192; A. B. Hart (ed.), *Commonwealth Hist. of Mass.,* I, ch. xvi; A. H. Hill, *Trade and Commerce of Boston;* John Robinson and G. F. Dow, *Sailing Ships of New Engl.,* 1607–1907; W. B. Weeden, "Early African Slave Trade in New Engl.," in *Am. Ant. Soc. Proc.,* n. s. V, and *Early Commerce of Providence.* (j) RELIGION AND MORALS. (Bibliography, see T. J. Wertenbaker, *First Americans,* 325, 333, 336; see refs. under "General Social" in ch. iv (esp. Calhoun), and "General Accounts," "Pilgrims," "Puritans," and "Separate Colonies," in ch. v; "Religion and Morals" in ch. xv, and E. B. Greene, *Prov. Am.,* 331–332); Brooks Adams, *Emancipation of Mass.;* H. B. Adams, "Saxon Tithingmen in Am.," in *J. H. Studies,* ser. I; Champlin Burrage, *The Church Covenant Idea;* E. H. Byington, *Puritan as a Colonist and Reformer;* Everett Gates, *Relig. Liberty in Mass.,* M. L. Greene, *Devel. of Relig. Liberty in Conn.;* R. P. Hallowell, *Quaker Invasion of Mass.;* E. D. Hanscomb, *The Heart of the Puritan;* P. E. Lauer, "Church and State in New Engl." in *J. H. Stud.,* ser. X; W. De L. Love, *Fast and Thanksgiving Days of New Engl.,* and *Samson Occum and the Christian Indians of New Engl.;* J. W. Platner, and others, *Relig. Life of New Engl.;* G. L. Walker, *Aspects of Relig. Life of New Engl.;* Williston Walker, *Hist. of Congregationalism,* and "Services of the Mathers in New Engl. Relig. Devel.," in *Am. Soc. Church Hist. Papers,* ser. I, vol. V, 61–85. (k) WITCHCRAFT DELUSION: S. G. Drake, *Witchcraft Delusion in New Engl.;* A. B. Hart (ed.), *Commonwealth Hist. of Mass.,* II, ch. iii; W. S. Nevins, *Witchcraft in Salem Village;* Wallace Notestein, *Hist. of Witchcraft in Engl.;* J. M. Taylor, *Witchcraft Delusion in Conn.,* 1647–1697. (l) CRIME AND PUNISHMENT: A. M. Davis, "Law of Adultery and Ignominious Punishments," in *Am. Ant. Soc. Proc.,* n. s. X, 97–127; A. M. Earle, *Curious Punishments of Bygone Days;* C. F. Gray, "The Body of Liberties," (1641), in *Mass. Hist. Soc. Collecs.,* ser. III, vol. VIII, 216–237; also "Early Laws," *Ibid.,* 191–215; John Noble, "Notes on the Trial and Punish. for Crimes in Mass.," in *Colonial Soc. of Mass. Pubs.,* III, 51–56. (m) INTELLECTUAL AND EDUCATIONAL. (See "General Social" in ch. iv); F. B. Dexter, "Influence of Engl. Univs. on the Devel. of New Engl.," in *Mass. Hist. Soc. Pro.* XVII (1880); Edward Eggleston, *Transit of Civilization,* ch. iv; P. L. Ford, *New Engl. Primer;* W. C. Ford, *Boston Book Market, 1679–1700;* White Greenough, *Sketch of Philosophy of Am. Literature;* G. L. Jackson, *Evolution of School Support in Mass.;* M. W. Jernegan, "Beginnings of Publ. Educa. in New Engl.," in *School Review,* XXIII, and other articles on education in *Ibid.,* XXVI–XXVIII; A. L. Jones, *Early Am. Philosophers;* G. E. Littlefield, *Early Schools and School Books of New Engl.* and *Early Mass. Press, 1638–1711* and *Early Boston Booksellers;* G. H. Martin, *Evolution of the Mass. School System;* Josiah Quincy, *Hist. of Harvard Univ.;* I. W. Riley, *Am. Philosophy — the Early Schools* and *Puritanism to Pragmatism* and *American Thought* (1923); R. F. Seyboldt, *Apprenticeship in Colonial N. Y. and New Engl.;* W. H. Small, *Early New Engl. Schools;* Henry Suzzalo, *Rise of Local School Supervision in Mass.* (1635–1827); Harlan Updegraff, *Origin of Moving Sch. in Mass.;* T. G. Wright, *Literary Culture in Early New Engl.*

Biographies. — See ch. vi.

Contemporary Accounts. — (a) BIBLIOGRAPHY: Channing, Hart and Turner, *Guide,* §§ 42–43, 127–146; see lists of sources in J. T. Adams, *Prov. Society,* 326–328, and T. J. Wertenbaker, *First Americans,* 321–322; W. P. Trent (ed.) *Camb. Hist. Am. Lit.,* I, 398–424 (Mathers); see also bibliographies under "Contemporary Accounts" esp. in chs. v, vi, x, xii, xiv, xv. (b) DOCU-

MENTS AND COLLECTIONS: see ch. iv, "Contemp. Accts.," under Jameson, *Privateers, etc.* and Clews, *Educational Admin., etc.*: E. L. Bogart and C. M. Thompson, (eds.), *Readings in Am. Econom. Hist.*, chs. i-iv; Ralph Gabriel (ed.), *Pageant of America;* A. C. Goodell (ed.), *Essex County Court Records* (Mass.), I-VIII, 1635–1683; A. B. Hart (ed.), *Contemporaries*, I, chs. xiv, xx, xxi and II, ch. iii (Witchcraft); "Harvard College Records, 1638–1750," in *Colonial Soc. Mass. Pubs.*, XV, XVI; Gertrude Kimball, *Pictures of Rhode Island in the Past;* John Noble (ed.), *Recs. of Court of Assistants of Mass., 1630–1692;* W. H. Perry, *Hist. Coll. Relat. to Am. Colonial Church* (Mass.); L. B. Schmidt and E. B. Ross (eds.), *Readings in Econom. Hist. of Am. Agriculture;* Williston Walker, *Creeds and Platforms of Congregationalism.* (c) NARRATIVES, LETTERS AND DIARIES: John Dunton, "Letters from New Engl." in *Prince Soc. Publications*, IV; (for criticism see C. N. Greenough, in *Colonial Soc. Mass. Pubs.*, XIV, 213–257); J. F. Jameson (ed.), *Narratives of Early American Hist.*, esp., G. L. Burr, *Nars. of Witchcraft;* Cotton Mather, *Magnalia Christi Americana* (1702), reprint 1853 and "Diary," in *Mass. Hist. Soc. Coll.*, ser. VII, vols. VII–VIII, and *Wonders of the Invisible World* and Robert Calef, *More Wonders of the Invisible World* are reprinted by S. G. Drake, *Witchcraft Delusion in New Engl.*, and in part in E. C. Stedman and E. M. Hutchinson, *Lib. of Am. Literature*, II; Samuel Sewall, "Letter Book," in *Mass. Hist. Soc. Colls.* ser. VI, vols. I–II and Diary, in *Mass. Hist. Soc. Coll.*, ser. V, vols. V–VI.

54. Population, Towns, and Counties

THOUGH New England had only one eighth of the area of the southern colonies, yet by 1700 the population was about equal to that of the South. In 1690 there were 77,000, and by 1715, 161,000. At the latter date the southern colonies had only 145,000 white inhabitants. Massachusetts, during the seventeenth century, counted about two thirds of the total population of New England. The people were almost wholly derived from middle-class English stock, a fact that made for uniformity in political, religious, and social life.

Population, Number and Distribution

The leaders of the Massachusetts Bay Colony were

united on the desirability of preventing a dispersion of
the population over a wide area, and in promoting the
township or community type of settlement. In 1634 the
general court enacted that the major part of the magistrates should have power of " setting down men in any
new plantation," viz., to found towns. Winthrop also
remarked that it was " prejudicial to the commonwealth
if some go far off for land while others had much and
could not make use of it." The town then becomes of
great significance in relation to the distribution of population. To understand important characteristics of the
economic and social life of New England, one must
understand the constitution of its towns, its land system,
its congregations, and its schools.

The New England town was in part a product of inherited ideas and practices of local government; in part
it was an indigenous institution arising out
The Towns   of the immediate needs of the people. The
essential things to note are these. (1) The town was
a distinct geographical entity covering usually about
forty square miles. (2) In Massachusetts, after 1635,
towns were established by the general court. (3) They
arose through that body granting a tract of land for
a town, sometimes only a " plantation right," authorizing settlements. The grant was made usually as the
result of a petition, to a group of men, perhaps ten,
more or less.

These men were made the sole " proprietors " of the
land with power to dispose of it. They could admit new
Economic   proprietors, keep their own records and
Aspect   choose their own officers. Such towns were
thus land companies, each proprietor owning an undivided share in the " common lands."

If granted a " town right " the town was entitled to
representation in the general court. The proprietors

were also given powers of town government: for example, the power to levy taxes, choose officers, impose

Political Aspect

penalties, and "make such orders as may concern the well ordering of their own towns," including the power to admit newcomers to citizenship. The man who had a right to share in the division of the lands, if a resident, was usually a voter in town meeting. Not all persons who were citizens and voters, however, had a right to share in the common lands. This privilege was reserved to the proprietors unless specifically granted by them to all or a part of those who were admitted as citizens, or to others.

In Massachusetts the unenfranchised class in the seventeenth century constituted about four-fifths of the

Religious Aspect

free male white residents. Such could not vote for the magistrates or deputies to the general court because an early law (lasting till 1691) granted this privilege to church members only. Such persons thus became "freemen" of the colony. The non-freemen were the male adults, not including servants or slaves, who were permanent residents of the town. By the charter of 1691 the colony franchise was given to those who held a freehold estate worth £2 a year, or £40 in personalty. The religious qualification for voting was thus abolished. The local franchise in Massachusetts was granted to a citizen of each town taxable at £20 estate.

In 1640 the general court of Massachusetts voted to grant land only to such as would form a church. Though the town was responsible for building the church and for the support of a minister, church membership was distinct from that of the land or political group. Church meetings were held separately and neither church nor church officials had power over corporate town business, except that certain members of the church were citizens of the town.

Thus while the non-church member was disfranchised in part, yet he was taxed for the support of the church. Of whatever faith, he was forced to attend church services in the town church, under penalty. In 1663 a Massachusetts act declared that Quakers and others refusing to attend the public worship of God " shall and hereby are incapable of voting in all civil assemblies during their obstinate persisting in such wicked ways and courses and until certificate be given of their reformation." The clergy were of great political importance, because no one was likely to be admitted to membership in the church, except with their consent.

The town meeting was the main agency for the regulation of the political and economic life of the community. It was here that taxes were levied, lands divided, and officers chosen to promote the general welfare of the community. In town meeting provision was made for the care of the poor, for the building and repair of roads, for the promotion of industries, through grants of land or monopolies, for the regulation of prices, and a host of other things. Thus the town meeting registered the will of the majority. This majority had the power to compel citizens to contribute, in the form of taxes, to measures that would promote the good of the whole group.

The county was the unit for judicial purposes and for the recording of deeds and wills. The main business of the county courts was the trial of small causes — drunkenness, stealing, etc., and the settlement of civil disputes. The officers were the justices of the peace who sat as judges, the sheriff and other court officers. The grand jurors, chosen in town meeting, met quarterly at the county seat and drew up a list of " presentments " or indictments against persons or towns violating the laws.

55. Land and Labor

The title to all land was originally held through grants made by the crown. Land was then granted to

Title to and Tenure of Land

groups or individuals in " fee simple," viz., free from all forms of feudal tenure or services, such as quit rents. Thence followed the idea of independent ownership of land; that it was freely alienable, that it would normally be divided into equal shares in the case of intestate estates. Thus the system of primogeniture was unimportant in New England. This land system promoted the development of small tracts, widely distributed, and was one cause for the rise of a democratic society.

When a grant of land was made for a town conditions of settlement were prescribed and included

Conditions and Purposes of Granting Land

various provisions: for instance, that the grant be taken up and improved within two or three years; that 20 families, more or less, settle and erect houses in one to three years; and that the town should support a minister. Where the proprietors and citizens were one body, as in many towns, the allotment of town land to encourage needed industries was very common. Land was granted by the proprietors or town to artisans to encourage them to ply their trade, such as blacksmiths, and shoemakers; to stimulate industries or manufactures, such as salt works, brickworks, gristmills, and sawmills. One of the important uses to which the town land was put was to reserve a certain portion for social betterment. Stephen Daye, of Cambridge, " being the first to set up printing," was granted 300 acres of land. It was common for the larger towns to set apart a tract of

land, the income to be used for the support of a free
school, as was the case of Boston in 1641. Land was
also granted outright to schoolmasters and ministers
who would agree to settle in the town. In the early 18th
century it was common to divide a township into 63
shares, especially in Maine; one for each of the sixty
prospective settlers, while one was reserved for the
first minister, one for schools, and one for the ministry.

Most of the farms were small, fifty to two hundred
acres, and the work was performed by the head of the
Labor   family and his sons, with perhaps a "hired
Conditions   man." There were always some indentured
servants and after 1639 some negro slaves in Massachusetts; and soon after in the other New England
colonies. The apprenticeship system was also speedily
developed, and was one of the principal sources of
supply for artisans.

The practice in New England was to form compact
settlements, villages, and towns. This tended to produce a division of labor, a combination of agriculture
and industry and a population that represented many
types of economic well-being. The artisan class was one
of the products. Thus the town of Newbury, Massachusetts, in 1634, included ninety-one grantees. Among
them were two clergymen, eight "gentlemen," two or
three merchants, one physician, one schoolmaster, one
sea captain, one mate of a ship, one dyer, one glover,
three or four tanners, seven or eight shoemakers, two
wheelwrights, two blacksmiths, two linen weavers, one
cooper, one saddler, one lawyer, and two or three carpenters. It will be remembered that Benjamin Franklin
was born in Boston in 1706, the son of a tallow
chandler and was apprenticed to his brother James
as printer.

56. Industries and Occupations

While agriculture was necessarily of primary interest, several other types of industry were of importance: the

Diversifica-
tion of
Industries

fisheries, extraction and exportation of raw materials, principally forest products; trading, especially the fur trade; manufacturing, such as shipbuilding and textiles; and shipping, particularly the development of the carrying trade for other colonies. This diversification of industry is one of the striking features of the life of the New England colonies, and had important political, economic, and social consequences.

Unlike the southern colonies the system of agriculture was intensive rather than extensive. That is, for

Agriculture

the most part, the unit was the small farm of one hundred acres more or less, worked by the labor of the family, and producing hardly more than sufficed for the support of the family. In other words New England agriculture was not based on the principle of producing a large surplus for export because the climate, soil, character of the crops and nature of the labor force made this unprofitable if not impossible.

The grantees or proprietors of a town first laid out " home lots " five to twenty acres, near the " place for

Division
of Land

Sabbath Assembly; " then larger tracts on the outskirts of the town for farms. The allotment of lands included tracts of arable land or " meadow land," ten to twenty acres, " upland," twenty-five acres or more suitable for pasturage, and often woodland. Besides these were the common fields or lands in which each proprietor had a share or right to use them for special purposes; for example, a " cow common," " pasturage common," common " woodlot," " meadow," or " marsh."

The early settlers relied on Indian corn or maize as their chief crop. In the early years of settlement when corn could be exchanged for beaver, the profits were large. A bushel of corn was traded for skins worth eighteen shillings. By the middle of the century, however, these early profits were impossible, due to depletion of the soil. The constant "cropping" of the older lands caused a deterioration in crops. Generally speaking, agriculture seldom expanded beyond the wants of each household; and by the end of the seventeenth century was, as a producing factor, subordinate to commerce.

Crops

The "sacred codfish" is the emblem or seal for all official documents of Massachusetts and an image of a large codfish may still be seen over the desk of the speaker of the House of Representatives of Massachusetts. The largest Cape on the New England Coast was named Cape Cod by Gosnold because of the immense number of codfish in that region. These facts are a reminder of the great importance of the fisheries in the economy of New England.

The Fisheries

One of the greatest fishing grounds in the world was the "Grand Banks" off Newfoundland almost at the door of New England where codfish, mackerel, etc., abounded. The fisheries in the course of the century became the keystone to the arch of New England commerce, and affected many aspects of life — the shop, shipyard, farm, and system of manufactures. The fisheries were the basis of the distilling industry, the slave trade, and much of the profitable commerce with the West Indies, and the Catholic regions of Europe. Later, fish became one of the important "ingredients" of the American Revolution.

The fisheries also stimulated the important industry

of shipbuilding, and made practical the utilization of New England's great natural resource, her forests. Randolph, in his report of 1676, names Boston, Charlestown, Salem, Ipswich, Salisbury, and Portsmouth as the chief places for building in Massachusetts, with 30 master builders, carpenters, and other workmen in proportion. He estimated that 730 vessels ranging from 6 to 250 tons were " built in and belong " to that colony.

Shipbuilding

Next to agriculture and fishing, products of the forests were of the greatest importance in New England. The forests provided employment for thousands; lumberjacks who cut down trees for masts and spars, and for the stave makers, " clapboard cleavers," and " sawyers." After sawmills were set up immense quantities of sawed boards, planks, and ship timbers were produced. Thomas Lechford, a lawyer in Boston, records a contract (1640) for the delivery of 7000 pipe-staves at Portsmouth at £18 per thousand. This item indicates the importance of the lumber industry at this early date.

Forest Products

The General Court of Massachusetts in 1640 passed acts to encourage the manufacture of linen, woolen, and cotton cloth for three years, if spun and woven of " wool or linen grown here." Still manufactures did not develop rapidly in the second half of the seventeenth century. It was more profitable to concentrate on shipbuilding, fishing, and trade, and with the profits to purchase manufactured goods in the English markets or smuggle them in from Europe. " Homespun " industries of the rougher sort did arise, but not on any considerable scale. An act of 1656 required the selectmen to see that spinners spun for 30 weeks every year a pound of linen, cotton or woolen per week under penalty of " 12d for every pound short." Fulling mills

Manufactures

were erected and woolen cloth was manufactured more and more. Efforts were made by both Massachusetts and Connecticut to further the textile industries. The latter in 1670 ordered every person to work one day each year in clearing the underwood to benefit pasturage and the former (1673) reduced the tax on sheep. Other manufacturing industries were stimulated by grants of land, as previously described.

57. Trade and Commerce

The trade and commerce of New England developed rapidly and had several aspects; (1) that with the Indians, mostly the fur trade; (2) intercolonial trade; (3) ocean traffic, or trade with the West Indies, England, Europe, and other countries, based largely on fish and lumber products. The return cargoes consisted of molasses, sugar, slaves, and European manufactured goods. Trade and commerce were regulated by the town, by the colony, and by England.

Nature of Trade and Commerce

From the middle of the seventeenth century came a great expansion of the fishing industry. Thus in 1664 it was said that Boston had a "great trade" to Barbados in fish and other provisions and that 1300 boats fished in the waters about Cape Sable. The first-class fish were sent to the Catholic regions of Southern Europe, those of second quality to the Portuguese Islands, and the poorest to Barbados to feed the negro slaves.

Codfish and Commerce

In 1660 English merchants complained that clapboards, pipe-staves, timber, fish, and other commodities from New England could be sold to greater advantage in other regions than England. English vessels came to Boston and other ports as early as 1651 in search of masts for the royal

Export of Forest Products

navy. In 1665 the commissioners sent over to New England reported that seven or eight ships were in harbor at Portsmouth, New Hampshire, and there was "great store of masts." The King's surveyor marked with a broad arrow the white pines twenty-four inches in diameter three feet from the ground, thus giving notice that such trees were reserved for the royal navy.

By 1660 the British Empire was already a "far flung" Ocean Empire stretching in the new world from the Caribbean Sea to Newfoundland, with numerous scattered possessions in Europe, Asia, and the Pacific. The problem for England was to defend, control, and make this empire pay, to protect colonial territory and trade routes, to supervise local governments and legislation in the interest of England and the empire as a whole, and especially to develop a profitable foreign trade in competition with rival powers. These policies brought the New England colonies, as it did others, into conflict with England, because of the insistence of the colonies on local self government and their own economic advantage. In other words the problem from the standpoint of the empire was whether the needs and demands of one colony, or a group, should be allowed to prejudice the interests of England and the empire as a whole.

The Problem of Foreign Trade

In the discussion of the effect of the Restoration after 1660 on the southern colonies, it was observed that one of the methods of stricter economic control was the enactment of navigation laws, partly for revenue, partly as a means of preventing competition, and partly to develop sea power and a merchant marine — the last two being the indispensable conditions of an ocean empire. By 1664 the mercantile theory, the foundation for a system of

The Balance of Trade

national state making and economy, had for one of its central features, a balance of trade favorable to England. Thomas Mun in his book *England's Treasure by Forraign Trade* (1664), says the best method to "increase our wealth and treasure is by Foreign Trade, wherein wee must ever observe this rule; to sell more to strangers yearly than we consume of theirs in value." The English theory involved the principle that all parts of the empire ought to subordinate their special desires, in order that England might establish a favorable balance of trade. This was an ideal which the nature and extent of the empire might have made possible, had the colonists been unselfish in their economic desires and prouder of the empire than of their own particular colony.

The New England colonies embraced a region that had more points of conflict and competition with England than any other group. Her principal industries — agriculture, fishing, and shipbuilding competed directly with those of England. Moreover New England tended, to an increasing extent, to produce some of her own manufactured goods. Having little to sell directly to England in exchange for goods purchased, she was forced to develop her trade in other areas, notably the West Indies. Only in this way could she obtain the money to pay her annual debt to English merchants. Hence it is clear that great resistance to a more strict economic control would develop in New England.

New England soon discovered that the great opportunity for expansion of her foreign trade lay with the West Indies. These islands needed provisions, horses, fish, and lumber. In return the colonists could obtain tropical products, molasses, sugar, indigo, etc. Eleven vessels sailed (1660) from New England with lumber for the West Indies. Very significant in the West Indian trade was the return of specie, largely Spanish silver, with which debts due British merchants could be settled. Buccaneers who preyed on Spanish commerce also brought in goods and specie. Bradford tells of the arrival at Boston of three such ships and eighty men, and says " They spente a great deale of money among ye people, and yet more sine (I fear) than money." One scribbler summed up the character of the trade thus:

" Heaps of wheat, pork, bisket, beef and beer,
Meats, pipestaves, fish should store both far and near,
Which fetch in wines, clothes, sweets and good tobac."

This rapid expansion of trade worried some of the Puritans. Edward Johnson declared that " Merchants, traders, vintners, would willingly have had the Commonwealth tolerate divers kinds of sinful opinions to intice men to come and sit down with us, that their purses might be filled with coyn, the civil government with contention, and the Church of our Lord Christ with errors." Thus did religion and morals compete with trade and profits.

58. Social Conditions

In the composition of the population of New England may be traced two important characteristics; first, the racial stock was remarkably pure, al-
Composition of the Population
most wholly English; second, the middle class in the seventeenth century, was large and important in comparison with that of other sections. This unmixed English derivation promoted unity of thought, habits, and customs, with similar political, religious, and social ideals. The large middle class hindered on the one hand the growth of a power-

ful upper class, such as existed in Virginia, and on the other was unfavorable to a large servile lower class. Besides the handicraftsmen in the towns, the middle class was represented chiefly by the small independent farmer.

By the structure of society is meant the relative power, influence, and prestige of the various classes and Structure of groups of the population. The transfer from Society England of twenty or thirty thousand people did not at first essentially change the relation of people and groups to each other. The social process, however, influenced by the new environment did gradually rearrange the people into new groups and classes. In the seventeenth century New England was not a region where the people were granted equal economic, political, religious, and social privileges. In fact a minority was in control, while the majority was struggling for more opportunity and freedom. John Winthrop and John Cotton were both opponents of a democratic government. The former remarked that democracy was among most civil nations "accounted the meanest and worst" government. The latter said, "Democracy, I do not conceyve that ever God did ordeyne as a fitt government, eyther for church or commonwealth. If the people be governors, who shall be governed." These two men well represent the ideals of the leaders in state and church.

The division of society in the towns into economic, political, and religious groups, each with particular privileges and powers has already been partly described. These inequalities were the basis for social groups. From a social standpoint there were superior and inferior individuals, and various customs and devices show how much the New Englanders prized social prestige. This may be illustrated by a description of the interesting custom of " seating " in the church, and laws on " excess apparel."

Social distinctions were common in New England and a somewhat elaborate system was developed to
Social mark off the upper classes of society from
Distinctions the lower. This is shown in the plan used for seating the inhabitants in the church. In general the best seats were assigned on the basis of age, family rank and descent, office, wealth, social standing, and usefulness to community. Whittier has described " seating " as follows:

" In the goodly house of worship, when in order due
    and fit,
As by public vote directed, classed and ranked the
    people sit.
Mistress first and good-wife after, clerkly squire
    before the clown.
From the brave coat lace embroidered to the gray
    coat shading down."

The early New Englanders also believed that one of the functions of dress was to emphasize class distinc-
Sumptuary tions so that the social prestige, rank or
Laws breeding of a person might be known. The upper crust of society was jealous when common people commenced to wear fine clothing, " above their station " in life. In a Massachusetts Act, 1651, the " intollerable " excess of apparel was complained of thus:

" We declare our utter detestation and dislike that men and women of meane Condition should take upon themselves the garb of gentlemen, by wearing gold or silver lace or buttons, or points at their knees or to walk in bootes or women of the same rancke to weare silke or tiffany horlles or scarfes, which though allow-able to persons of greater estates, or more liberal education, yet we cannot but judge it intollerable in persons of such like condition."

Such laws did not apply to magistrates or public officers, or their wives or children, or anyone above ordinary degree or whose estate was once considerable but "now decayed," or to those of "liberal education."

59. Religion and Morals

The process of organizing a church generally followed in New England consisted in the drawing up of Religious what is known as a church "covenant" or Organization confession of faith — a system of discipline which each member bound himself to follow. The importance of the system established, known later as "Congregationalism," is this. The whole constitution of the English Establishment and its hierarchial order was rejected. No Church of England services were allowed, and, as we have seen, persons who disputed the Puritan creed, were likely to be banished from the colony. The covenant was democratic in its effect, because every local church was thus independent and self-governing, with power to admit members, make choice of a pastor, and other officials.

The conflict of the ideals underlying extreme Puritanism and democratic church organization both operating in the same community needs further Puritanism explanation. Originally the Puritan party in and Congregationalism England desired religious toleration for themselves and a more democratic government centered in Parliament. In New England, however, these principles were rejected in favor of intolerance and oligarchical government, in order to secure unity and preservation of the faith intact.

A striking feature of life in Puritan New England was the variety and number of agencies and methods es-

tablished for the purpose of regulating the religious and
moral life of the individual and the community. The
Regulation   Puritans seemed to believe that saints could
of Morals   be made by laws vigorously enforced.
So state and church were active in ferreting out and
punishing wickedness. The General Court enacted a
severe code of laws and set up an elaborate judicial
system. The church watched over its own members or
as Bradford says: " Ye churches look narroly to their
members and ye magistrates over all." Puritan public
opinion was extremely hostile to the wrongdoer and
supported the officers of the law in their efforts to punish crimes by informing against evildoers. The typical
Puritan was anxious not only with respect to his own
conduct but that of his neighbor. He was his " brother's
keeper." The influence of the " New England Conscience " then was a very important agency in maintaining the accepted religious and moral code.

Notwithstanding this system of espionage, plenty of
" sin " was committed and punished, in both the Plym-
Bradford and   outh and Puritan colonies. William Brad-
Winthrop on   ford remarks in his journal " Marvilous
Morals   it may be to see and consider how some
kind of wickedness did grow and break forth here, in
the land where the same was so much witnessed against."
And John Winthrop explained a general fast, ordered
by the General Court in 1642, because of the " danger
we conceive our native country was in and the foul
sins which had broken out among us." He said further
" As people increased, so sin abounded." The court
records show how much time and energy were consumed in punishing crime. In fact, as might be expected, not all the people of New England had high
moral and religious ideals. This accounts for the vigorous measures taken to remedy the evil.

The criminal codes of the New England colonies were extremely minute and severe. They not only regulated habits, food, drink, dress, and industry, but particularly the thought and practices of the people with respect to their religion and morals. The first code of Massachusetts, the famous Body of Liberties, 1641, named ten crimes as capital offenses, viz: heresy or idolatry, witchcraft, blasphemy, murder, poisoning, bestiality, sodomy, adultery, manstealing, and treason. The code followed closely that of Hebrews as outlined in Exodus, Leviticus, and Deuteronomy. The severity of the English criminal code and the authority of the Bible helped to justify the Puritan theory of punishment. Four New England colonies, Massachusetts, Plymouth, Connecticut, and Rhode Island, between 1641 and 1701, enacted fifty-seven different laws declaring that thirty different crimes, at various times, should be punished with the death penalty. Besides those mentioned above, piracy, rioting, kidnapping, robbery, selling arms to Indians, and conspiracy, were capital offenses.

The Laws and Capital Crimes

In addition to their faith in the efficacy of capital punishment, the Puritan leaders of the New England colonies thought that physical mutilation of the criminal would deter persons from crime. Twenty-four different crimes were punishable by such penalties as branding with a red-hot iron, cutting off the ears, slitting the nose, or boring the tongue. Among these were assault, arson, profanity, forgery, Sabbath breaking, speaking evil of preachers or officers, and drunkenness. Whipping, gagging, and nailing the ears of the offender to the pillory were the more moderate forms of inflicting physical pain.

Physical Mutilation

A third method of punishing evildoers was based on a belief in the effectiveness of shame and public ig-

nominy as a deterrent to crime. The agencies of correction were the stocks, pillory, ducking stool, and the
Publicity wearing of a badge or letter indicating
and Shame the nature of the offense; such as A for
adultery, D for drunkenness, T for theft. This custom
is well illustrated in Hawthorne's *The Scarlet Letter*.
Exposing the victim in the public square or before the
meeting house, especially on Sundays or court days,
was thought to be especially efficacious. The underlying
basis of criminal justice was the belief that society must
be revenged on the individual for his wrongdoing — an
eye for an eye and a tooth for a tooth. Little or no conception of reforming the criminal can be discerned in
these customs.

One of the chief elements of morality, truthfulness,
was also minutely regulated. The Massachusetts law
Falsehood stated that for a lie a fine of ten shillings
should be imposed for the first offense, or
the culprit should sit in the stocks two hours. For the
second offense the penalty was twenty shillings or
" whipped on the naked body not exceeding two houres;
for the third offense forty shillings or whipped with
more stripes." One Mr. Joseph Taubor for example
was sentenced to sit in the stocks one and one-half
hours, for saying there were " seven or eight liars in the
church and if anyone would lie soundly he would be fit
for the church." Even such petty matters as internal
family troubles were regulated, as when a wife who
had called her husband " an old Devil " was sentenced
to stand with her husband back to back in the market
place, both being gagged.

Besides the sheriff, the grand jury men, and the
county court, the usual agencies for apprehending, trying, and punishing offenders, there were the town officials — the constables and tithing men. The former

had power to arrest and commit to prison " such as are overtaken with drinke, swearing, breaking ye Sabbath, Control of Morals by Town and Church lying, vagrant persons," etc. The latter watched over family life, one for every ten families, and looked after tippling, Sabbath breaking, gaming, and idleness.

The church also watched out for its own members; and in fact acted as a court. Particular attention was paid to those committing moral offenses — lying, drunkenness, stealing, etc. The pastor called the offender to stand before the pulpit and admonished, suspended, or even excommunicated him from the church. Confession in the church was sometimes enjoined by the county court, as was true of John Sell, 1638, " for uncleanliness to sit in stocks at Lynn training day . . . and make confession in church." Such a system produced a distinct type of people and one can understand why this aspect of Puritanism was such a powerful force in the regulation of public and private morals.

The struggle for religious liberty in New England is illustrated by the famous Quaker episode. The Quakers were democratic in tendency while the Persecution of the Quakers Puritans were aristocratic. The Puritans believed the Bible to be the complete and final revelation of God, while the Quakers believed in the " inner light," a special divine revelation for each individual. The Puritans looked upon their clergy as beings of a superior order, while the Quakers believed anyone could be " called to God " as a religious leader. The life of the Puritans was based largely on the Old Testament, that of the Quakers on the New.

Suspicion and hatred towards Quakers led Massachusetts to pass a law providing for a fine of £100 on a master of a ship bringing a known Quaker into the colony. Another law imposed the death penalty on those Quakers who returned a third time after banishment. Three did return in 1659, Mary Dyer, William Robinson, and Marmaduke Stevenson. The men were soon executed and a year later the woman. In general the persecution of the Quakers resulted in a considerable number being whipped, imprisoned or banished.

The Puritan argument in defense of their drastic policy was similar to that advanced to defend their attitude towards Roger Williams. The Quakers were looked upon as a real danger to the success of the Puritan ideals of religion and government. They were considered "malignant and assiduous promoters of doctrines directly tending to subvert both Churches and State." Of the legal right of the Massachusetts leaders to punish, banish, or even hang those who disobeyed their laws there can be no question. It is the wisdom and humanity of the policy that is matter for argument.

60. The Witchcraft Delusion

The witchcraft delusion, famous in New England annals, may be considered as one phase of the religious and moral problem. For in theory the punishment of witches was a war against sin, in that the Devil had been allowed to work his evil deeds through the witch. In other words the witch was "possessed of the Devil." Puritanism was not responsible for witchcraft in New England inasmuch as it had existed in England and Europe for centuries, and was known in other colonies. Hence the problem of witchcraft was inherited, while other factors influenced the outbreak of a movement to punish witches for supposed practicing of evil deeds. The nature of the Puritan theology, the hardships, privations, and discouragements growing out of the Indian wars and the Andros régime,

The Problem

were conditions that led to intensified war on the Devil and his agents, the witches.

Between 1647 and 1692, the latter the date of the outbreak of the Salem witchcraft, several accusations Early Cases   of witchcraft were made in Plymouth, New of Witchcraft   Hampshire, Massachusetts, and Connecticut. In the two latter colonies executions for alleged witchcraft occurred. In May 1681, some of the clergy of Massachusetts, according to Increase Mather, then President of Harvard College, sent out a paper with a request to collect facts concerning witchcraft and other " strange apparitions." Mather published a book in 1684, *An Essay for the Recording of Illustrious Providences,* in which he gave an account of various cases of witchcraft.

The community was thus attuned to the outbreak in Salem which occurred in March 1692. Several young Salem   girls, one only nine years old, a daughter Outbreak   of Samuel Parris, minister of Salem Farms, became interested in stories of witches perhaps found in a book owned by the minister, called *A Discourse of the Damned Art of Witchcraft.* They commenced to act like the witches described; to utter queer sounds and to force their limbs into postures which produced cramps and spasms. One Ann Putnam, a girl of twelve, called aloud in church to the minister, " There is a yellow bird sitting on the minister's hat, as it hangs on the pin in the pulpit." Ministers and physicians declared that " witchery " was the cause of such actions.

The children, who, it is now believed, were perpetrating a fraud consciously or unconsciously, finally named three women as the witches; one a servant, half Indian and Negro; one a miserably poor old woman and a third who was nervous and bed-ridden. These three were solemnly tried March 1st before a court in the meeting house of Salem Village, with the children as witnesses. The judge told the children to look at one of the accused women "and so they all did. . . And presently were all tormented." Others were tried in a similar manner; and by the middle of May one hundred were in jail awaiting trial. The new Governor, Sir William Phips, a superstitious and excitable man, called a special court of seven Magistrates among whom was the famous Judge Samuel Sewall. Various sessions of the court were held in which, after trial, sentence of death was pronounced and executed on at least twenty persons. Then came a reaction and fifty-five who confessed to being witches were pardoned.

A few years later reason returned. Members of juries acknowledged their fault, and the famous Judge Sewall rose in his pew in the Old South Church, Boston, January 14, 1696, and acknowledged his great offense in participating in the convictions. The extent of the movement was due in part to the opportunity it gave to disgruntled persons to vent against their enemies personal vindictiveness and malice, growing out of previous quarrels. Anyone might thus be accused of witchcraft. It is believed also that some of the "witches" had hypnotic power, and used this power to bring trouble on those whom they disliked. From a political standpoint, the witchcraft movement was an effort on the part of the old clerical order to retain their influence and power.

61. Intellectual Life

The intellectual development of the New England colonies was one of the striking features of the life

Evidences of Intellectual Life

of this section. Mental activity was most noticeable in theology and education; in the publication, importation, and dissemination of books, and in the gathering of libraries. In

Massachusetts, particularly, many important events took place which stimulated the intellectual life. In 1635 the first town or public school was proposed, and in 1636, Harvard, the first college in the English colonies was founded. In 1639 the first printing press was set up in Cambridge and a book published. In 1642 the first law was passed on compulsory education of children. In 1647 the first public school system was founded. In 1650 the first bookshop was opened. From the press came numerous books and pamphlets growing out of the religious controversies of the period. The clergy preached sermons from their pulpits every Sunday and on other days, not only on theology but often on matters of political, educational, and social interest. These sermons were .often printed in large editions.

This outburst of intellectual activity was due to the influence of several factors; such as the close relation of religion and education; the large number of educated clergymen; the community type of settlement — village and town; the nature of local government — the town meeting; the nature of the land system which made possible the use of common or town lands for religious and educational endowment and the tendency of the Puritans to emphasize the good of the group. The desire to read and study the Bible as a means of forming independent judgments, to have children brought up in the true faith, and to enjoy an educated clergy also provided powerful religious motives for education.

The source of the Puritan migration in the excellent middle class English stock, was a very favorable intellectual condition. Rev. William Stoughton of Massachusetts declared (1668) that "God sifted a whole nation that he might send choice grain over into this wilderness." A second fortunate circumstance was the un-

usually large proportion of educated clergymen, graduates of Cambridge and a few from Oxford. Over one
hundred and thirty arrived in New England before 1647.
For most of the period there was more than one for
every forty families. So large a number were located
within a short distance of Boston, that we may safely
say that such a concentration of educated men in a
new settlement, in proportion to the population, has
never occurred before or since.

The founding of Harvard College, within a few years
after the settlement of Boston, was an event of the
Harvard greatest significance. The general court of
College Massachusetts appropriated £400 in 1636
and John Harvard gave his library and much of his
fortune in aid of the project. A contemporary author
stated in 1643 that after building houses, and providing
for necessaries for livelihood, after building churches
and establishing civil government, the next thing desired was " to advance *Learning* and to perpetuate it to
posterity; dreading to leave an illiterate ministry to the
churches, when our present Ministers shall be in the
Dust." The entrance requirements were ability to understand and " to make and speake true Latin in verse
and prose "; also to decline the paradigms of nouns and
verbs in the " Greek tongue." Latin, Greek, Hebrew,
Rhetoric, Logic, and Mathematics were the main subjects of study.

Between 1630 and 1645 a number of towns in the
New England colonies encouraged the establishment of
Means of schools, such as Boston in 1635, which
Education voted that " our brother Philemon Por-
mont, shalbe intreated to become scholemaster, for the
teaching and nourtering of children with us." Charlestown voted (1636) that Mr. William Witherell be
agreed with " to keepe a schoole for a twelve month to

begin August 8, and have £40 this year." Dorchester, Dedham, and Salem in Massachusetts, New Haven and Guilford in the New Haven Colony, Hartford in Connecticut, and Newport in Rhode Island, all took action in town meeting before 1645, providing for the establishment or support of schools.

In 1642 the general court of Massachusetts, "taking into consideration the great neglect of parents and masters in training up their children in learning and labor," passed an act requiring selectmen to see whether the children of parents and masters had the ability to read and understand the principles of religion and the capital laws of the country. In 1648 this act was revised so that children must be able "perfectly to read the English tongue," or selectmen might be fined twenty shillings for neglect. Similar acts were passed by Connecticut in 1650, New Haven in 1655 and by Plymouth in 1671.

The first school system in the colonies was established in Massachusetts by the act of 1647. Two important School reasons may be given for the passage of Systems this law, first that learning might "not be buried in the grave of our fathers in Church and commonwealth"; second, that means might be provided to fit boys for Harvard College in order that a continual supply of educated ministers might be available for the churches. The act provided: first, that towns of fifty families should appoint one within their town to teach all such children as should resort to him to read and write; second, that in towns of one hundred families there should be "set up a grammar school [that is what was called a Latin grammar school] the master whereof, being able to instruct youth so far as they may be fitted for the University." It was left optional with the towns to vote whether the salary of the teacher should fall on the parents of those who sent their children to the school, or be paid by the "inhabitants in general," that is, possibly by taxation, a plan that had already been tried out by a number of towns. Another remarkable feature provided that any town neglecting to comply with the act above a year, must pay a penalty of £5, increased in 1692 to £10.

The general effect of this act was to stimulate the founding of schools, particularly after the county courts commenced to impose the penalty on towns for failure to comply with the act. Connecticut, in 1650, passed an act similar to that of Massachusetts, and later New Hampshire, so that by 1689 most of the territory of New England was under a system of compulsory education and schools. Rhode Island was the only exception.

It is clear that New England was much more fortunate than the southern colonies in favorable conditions Conditions of Social Progress for rapid social progress; the towns and town meeting, the land system, especially the use of land for social and economic betterment of the whole group; the diversification of industries, the degree of unity which existed; and the large proportion of educated leaders in church and state. These educated leaders were determined that the two most important agencies of social progress, the church and the school, should be widely accessible. With such favorable factors we can understand why New England advanced so rapidly in intellectual and social well-being.

CHAPTER VIII

COLONIZATION AND DEVELOPMENT OF THE MIDDLE COLONIES TO 1689

62. References

Bibliographies. — See refs. under bibliographies in ch. ix; J. T. Adams, *Prov. Society*, 324–356; C. M. Andrews, *Colonial Self-Govt.*, 339–340, 341–342, 347–351; H. E. Bolton and T. M. Marshall, *Coloniza. of North Am.*, 178, 215; Channing, Hart and Turner, *Guide*, §§ 31–34, 36–39, 42–43, 45, 48, 96–97, 99, 108–109, 122–126, 141, 163–164; S. G. Fisher, *The Quaker Colonies*, 231–234; M.W.Goodman, *Dutch and English on the Hudson*, 231–233; E. B. Greene, *Prov. Am.*, 325–340, and *Foundations of Am. Nationality*, 153–154, 177; Grace Griffin, *Writings on Am. Hist.*, 1906–1923; J. T. Jennings, *Bibliog. of N. Y. Colo. Hist.* and *List of Books relat. to state of N. Y.*; J. N. Larned, *Lit. of Am. Hist.*, 69–76, 92–100, 365–375; H. J. Priestly, *The Coming of the White Man, 1492–1819* (Am. Life Series I), ch. xiii; Justin Winsor, *Nar. and Crit. Hist. of Am.* (critical essays on authorities in III–V).

Historical Maps. — Nos. 1 and 2 of this vol.; H. E. Bolton and T. M. Marshall, *Coloniza. of North Am.*, 168, 176, 200, 222; Channing, Hart and Turner, *Guide*, §§ 33–34, 96–97 (bibliography); D. R. Fox, *Atlas of American Hist.*, 8–13; S. G. Fisher, *Quaker Colonies*, 84 (Delaware region 1665–1774); Justin Winsor, *Nar. and Crit. Hist. of Am.*, Maps in III–IV.

General Accounts. — (For Engl. and European background see refs. to chs. i and v, vii, under "General" and "Special Accounts"); W. C. Abbott, *Expansion of Europe*, I, ch. xviii, esp. 419 ff.; C. M. Andrews, *Colonial Self-Govt.*, chs. v–viii, xi–xii, xvii; G. L. Beer, "Cromwell's Economic Policy," in *Polit. Sci. Quart.*, XVI, 582–611, XVII, 46–70; H. E. Bolton and T. M. Marshall, *Coloniza. of North Am.*, chs. ix, x, xi; Edward Channing, *Hist. of the U. S.*, I, chs. xvi–xvii, II, chs. ii–iv; F. C. Dietz, *Polit. and Social Hist. of Engl.*, ch. xviii; J. A. Doyle, *Engl. Cols. in Amer.*, IV, chs. i–ix; S. G. Fisher, *Quaker Colonies*, chs. i–ii, viii, x, xii–xiii; John Fiske, *Dutch and Quaker Colonies*, I–II; M. W. Goodman, *Dutch and English on the Hudson*, chs. i–iv, vi–ix; E. B. Greene, *Foundations etc.*; chs. vii–viii; C. J. H. Hayes, *Polit. and Social Hist. of Mod. Europe*,

I, ch. ii; R. M. Jones, *Quakers in Am. Colonies;* H. E. Osgood, *American Colonies in 17th Cent.*, II, chs. i-ii, vi-viii, xi, III, ch. xii; H. I. Priestly, *1492–1819* (Am. Life Series, I), ch. xii; Justin Winsor, *Nar. and Crit. Hist. of Am.*, III, chs. x-xii; IV, chs. xiii-ix.

Special Accounts. — (a) NEW NETHERLAND AND NEW YORK: J. R. Broadhead, *Hist. of the State of N. Y.*, I; W. E. Griffith, *Story of New Netherland;* J. H. Inness, *New Amsterdam and its People;* T. A. Janvier, *Dutch Founding of New York;* A. E. McKinley, "Engl. and Dutch Towns of New Netherland," in *Am. Hist. Rev.*, VI, 1–18; E. B. O'Callaghan, *Hist. of New Netherland*, I–II; H. L. Schoolcraft, "The Capture of New Amsterdam," in *Engl. Hist. Rev.*, XXII, 674–693; A. J. F. Van Laer, "The Patroon System under the Colony of Rensselaerswyck, in *N. Y. Hist. Assoc. Proc.* VIII, 222–243; J. G. Wilson, *Memorial Hist. of the City of N. Y.*, I–II. (b) NEW JERSEY: E. J. Fisher, "New Jersey as a Royal Province," 1738–1776; *Columb. Stud.*, XLI; E. P. Tanner, "Province of N. J." (1664–1738) in *Columb. Studies*, XXX; W. A. Whitehead, "The English in East and West Jersey," in Justin Winsor, *Nar. and Crit. Hist.*, III. (c) NEW SWEDEN AND DELAWARE: Amandus Johnson, *Swedes on the Delaware;* G. B. Keen, "New Sweden," in Justin Winsor's, *Nar. and Crit. Hist. of Am.*, IV, ch. ix; J. T. Scharf, *Hist. of Del.*, *1609–1688;* Francis Vincent, *Hist. of Delaware*. (d) PENNSYLVANIA: S. G. Fisher, *Making of Pa.;* W. T. Root, *Relations of Pa. with the Brit. Govt.*, *1696–1765;* W. R. Shepherd, "Hist. of Proprietary Govt. in Pa." in *Columb. Stud.*, VI.

Biography. — E. M. Brown, *Henry Hudson;* S. G. Fisher, *The True William Penn;* Thomas Hodgkin, *George Fox;* J. F. Jameson, "Willem Usselinx," in *Am. Hist. Assoc. Papers*, II, no. 3; Isaac Sharpless, *Political Leaders of Pa.;* Bayard Tuckerman, *Peter Stuyvesant.*

Contemporary Accounts. — (a) BIBLIOGRAPHY: See "Contemporary Accts." ch. ix and lists of sources in J. T. Adams, *Provincial Society*, 326–328; Channing, Hart and Turner, *Guide*, §§ 42–43, 122–126; A. R. Hasse, *Materials for a Bibliography, etc.; Hist. Sources in Schools*, §§ 55–57, 69–70. W. P. Trent (ed.), *Camb. Hist. of Am. Lit.*, I, 365–384. Milton Waldman, *Americana, etc.*, ch. viii; (b) NARRATIVES: Thomas Budd, *Good Order Established in Pa. and N. J.* (1685), ed. 1902; Daniel Coxe, "Account of New Jersey" in *Pa. Mag. of Hist.*, III, 327–329; Daniel Denton, *Brief Description of N. Y.* (1670), ed., 1903; J. F. Jameson (ed.), *Orig. Narratives of Early Am. Hist.* (*Nars. of Early Pa. and West New Jersey and Delaware;*

Journal of Jasper Danckaerts) 1679–1680); *Nars. of the In-surrections; Nars. of Indian Wars*); G. P. Winship (ed.), *Sailors Nars. of Voyages along the New Engl. Coast, 1524–1674.* (c) RECORDS AND COLLECTIONS: B. E. Fernow (ed.), *Records of Burgomasters of New Amsterdam, 1653–1674*, (7 vols.); Peter Force, *Tracts, etc.;* Ralph Gabriel (ed.), *Pageant of America;* A. B. Hart (ed.), *Contemporaries,* I, chs. xxii-xxv; Aaron Leaming and Jacob Spicer, *Grants and Concessions and Original Constitutions of the Province of N.J.;* "Leisler Papers," in *N. Y. Hist. Soc. Coll.,* 1868; William Macdonald (ed.), *Select Charters,* nos. 9, 29–31, 35–41; S. Munsell, *Annals of Albany;* E. B. O'Callaghan, *Laws and Ordinances of New Netherland, 1638–1674;* H. E. Osgood (ed.), *Records of Common Council of N. Y. City* (8 vols.) 1675–1676; collections of docu-ments are in *Docs. Relat. to Colonial Hist. of N. Y.,* 15 vols., *Archives of New Jersey,* 27 vols., and *Pa. Archives.*

63. New Netherland (1609–1629)

As compared with New England the Middle Colonies had a larger area with a greater proportion of fertile soil. They were therefore more nearly self-supporting agriculturally. New York had access to the great fur country via the Hudson and Mohawk valleys, and also possessed the best harbor on the coast. Pennsylvania included many extensive and fertile valleys, but economic progress was retarded be-cause of the difficulties of transportation. Her great natural resources of coal and iron were of slight im-portance in the period under consideration. Forest re-sources, however, in both New York and Pennsylvania were extensive. Most of New Jersey was not a region of rich soil, compared, for example, with the tide-water region of Virginia. Her greatest advantage in this early period was her position in relation to New York harbor. From this, northern New Jersey benefited greatly in economic and social development. The physical en-vironment of the Middle Colonies in relation to po-litical, economic, and social institutions promoted a

Physical Environment

cosmopolitan population. This was due in part to loca-
tion and the importance of New York and Philadelphia
as ports of entrance for immigrants.

The Dutch commenced to lay plans for colonies
about the same time as the English. This seafaring
people, made wealthy by trade, commerce,
and manufactures, naturally cast longing
eyes toward America. For the Dutch, like
Spain, France, and England, wished to share in the
rich spoils of the new world. As early as 1597 companies were formed to trade in the West Indies; and in
1602 the great Dutch East India Company was chartered with extensive powers of conquest, colonization,
and government. This company was a model for the
rival French and English companies. It was in 1609 that
a twelve-year truce was concluded between the con-
federated states of the Netherlands and Spain. Thus the
long and heroic struggle for liberty, begun in 1559,
bore fruit in at least a temporary victory for the Dutch.
This spirit of liberty was brought to America by many
of the Dutch colonists.

In 1609 Henry Hudson, an English navigator and
explorer, offered his services to the Dutch East India
Company, and sailed from Amsterdam in
the ship *Half Moon* to search for a northeast passage to India. Failing in this project, he sailed west towards Newfoundland, then to
the south, and by July was off the coast of Maine.
He landed on Cape Cod, followed the shore line, and
finally entered New York Harbor. Then he sailed up the
majestic and beautiful river which now bears his name
as far as the present Albany, still in search of a passage
to India. Through friendly intercourse with the Indians
he became acquainted with the prospect of the lucrative
fur trade. It may be noted that in this same year

Champlain was in contact with these same Indian tribes in the North. Soon the West India Company sent other trading ships to the Hudson. It was on the basis of Henry Hudson's voyage and those of other navigators, notably that of Block (1614) that the Dutch laid claim to much of the southern New England coast.

In 1614 the States General granted a charter to a company of merchants, giving them a three-year monopoly, renewed year by year till 1621, of trade from Virginia to New France, between 40° and 45° of latitude. The region was named New Netherland. It was in this year that Captain John Smith explored the same region and called the northern part of it New England. The Dutch built a fort and trading house at "Fort Nassau," near the site of Albany, and thus prepared the way for a permanent Dutch settlement on the Hudson.

The New Netherland and Dutch West India Companies

This first company was succeeded by the Dutch West India Company, which secured a charter in June 1621 with exclusive privileges to trade and found colonies in America, Africa, and other specified regions, including powers of government. Colonization was not at first the main object of the Dutch West India Company. The charter did not make a specific grant of territory, nor did it even describe in detail the area in which trade was to be carried on. Protests were made by England against this intrusion on territory claimed by the English.

In the spring of 1623 the *New Netherland* sailed with thirty families, Dutch and Walloons, Protestants, the latter fugitives from the Belgian provinces. Two forts were built; another "Fort Nassau" on the "South River" (Delaware) near the present site of Camden, New Jersey, and Fort Orange on the present site of

The Expedition of 1623 and the Purchase of Manhattan Island

Albany, where eighteen families settled. Immigration continued for the next three years so that by May 1625 the colony numbered about 200. In 1626 Peter Minuit arrived, commissioned as Director General, and made his famous purchase of the island of Manhattan from the Indians for twenty-four dollars. A third fort was built by the company at the southern end of the island which took the name of New Amsterdam.

The Dutch made peace with the Indians and with the colony of New Plymouth, though Governor Brad-

Progress to
1629

ford warned them that they were within a region claimed by the English and had no right to trade or set up a colony there. By 1629 New Netherland had a European population of about three hundred and fifty, and in this year arrived Jonas Michaelius, the first clergyman who established a church. The Dutch colony was based very largely on the fur trade. Beaver and other skins, brought by the Indians from the North and West, were the chief source of its prosperity, rather than agriculture. The company estimated the average value of the fur trade at 50,000 guldens.

64. Government of New Netherland (1629–1664)

The West India Company became the object of greater state control in 1629. In this year the govern-

Charter of
Privileges
(1629)
and the
Patroonship

ing board of the company issued a charter of privileges, designed to facilitate colonization by the establishment of " patroonships." Proprietaries would more accurately describe these grants. Anyone who established a colony of fifty adults became a lord of the manor, or " patroon," with absolute ownership, of a tract of land extending sixteen miles on one side of the Hudson river or eight miles along each bank, stretching for an indefinite distance into the interior East and West.

The patroons were given large governmental and judicial powers and were advised to provide ministers and a schoolmaster. Colonists who emigrated under the patronage of the patroons were to be exempt from taxation for ten years.

The West India Company was divided into five branches or chambers; that in Amsterdam was given the supervision of the New Netherland. The directors of this chamber proceeded to obtain for themselves patroonships and huge grants of land. One secured in 1630 ran thirty miles in length. More famous was the grant to Killian Van Rensselaer, who obtained an enormous tract near Albany, nearly fifty miles square, called Rensselaerwyck. Another director bought the whole of Staten Island with other territory. Thus the Dutch theory and practice of colonization permitted a monopoly of government, trade, commerce, and land to pass into the hands of relatively few men. Little was left for the independent colonist. Moreover these great proprietors were often in conflict with the central government.

The Dutch also occupied a portion of what is now Delaware, and in 1635 established themselves on the
Expansion of the Dutch in Delaware and Connecticut
Connecticut River near Hartford and built a fort. Between 1632 and 1647 they were hard pressed with Indian warfare brought on by Governor Kieft and dishonest traders who provided the Indians with too much liquor. It was not until Governor Peter Stuyvesant arrived in 1647 that the colony of the New Netherland commenced to develop rapidly.

The Dutch governors and most of the Directors were selfish and did little to promote the welfare of the mass of the people. One of the reasons for recalling Governor Kieft was due to the part he played in bring-

ing on Indian warfare. The "Remonstrance" of 1649
lists the woes of the colony. It was asserted that
The Dutch   colonization had not been properly encour-
Governors   aged; that trade had fallen off, due to
smuggling; that goods were high in price; that the mill
was neglected, and the church unbuilt. According to
this document disorder and discontent prevailed. There
was lack of public revenue, and conflicts between patroons and central government.

Peter Stuyvesant, governor, 1647-1664, was arbitrary, harsh, and stubborn, but many reforms were
needed. He checked a profitable but illegal business viz.,
the sale of liquor to the Indians. He also checked the
smuggling of furs into New England and of European
goods thence into New Netherland. He levied a tax to
obtain revenue to improve the town. He endeavored to
foster the foreign trade of New Netherland, and tried
to keep the peace with his New England neighbors.

In internal affairs he was unsuccessful. He appointed
some of his own men to be the members of the city government. His chief assistant, the "schout," was Cor-
nelis Van Tienhoven, a sort of sheriff, district attorney,
and chief officer next to the governor. He is described
in the Remonstrance of 1649 thus: "He is subtle,
crafty, intelligent, sharp witted for evil . . . he is a dis-
sembler, double faced, a cheat; the whole country pro-
claims him a knave, a murderer, a traitor — he fleeces
the people."

In December 1653 a popular convention of nineteen delegates met at New Amsterdam to remonstrate
Complaints   against the existing government. Delegates
against the   came from Dutch and English towns. They
Government   complained of arbitrary government, orders and ordinances "without the knowledge or consent
of the people," and "odious to every free born man

and especially so to those whom God has placed under a free state in newly settled lands." This has the true ring of the Dutch and Anglo-Saxon spirit of liberty. The reply of Stuyvesant denied the right of the delegates to assemble. He said: "We derive our authority from God and the Company, not from a few ignorant subjects; and we alone can call the inhabtants together."

In New Netherland and later in New York, the government was largely centered in the governor and council, autocratic and aristocratic in theory and practice. Popular tendencies and forces existed, but New Netherland and New York failed to obtain a popular legislature until late in the seventeenth century (see p. 205). Like Virginia, it was a proprietary province, the Dutch West India Company being the proprietor. The immediate control was lodged in the chamber of Amsterdam; but the States General of the United Provinces maintained a close supervision of the company. Hence the province was really under joint control of these two bodies. The director general of New Netherland presented full reports to the Amsterdam Chamber; and received directions and orders concerning such matters as grants of land, admission of immigrants, trade relations, Indian affairs, and patroons.

Colony and Local Government

The Director General with a local council of about five, whom he virtually appointed, and a small number of officials, administered affairs within the colony. They made and executed the laws and sat as the highest judicial court in the province. Some of the directors, like Kieft and Van Twiller, acted autocratically and independently of the council. One of the council complained that the power of the director in New Netherland was greater than that of the Prince of Orange in the

Netherlands, and Stuyvesant was known as the "great Muscovy Duke." In the remonstrance of 1653 it was declared that "the entire government of this country is directed and controlled exclusively according to the pleasure and caprice of Dr. Stuyvesant and one or two of his favorite sycophants."

The local governments also had their origin in grants of privileges from the director and council. A village system similar to that of the Netherlands was established. In the revised "Freedoms and exemptions" (1640) provision was made for the establishment of colonies under masters each of whom was required to bring over five adult colonists and settle them in the province. As they developed into villages, the company agreed to grant them powers of local government — by village rights or charters, which provided for magistrates and ministers of justice, appointed by the director and council, from lists of nominees presented by the freemen of the village. These magistrates formed a town board and had authority to pass ordinances concerning lands, highways, schools, churches, and other local affairs, subject to the approval of the directors and council. They also acted as a local court. It will thus be seen that, unlike the New England towns, the inhabitants had little or no powers of local self government, nor anything corresponding to the town meeting. The colony or patroonship of Rensselaerwyck exercised almost independent powers. The patroon or court appointed all the officials, who were independent of the director and council.

65. New Sweden (1626–1655)

Sweden was the fifth European power that attempted colonization of the Atlantic coast. The projector of this movement was William Usselinx, who laid a plan before Gustavus Adolphus for a commercial company, similar to the Dutch West India Company. He urged the advantages of trade and commerce and the enlargement of the kingdom. A charter of privileges was signed by the king, June 6, 1626, establishing a company with power to make settlements. The project for founding an American colony advanced slowly, perhaps hindered by the death of Adolphus in 1632 and the absorption of Sweden in the Thirty Years' War. It was not until 1638 that an expedition of about fifty colonists finally set out under Peter Minuit. They settled on the Delaware, purchased of the Indians lands claimed by the Dutch, built a fort near the present site of Wilmington and called it Fort Christina. Between 1638 and 1656, twelve expeditions were dispatched to New Sweden, but the colony remained a feeble one. In 1653 the settlement numbered only two hundred souls, men, women, and children. The Governors were given extensive powers in justice and government, but there was really little need of laws for the government of a few people living a simple frontier life.

The Swedes were at a great disadvantage because overshadowed by the more populous Dutch and English colonies, who interfered with their development. In 1655, the Dutch seized their settlements and forts with little or no opposition. Though the hopes of Sweden were not realized in the development of her empire or in the enlargement of her trade and commerce, yet these industrious, religious, and honest people played their part well in establishing the beginnings of the civilization later carried out by Penn and his followers in Pennsylvania, Delaware, and New Jersey. When Penn arrived in 1681 he found nearly a thousand settlers on the Delaware, more than half of whom were Swedes.

66. New York (1664-1691)

By 1655 the eastern end of Long Island surrendered by Stuyvesant under the terms of the Treaty of Hartford (1650), was under English control. Encroachment on Dutch Territory by the English To the north, Massachusetts was seeking to tap the Dutch fur trade at its source, Albany. Maryland was pressing the Dutch from the south, and ordering them out of the lands on the southwest side of Delaware Bay. The Connecticut settlers were also pressing the Dutch and in 1662 sought to have included in their charter all the lands " westward to the Bay of Delaware."

In March 1664, Charles II granted all the territory between the Connecticut and Delaware Rivers, including Conquest of New Netherland by the English Long Island and Martha's Vineyard, Nantucket, and the Elizabeth Islands, to his brother the Duke of York. The bitter commercial rivalry between Holland and England for control of the seas and the profits of commerce, led the Duke of York to dispatch a fleet to New Netherland to seize the territory from the Dutch. This act of aggression was a part of the plan of England to enforce the navigation acts. Otherwise there would have been illegal trading with the Dutch, especially by Virginia and Maryland. Moreover, England had in mind not only commercial control of the area of the Dutch colony, but planned to bring the new territory to be acquired as well as the colonies already established, under the more strict control of the king, as already described in Chapter VI.

Stuyvesant was forced to capitulate and New Netherland became an English colony August 26, 1664. The property, civil rights and religion of the Dutch settlers were guaranteed. A code of laws known as the Duke's laws was enacted, including trial by jury and equal taxation. For a brief period, 1673–74, during the war between Holland and England, New York was under Dutch control but was restored to England in 1674.

Under the royal charter of 1664 the Duke of York became proprietor of a vast region. He also received The English rights of government, without mention Government of a popular legislature. A governor (Nicolls) and a council were appointed. The latter became aristocratic and exclusive in character. Counties were organized (1683) and county officials appointed — sheriff, deputy sheriff, and justices of the court of sessions. In the villages increased self government was granted by a provision that each town should elect a board of eight overseers and a constable, with power to act as a court. The English parish system was also introduced. The governor and council regulated the formation of new villages and towns, and in the Dutch sections appointed local magistrates and established local courts. Taxes, according to the Duke's laws, were regulated by the same authority which also made an annual levy and ordered the sheriffs and constables to collect the taxes.

A demand for a legislative assembly had been made on several occasions under Dutch rule, but to no purpose. The famous "Remonstrance of New Struggle for an Assembly Netherland," 1649, complained of autocratic government, lack of colonists, and demanded more liberal local self-government. Again in 1653 a meeting of delegates from various towns drew up another protest which complained that " 'Tis contrary to the first intentions and genuine principles of every well regulated government, that one or more men should arrogate to themselves the exclusive power to dispose, at will, of the life and property of any individual, and this by virtue or under pretence of a law or order he or they might enact, without the consent, knowledge or election of the whole Body, or its agents as representatives. . . We humbly submit that 'tis one of our privileges that our consent or that of our representatives is necessarily required in the enactment of such laws and orders."

The notion that the people had a right to a representative assembly is important, as it is typical of the growth of such a sentiment in other colonies. A Dutch assembly did meet April 10, 1664, but disagreements arose between the director and council over furnishing supplies for a regular military force which the assembly declined; and it soon adjourned. When Governor Lovelace arrived in 1669, demands for an assembly were made and again under Governor Andros in 1675. The Duke of York opposed it because he considered that such bodies were likely to prove dangerous, assume too many privileges, and thus disturb the peace of the province. In the spring of 1681 the court of assize, during the absence of Andros, petitioned the Duke that the province in the future might be ruled by a governor, council, and assembly, to be elected by the freeholders, as was the custom in some of the other colonies; that the inhabitants "groaned" under arbitrary and absolute power; that, by means of revenue exacted against their wills, their trade had been burdened and their liberty destroyed, until they had become a "reproach" to their neighbors in the other colonies.

Finally Governor Thomas Dongan was given authority to call an assembly (1682), with the stipulation that no tax should be levied without its sanction and the approval of the Duke of York. This assembly first met October 17, 1683, and passed several laws and also the important "Charter of Franchises and Liberties." One

provided for county representation in the assembly and
county and local courts. Trial by jury and other civil
rights were also subjects of legislation. When James became king (1685) he abolished this assembly and New
York became a royal province. Power of legislation and
taxation was now given to the governor and council. In
1688 Andros arrived on his mission to consolidate the
northern colonies under one government.

When the news of the revolution of 1688 arrived
and Governor Nicholson angered the people by
Leisler   his actions, they revolted (May 1689),
Rebellion   under Jacob Leisler, a German merchant,
who seized the fort and proclaimed William
and Mary. Leisler practically assumed a dictatorship over the southern part of the province of New
York, and later extended his control over Albany
and Ulster County. Being in need of revenue, he summoned a convention of delegates from seven counties.
This body appointed him commander-in-chief of the
province with large powers. With the arrival of Governor Sloughter in March 1691, Leisler surrendered and
was put to death. New York's chief gain was a representative assembly, which met April 9, 1691.

67. New Jersey (1664–1689)

Soon after the Duke of York received his grant from
Charles II, he granted (1664) the territory known as
Establishment New Jersey to two favorites, Sir John
of the   Berkeley and Sir George Carteret, who as
Jerseys   proprietaries believed they possessed powers similar to those granted to the proprietors of Carolina. No specific powers of government were enumerated. The proprietors in 1665 issued a document
called " Concession and Agreement " which provided
for a governor, council, and assembly of representatives,

with the power to frame laws. No taxes could be levied without legislative consent, and liberty of conscience was guaranteed. Philip Carteret was the first governor.

There were various settlements, the Dutch at Bergen, and later settlers from New England at Elizabethtown, Newark, and Woodbridge. These towns were granted rights of local self government. In a number of them town meetings were provided for, similar to those in New England. Thus a larger degree of local liberty was conceded by the proprietors than in New York. Justices of the Peace, important local officials were, however, appointed by the governor and council, and occasionally the constables, and other officials.

An assembly met at Elizabethtown, 1668, and passed a number of severe capital laws, voted taxes to be levied The First on the towns, and provided for Indian Assembly legislation. The usual friction between the assembly and the council appeared in New Jersey as in other colonies, showing at this early date the independent attitude of the lower house. In a message to the council the deputies complain that the former body had "Expectations that things must go according to your opinions, though we see no reason for, much less Warrants from the Concessions."

Berkeley sold his undivided share in New Jersey (1674) to Edward Byllynge, a Quaker, for £1000. Later West and East West New Jersey (1675), as it was called, New Jersey came into the possession of William Penn and two of his Quaker brethren. Colonists who came in 1677 brought with them "Concessions and Agreements," probably draughted by Penn, granting civil liberties, including an assembly, trial by jury, and religious freedom. Soon after the death of Carteret, the other proprietor under the Duke's grant, East New Jersey was sold for £3,400 (1682). This became the property of William

Penn and eleven associates, Quakers. These new proprietors drew up a frame of government called the
"Fundamental Constitutions," but it was never put
into effect. The plan of the king to unite the northern
colonies into one government under Andros led to the
annexation for a short time of both Jerseys to New
York; but with the revolution of 1688 and the overthrow of the Andros government the proprietors re-
sumed control, though they were not very well obeyed.
The progress of the Jerseys was delayed because of the
effort of the proprietors to use them as sources of profit
and revenue.

68. Pennsylvania (1681–1689)

William Penn, son of the wealthy Admiral Penn,
while at Oxford University, became interested in
Quakerism, and indeed was expelled for
attending unauthorized religious meetings.
After traveling in France, Italy, and other European
countries he returned to England and became thor-
oughly wedded to the religious ideas of the Society of
Friends (1667). George Fox had been preaching now
for twenty years or more and the time was ripe for the
"Holy Experiment."

William Penn

Penn was a firm believer in the old English ideas of
freedom and representative institutions, guarantees of
property and jury trial. Unlike all other great colonial
proprietors, he urged the people " not to give away anything of Liberty and Property that at present they
do . . . enjoy . . . and understand that it is easy to
part with or give great privileges, but hard to be gained
if once lost." Penn also wrote (1681), " For the matters
of liberty and privilege I propose that which is extraordinary, and to leave myself and successors no power of
doing mischief; so that the will of one man may not

hinder the poor of the whole country." Because of his birth and social position he associated with people of rank. Though rich, talented, and educated, he was at home among the middle and poorer classes, from whom he won the bulk of the converts to Quakerism.

In general with other Quakers the central point of Penn's religion was obedience to the "inner light," or The "Inner Light" direct inspiration. This "inner light" was a guide to the understanding of the Bible, to be applied to the affairs of daily life, and in part to government, laws, and institutions. The effect of this doctrine in some cases made the words of a poor and even illiterate Quaker of as great importance as one who was rich and educated. Thus Quakerism tended to reduce all ranks of society to a spiritual level — a spiritual democracy.

Such was the man to whom the king granted Pennsylvania (1681) in consideration of "the debts due Grant of Pennsylvania him and his Father from the Crown," estimated at £16,000. Through his connection with New Jersey Penn was already interested in colonization. He now found it possible to try out his ideas on a large scale. More land was secured the next year when he obtained title to the Delaware region, which he annexed to his own dominion. The grant was the subject of much dispute because of overlapping claims, particularly those of New York and Maryland. The boundaries in fact were not finally agreed upon until 1760, and it was not until 1767 that the southern boundary with Maryland, the famous Mason and Dixon Line, was drawn. Some settlers, Dutch and Swedes mainly, were in Penn's territory before 1681. To these people he dispatched a letter promising an assembly to make laws for their government. He arrived in the ship *Welcome* with about one hundred emigrants October

27, 1682, and proceeding up the Delaware founded Philadelphia.

By the royal charter of 1681 Penn was made absolute proprietor of Pennsylvania. Laws passed were subject to the approval of the crown, that is the royal veto was provided for, and the supremacy of Parliament was recognized. Laws were to be made and taxes were to be levied only with the consent of the governor and an assembly. In a letter to the settlers (1681), he said that "he had an honest mind to do uprightly." "You shall be governed by laws of your own making . . . I shall not usurp the right of any, or oppress his person." Again he declared that "any government is free to the people under it . . . where the laws rule and the people are a party to these laws, and more than this is tyranny, oligarchy, or confusion. . . Liberty without obedience is confusion, and obedience without liberty is slavery."

Charter and Frame of Government

Penn issued a Frame of Government April 25, 1682, to "preserve the magistracy in reverence with the people and best keep it from being hurtful to them." He proposed a governor, deputy-governor and a council of seventy-two members; persons of wisdom, virtue, and ability, chosen by the freemen, one third to be elected each year; the overlapping principle of the present United States Senate. He proposed that the freemen, being persons who owned land or paid taxes, should also elect an assembly who should give their assent or dissent to laws prepared by the council. Penn also drew up a code or body of laws "agreed on in England" which provided for religious freedom and a mild criminal code.

Soon after his arrival (October 1682) Penn proceeded to organize a government without following exactly the charter, draft, frame of government, or pro-

posed laws. A General Assembly met at Chester in
December 1682, and adopted the "Great Law" agreed
on in England, and passed other laws. Social legislation included the abolition of
alehouses, horse racing, bull and bear baiting, cock-
fighting, games of cards and dice, stage plays, lotteries,
and duelling. Children were to be taught useful trades
and the laws were to be taught in the schools. Provision
was also made for the care of the poor, and insane
prisoners were also provided for. Liberty of conscience
was guaranteed and a very mild criminal code enacted.

The First Assembly

The frame of government was several times modified
(1683, 1696, and 1701) in the direction of more popular freedom. Both executive and judiciary depended
for their support on the people, who also elected subordinate officers. One striking feature is the absence
of laws providing for forts, armed forces, militia, established church, and restrictions on immigration.

Thus the important motive of Penn and his followers in emigrating was to escape from religious persecution, as was true of Lord Baltimore and
the Catholics, John Winthrop and the Puritans. In 1680 Penn presented to king and Parliament
a compilation of the sufferings of the Quakers. Ten
thousand had been imprisoned, and 243 had died mainly
from cruel usage. Their estates had been confiscated
and exorbitant fines imposed. But the Quakers were
made of the stuff of martyrs and acted in the spirit
of Penn's remark, "My prison shall be my grave before
I will budge a jot, for I owe obedience of my conscience
to no mortal man." Immigration occurred on a large
scale and by 1685 Pennsylvania boasted some 8000 inhabitants, about one half English and the others mainly
Dutch and Germans. Philadelphia had nearly 400 houses
and was the largest town in the colonies. Penn said in

Character of Settlers

1684: "I have led the greatest colony into America that ever any man did upon a private credit, and the most prosperous beginnings that ever were in it are to be found among us."

Penn returned to England in 1684, and this was the signal for trouble between the assembly and the Gov-
Opposition to Proprietary Government
ernor and council. The proprietary system became unpopular and the assembly tried to assert more authority. Continual disputes occurred between the assembly and the council over the promulgation of laws " by the authority of the President and council." The assembly, contrary to the frame of government, commenced to initiate legislation and amend bills. Thus the dispute between the popular branch of the legislature representing the people, and the upper house representing the proprietor, was similar to that in other colonies. Penn was greatly disturbed at the turn of affairs, and did his best to bring about harmony but without much success. In the confusion incident to the English revolution (1668–89) the disputes continued; but finally Penn's appointee, Blackwell, resigned as President of the Council and the council elected its own president.

69. Delaware

The region now known as Delaware was that first occupied by the Swedes, conquered by the Dutch and brought under the control of the Duke of York by the conquest of New Netherland. Penn's boundaries by the charter of 1681 did not include the district about Newcastle. Nevertheless he not only claimed the lands on the Delaware previously settled by the Dutch and Swedes, but felt that he must have more in order to secure access to the water and shores of Delaware River, Delaware Bay, and so on to the ocean. In 1682 the Duke of York by deed granted the three counties of Delaware " the Territories " and Penn annexed them to his dominion. An act was passed by the Assembly of 1682 called the Act of Union, uniting the Territories to Pennsylvania. Both had the same governor and assembly, though Delaware later (1702) secured a separate assembly and in due time became a separate state in the union.

CHAPTER IX

ECONOMIC AND SOCIAL DEVELOPMENT OF THE MIDDLE COLONIES TO 1689

70. References

Bibliographies. — See refs. to chs. iv, vii-viii, x, xii, xiv-xv, under bibliography; J. T. Adams, *Prov. Society*, 324–356; C. M. Andrews, *Colonial Folkways*, 239–243, and *Colonial Self-Govt.*, 341–342, 347–351; Channing, Hart and Turner, *Guide*, §§ 36–39, 42–43, 45, 48, 96–97, 122–126, 161, 163–165; H. U. Faulkner, *Am. Econom. Hist.*, 76–77, 100–101, 115–116; S. G. Fisher, *The Quaker Colonies*, 231–234; M. W. Goodman, *Dutch and English on the Hudson*, 231–233; E. B. Greene, *Prov. Am.*, 331–340; Grace Griffin, *Writings on Am. Hist.*, 1906–1923; J. N. Larned, *Lit. of Am. Hist.*, 69–76, 92–100, 365–375.

Historical Maps. — See references, ch. viii.

General Accounts. — See references under "General Accounts" in ch. viii; J. T. Adams, *Prov. Society*, chs. i-vi; C. M. Andrews, *Colonial Folkways and Colonial Self-Govt.*, chs. viii-xix; Chas. and Mary Beard, *Rise of Am. Civiliza.*, chs. ii-iii; Carl Becker, *Begin. of Am. People*, 134–146; J. A. Doyle, *Engl. Col. in Am.*, IV, chs. i-v; H. U. Faulkner, *Am. Econom. Hist.*, chs. i-v; S. G. Fisher, *The Quaker Colonies*, chs. ii-iv, ix; M. W. Goodman, *Dutch and English on the Hudson*, chs. ii, v-vi; H. L. Osgood, *Am. Col. in the 17th Century*, II, chs. ii, xiii.

Special Accounts. — (a) ECONOMIC AND SOCIAL. (See refs. under this heading, ch. iv and ch. vii, appropriate chs. on the Middle Colonies; see also "Special Accounts," ch. viii); A. M. Earle, *Early Colonial Days in New York;* M. A. Hanna, *Trade of the Delaware District before the Revolution;* Esther Singleton, *Dutch N. Y.* (b) LAND AND LABOR. H. S. Cooley, "A Study of Slavery in New Jersey," in *J. H. Stud.*, ser. XIV; Irving Elting, "Dutch and Village Communities, *etc.*," in *J. H. Stud.*, ser. IV; C. A. Herrick, *White Servitude in Pa.;* W. P. Holcomb, "Pa. Boroughs," in *J. H. Stud.*, ser. IV; E. V. Morgan, "Slavery in New York," in *Am. Hist. Assoc. Papers*, V, 335–350; R. F. Seyboldt, *Apprenticeship in Colonial N. Y. and New Engl.;* W. R. Shepherd, *Hist. of Proprietary Govt. in*

Pa. in *Columb. Stud.*, VI (land system, chs. i-v); C. W. Spencer, "Land System of Col. New York," in *Proc. N. Y. State Hist. Soc. Assoc.*, XVI, 15–164; Edward Turner, *Negro in Pa.* (c) RELIGION AND EDUCATION. (See refs. to ch. xii and xv, "Special Accounts"); Lucy Bittinger, *German Religious Life in Colonial Times;* E. T. Corwin, *Hist. of Dutch Reformed Church;* W. H. Kilpatrick, *Dutch Schs. of New Netherland and Colonial N.Y.;* Thomas Woody, *Hist. of Quaker Education in Pa.* and *Hist. of Quaker Education in N. J.;* F. J. Zwierlein, *Religion in New Netherland.*

Biographies. — (See references to ch. viii); M. D. Learned, *Life of Francis Daniel Pastorius.*

Contemporary Accounts. — (a) BIBLIOGAPHY: Channing, Hart and Turner, *Guide*, §§ 42–43, 122–126; W. P. Trent (ed.), *Camb. Hist. Am. Lit.*, I, see "Contemp. Accts.," ch. viii. (b) RECORDS AND COLLECTIONS: E. L. Bogart and C. M. Thompson (eds.), *Readings in the Econom. Hist. of U. S.*, chs. ii-v; A. B. Hart (ed.), *Contemporaries*, chs. xxii-xxvi; Hugh Hastings (ed.), *Ecclesiastical Records of State of N. Y.* (7 vols., 1621–1810); C. H. McIlwain (ed.), Peter Wraxall, "An Abridgment of the Indian Records of New York" (1678–1751), (*Harvard Stud.*, XXI); Mennonite protest on slavery, in *Pa. Mag. of Hist.*, IV, 28–30; L. B. Schmidt and E. B. Ross (eds.), *Readings in Econom. Hist. of Am. Agricult.*

71. Conditions of Settlement and Development

THE development of the middle colonies was retarded by several factors. The Dutch and the Swedes
Retarding Influences failed to colonize on a large scale. The richest part of New York, the Mohawk Valley, was not yet open to settlement, because it was held by the Iroquois Indians. The land in the Hudson Valley was largely monopolized by a comparatively few great land owners, thus retarding the rapid growth of population. In Pennsylvania, in Delaware, and most of New Jersey, the settlers were few until late in the century. Hence relatively little economic and social progress had been made in this part of America, except at a few centers of population, such as Philadelphia, northern New Jersey, and New York City. One factor

of great influence was the diversity of racial stocks and of religious sects that settled in this region. The result was a complex and bewildering variety of political and social ideas and institutions. The contrast in comparison with the South and New England was striking.

Other influences which retarded early development in this section were the following: lack of any legislative assembly in New Netherland and New York; slow development of local self-government; the scarcity of educated leaders in church and state; resulting slow progress of intellectual life; the lack of a press and inadequate educational facilities. The whole region was under proprietary forms of government, with its attendant disadvantages, especially with respect to the distribution of land; since all unassigned lands were the property of the proprietor.

The town of New Amsterdam, after 1664 called New York, dominated this region for most of the century. Economic and Social Factors It was a commercial port with the main interest in trade and commerce. Ship-owners and agents, sailors and innkeepers, traders, manufacturers, and artisans were in evidence. Agricultural progress was slow at first, because of the great interest of the Dutch in the fur trade and the difficulties the small land holder labored under. The cosmopolitan character of the population made for toleration and a more flexible and joyful social life, with a less provincial attitude towards most problems than in Puritan New England for example.

The number of people in the middle colonies during the seventeenth century was considerably less than in Number, Character, and Distribution the other two sections. The region developed slowly because of the economic and social influences just mentioned. When the Dutch lost their colony in 1664 perhaps 7000 people were living in this territory — not a quarter as many as in Massachusetts. In 1689 the white population of New York reached 16,000 and that of New Jersey 14,000. The population of Virginia at the same time was 60,000. Before Penn arrived in 1682 perhaps a thousand people were settled in the Pennsylvania-Delaware region. Immigration into Pennsylvania and Delaware increased somewhat, so that by 1689 the population rose to about 12,000. At this date the total population of the middle colonies was perhaps 45,000, about half that of either New England or the South. In this population many racial elements appeared and many religious beliefs were held.

The middle colonies were known as the "bread colonies" and from an agricultural standpoint they were the great producers of cereals. Farmers, traders, and artisans made up the bulk of the population. While numerous large landed estates existed especially in New York, the small farm predominated in the other middle colonies. The servile and semi-servile classes — negroes and white indentured servants, were more numerous than in New England but much less so than in the Southern colonies. The great bulk of the population was concentrated in New York City, northern New Jersey, and Philadelphia, leaving the great western regions of Pennsylvania and New York unoccupied.

72. Land Problems

The land systems in the middle colonies, quite unlike those of New England, were based on the principle

The Proprietary System of income or profit to the proprietors, who looked on their provinces as private estates. They expected a return from their property, and hence were eager to sell land for cash or to impose some form of rental for its use— such as annual quit rents. Moreover a proprietor might dispose of an entire province; or by process of inheritance it might be divided among many heirs. Thus the Duke of York sold New Jersey, 1664, a part of his great estate, to Lord Berkeley and Sir George Carteret, and later many new proprietors were added. William Penn at one time mortgaged the great colony of Pennsylvania for £6600. It was the proprietor who granted lands, erected manors, fixed the price, rental, and in other ways determined the conditions on which land might be granted to colonists. The proprietors, however, were anxious to encourage immigration in order to enhance the price of lands; therefore in the early years of settlement land was granted very freely and on easy terms.

New Netherland, for example, was a proprietary province, the West India Company being originally the Large and immediate or actual proprietor, while ab-Small Grants solute title was in the Dutch government. In 1629 the " Charter of Freedoms and Exemptions " gave rise to the form of grant known as patroonships, already described. They consisted of immense tracts along the river, indefinite in size, but some reached to 200,000 acres. This form of grant, however, declined under the Dutch. A provision in the " Charter of Exemptions " allowed for smaller grants to private persons who settled on their own account. With the consent of the director and council, a colonist might take as much land as he could properly improve. In 1640 greater stress was laid on these small tracts so that grants of moderate size increased in the province as a whole.

The Dutch did not develop a definite system of quit rents, though in some of the patents the payment of Tenant a tenth of the product of the soil was re-Farming quired. The farms of the colony of Rensselaerswyck for instance were let out at a fixed rent payable in grain, beaver, wampum, or else let out on shares at halves or thirds. The tenant was bound to keep the buildings and tools in repair.

In New Netherland, individuals and families also pushed into unoccupied territory, extinguished Indian titles, and later obtained the sanction of Town Grants the company. When settlers in sufficient numbers had bought or leased land within a given area and built dwellings, rights of local government were bestowed by the director and council; and the settlements became a village or town, for example Brooklyn. After town patents were issued, the town itself granted land within its boundary, and in some towns a system of common lands, fields, pastures, woodland, etc., arose as in New England. Thus a democratic element existed, even in the Dutch period, based on the ownership of small grants, in opposition to the aristocratic large landholders.

Complaint was made as early as 1654 that illegal title to large tracts of land had been obtained from the Indians and then conveyed to others without Illegal Claims to out any record made in the office of the Land secretary of the province. This practice in connection with the huge proprietary grants, delayed settlement and the increase of population. Lands were held for speculative purposes and remained "for long years wild and waste without considerable improvement." Little land was for sale except at exorbitant prices. The director general and council therefore annulled many claims except "whatever by fair account they can show they have paid and given for said lands."

When the English seized New Netherland, Governor Nicholls confiscated the estate of the West India Company, thus securing for the Duke of York all the unoccupied land in the province. Large grants were speedily made by the English governors, which came to be known by special names; such as Fordham, Pelham, Phillipsburgh, organized somewhat like manors. The Van Cortland family acquired fifteen thousand acres of land for example. Under Governor Dongan there developed the famous Livingston Manor.

Grants Under the English Governors

This tendency towards the manorial form of grant became a basis for a social and political development of New York, extended by family alliances and a system of tenant rights which existed for several generations. Group settlements also developed, largely on the model of the New England town, as those on Eastern Long Island, and in Westchester County. From the time of the administration of Governor Dongan (1686) patents or deeds recorded contained a provision for a quit rent.

It was said of the English Governor Fletcher (1693) that " the most extraordinary favors of former governors were but petty grants in comparison to his. He was a generous man, and gave the King's lands by parcels of upwards of one hundred thousand acres to a man, and to some particular favorites four or five times that quantity." To Captain John Evans he granted a large tract of unappropriated land eighteen miles in length on the Hudson river, and extending thirty miles inland. Lord Bellomont, Fletcher's successor, declared " that this whole province is given away to thirty persons," and that the best lands were held by a few; that therefore it " can never be well peopled, for men will never care to become tenants to proprietors of land in this province, when they can buy fee simple lands in the Jerseys for five pounds per hundred acres, and I believe as well in Pennsylvania."

The grant of Pennsylvania to William Penn by Charles II was in the nature of a fief, a feudal principality, such as still existed in England at that time. Penn and his heirs were absolute proprietors who might dispose of their land as they saw fit. Penn's early plans for distribution provided for the sale and rental of land. To every master of a family he promised 200 acres at a rental of one penny per acre. He also offered 50 acres per head for every man and maid servant at the same rental. Poor servants paid one penny to one half penny per acre rental after they became free. Thus land was not granted on the basis of free tenure; the estate was perpetually subject to a quit rent; and also to forfeiture under certain conditions. The purpose of Penn is shown by a letter to a friend in which he said that he must either be paid by purchase or secure a rent from his land for other use. Else, "I should make nothing out of my country."

William Penn and Land Grants

Penn was absent from his colony from 1684 to 1699, with the result that many titles were disputed, many frauds were committed and many quit rents uncollected. Grants were made in loose fashion and when later surveys were made there was great confusion, due to overlapping grants. "Squatting" occurred from the first, and this added to the confusion.

Abuses of the System

The weakness of the land system was the lack of supervised settlement, and of pre-surveys; and a poor administrative system that made "squatting" possible and hindered the collection of quit rents. Later, great trouble arose between Penn, his heirs, and the Assembly over the taxation of proprietary lands and the collection of the quit rents. The distribution of land was haphazard, wasteful, and encouraged speculation; that is, much of the land granted was not taken up for settlement but to hold for a rise in price. The revenue features irritated the colonists and became one of the great grievances of the frontiersmen in this as in other colonies.

The rights of the two original proprietors, Lord Berkeley and Sir George Carteret, to East Jersey were

The Land Problem in New Jersey

sold to William Penn and his associates in 1682. "Concessions" were published providing for moderate-sized grants for colonists and large estates for the proprietors. The proprietors gradually divided the unimproved lands among themselves and sought to plant colonists on a part of their shares.

West Jersey was also sold to Penn and his associates, in 1674 and 1676. In 1677 regulations for land grants were proposed by Penn, including plans for the sale of land in lots of a thousand acres. Land in lots of 5000 acres was organized into townships with reserves for the proprietors and a system of headrights similar to that in Pennsylvania. Settlement was required within six months after the survey. The most striking characteristic of the land systems of the Middle Colonies is the revenue feature and the large amounts of the best lands that were reserved for the proprietor or granted to wealthy men in large tracts.

73. Industries and Occupations

The industries and occupations of the Dutch and English were conditioned in part by the attitude of the

Dutch Policy and Accomplishments

mother country. The Dutch looked on New Netherland much as England looked on her colonies. As early as 1630 it was provided that colonies should not make woolen, linen, or cotton cloth, "nor weave any other stuffs on pain of being banished." The Dutch also encouraged the production of naval stores, and ship timber formed one of the early items of export from New Netherland. The Dutch set up two sawmills on Manhattan Island as early as 1628, and other mills were erected, especially at Albany, which became a center of lumber trade. Another industry started by the Dutch was distilling. When the English took possession of the New Netherland in 1661 several breweries and distilleries were in operation.

New York under the English was subject to the Navigation Acts, and in so far as they were enforced, the colonists of New York were diverted from manufactures. The middle region was that of the "bread colonies." It contained large natural resources including forests — for lumber, ships, and stores. A few ships were built at New York before 1678. Lord Cornbury stated in 1708 that most of the ships used in New York trade were made in the local shipyards. But the New England builders constructed at less cost, so that shipbuilding developed slowly.

Progress in New York under the English

The naval stores industry hardly got started before the eighteenth century, but some production of masts and ship timber occurred as early as 1698. Lumber products, however, were made in large quantities; a report of 1701 declared that there were forty sawmills in the colony. One on the Livingston Manor was operating with twelve saws. The cost of a small mill was about $1000; operated by one man and a boy it could saw 1000 feet of boards a day. Other lumber products were clapboards, shingles, and staves, largely produced for the West Indian trade.

Lumber Products

Cloth making was widespread as early as 1670. Daniel Denton reports, "They sowe a store of flax, which they make everyone cloth of for their own wearing, as also woolen cloth, and lensey-woolsey." And Governor

Cornbury informed the Lords of Trade in 1705 that linens and woolens are made: "As for the woolens they are already too good; the colonials are making coarse cloth; good serges are being made. I fear that England will not long be needed to supply cloth for this colony."

Cloth Making

Little progress was made in the non-agricultural industries in New Jersey and Pennsylvania before 1689. One writer reports "one Iron Work already in East Jersey by 1685," and iron manufacturing was started in Pennsylvania in 1692, according to the printer Andrew Bradford, who said,

Industries in New Jersey and Pennsylvania

> "A certain place here is where some begun,
> To try some mettle and have made it run,
> Wherein was Iron absolutely found
> At once was known about some forty pounds."

From such small beginnings grew one of the greatest industries in the United States.

The lumber industry was established also in Pennsylvania and New Jersey. Another writer describes (1685) "The Pine Tree growth here, out of which is made Pitch, Tar, Rosin and Turpentine." William Penn wrote in 1683: "Two ships have been freighted to the Barbados, with house and pipe staves since my coming." In 1693 the assembly passed a law that all staves should be of "good sound well seasoned white oak timber, for hogsheads, tierces, and barrels." A tannery was also in use in Philadelphia as early as 1683, and nearby "several sorts of good clay of which bricks, Earthenware, and Tobacco Pipes are made." Other evidence of manufactures in the middle colonies will appear in the discussion of trade and commerce.

74. Trade and Commerce

The Dutch Colony of the New Netherland was largely based on the fur trade, and to 1638 it was monopolized by the West India Company. Throughout the period of Dutch rule, furs could legally be exported only to the Netherlands. Further regulation of trade occurred through a proclamation issued by the governor in 1638. It prohibited persons in the employ of the company from trading in peltries; from exporting furs without permission; from " clandestine " traffic, and from selling powder or guns to the Indians. Duties were placed on imports from and exports to the Netherlands. In 1640 all goods shipped from New Netherland were to be landed at the Company's warehouse. In 1645 private merchants were allowed to trade, but under strict regulation, such as a requirement for the examination of cargoes by customs officials. A report on the fur trade in 1626, shows that one cargo consisted of 7246 beaver skins, nearly a thousand otter skins, besides others valued at $25,000.

By this time also trade was carried on between New Netherland and New England and tobacco was imported from Virginia. This trade increased after 1652. The Dutch West India Company wished trade only between the colony and the mother country. Not until 1659 did the company allow the experiment of trade wth France, Spain, Italy, the Caribbean Islands, and elsewhere. The next year the Amsterdam directors approved of trade with the English colony of Virginia. "A free and unshackled commerce with that nation must be conducive to the propriety of your city and its inhabitants." In fact complaints were made in 1647 that the revenue had been "greatly defrauded" because of smuggling of furs to New England and Virginia, for shipment thence to England, and by the introduction of foreign merchandise in vessels which ran past Fort Amsterdam during the night." The next year complaint was made of Scottish merchants and small traders who were "underselling" and ruining the trade. They were prohibited from trading further unless they built houses in New Amsterdam and lived there for three consecutive years. In the early period little was exported except furs. Indeed in 1638 it was said that "nothing comes from New Netherland, but beaver skins, mincks, and other furs." Nor does the export trade seem to have developed much up to the time of the loss of the colony to England.

Commerce developed slowly under English control. Indeed as late as 1679 a traveler remarked that "this country yields in abundance everything most essential for life if the inhabitants so apply it. Its shipping does not amount to much, for the reason they have everything at home, and have little occasion to borrow or buy from their neighbors." A report of Governor Andros in 1678 gives some idea of the nature of the trade at this date. "Our produce is land provisions of all sorts as of wheat exported yearly about 60,000 bushels, pease, beefe, pork, and some refuse fish, tobacco, beaver, peltry, or furs from the Indians, Deale Oak timber, planks, pipe staves, lumber, horses, and pitch and tarr lately began to be made. Comodityes imported are all sorts of English manufacture for Christians, and blanketts, Duffells, etc., for Indians about 50,000 lb. yearly. Pemaquid (Maine) affords merchantable fish and masts." Governor Dongan the next year comments on the West Indian trade as made up of "Flour, Bread, Pease, Pork and some times horses; the return from thence for the most part is rumm, which pays the king a considerable excise, and

Progress of the English

some molasses which serves the people to make Drink and pays no custom."

An interesting account of the trade of Pennsylvania is given by Gabriel Thomas, in his account of Penn-
Early trade sylvania (1698), which describes the trade
of Pennsyl- as follows: "Horses, Pipe-Staves, Pork
vania and
New Jersey and Beef Salted and Barrelled up, Bread
and Flower, all sorts of Grain, Pease, Beans, Skins, Furs, Tobacco, Pot-Ashes, Wax etc., which are bartered for Rumm, Sugar, Molasses, Silver, Negroes, Salt, Wine, Linen, Household-Goods etc." This same writer says that as a result of this trade, silver is more plentiful in Pennsylvania than in England, considering the number of people. The New Jersey trade as described by this same writer, consisted mostly of skins, tar, pitch and rosin, rice, cranberries, oil and whalebone, and live-stock sent to Philadelphia.

75. Social Conditions

Perhaps the most important social characteristic of the middle colonies was the cosmopolitan character of
Racial the population together with the great va-
Diversity riety of racial elements and religious sects
to be found in this section. This was true from the founding of New Netherland. Holland had been noted for a century and more as a land where civil and religious liberty had advanced farther than in any other country of Europe. Hence the middle colonies under the Dutch government were an asylum for every sect; and representatives of almost all the European races had taken up their residence in this free country.

It was natural that colonies founded by the Dutch should resemble the mother country. As early as 1664 it was reported that fourteen languages were spoken on Long Island, and by 1674 eighteen nationalities were represented in New York. Another report reads "we are, if I may be allowed to say so, born cosmopolite." John Miller who described New York in 1692 said, "Our chief unhappiness here is, too great a mixture of nations, and English the least part; French Protestants, Dutch, etc." In the seventeenth century representatives of the following races lived in New Netherland and New York. The Walloons, from the southern provinces of the Netherlands, now Belgium, spoke French. They had sought refuge in Holland and furnished some of the first emigrants to New Netherland. They were skilled in the art of manufacturing linen and woolen cloth. Other elements besides the Dutch, were English, Welsh, Jews, Swedes, French, Germans, Scotch, Irish, Scotch-Irish, Negroes and Indians.

Delaware, New Jersey, and Pennsylvania were also greatly influenced by the variety of races that settled in these regions. The Dutch were on the "South River," the Delaware, as early as 1623; and were followed in 1638 by the Swedes. After the English conquest in 1664, Englishmen and New Englanders entered the territory. When Penn arrived in 1682, a thousand or more people had already settled along the Delaware, near Philadelphia, Wilmington, and on the West Jersey shore. The Dutch had also settled several towns in northern New Jersey. After 1664 New Englanders settled along the Passaic River, and English and Scotch in the Perth Amboy region, New Jersey. English Quakers occupied the territory in southwest New Jersey, so that by 1681 there were 1400 in this region opposite Philadelphia.

The English Quakers admitted to Pennsylvania many Germans and later other races. In fact William Penn advertised his province extensively in Germany in order to attract immigrants. The Germans who came to Pennsylvania before 1700 tended to settle in compact groups. Since there was little intermarriage with other races, they preserved to a large extent their language, religion, educational and social ideals. Several German religious sects arrived early; the more important being the Mennonites. The main body of the Germans who arrived later belonged to the two principal German churches, the Reformed and the Lutheran. The smaller German religious sects were, generally speaking, liberal in their views, opposed to dogma, and individualistic in their interpretation of the scriptures. The Mennonites of Germantown held views very similar to the Quakers. Thus they were opposed to war, higher education, and negro slavery, and in favor of religious liberty. Francis Daniel Pastorius was their most important leader, a teacher, a master of seven or eight languages, and well read in science and philosophy. He had studied jurisprudence at the University of Strasburg, Basle, and Jena and was for a time a lecturer on law at Frankfort.

One other racial group migrated to Pennsylvania in considerable numbers before 1689, a body of Welsh Quakers, settled in a compact group retaining their native language. Thus each of four languages was spoken by a considerable number of people — English, German, Welsh, or Swedish in Philadelphia and the surrounding territory. The Welsh supplied most of the physicians in the early days of the province, and numbered among their leaders Thomas Lloyd, deputy governor of Pennsylvania. Few Scotch, Scotch-Irish, or Irish, appeared in Pennsylvania until later in the eighteenth century.

This diversity in race, language, and religion is one of the important factors that affected the political, social, and economic development of the middle colonies. It was this factor that accounts so largely for their pe-

culiar religious and educational history. The various races and sects reacted on each other, and thus pro-
Social duced a great variety of habits, customs,
Ideals and institutions. One effect of liberal and varied ideas and institutions was the absence of a narrow provincial spirit, prominent particularly in the Puritan colonies.

In Pennsylvania particularly we find the striking effects of racial and religious diversity. Religious liberty or the absence of religious persecution and of such crowd obsessions as the witchcraft delusion may be noted. A humanitarian impulse can be seen in the mild criminal code enacted by the Assembly, in which the only crimes punishable by death were treason and murder. At the same time in England two hundred or more capital crimes stood on the statute books; and nearly forty were punishable by death in the New England colonies. Penn also wished to abolish primogeniture and imprisonment for debt.

The attitude of the Quakers towards the Indians is shown in the " Great Treaty " made by Penn in 1683. It resulted in seventy years of peace and friendship, in contrast with almost perpetual warfare in most of the other colonies. Land purchases were always made of the Indians before land grants were made. The opposition of the Quakers to war was of course one of the important reasons for the friendly relations they established with the Indians. It may be noted also that the first important public protest against negro slavery was made by the Germantown Friends (Mennonites) in 1688.

The aristocratic organization of society of the old world was mirrored more or less in New Netherland and New York. The Patroons, manorial lords, and large land holders took the place of the nobility. These were

the "gentlemen." Alongside them were also yeomen
or small farmers, servants and slaves. The Dutch West
Structure India Company encouraged the importa-
of Society tion of slaves, and in 1640 promised to
"exert itself to provide patroons and colonists, on their
order, with as many "Blacks as possible." Under the
Duke's Laws of 1664 in New York, slavery existed, and
a servant could be held by indenture for a term of
years or for life.

In New Jersey and Pennsylvania the great bulk of
the people were small farmers, land being plentiful
and cheap. Thus, originally, society, in these colonies,
was less sharply divided into classes than in New York
and hence was more democratic. Another influence that
affected social structure was the relation of the clergy
to society. Among the Quakers and some of the other
religious sects the line between the clergy and the lay
religious leaders of the people was, contrary to the Puritan ideal, almost indiscernible. No combination of
clergy and magistrates sought to maintain an oligarchy like that of Massachusetts. The opposition to a
division of society into ranks of social superiors and
inferiors explains the refusal of Quakers to doff the
hat in the presence of a magistrate (or even a king), a
serious offense in Massachusetts at this time.

76. Religion and Morals

The state of religion and morals in New Amsterdam
is set forth by Pastor Backerus who wrote to the Classis
Lack of of Amsterdam in 1648, that in his congre-
Churches and gation "most of them are very ignorant
Ministers in
New Nether- in regard to true religion, and very much
land given to drink. To this they are led by the
seventeen tap-houses here. . . If you could obtain
from the honorable Directors an order for closing

these places, except three or four, I have no doubt the source of much evil and great offense would be removed." The population of New Amsterdam at this date was hardly more than 600. The Directors of the Dutch West India Company also wrote a letter to Governor Stuyvesant (1652), complaining that the " clime does not reform well the manners of individuals, and that many complaints were received for drunkenness and other vices " even among high officials. As late as 1649 no church building had been erected, money previously collected for this purpose having been misapplied by the Director General, and the church was without revenue.

Up to 1654 no Dutch towns, clergymen, nor churches existed other than at New Amsterdam, Albany, and in two of the Patroonships. The people attended worship at New Amsterdam and came to communion and other services "at their great inconvenience. Some had to travel three hours to reach this place." Up to 1660 only two additional ministers arrived, making four altogether for the whole colony. By 1664, however, there was more rapid development; and when the English took control there were twelve Dutch Reformed churches in the colony.

The complex religious character of the population in 1655 is set forth by the pastor of the Dutch Reformed church, New Amsterdam. He said: " We have here Papists, Mennonites, and Lutherans among the Dutch; also many Puritans or Independents, and many Atheists and various other servants of Baal among the English under this government, who conceal themselves under the name of Christians." He mentions also that a number of Jews had arrived.

Variety of Religious Beliefs

Under the English government, after 1664, the Anglican Church made slow progress. Only a chapel existed in 1676; the Church of England was not really established until 1693, and then it was set up only in Religious
Progress
under the
English four counties, New York, Westchester, Queens, and Richmond. Several Congregational churches existed at the eastern end of Long Island, and in the so-called English town at the west end of the island. By 1670 several flourishing Quaker settlements were made on Long Island. The Lutherans had also established two churches by 1668. In the Delaware region the Swedish Lutherans had established four churches before Penn arrived in 1682. Governor Andros, describing New York in 1678, says that it contained twenty-four towns or villages and "religions of all sorts — one church of England, several Presbyterians and Independents, Quakers, Anabaptists of several sects, some Jews, but Presbyterians and Independents most numerous and substantial."

The Fundamental Constitutions granted by Berkeley and Carteret in 1683 for New Jersey provided that the Religious
Liberty in
New Jersey people "shall in no way be molested or pre-judged for religious persuasions and exercise in matters of faith and worship, nor be compelled to frequent and maintain any place of worship or ministry whatsoever." Thus religious liberty was practically guaranteed in New Jersey, and Quakers, Congregationalists, Dutch Reformed, and Baptists and other sects soon set up their churches.

In earlier chapters it was pointed out that no one can appreciate colonial Massachusetts without an understanding of "Puritanism," particularly William Penn
and Religious
Liberty with respect to its hostility to religious liberty. In like manner, to appreciate Pennsylvania one must understand the spirit and methods of "Quakerism" in its relations to this same fundamental problem. The principles on which the founders of Pennsylvania based their government, and those on which (in the early years at least) the leaders acted, were quite in contrast with the principles of the founders both of Virginia and Massachusetts. The religious and political ideas developed by George Fox and William Penn were essentially based on the principle of religious liberty. Penn wrote (1670) a book called "*The Great Case of Liberty of Conscience Briefly Debated and Defended.*" He planned his colony as an asylum for the persecuted of all faiths. Unlike the Puritans, the Friends stood for the principle of religious liberty for all men, not merely for the establishment of their own peculiar ideas of truth. Said Penn, "Every person that does or shall reside therein shall have and enjoy the free possession of his or her faith and exercise of worship towards God, in such way and manner as every person shall in conscience believe is most acceptable to God." Thus there was perfect liberty of conscience, which made possible the variety of religious sects found in Pennsylvania from its first settlement.

77. Intellectual Life

A responsibility for the education of the children of settlers in the New Netherland was recognized by the

Dutch Theory of Education

Dutch West India Company, by the States General, and by the Dutch Reformed Church. The latter had been the established church of Holland from 1581. The educational ideals and motives which prevailed among the leaders of the Dutch Reformed Church appear in the legislation of the Synod of Dort (1618–1619). One article reads: "Schools, in which the young shall be properly instructed in the principles of Christian doctrine, shall be instituted, not only in cities, but also in towns and

country places, where heretofore none have existed.
The Christian magistracy shall be requested, that well
qualified persons may be employed, and enabled to de-
vote themselves to the service, and especially that the
children of the poor may be gratuitously instructed,
and not be excluded from the benefit of the schools."
Another article reads, "The consistory in every congregation shall be careful to provide good schoolmasters
who are able, not only to instruct children in reading,
writing and grammar, and the liberal sciences; but also
to teach them the Catechism, and the first principles of
religion." It is thus clear that the Dutch theory of
education provided for parochial, religious elementary
schools in towns and villages, under the control of the
Dutch Reformed Church, free to children of poor parents; a system quite as liberal as that of New England
in this period.

The educational and religious affairs of the Dutch
West India Company were placed under the direction
Progress in   of the Classis of Amsterdam, an eccle-
New Nether-   siastical body with representatives from a
land   a group of churches. It was provided in
the charter of the Company that it should bind itself
"to maintain good and fit preachers, school masters,
and comforters of the sick," the latter to act as assistants to the pastor. Two other officers of the church
were the "voorlezer," or reader and church clerk, and
the "voorsanger," or chorister. These two offices were
often combined with that of teacher, so that the latter
was in reality a church official.

The Company tried to shift the responsibility for religion and education in the "Charters of Freedom and
Exemptions" (1629) by providing that patroons and
colonists "should endeavor to find out ways and means
whereby they may support a minister and schoolmas-

ter." Very little was accomplished by this method. In fact only two of the colonies, other than that settled by the Company, appointed a teacher, one at Rensselaerwyck and one on the " South " or Delaware River.

Finally in 1638 the West India Company appointed a teacher, at New Amsterdam, and thus the first school was established. Owing to the weakness of the church, it was supported or managed by five groups, the West India Company, the Classis of Amsterdam, the Dutch Reformed Church in New Amsterdam, the Governor and Council, and (after 1653) the Burgomasters of the City of New Amsterdam. During the Dutch period a small salary was paid by the West India Company. Those pupils who were able paid tuition fees, as was the case in some towns in New England. " The poor and needy who ask to be taught for God's sake he shall teach for nothing." Later the school came entirely under the control of the church. The West India Company also provided for a Latin School in 1659, and sent over a teacher who received an annual salary of about two hundred dollars.

Ten out of the twelve Dutch settlements had established schools before the English occupation in 1664, all of the same general type. The teacher held one or more positions in the church, and was also the court messenger or town clerk. Support usually came from a number of sources: a small grant made by the town, tuition fees, from the director general and council, and from the church. Control was exercised jointly by the church and local court. Thus were reproduced in New Amsterdam the principal features of the school system of the mother country — an elementary school for reading and writing, and sometimes arithmetic; together with the catechism and other religious instruction; jointly managed and supported by church and civil authorities.

In New Jersey the first action on education was taken by the Assembly of West Jersey in 1682. State aid in the form of land was inaugurated by the grant of an island to the town of Burlington, the income of which was to be employed by the overseers to be appointed "for the maintaining of a school for the education of Youth within the said town." In 1693, after the union of East and West Jersey under one governor in 1690, a new act was passed. The preamble admits that "learning" had been much neglected in the province; and provided that the inhabitants of any town "shall and may" by a warrant from a justice of the peace meet and choose three men "to make a *rate* [tax] for the salary and maintaining of a schoolmaster within the said town." A majority vote could bind all inhabitants to pay their proportion of the tax, and in case of refusal on non-payment by an inhabitant his property could be sold for taxes due. A few towns had established schools on their own initiative before this legislation, particularly Bergen, Newark, and Woodbridge.

Educational Legislation of New Jersey

Some effort was made by the Swedes to found schools. Governor Printz (1642) was instructed to "urge instruction and virtuous education of the young," but there is no record of the establishment of a school before the loss of the colony in 1655. The Dutch, however, did establish a school at New Amstel, now Newcastle, Delaware. The City of Amsterdam purchased the region, and agreed to colonize it and pay the salary of a teacher. A letter from the teacher in 1657 says, "I am engaged in keeping school, with twenty-five children in it, but I have no paper

New Sweden and Delaware

nor pens for the use of the children, nor slates, and pencils."

The ideals of higher education among the mass of the Quakers were decidedly weak, due especially to the fact that, unlike the Puritans, they did not believe that an educated ministry was a necessity. William Penn himself was interested in elementary education, and his original plan for schools and education is set forth in the Frame of Government (1682). The governor and provincial council were to "erect and order all public schools." The Assembly provided in 1683 that parents and guardians should have their children taught to read and write by the time they were twelve years of age, under penalty of £5. The council also, this same year, "sent for Enoch Flower, a schoolmaster, and agreed with him to teach reading, writing and casting accounts" on a tuition basis. The Philadelphia monthly meeting established a school in 1689 and employed George Keith at a salary of £50 for one year, the poor to be taught gratis.

While Penn's ideas included public education, the character of the settlers in Pennsylvania and in the other middle colonies made it difficult to carry out such a plan. With Dutch, Swedes, Germans, English, and Welsh, representing the Dutch Reformed, Lutheran, Anglican, and Quaker faiths, the tendency was for each sect to develop schools in connection with its own church.

It is thus clear that in the middle colonies the problem of education was thought of as in large part the duty of the church, sometimes aided by the civil authorities. The diversity of races and sects was a factor that hindered the growth of public education in this region.

78. Accomplishments and Problems of the Colonies in 1689

We have now completed a survey of the establishment and practices of the colonies founded or acquired Territorial by England during the seventeenth century. Acquisitions tury. What were the chief accomplishments of this effort at colonization and what the important problems still unsolved? The great accomplishment was the occupation of the Atlantic Seaboard from Maine to the southern boundary of South Carolina; the ousting of rival nations, Spain, France, and Holland, and the cancelling of their claims to territory; the successful establishment of eleven colonies; the expansion of a settled area to the region of the fall line; and the setting up of a line of defense against the Indians who had gradually been pushed back as the frontier advanced.

The English population had increased from zero in 1607 to about 220,000 in 1689; viz., New England, Diversification 80,000; middle colonies, 45,000; south- of Industries ern colonies, 95,000. Much land was distributed to many individuals and some progress had been made in exploiting the natural resources of the region. Labor systems suitable to the needs of the various sections had been developed, plantations and small farms established, trade and commerce developed, and even manufactures had commenced. Already diversification of industries had begun, especially in the northern colonies. While agriculture was the main interest, yet many important activities not strictly agricultural had been established; such as production of naval stores, shipbuilding, fishing, and textile manufactures. This diversification of industries is one indication of an advancing and complex civilization.

The development of political life and institutions is important. Of great consequence was the tendency Political of the popular assemblies to resist royal Tendencies authority and acts of Parliament, considered prejudicial to their interests.

In their religious life the colonists had made more progress than is ordinarily the case in the settlement Religious of new countries, because of the importance Toleration portance of the religious motive for colonization. While intolerance was the general rule at the beginning of settlement, toleration had made great progress, particularly in Rhode Island, Maryland, and Pennsylvania, and even in Massachusetts after the cessation of the persecution of the Quakers.

The unsolved problems were many. The struggle for the final control of the great interior between France Extent of and England was looming on the horizon English Control at the end of this period. The occupation of the frontier regions and the treatment of its future inhabitants were yet to be worked out. Rumblings of dissatisfaction were heard over land distribution; over the claims of the great proprietors; over the engrossing of large tracts by wealthy speculators, and over the inequalities of taxation and representation.

From England's standpoint certain economic developments were very unsatisfactory; particularly the non-enforcement and evasion of the navigation laws by smuggling, and the tendency of the colonists to increase their manufactures. Naturally also England viewed with alarm the increasing tendency of the assemblies to resist the royal prerogative and to object to a more effective control over the colonies.

So far the colonies had made little progress along cultural lines. In fact in some respects a retrograde movement, a drop in standards of culture was visible,

as a result of the process of occupying and developing
Slow Cultural Progress new lands. Literature, art, science, medicine, the number of learned men, and the agencies for transferring knowledge, such as books and libraries, schools and colleges, all these were distinctly on a lower plane than in the mother country. Moreover a distinct decline in religious fervor and perhaps in morals, particularly in New England, was a source of great anxiety to the clergy. In general, economic well-being had developed more rapidly than the intellectual, religious, and cultural aspects of life.

CHAPTER X

POLITICAL AND COMMERCIAL POLICY OF ENGLAND TOWARD THE COLONIES (1689–1750)

79. References

Bibliography. — See references under bibliog., chs. iii, vi, viii, xi, xiv; J. T. Adams, *Rev. New Engl.*, footnotes chs. ii, iv, v; C. M. Andrews, *Colonial Self-Govt.*, 339–340; Channing, Hart and Turner, *Guide*, §§ 36–39, 42–43, 45–48, 117, 119–121, 123–124, 126, 146, 149, 162–164; O. M. Dickerson, *Am. Col. Govt., 1696–1765*, 367–378; H. U. Faulkner, *Am. Econom. Hist.*, 115–116; E. B. Greene, *Prov. Am.*, 328–339, and *Foundations of Am. Nationality*, 255–256; Grace Griffin, *Writings on Am. Hist.*, 1906–1923; J. N. Larned, *Lit. of Am. Hist.*, 69–76.

Historical Maps. — No. 4 of this vol.; H. U. Faulkner, *Am. Econom. Hist.*, 76–77, 100–101, 115–116; D. R. Fox, *Atlas of Am. Hist.*, 12–16; E. B. Greene, *Foundations, etc.*, 224–225; Justin Winsor, *Nar. and Crit. Hist. of Am.*, maps in V.

General Accounts. — (a) BRITISH COLONIAL POLICY: See references to chs. vi, xi, xiv; C. M. Andrews, in *Cambridge Hist. of British Empire*, volume I; W. J. Ashley, *Introduc. to English Econom. Hist. and Theory*, I; and *Surveys, Historic and Economic* (smuggling, 309–335); and "The Commercial Legislation of England and the Am. Colonies, *1660–1760*," in *Quar. Journ. of Econom.*, XIV, 1–29; G. L. Beer, "Commer. Policy of Engl. Toward the Colonies," chs. iv-vii, in *Columb. Stud. in Hist.*, III, and *Old Colonial System*, I, chs. i-v; G. W. Chalmers, *Introduc. to the Hist. of the Revolt of the Am. Colonies* and *Opinions of Eminent Lawyers, etc.* (ed. 1858); William Cunningham, *Growth of Engl. Industry and Commerce*, I; F. C. Dietz, *Polit. and Social Hist. of Engl.*, ch. xvi; G. B. Hertz, *Old Colonial System*, chs. ii-iii, and *British Imperialism in the 18th Century;* J. W. Horrocks, *Short Hist. of Mercantilism;* W. T. Morgan, *English Polit. Parties and Leaders in the Reign of Queen Anne;* Thomas Pownall, *The Administration of the British Colonies;* C. G. Robertson, *England under the Hanoverians;* Gustav Schmoller, *The Mercantile System;* J. R. Seeley, *Expansion of Engl.*, ch. vi, and *Growth of Brit. Pol.*, II, pts. III–IV; G. M. Trevelyan, *England under the House of Hanover.*

(b) GENERAL ACCOUNTS: J. T. Adams, *Rev. New Engl.*, chs. ii-v; C. M. Andrews, *Colonial Period*, chs. v-vi, viii, and *Colonial Self-Govt.*, chs. i-iv, xvi-xviii; and "Colonial Commerce," in *Am. Hist. Rev.*, XX, 43–63; Carl Becker, *Begin. of Am. People*, 134–160, ch. v; H. D. Bolton and T. M. Marshall, *Coloniza. of North Am.*, ch. xix; Edward Channing, *Hist. of the U. S.*, I, ch. vi, II, chs. i, viii-ix; J. A. Doyle, *Engl. Col. in Am.*, I, ch. vi (101–112), III, ch. iv; H. U. Faulkner, *Am. Econom. Hist.*, chs. v, vii; E. B. Greene, *Provin. Am.*, chs. iii-vi, viii, x-xi, xvii; and *Provin. Governor*, chs. viii-ix, xviii; and *Foundations, etc.*, ch. vii 130–136, and ch. x; Ralph Harlow, *Growth of the U. S.*, ch. viii; W. S. McClellan, *Smuggling in Am. Colonies;* H. L. Osgood, *Am. Colonies in the 17th Cent.*, III, chs. v-vii, and *Am. Colonies in the 18th Cent.*, I, chs. i, iv-viii, xv, II, ch. xviii, pt. II, ch. i, and "England and the Colonies," in *Polit. Sci. Quart.*, XVI, 24; J. G. Palfrey, *Hist. of New Engl.*, II, ch. xv, III, ch. i. (c) COMMERCIAL CAUSES OF REVOLUTION: C. M. Andrews, *Colonial Background of the Revolution*, chs. i-ii, and "The Am. Revolution: An Interpretation," in *Am. Hist. Rev.*, XXI, 219–232; C. H. McIlwain, *The Am. Revolution, a Constitutional Interpretation*, chs. i-ii; C. H. Van Tyne, *Causes of the War of Independence*, chs. i-ii.

Special Accounts. — (a) BRITISH COMMERCIAL POLICY: C. M. Andrews, "Am. Colonial Hist.," 1690–1750, in *Am. Hist. Assoc. Rpt.*, 1898, 49–60; Herbert Bell, "West Indian Trade before the Rev.," in *Am. Hist. Rev.*, LXII, 272; Ralph Bieber, *Lords of Trade and Plantations, 1675–1696"; N. A. Brisco, "The Economic Policy of Robert Walpole," in *Columb. Stud.*, XXVII; Edward Channing, "Navigation Acts," in *Am. Ant. Soc. Proc.*, n. s. 1889, VI, 160–179; M. P. Clarke, "Board of Trade at Work," in *Am. Hist. Rev.*, XVII, 17–43; O. M. Dickerson, *Am. Colonial Govt., 1696–1765;* W. E. B. DuBois, *Suppression of the Af. Slave Trade, 1638–1870 (Harv. Stud.*, I); H. E. Egerton, "System of British Colonial Administration in 17th and 18th Cent." in *Royal Hist. Society Trans.*, 4th ser., I, 190–217; A. B. Hart (ed.), *Commonwealth Hist. Mass.*, II, chs. i, iv; D. O. McGovney, "Navigation Acts as Applied to European Trade," in *Am. Hist. Rev.*, IX, 705–734; L. P. Kellogg, "Am. Colonial Charter," in *Am. Hist. Assoc. Rpt.*, 1903, 187–341; Eleanor Lord, "Industrial Exper. in the Brit. Cols.," in *J. H. Stud.*, extra vol. no. XVII; L. M. Penson, "London Merchant's West Indian Interests in the 18th Cent.," in *Engl. Hist. Rev.*, XXXVI, 373–392; F. W. Pitman, *Devel. of Brit. West Indies*, 1700–1763; W. T. Root, *Relations of Pa.*

with the Brit. Govt., chs. i–vi; and "Lords of Trade and Plantations, *1675–1696*," in *Am. Hist. Rev.*, XXIII, 20–41; E. P. Tanner, "Colonial Agencies," in *Polit. Sci. Quart.*, XVI, 24–49. (b) BRITISH COLO. ADMINISTRATION: C. M. Andrews, "The Royal Disallowance," in *Am. Ant. Soc. Proc.*, n. s. XXIV; A. G. Dorland, "The Royal Disallowance in Mass.," in *Bulletin of Queens Univ.*, Hist. Dpt. No. 22; H. D. Hazeltine, "Appeals from Colonial Courts to the King in Council," in *Am. Hist. Assoc. Rpt.*, 1894, 299–350; E. B. Russell, "Review of Am. Colo. Leg. by the King in Council," in *Columb. Stud.*, LXIV; A. M. Schlesinger, "Appeals to the Privy Council," in *Polit. Sci. Quart.*, XXXVIII, 279–297; 433–450; G. A. Washburn, "Imperial Control of Administration of Justice," etc., (1684–1776), in *Columb. Stud.*, CV. —

Contemporary Accounts. — (a) BIBLIOGRAPHY: see bibliographies in Dickerson, Root, Russell and Washburn under "Special Accts." above; see references under "Contemporary Accts.," chs. vii and xiv; J. T. Adams, *Provincial Society*, 326–328; Channing, Hart and Turner, *Guide*, §§ 42–43, 45, 48, 117, 119–121, 123–124, 126, 146, 149, 162–164; A. R. Hasse, *Materials for a Bibliography*, etc.; *Hist. Sources in Schools*, § 73; J. N. Larned, *Lit. of Am. Hist.*, 69–76. (b) DOCUMENTS AND COLLECTIONS: E. L. Bogart and C. M. Thompson (eds.), *Readings, etc.*, 69–81, ch. iv; C. S. Brigham (ed.), "British Royal Proclamations Relating to America, 1603–1783," in *Transac. and Colls. of Am. Ant. Soc.*, XII; *Calendar of State Papers, Colonial and West Indies;* W. E. Grant (ed.), *Acts of the Privy Council, Colonial;* A. B. Hart (ed.), *Contemporaries*, II, ch. vii (Engl. Control); *Journal of the Board of Trade;* William Macdonald (ed.), *Select Charters*, nos. 22, 23, 25, 34, 43, (Nav. Act); 50 (Molasses Act); Edward Randolph, Report for 1698, is in *S. Carolina Hist. Colls.*, I; L. F. Stock (ed.), *Proceed. and Debates of the Brit. Parl. respect. North Am.*

80. Conditions in the Early Seventeenth Century

DURING most of the seventeenth century, England's political and economic control over the colonies was
Weakness of Control conspicuously weak. This was due to several influences already narrated; such as geographical isolation, the failure of English statesmen to comprehend local conditions, poorly developed administrative agencies, and inefficient officials.

It was accordingly difficult for the crown to formulate plans and policies suited to the colonies, and still more difficult to enforce them. Moreover, Parliament passed only a few laws touching colonial affairs, mainly for the purpose of regulating trade. Hence the colonists enjoyed wide latitude in their internal legislation.

While the crown encouraged the establishment of colonies, settlements were actually founded by individuals and private groups acting as proprietors and companies. English statesmen to 1660 had vague ideas of developments within the colonies, and hardly considered their exact relation to England. Policies did gradually develop, but rather as a reflex of experience and necessity, than from carefully considered plans. England was interested in the colonies as regions valuable for agricultural development, for raw materials and trade, rather than as political entities. Hence no permanent English administrative bodies were organized whose special business it was to exercise control over the colonies. Instead, England made use of various governmental agencies already organized, assisted by special temporary boards and committees, made up principally of members of the Privy Council.

Beginnings of Control

The main agency for the control of the colonies to 1660 was the King, assisted by the Privy Council and various executive boards. The king was not only the center of control but also the owner of the soil. Though the source of authority, he delegated many of his powers to others. He created proprietors and appointed governors. Special commissions relating to the colonies were also created. For example, Charles I, in 1634, created a " Board of Commissioners for Trade and Plantations."

During the civil war period (1641–1649) control over the colonies was weak, since the home government Early Attitude was engaged in the struggle between King of Parliament and Parliament. A Board of Commissioners for the Plantations, appointed by Parliament (1643), was given power to appoint governors and other officials and secure information concerning the colonies. It granted Roger Williams (1643) the Narragansett Patent; and a year later decided against the claim of Massachusetts to that region. Parliament passed some laws relating to the colonies in general between 1621 and 1650, mostly on regulation of trade. The act of 1650 declared that certain colonies, among them Virginia, " are and ought to be subordinate to and dependent upon England, and both ever since the planting thereof have been and ought to be subject to such laws, orders and regulations as are or shall be made by the Parliament of England." This act, however, seems to have had little influence between 1660 and 1750.

81. Plans of Control (1660–1689)

With the Restoration in 1660 the idea took root that the colonies ought to be subject to greater control. New Condi- The merchants and traders especially were tions becoming more interested in the colonies as sources of profit. Another problem was that of overcoming Dutch commercial competition. Still another problem was the desire to reduce English taxes and to pay off debts which had greatly increased in the twenty years from 1641 to 1660. Within the thirty years following 1660, a new problem arose, that of adequately defending the colonial frontier against the French and Indians.

In 1660 England commenced to experiment with new administrative organs. The King appointed a Com-

mittee of the Privy Council to look after colonial af-
fairs, and created two special subordinate councils, one
New   a Council of Trade and the other a Coun-
Administration cil for Foreign Plantations. For special
Agencies   purposes royal commissions were from
time to time appointed, such as those of 1664 and 1677.
In 1675 a standing committee of the Privy Council of
twenty-four members was organized, known as the
Lords of Trade, lasting till 1696. The principal business
of this body was to secure information pertaining to the
colonies. Through instructions given to these bodies the
commercial policy of England was gradually developed,
particularly the regulation of colonial trade for England's advantage; the execution of the acts of trade in
the colonies (p. 260); developing the colonies as sources
of raw materials; drawing up instructions for colonial
governors; protecting and advancing shipping; and en-
couraging the development of English manufactures.

The rise of two political ideas has been previously
discussed (p. 156). One was a plan to substitute a sys-
Plans for   tem of royal provinces in place of proprie-
Royal   tary and corporate colonies, since the latter
Colonies   especially could not be depended on to
enforce the orders of the King. To English statesmen
and merchants it seemed reasonable that national
wealth and power should have preference over that
of the colonies. Hence trade between England and
foreign countries, and that with her colonies, should
be developed and protected by the central authority.
To accomplish this result, it might be necessary to
sacrifice the special interests of individual colonies, and
govern them through royal officials, who should be solely
responsible to the King. This idea explains the increase
in the number of royal colonies (1675 and 1692). The
" Dominion of New England " was a plan to create a

very large royal colony in order the more easily to enforce political and commercial policies.

82. Division of Powers

The effect of the revolution of 1688 was to take away power from the King and place it in the hands Underlying of Parliament. Though the theory of the Ideas absolute power of Parliament was developing in England, this was not true in the colonies. For the colonists continued to think of their connection with the mother country through the crown rather than Parliament. Nevertheless, though the power of the crown was weakening in England, the King endeavored to exercise his prerogative in the colonies much as if the English revolution had never occurred. The colonial assemblies on the other hand were influenced by the shifting of the balance of power in England from the King to Parliament, and sometimes acted as if their own assemblies bore much the same relation to the King, and his agent, the royal governor, as did Parliament to the King. While the assemblies rarely denied the legal right of Parliament to legislate for the colonies, they did not hesitate to evade and nullify its acts.

To understand the attitude of the colonies towards England, a picture of the division of powers between The Central the mother country and the colonies is es-Government sential. The center of government and chief source of power was the King, acting through various executive committees, councils, and boards. The colonies admitted, with some reservations, that the central government had the right to exercise the following powers: diplomatic relations with foreign countries; treaties; defense of the empire, war and peace, army and navy; patrol of the seas; coinage; post office; regulation of trade and commerce by general statutes and customs duties. The King and his officers carried out the laws of Parliament and formulated plans for the development and application of a national policy. Parliament passed acts, for the most part regulating trade and external relations; but the administration was in the hands of the King. He governed the royal colonies through royal officials. He granted commissions and gave instructions to royal governors. He administered the crown lands and made treaties with the Indians.

From England's standpoint the powers of the colonial assemblies were limited in many respects. First of all,

Limitations of Colonial Assemblies King and Parliament charters granted by the crown had from the first forbidden the assemblies to pass laws directly contrary to those of England. In most of the colonies the laws were subject to veto by the royal governor. In the next place the " King in Council " could review the legislation of most of the colonial assemblies; that is, he could approve or disallow their laws. The Privy Council could act as a Court of Appeals and reverse decisions of colonial courts. The assemblies could not impeach the royal governors. All these limitations were strictly legal and in accordance with charters, commissions, and instructions, and other acts, which determined beforehand the conditions on which the King allowed colonies to be established and to develop.

The colonists insisted that there were also limitations on the King, on his prerogative, and on Parliament. These limitations were based on the colonial interpretation of Magna Carta, and of their own charters; on the rather vague phrase " rights of Englishmen," and on the doctrine of natural rights. This latter doctrine was discussed before 1750, and was identified with the notion that the authority of the King was limited by what was just and reasonable. Because Parliament seldom meddled with strictly local concerns up to 1750, but confined its acts principally to the regulation of trade, the question of division of power arose usually between the King and the assemblies, rather than between the assemblies and Parliament.

83. King, Council, Boards, and Parliament in Action

The King, acting through his agents, was the source of authority. He controlled the crown lands in the royal colonies. When granted or sold they were subject to quit rents and other fees which would bring in royal revenue. In 1689 the only royal colonies were Virginia, New York, and New Hampshire; by 1754 four more had been added: New Jersey, North Carolina, South Carolina, and Georgia. In addition, Massachusetts was a semi-royal colony from 1692, and Maryland was a royal province from 1691 to 1715. The King, through proclamations, orders in council, commissions and instructions to royal governors, exercised great power. (See p. 273.)

One of the first pronouncements of James II was that the colonists did not " need general assemblies, and ought not to have them." Thus the plan of a government by governor and council, without assemblies, was tried out, as we have seen, in the experiment of the Dominion of New England under Andros. This failed but emphasis continued to be laid on the King's " prerogative." This term was broad and elusive, and to the colonists it seemed very dangerous.

Blackstone declared (1753) that the prerogative was that "special preëminence which the king hath over and above all persons, and out of the course of common law, in right of his regal dignity . . . that it can only be applied to those rights and capacities which the king enjoys alone in contra-distinction to others." In practice, as embodied in royal instructions, it embraced the whole field of administration and hence was distinctly hostile to the principles of self-government which the colonists wished to develop. Thus, when the New York assembly passed a law requiring triennial elections, in order to lessen the power of the governor, the act was disallowed by the Privy Council on the ground that it was a "very high infringement upon the prerogative of the crown."

The Privy Council, acting for the King, issued "orders in council," on a great variety of subjects. The The Privy commissions and instructions for royal governors, drawn up by the Board of Trade, were approved by the Privy Council. The standing council of the Board of Trade examined laws passed by the colonial assemblies, occasionally even those of Connecticut and Rhode Island, and then a report was made to the Privy Council. Those found to be contrary to royal prerogative, to acts of Parliament, to English common law, and others thought to be prejudicial to England's economic interests were disallowed. Nevertheless the records mention only 469 cases of actual disallowances of colonial laws out of 8563 submitted. Thus the assemblies were to a large degree actually self-governing. The Privy Council sitting as a court of appeals heard cases appealed from colonial courts, some of which were of great significance. The actual number of such appeals appears to have been only 65.

Besides the King and Privy Council, numerous other English agencies and boards, all of them under the authority of the crown, were active in carrying out England's political and economic policies. For example, the executive departments, whose heads made up the cabinet, gradually became more and more influential.

Departments and Boards Officials The Treasury Board, with its First Lord of the Treasury, had control of finance, revenue, etc. Subordinate to this board was the Customs Board or Commissioner of Customs, responsible for the enforcement of the navigation acts and the collection of the duties levied on goods exported or imported. Under its authority were the officials of the customs service. In the colonies royal officials such as the naval officers, collectors, and customs house officials, were stationed at the customs houses established at various ports along the Atlantic coast, and in Virginia and Maryland on the important rivers.

Collectors of customs were appointed from England as early as 1676. Edward Randolph, the first Collector of Customs for New England, had a hard time in making the Massachusetts officials recognize his authority. His reports on the evasion of the navigation acts had much to do with the revocation of the charter of Massachusetts in 1684. Other officers attended to the King's revenues, arising from fines, forfeitures, prizes, quit rents, license fees, etc.

Another important organ of control was the Admiralty Board, with its First Lord of the Admiralty. This board administered the navy and naval affairs; protected commerce by convoys; looked after pirates and privateers; and helped in the enforcement of the trade laws. It issued warrants for vice-admiralty officers, for letters of marque, and particularly managed the vice-admiralty courts that had charge of cases of smuggling.

The Secretary of State for the southern department exercised jurisdiction over the colonies. This official grew in influence and initiated important policies, especially along administrative and military lines. He was influential in appointing royal governors and other officials. He had close relations with the crown and was an intermediary between King and Parliament. He corresponded with officials in the colonies. Addresses to the King from the colonial legislatures were sent through the Secretary of State, and orders were transmitted by letter from the Secretary of State to the colonial officers. The important officers of state formed the ministry or cabinet. Such men as Sir Robert Walpole, Prime Minister, and the Duke of Newcastle, long Secretary of State, determined the large policies, in the name of the King, while various boards executed them.

An important agency was the Board of Commissioners for Trade and Plantations, or the Board of Trade, established by the king in 1696. It took the place of the old Committee of the Privy Council known as the Lords of Trade (1674–1696). It consisted of eight of the principal officers of state, ex-officio members, and eight active members not connected with the ministry. John Locke, the philosopher, was a member for a time. While the Board of Trade had little authority, it was an important body in securing information, formulating plans, and giving advice in connection with instructions to royal governors. It sent " queries " to and received replies from the royal governors, draughted their instructions, and made recommendations for the appointment of royal officials. It called on other agencies for information, such as the Treasury, Admiralty, and War Office.

Several other boards and agencies had contact with the colonies. Among them was the War Office, with a Secretary at War, who had to do with the welfare of the army, fortifications, supplies, etc. Four companies of English troops, partially raised in New York, were garrisoned at New York and Albany from about 1695. Among other duties

Other
Agencies
of Control

the law officers of the crown examined laws and reported their opinion as to whether they were contrary to acts of Parliament. The Bishop of London exercised special supervision over the affairs of the Anglican Church within the colonies.

The membership of the lower house of Parliament, as well as the ministers of state who had seats in this body, were greatly influenced in the eighteenth century by the advancing class of wealthy merchants. This fact must be kept in mind in order to appreciate the plans for both political and economic control of the colonies. Though mainly interested in the colonies as regions useful to advance the trade and wealth of the mother country, Parliament legislated on a variety of matters, such as naturalization, importation of convicts and slaves, limitation of manufactures, especially of woolen cloth, hats, and iron. It passed the piracy act (1700) and established (1708) the rates at which foreign coins should circulate and the rates of service for the post office (1710). It made lands and slaves liable for debt (1732), and enacted the famous molasses act of 1733, which threatened to ruin the New England West Indian trade. It forbade the issue of paper currency (1751). Several bills were introduced into Parliament (1701–22) to annul the charters of various colonies. Parliament also received petitions and took testimony on colonial affairs, called on officials and boards to furnish information, and appointed committees to investigate affairs within the colonies. In spite of this activity, however, it was not Parliament and its laws, but rather the King and his prerogative that troubled the colonies most. The King, not Parliament, administered colonial government and executed the laws. While the ultimate control of national affairs after 1689 was in Parliament, the actual administration was in the King and this was what touched the colonists most closely.

Thus in the eighteenth century great effort was made to extend political and economic control over the colonies by various means; through disallowance of laws and appeals from colonial courts to the Privy Council; through the appointment of numerous royal officials resident in the colonies; especially through the royal governor and those whose duty it was to enforce trade acts and collect revenue; through the establishment of special vice-admiralty courts to try smuggling cases, and through the military officials and troops sent over or raised for defense during the French wars.

84. Defects of the System and Proposed Remedies.

In spite of this elaborate system English governmental control was inefficient. There was too much overlapping of powers, and the system was cumbersome. Ideals of public service were low, bribery was common, and the actual work in the colonies was not always done by the original appointees, many of whom remained in England, received a salary, and had their work done by deputies. Lack of coöperation was common. Thus the War Office could plan defenses but they might remain unbuilt because the Treasury Board failed to supply funds. The struggle of the colonial assemblies to encroach on the power of the royal governor and obtain control of the purse, was important because it hindered efficient control. In fact the governor often failed to veto acts which his instructions bound him to prevent. In spite of the Board of Trade and royal governors, English officials lacked exact knowledge of conditions within the colonies and often misunderstood them. It should be noted that none of these agencies and boards were created solely for the control of the colonies. Hence all of them had other, and often more important, duties and so could not give their undivided attention to the colonies. Colonial government in England was impersonal, and lacked centralization. In this direction the personal government of King and Privy Council during the seventeenth century was largely supplanted by a government by departments and officials. The great officers of state were the guiding factors.

Some effort was used to remedy the defects of the system by attempts to enlarge the power of the King.

Efforts to Increase the Royal Power

Among them was a renewed attack on those colonies still holding charters, because of "the independency they thirst after." In fact in 1701 an attempt was made to push a bill through Parliament directing that the chartered colonies might be reunited to the crown. Another similar bill was introduced in 1706, and another in 1715 was designed to amend the charters so that the crown would have greater control. All these bills failed, due to determined opposition in Parliament. After 1700 this body was commonly opposed to an increase of royal authority and prerogative. Thus the charters of the colonists were protected by Parliament, while at the same time at home it was encroaching upon the powers of the king. The effort to gain the assistance of Parliament having failed, the crown attempted to secure the annulment of charters "either by purchase, agreement, or otherwise," as in the case of Massachusetts in 1684. This policy was successful in the Jerseys when the proprietors surrendered their rights of government in 1702. In the Carolinas all the eight proprietors excepting Lord Granville, in 1729, gave up their claims. The charter of Georgia was surrendered in 1752. Thus in this year all of the colonies excepting Maryland,

Pennsylvania-Delaware, Connecticut, and Rhode Island were in the hands of the crown. Attacks were made on the charters of Connecticut and Rhode Island after 1720, but without result.

The attacks on the chartered colonies called forth a famous reply by Jeremiah Dummer, agent of Massachusetts in England, entitled *Defence of the New England Charters*. Dummer defended the colonists against the accusations brought against them; such as their alleged tendency towards independence, arbitrary government, passage of laws contrary to those of England, violation of the navigation acts, etc. He also maintained that justice and the interests of England necessitated the retention of the charters.

85. The Commercial Policy of England (1606–1699)

During the eighteenth century the mercantile doctrine developed rapidly. The problem was how to enrich England at the expense of rival states, and partly at the expense of her own colonies. Two important features of the doctrine were, first, the regulation of the trade, commerce, and manufactures of the colonies by acts of Parliament for the purpose of enriching England, in other words to prevent rival states from sharing in the wealth of her colonies; and second, the enforcement of these acts by the various agencies of government previously mentioned — Privy Council, Treasury, and Admiralty Boards, Secretary of State, and the subordinate officials connected with these agencies in England and in the colonies.

The American colonies, it must be remembered, were only one element in a far-flung empire that ranged over nearly the whole world. The commercial system and the machinery of the empire were devised to regulate and expedite trade and commerce so that all of the subordinate parts of the empire, including the American colonies, would contribute to the mother country. England not only expected the colonies to obey the navigation and other acts, but she also expected them to produce those particular raw materials that would best contribute to the prosperity of the mother country. In the exchange of products it was essential that the colonists should buy more in value than they sold, so that a favorable balance of trade for England would result, which must be paid to the English in specie.

The mercantile system was bound to lead to international rivalry, because it involved competition for colonies, in order to secure raw materials. This meant especially that a struggle was bound to occur between France and England. Mercantilism would also lead to conflict of interest among different colonies, as in the case of New England and the English West Indies. England was practically compelled to regulate trade in the interest of the English merchants, else she would have to admit that the colonies existed as much for the benefit of the colonists and her greatest rivals, Holland and France, as for herself. This was contrary to the whole theory of colonization. Between 1660 and 1690 England, through the navigation acts (p. 62), succeeded in greatly weakening the maritime power of the Dutch.

Nevertheless her own weak and inefficient administrative system was continued. In order to make the mercantile theory effective and to win an economic victory over rivals, England needed to develop a better system of commercial control. In addition, the increase and expansion of English trade, the growth of the navy, and the outbreak of the war with France (1689) made more revenue desirable. Mercantilism then was essentially a policy designed to make England a richer and more powerful national state. But this policy called for a large income, population, merchant marine, navy, raw supplies, and manufactures. The colonies could contribute especially, raw materials, revenue, and markets, and it was hoped a favorable balance of trade which would be paid in specie. Mercantilism was bound to sacrifice the colonies in the interests of the central state — " England, Wales, and Berwick-upon-Tweed," and after 1707 Scotland. The great point was this: the colonies must not be competitors, but rather feeders, of the mother country.

It must be remembered that the commercial policy of England was two-sided, and included both restriction British Policy and stimulation. In the first case the main Two-Sided effort was to check, so far as possible, competition with her own industries, whether it arose in rival countries or in English colonies. This explains the passing of the navigation and trade acts, and those prohibiting certain kinds of manufactures in the colonies. On the other hand England was anxious to stimulate those colonial industries which would not compete with their own, such as naval stores, and the production of commodities which she could otherwise obtain only from foreign countries.

The formation of the Board of Trade in 1696 and the passage of the navigation act in that same year Policy of are important in their relation to the deBoard of velopment of England's commercial polTrade icy in the eighteenth century. The Board of Trade was instructed to secure information which would help improve and extend trade and manufactures useful and beneficial to England, and to discourage such manufactures as were harmful.

The effects in the colonies were seen first in the effort to discourage the manufacture of certain products, such as woolen cloth (1699), usually furnished by England, which might compete with her own products; and second, in the effort to develop the naval stores and staples which Great Britain had been importing from other states. The information obtained by the Board of Trade enabled Parliament to enact laws to further these policies, and aided the administrative agencies to carry out such laws.

A standing complaint in England was the evasion of the navigation acts. New England and Virginia were

Navigation Act of 1696

carrying on illegal trade with Holland and other countries. Tobacco was exported to Scotland in large quantities. The trade act of 1696 had for its main purpose the preventing of frauds and the regulation of the " abuses of the plantation trade." Hence the substance of the former navigation laws was reënacted in principle. Governors were to be sworn to enforce the acts, including the governors of the chartered colonies, under a penalty of removal from office and a fine of £1000. Customs officers were empowered to seize smuggled goods. Writs of assistance were authorized, a type of general search warrant which later caused an uproar at the beginning of the revolutionary movement. Vessels in the colonies were subject to search and seizure and royal officials were given the same powers for collecting revenue in the colonies which they had in England.

In order to enforce the act more effectively, England enlarged the customs service in the colonies and new instructions were issued to collectors. Provision was also made for the trial of smuggling cases in vice-admiralty courts. The important point here is the fact that (after 1700) cases of this sort were taken from the common law courts with juries, and transferred to courts without juries, in which the judges were appointed by the English authorities. The colonies were soon divided into two and later some ten or more admiralty districts, northern and southern, and an admiralty judge was appointed for each. The purpose was to check illicit trade and aid the customs officials.

86. Eighteenth Century Economic Policies

The obnoxious molasses act of 1733, was designed to compel New England traders to sell their produce to the English West Indies, Barbados and Jamaica, rather than to the French islands, and to compel them to purchase their molasses and sugar in the English colonies. Heavy duties were levied on sugar and molasses imported from the foreign West Indies.

Later Acts Regulating Trade

This policy was intended to protect and develop the British West Indies at the expense of New England and the French colonies. This law was enacted despite the fact that the English West Indies could not consume the surplus products, provisions and fish of the continental colonies, nor could they supply them with the sugar and molasses desired. For the total exports of the British islands, mainly molasses and sugar, scarcely equalled two-thirds of the amount consumed annually by the colony of Rhode Island alone. In fact, this output was estimated at about one eighth of the amount used by the continental colonies annually.

During the eighteenth century England extended the list of "enumerated" goods, those that must be shipped to England only. The original list included sugar, tobacco, cotton, wool, indigo, and dye woods. In 1705 rice was included, but later (1731) it was relaxed. So also were added in this year molasses and naval stores. Later copper and furs were enumerated. Other acts imposed duties on goods exported from the colonies into Great Britain, similar to those levied on tobacco. Still other acts prohibited the exportation to England of certain agricultural products, cereals and salt provisions. The purpose here was to protect the English farmers.

The object of the new acts was to apply the principles of mercantilism more effectively. The colonists offered resistance because the policy interfered with local desires and needs. This conflict of ideas helps to explain the workings of the English commercial policy in the eighteenth century, and makes clear some of the reasons for colonial opposition to England's policy.

Besides the plans for restrictions on trade, the Board of Trade made a special report to the House of Commons on the woolen industry in the colonies, and this led to the "Woolens Act" of 1699. The purpose was to prevent the growth of woolen manufactures within the colonies. Heavy penalties were provided to prevent the exportation of wool or woolen goods produced or manufactured in the colonies, even from one colony to another. This act did not apply to household manufactures for home consumption only.

Attitude of England Towards Colonial Manufactures

The manufacture of several other articles was restricted at later dates; such as hats (1732) and iron (1750). No mill was to be erected for the rolling of iron, and no forge nor furnace. The object here was to prevent the making of tools, implements, and hardware in the colonies. Casting furnaces were allowed for the production of kettles, salt pans, and cannon.

The purpose of the restrictions on manufactures was twofold. First, if allowed to manufacture, the colonies would not produce raw materials for export in such large quantities; and much of what was produced would be consumed at home. Second, it was England's desire to prevent competition with her own products and those from the continent which by law must first be landed at an English port. Closely allied to the restrictions on manufactures were acts to prevent the "enticing" of free artificers to emigrate (1718); of exporting utensils used in woolen or silk manufacture (1750), backed up with fines of £100 and £500 respectively with twelve months imprisonment.

On the other hand the British commercial policy included the stimulation of certain colonial industries; and much favorable legislation was passed to this end. From England's standpoint it was desirable to divert some of the energy of the colonies into such industries for several reasons. England would benefit by keeping trade within the empire. The colonists would diversify their economic life, and hence they would be enabled the more easily to overcome any adverse balance of trade against them. The policy of stimulation would also divert the colonists from producing those goods which competed directly with those manufactured in England.

One of the great desires of England was to stimulate particular industries such as "naval stores," based Naval Stores mainly on the forest resources of the col-Industries onies. Included in this term were such products as tar, pitch, turpentine, masts, spars, and hemp. Before 1700 England obtained such articles from the Baltic regions, especially from Sweden. The outbreak of the French wars, and the formation of a company in Sweden to monopolize the trade in pitch and tar, spurred England on to develop the naval stores industries in the colonies. It is to be noted that the Massachusetts charter of 1691 provided that trees on ungranted lands, twenty-four inches in diameter one foot from the ground, should be reserved for the King's use; a provision very difficult to enforce.

In October 1700 the Board of Trade sent in an

elaborate report on naval stores and the resources of New England and New York. Finally a bill was passed in 1705 providing for bounties on the importation of naval stores into England; £4 per ton on tar and pitch, £3 on rosin and turpentine, £6 on hemp, and £1 per ton on masts, yards, and bowsprits. Such articles were enumerated and could be shipped to England only. By 1718, 82,000 barrels of tar and pitch were exported from the colonies annually, while the amount received from Sweden and elsewhere declined. In the Carolinas the naval stores industry was large, especially the production of tar and pitch. That of South Carolina for three years (1721–1724) amounted to 78,744 barrels.

Other products needed by England from time to time received encouragement by bounties and draw-back duties. Some goods were freed from import duties, such as pig and bar iron, lumber and other goods. Bounties were granted for the production of indigo and hemp. Rice could be exported freely to Spain, Portugal, and the Mediterranean, while no restrictions were placed on the export trade to the West Indies of fish, lumber, provisions, and other articles.

Encouragement of Other Industries

That part of England's policy which we have called restrictive was not wholly prejudicial. In fact most of her trade acts tended, to some extent, to stimulate industries and manufactures in the colonies, even those which England hoped to prevent. For example, the navigation acts stimulated shipbuilding and allied industries, such as cordage, lumber products, provisioning, and iron manufactures. High prices of manufactured goods, arising in part because of the prohibition of direct trade with the continent, often led to the production of manu-

Effects of Commercial Policy

factures (woolen cloth for example) in order to escape these high prices. The enumerated articles sent to England only, were often sold in a glutted market and at low prices, especially in the case of tobacco. This led to diversification of industry and the production of articles in the colonies that England wished to furnish herself. Likewise the woolens act of 1699, by preventing the export of wool, tended to stimulate woolen manufactures. For if the wool could not be sold abroad, the only recourse was to manufacture it into cloth at home. The Board of Trade was greatly worried concerning the extent of manufactures in the colonies, as is shown by its numerous reports on the subject. They recognized the necessity of some manufacture, but endeavored to limit it to the needs of the individual home.

A report of the Board of Trade in 1721 estimated that the trade of the American colonies as a whole furnished employment to one third of the shipping of the United Kingdom. The report stated that the value of the exports to the colonies exceeded the value of the imports to England by £200,000 per annum. Most of this unfavorable balance fell on the northern colonies, which, however, paid it through the profits of their West Indian trade. On the whole, it does not appear that down to 1750 the colonists suffered much from the British commercial policy. The navigation and trade acts were not only evaded but they tended to stimulate many industries profitable to the colonies. The acts restricting manufactures amounted to little because they were neither enforced nor obeyed. The northern and middle colonies had little direct trade with England and were left free to trade with the West Indies, and so to obtain the money to pay their balance due England. Both England and the colonies, in varying degrees, prospered in the eighteenth century. The southern colonies felt the ill effects of the system most. Whether the colonies would have prospered more and England less without any restrictions on colonial trade and manufactures, or what would have been the effect on colonial prosperity had the acts been rigidly enforced, are interesting questions for speculation.

CHAPTER XI

CONSTITUTIONAL AND POLITICAL DEVELOP-
MENT OF THE COLONIES (1689–1750)

87. References

Bibliographies. — J. T. Adams, *Rev. New Engl.*, footnotes to chs. ii, iv, vi, and *Prov. Society*, 336–337 (law and legal insts.); C. M. Andrews, *Colonial Self-Govt.*, 337–347; J. F. Burns, *Controversies between Royal Govs. and their Assembs. in Northern Am. Cols.*, 423–427; Channing, Hart and Turner, *Guide*, §§ 36–39, 42–43, 45–48, 117, 119–121, 123–124, 126, 146, 149, 162–164; E. B. Greene, *Prov. America*, 329–331, and "Prov. Gov. in the Engl. Cols. of North Am.," (*Harv. Stud.*, III), 271–278; and *Foundations of Am. Nationality*, 205–206, 255–256; Grace Griffin, *Writings on Am. Hist.*, 1906–1923; J. N. Larned, *Lit. of Am. Hist.*, 69–76.

Historical Maps. — No. 4 of this vol.; D. R. Fox, *Atlas of Am. Hist.*, 12–16; Justin Winsor, *Nar. and Crit. Hist. of Am.*, V (maps).

General Accounts. — (See references under "General Accts." to chs. iii, v, vi, viii and x); J. T. Adams, *Rev. New Engl.*, chs. iii–iv, vii–viii; C. M. Andrews, *Colonial Self-Govt.*, chs. x, xii, xvii, *Colonial Period*, chs. vii, ix, and *Colonial Background of Am. Rev.*, chs. i–ii; Carl Becker, *Begin. of Am. People*, 184–200; Edward Channing, *Hist. of U. S.*, II, chs. vii, x–xii; J. A. Doyle, *Engl. Col. in Am.*, V, chs. i–ii, viii; E. B. Greene, *Prov. Am.*, chs. v, xi–xiii, xv, and "Provincial Governor" (*Harvard Studies*, III), esp. chs. viii–ix; Ralph Harlow, *Growth of U. S.*, ch. ix.; H. L. Osgood, *Am. Colonies in the 18th Cent.*, I, chs. iii, ix–xii, II, chs. xix–xxiv, pt. II, chs. ii–v, vii, III, chs. viii–ix, xii–xvi, pt. III, ch. iv, IV, chs. v–x; J. G. Palfrey, *Hist. of New Engl.*, IV, chs. iii, v–xi, bk. V, chs. i, vii; Justin Winsor, *Nar. and Crit. Hist. of Am.*, V, chs. ii, vi.

Special Accounts. — (a) POLITICAL THEORY: J. F. Burns, *Controversies, Between Royal Govs. and Their Assembs. etc.*; Richard Frothingham, *Rise of Repub. of U. S.*, chs. i–iv; C. E. Merriam, *Am. Polit. Theories*, ch. i; G. L. Scherger, *The Evolution of Modern Liberty*. (b) COLONIAL AND LOCAL GOVERNMENT: C. F. Bishop, "Hist. of Elections in the Am. Colonies," in *Columb. Stud.*, III; Edward Channing, "Town and County Govt. in the Am. Colonies," in *J. H. Stud.*, ser. II; Ralph Harlow, *Hist. of Leg. Methods before 1830;* G. E. Howard, "Introduction to Const. Hist. U. S.," in *J. H. Stud.*, extra vols. IV–V; P. L. Kaye, "Engl. Colo. Admin.," in *J. H. Stud.*, ser. XXIII; A. E. McKinley, *The Suffrage Franchise in the Thirteen Engl. Colonies;* F. H. Miller, "Legal Qual. for Office" (1619–1899), in *Am. Hist. Assoc. Rpt.*, 1899, I, 87–153; T. F. Moran, "Bi-Cameral System," in *J. H. Stud.*, ser. XIII; Hubert Phillips, *Devel. of Residential Qual. for Representation in Colonial Legislatures;* E. P. Tanner, "Colonial Agencies in Engl. in 18th Cent.," in *Polit. Sci. Qr.*, XVI, 24–49. (c) Charters and Law: C. M. Andrews and others, *Select Essays in Anglo Am. Legal History* (3 vols.); A. H. Carpenter, "Habeas Corpus in the Colonies" in *Am. Hist. Rev.* VIII; L. P. Kellogg, "Am. Colonial Charter," in *Am. Hist. Assoc. Rpt.*, I, 1903; P. S. Reinsch, "Engl. Common Law in the Early Am. Colonies," in *Univ. of Wis. Bull.*, no. 31; C. W. Warren, *History of the Am. Bar;* for royal disallowance see references in ch. x, "Special Accts." under Andrews, Dorland, Hazeltine, Russell, Schlesinger, and Washburn.

Special Accounts by Colonies. — Bibliography in Channing, Hart and Turner, *Guide*, § 37. (a) New England Colonies: C. M. Andrews, *Conn. and the British Govt.;* S. G. Arnold, *Hist. of Rhode Island;* Charles Borgeaud, *Rise of Mod. Democracy in Old and New England;* W. H. Fry, "New Hampshire as a Royal Prov.," in *Columb. Stud.*, XXIX; A. B. Hart (ed.), *Commonwealth Hist. of Mass.;* II, chs. i, v; G. H. Haynes, *Suffrage and Rep. in Mass.*, in *J. H. Stud.*, ser. XII; Thomas Hutchinson, *Hist. of Prov. of Mass. Bay*, 1691–1750; Justin Winsor, *Memo. Hist. of Boston*, II, ch. ii. (b) Middle Colonies: Carl Becker, *Polit. Parties in New York*, ch. i; E. J. Fisher, "New Jersey as a Royal Province," 1738–1776, in *Columb. Stud.*, XLI; W. T. Root, *Relations of Pa. and the Brit. Govt.;* W. R. Shepherd, "Hist. of Proprietary Govt. in Pa.," in *Columb. Stud.*, VI; C. W. Spencer, *Phases of Royal Govt. in New York, 1691–1719;* E. P. Tanner, "Province of New Jersey," in *Columb. Stud.*, XXX. (c) Southern Colonies: J. S. Bassett, "Const. Beginnings of North Car.," in *J. H. Stud.*, ser. XII; J. A. C. Chandler, "Representation in Va.," in *J. H. Stud.*, ser. XIV; V. W. Crane, *The Southern Frontier, 1670–1732;* P. S. Flippin, "Royal Govt. in Va.," 1624–1775, in *Columb. Stud.*, LXXXIV, and "Financial Admin. of Col. of Va.," in *J. H. Stud.*, ser. XXXII; J. R. McCain, *Georgia* *as a Proprietary Province;* Edward McCrady, *Hist. of South Carolina under the Royal Govt., 1719–1776;* and *Hist. of S. C. under the Proprietary Govt., 1670–1719;* N. D. Mereness, *Md. as a Propri. Province;* E. I. Miller, *Legislature of Prov. of Va.;* C. L. Raper, *North Carolina, A Study in Engl. Colonial Govt.;* W. Z. Ripley, "Finan. Hist. of Va." in *Columb. Stud.,* IV; W. A. Schaper, "Sectionalism and Representation in South Carolina," in *Am. Hist. Assoc. Rpt.,* 1900, I, 237–463; St. G. L. Sioussat, "Engl. Statutes in Md.," in *J. H. Stud.,* ser. XXI; W. R. Smith, *South Carolina as a Royal Prov., 1719–1776.*

Biographies. — (See references to chs. vi, viii, xii, xiii-xv, and Channing, Hart and Turner, *Guide,* § 39); Henry Bruce, *Life of James Oglethorpe;* W. C. Bruce, *Benjamin Franklin Self-Revealed;* E. B. Greene, *Provincial Am.,* ch. xiii (provincial leaders); Everett Kimball, *Public Life of Joseph Dudley, 1660–1715;* D. E. Motley, *Life of Commissary James Blair;* K. B. Murdock, *Increase Mather;* Isaac Sharpless, *Polit. Leaders of Provin. Pa.;* W. L. Stone, *Life and Times of Sir William Johnson;* G. A. Wood, "Public Life of William Shirley," in *Columb. Stud.,* XCII.

Contemporary Accounts. — (a) BIBLIOGRAPHY: See refs. under "Contemp. Accts.," ch. x; Channing, Hart and Turner, *Guide,* §§ 36–39, 42–43, 45–48, 117, 119, 120, 121, 123–124, 126, 146, 149, 161, 162; *Hist. Sources in Schs.,* § 73; see list of sources in J. T. Adams, *Prov. Society,* 326–328. (b) OFFICIAL CORRESPONDENCE: Gov. Belcher Papers, 1731–1743, in *Mass. Hist. Soc. Coll.,* ser. VI, vols. VI–VII; Cadwalader Colden, Papers, in *N. Y. Hist. Soc. Colls.,* I–IV (1917–1920), 1711–1754; G. S. Kimball, *The Correspondence of the Colonial Govs. of R. I.* (1723–1775); Law Papers, 1741–1750, in *Conn. Hist. Colls.* XI, XIII, XV; C. H. Lincoln (ed.), *William Shirley, Correspondence* (2 vols.), 1731–1760; Lewis Morris, Papers, 1738–1746 in *New Jersey Hist. Soc. Colls.,* IV; Penn-Logan Correspondence in *Pa. Hist. Soc. Memoirs,* IX–X; Alexander Spottswood, Official Letters (2 vols.), in *Va. Hist. Soc. Coll.,* n. s. I–II. (c) RECORDS AND COLLECTIONS: *Collection of Proceed. of Great and Gen. Court of Mass., etc.,* 1729; Jeremiah Dummer, *Defence of New Engl. Charters* (1721); Benj. Franklin, *Hist. Rev. of the Const. and Govt. of Pa. etc.,* in *Works* (ed. Sparks), III; A. B. Hart (ed.), *Contemporaries,* II, chs. viii (Colonial Govt.), ix (Assemblies), x (Courts), xi (Local Govt.), and no. 122. (Peter Kalm on independence, 1748); Mabel Hill (ed.), *Liberty Documents,* chs. ii, vi, viii, ix, xi; *Journal of House of Rep. of Mass.,* 1715–1727 (7 vols.); William Macdonald (ed.), *Select Charters,* nos. 45, 47, 48.

88. Underlying Conditions and Ideas

ONE important influence on colonial development was the political and commercial policy of England toward the colonies. The main effect of this policy was to place the colonies under various restraints — political, economic, religious, legal, and judicial. Much of the constitutional and political history of the colonies in their relations with England, is the story of their efforts to evade, nullify, or abolish various forms of restraint. From the political standpoint, great opposition was bound to arise against the extension of the prerogative of the king lest rights previously conferred or claimed should be violated. The substitution of the royal type of government for proprietary and corporate colonies tended to magnify and extend the powers of the King. This helps to explain the hostility of the colonists to the royal governor and his instructions.

English Policy

In spite of the instructions to the governors and the number of royal officials, there was lax enforcement of laws and executive orders. This fact tended to breed in the colonists disrespect for King and Parliament. The fact is many colonists did much as they pleased in spite of England's elaborate system, on paper, of political and economic control. It is largely for this reason that we have an apparent paradox. What appears to have been a rigid and burdensome system, was in fact so flexible that the colonies prospered in spite of it. It must be remembered too that the British commercial policy was in some respects highly favorable to colonial prosperity (p. 259). These facts explain the apparent willingness of the colonists to admit, without much question, the legality of British control and their own

Non-Enforcements of Laws

subordination. As long as the actual enforcement of the system was so weak, they could outwardly appear to be "loyal subjects."

Among various tendencies in the colonies one of great importance was the tendency of colonial political institutions to diverge from those in England. In the mother country the executive and representative branches of government tended to work in harmony, through the development of the cabinet system. The chief ministers of state and some other executive officials occupied seats in one or the other of the Houses of Parliament. The Cabinet was really a committee of the party with a majority in the House of Commons. In the colonies, on the other hand, the royal governor and other officials were likely to be in conflict with the assemblies, because in many respects their interests were antagonistic. English statesmen looked upon the colonies as having somewhat the legal status of municipal corporations. They considered that the assemblies were similar to the English borough (or municipal) councils, which derived their powers from royal charters. The colonists on the other hand thought of their colonial assemblies as if they were miniature Houses of Commons. The first assembly of Massachusetts under the new charter passed, October 15, 1692, an act which declared that "no aid, tax . . . or imposition whatsoever" should be "levied on any of their Majesties' subjects or estates, on any pretence whatsoever, but by the act and consent of the Governor, Council, and Representatives of the people assembled in General Court." This was in effect a denial of the right of Parliament to legislate for Massachusetts in this particular.

The frontier affected constitutional and political developments in each colony. Though it bred notions of

Diverging Political Institutions

equality and of a government resting on the consent of the governed, viz., on numbers; in fact the laws Influence of regulating suffrage, representation, and of-Environment fice-holding were based on a different principle, viz., ownership of real or personal estate. Thus many living on the frontier were disfranchised, especially the squatters; and the small farmer was deprived of equal representation and to a great extent prevented from holding important offices. Most important was the fact that though the assemblies in theory represented the people as a whole, in fact from the foundation, in all the colonies, they failed to represent a large part of the people, because of unequal representation.

The general effect of their environmental conditions in relation to England, was to cause the colonists to lose their identity as Englishmen, although they continued to speak of themselves as such. This was even true among the original settlers, those descended from pure English stock. It was still more true of the large number of non-English racial stocks that migrated to the colonies in the eighteenth century, such as the Scotch-Irish, Irish, Germans, and others. Since these racial groups were located largely in the back-country they had little contact with or respect for England's authority.

The early eighteenth century from 1715 to 1754 was a period in which the wealth of the colonists increased Material rapidly partly because of rich natural Prosperity resources, partly from non-enforcement of laws, and partly because of favorable features of England's commercial system. The fur trade flourished, commerce expanded, new lands were occupied, natural resources, especially the forests, were utilized, and manufactures increased. In fact the tendency towards self-government was hastened by material prosperity, for it bred the idea of economic independence.

89. Structure of Colonial Governments

Ten of the colonies by 1754 had essentially the same type of government. Of these, six were the so-called Types of Colonies and Government royal colonies: New Hampshire, New York, New Jersey, Virginia, North Carolina, and South Carolina, all without charters. Massachusetts was semi-royal, under a charter, but the crown appointed the governor. Pennsylvania-Delaware and Maryland were organized under proprietary charters, the proprietor naming the governor. Georgia, for a time under a charter operated by trustees, was made a royal colony in 1752. Connecticut and Rhode Island were corporate colonies under their original charters and completely self-governing. They elected their own governors, and their charters did not require them to send their laws to England for approval. The middle and southern colonies differed from those in New England (except New Hampshire) because the unoccupied land was owned by the crown, or proprietors, and the land when granted was held not in full ownership but with obligations on the tenant to pay quit rents.

Thus by 1753, all the colonies excepting Connecticut and Rhode Island, Pennsylvania-Delaware and Maryland, were in the hands of the crown. Moreover, when the proprietary colonies were returned to their owners after a brief possession by the King — Pennsylvania in 1694 and Maryland in 1715 — a part of the royal control survived. Deputy governors, appointed by proprietors, had to be confirmed by the crown. The proprietor of Pennsylvania could no longer veto the laws of his colony. Maryland was expected to send its laws to England for the King's approval, though this requirement was seldom obeyed. In the royal colonies the governor and council, appointed by the King, represented the royal prerogative, while the assembly, chosen by those who were granted the franchise, represented the people.

The great conflict arose over the relative importance and power of these two branches of the government, the executive and legislative — the King and the people. The prime object of the King and his agents was to prevent the assembly from encroaching on the powers of the executive; the object of the assembly was to increase its power largely at the expense of the King and the royal governor. As already explained (p. 251) the royal prerogative was somewhat vague and elusive, but the King's "royal will and pleasure," was nevertheless very important, as interpreted by the royal governor.

In the royal colonies the governor was appointed by the King, and so also was the council, except in Massa-
The   chusetts. The King, however, usually
Council   took the advice of the governor in
the appointment of councillors. The proprietor of the proprietary colonies nominated the governor and council, subject to approval by the crown. The council exercised executive and judicial functions, and as an upper house had equal power with the assembly in making the laws. It was usually made up of men drawn from the more wealthy and aristocratic landholders, recommended by the governor. The main business of the council was to advise the governor, act with him in approving or disapproving legislation, and to sit as the highest court of appeals in the colony. The principal conflict between the council and the assembly was the denial by the latter of the right of

the council to initiate money bills. Acting with the governor the council served as a court of appeals in civil cases.

The lower house, usually called the assembly, was elected by the people, viz., by a limited electorate based on a property qualification. It has been estimated that hardly more than a sixth of the population had the right to vote; and that commonly not more than a tenth voted. The assembly had the sole power to initiate bills for taxation and no taxes could be levied without its consent. Hence it had great power over the governor and council since it could withhold salaries and supplies. Its speaker was often the head of the opposition to the governor. The assembly was usually organized on the committee system, and committees, like a caucus, decided on the program of legislation. The assembly was looked on by English officials as a subordinate body; the governor and council being the important branch of the government. Needless to say this was not the view of the assembly.

The Assembly

The assembly tried to protect its rights by appointing agents to reside in London to look out for the interests of the colony. The agent was especially active in presenting and defending the claims of the colonies before the Board of Trade. He often listened to debates in Parliament and protected the colonies from adverse legislation. Benjamin Franklin is the most noted of the later colonial agents, and at one time represented several colonies. The power of the assemblies was checked by the fact that their acts required the consent of the council acting as an upper house, and were subject to the veto of both the governor and the King in council.

The royal governor represented a principle hostile to

colonial interest and desires; the principle of external
control. His power was based on his commission and
The Royal his instructions, both granted by the King,
Governors which often provided for his action in
minute detail. The royal instructions finally became
an elaborate document which included many clauses
favorable to the crown. In some ways they took the
place of a charter for the royal colonies. The governor
was usually instructed not to approve certain types
of laws, such as those involving the King's prerogative;
the regulation of trade prejudicial to England; laws contrary to those of Parliament; those interfering with
the bringing in of slaves and servants; and those which
made paper money legal tender. His powers included
the right to convene, prorogue, or dissolve the assembly,
and to veto its acts. He appointed most officials —
judges, sheriffs, justices of the peace, and was commander of the militia. His general duty was to enforce
the laws and protect the interests of the crown.

Numerous royal officials besides the royal governor
were appointed by the king to represent and protect
British his interests. Most important were the
Officials surveyor-general, collector of customs,
vice-admiralty judges, surveyor of woods, attorneys
general and other officers. These officials were necessarily a thorn in the flesh of the colonists.

The workings of the colonial governments developed
serious friction, due to several causes. The fundamental
Divided Au- idea underlying the structure of the royal
thority and governments was authority divided be-
Conflicting
Interests tween two bodies having interests incom-
patible with each other. On the one side were the governor and council and other officials appointed by the
King and governor. The governor was the mouthpiece
of, and responsible to, the King; derived authority from

the King; was conservative, and often looked on the colonies as a minor part of the British empire, which ought to subordinate its interests to those of the empire as a whole. In some cases the councils supported the governors in their views.

On the other side stood the popular assembly, the mouthpiece of the people, deriving its authority from the people, tending towards radicalism, looking on the colony as more important than the empire, and pretending more and more to powers similar to those of the House of Commons. To make this system work harmoniously was like trying to mix oil and water.

90. Attitude of Colonies Toward English Control

In spite of the direct limitations on the power of the colonial assemblies, they were able to evade in a number of ways the King's prerogative and the acts of Parliament. Thus they sometimes passed laws which they knew were contrary to acts of Parliament, to remain in force for limited periods, particularly such as those relating to quit rents and paper money. When laws were disallowed in England, they were often reënacted in slightly different form. This was made possible because of the length of time it took to send laws to England and to receive an answer back concerning them — a matter of three or four months. Mail facilities were very poor, and captains of ships entrusted with dispatches were often careless.

Evasion of Control

Judicial decisions of the colonial courts, though reversed perhaps by the Privy Council, were often nevertheless enforced. The famous Connecticut case of Winthrop *vs.* Lechmere, appealed to the Privy Council (1728), declared invalid (1728) a law distributing property of intestates among heirs. A bitter controversy arose and finally the decision was practically reversed in

1745. Royal governors were forced to approve laws directly contrary to their instructions, or else wait in vain for their salaries. Juries in colonial courts frequently refused to convict smugglers. Merchants often disobeyed the navigation acts. Squatters settled on the King's lands and drove away officers sent to collect quit rents. Though the penalty for failure to pay the quit rent was forfeiture of the land, Virginia passed an act to forbid such forfeiture. Another example of resistance was the practice of using for timber the trees in the king's forests. Although those marked with a broad arrow were to be saved for masts for the royal navy the squatters cut them down by the hundreds.

A report of Edward Randolph, surveyor of customs, made in 1700, complained that the right of appeal to the King's Court was denied; that the assemblies refused to pass acts for the defence of the colonies; such as those providing forts, arms, and ammunition, sometimes in direct conflict with the instructions of the governor; that they encouraged woolen manufactures, refused to acknowledge vice-admiralty jurisdiction, and disregarded the value of coins as fixed by the King's proclamation.

It may be noted that great confusion prevailed as to exactly what the law was at any given time. Thus one writer in 1701 made the following complaint:

"It is a great unhappiness, that no one can tell what is law and what is not in the plantations. Some hold that the law of England is chiefly to be respected, and, where that is deficient, the laws of the several colonies are to take place, others are of the opinion that the laws of the colonies are to take first place, and that the law of England is of force only where they are silent, others there are who contend for the laws of

English Law and the Colonies

the colonies, in conjunction with those that were in force in England at the first settlement of the colony, and lay down that as the measure of our obedience, alleging that we are not bound to observe any late acts of Parliament in England, except such only where the reason of the law is the same here that it is in England. But, this leaving too great a latitude to the judge, some others hold that no late acts of the Parliament of England do bind the plantations but those only wherein the plantations are particularly named. Thus we are left in the dark in one of the most considerable points of our rights; and, in the case being so doubtful, we are too often obliged to depend upon the crooked cord of a judge's discretion in matters of the greatest moment and value."

The colonists laid stress on their charter rights, embodying their rights as Englishmen, which they claimed Charter and Natural Rights were inviolable; they insisted that once granted they could not be revoked. Gradually they set up the doctrine of " Natural Law; " that is, of inalienable or inherent rights. The essence of this theory was that King and Parliament were both limited in their power by an inherent unwritten body of self-evident principles; hence that their acts were invalid if contrary to justice and right — or, as Jefferson phrased it later, contrary to the natural rights of " life, liberty .and the pursuit of happiness."

From the standpoint of England, some of the claims of the colonists were on their face unreasonable. England declared that the colonists wished to secure all the general advantages of remaining within the empire; that while on the one hand they were eager for those laws passed by Parliament which were for their direct advantage, such as the protection given by the English army and navy from

attacks by Indians, French, and pirates; on the other
hand when Parliament passed acts regulating trade believed to be necessary for the prosperity of England or
the well being of the empire, the assemblies complained
that such acts were unfavorable to their own particular and local interests. Thus when Parliament made
rice an "enumerated" article South Carolina and
Georgia vigorously objected to the act as prejudicial
to their interests.

91. Encroachment of the Assemblies on the Powers of the Governor and Council

The central feature of the constitutional history of
the colonies is the constant encroachment of the assemblies on the powers of the governor and
council and thus indirectly on those of
the King. Briefly, the assemblies tried to
control the governor much as Parliament did the King.
The causes for the conflict were due to several factors.
First, to the inherited ideas that the representative assembly of the people should be the real source of power
and the protector of their liberties as against the power
claimed by the governor and conferred upon him by his
instructions granted by the King. Second, to the belief
that the governor and council and the assembly were
each trying to encroach on the respective rights and
privileges of the other. Third, to the antagonism of the
interests of the two bodies, already explained; and
fourth, to the character of some of the royal governors.
No doubt one cause of the conflict between the assemblies and the governors was the inherited background of the struggle between Parliament and the
King during the seventeenth century. The assemblies
could hardly forget the great protests of Parliament
against the arbitrary power of the King, such as those

in the Petition of Right, the Grand Remonstrance, and the Bill of Rights.

Appointments as royal governors were sometimes given to second- and third-rate men, not on the basis of real ability and experience but because of "political pull;" a reward for services to the crown, or because they were friends of high officials in England. Some looked on the office as a chance to recoup broken fortunes. Some governors never came to America but sent a deputy. Franklin describes the governors as "sometimes men of vicious character and broken fortune sent by a minister to get them out of the way." The New York assembly described their governors as entire strangers to the people, without money or interest in the welfare of the people; "all methods are used, and all engines set to work to raise estates to themselves and therefore should the public monies be left to their disposition, what can be expected but the grossest mis-application."

Character of the Royal Governors

On the other hand there were some very able governors, and many were honest, if mediocre, men, who tried to do their duty under great difficulties. The governors who brought discredit to themselves and England were such men as Fletcher and Cornbury. Men like Shirley, Nicholson, and Spotswood were able and fair-minded governors. The greater number of governors were neither very good nor very bad but on the whole were not the type of men who would advance greatly good relations between the colonies and England.

The royal governors accused the assemblies of encroaching on their legitimate powers, of seizing many of their executive functions, of trying to throw off their dependence on the crown, and of being animated by a spirit of disobedience, and even independence. The assemblies protested that they

Spirit of the Assemblies

were loyal, and were only trying to preserve their constitutional rights; their right of local self-government.
Still it is a fact that the colonies were rapidly outgrowing
the form of government imposed upon them by England,
and were gradually endeavoring to substitute one of
their own making. The Board of Trade in a report to
the Privy Council, as early as 1723, accused the inhabitants of Massachusetts, working through their assembly,
of " daily endeavoring to wrest the small remains of
Power out of the Hands of the Crown, and to become
independent of their Mother Kingdom."

In other words, while the assemblies resisted encroachment on what they believed to be their rights, they at
the same time were not averse to encroaching on the
legitimate power of the governor, without perhaps good
legal reason. From this standpoint they were attempting
to seize all the power possible, on the ground that it was
desirable for the prosperity and happiness of the people.
They chafed under the control of the King, Privy
Council, and the governor, especially with respect to
the vetoing of colonial laws. This system of veto had
its good points, however, since it prevented some ill-
advised legislation. The assemblies were also restive
under the limitations imposed on them in passing laws
which in any way discriminated against British merchants, trade, and the royal prerogative. The assemblies
felt that little allowance was made for their peculiar
environment and needs.

On the other hand it is a fact that they were subordinate bodies, and dependent on the will of the King
and Parliament. They objected to and evaded laws
and the King's instructions, but based their argument,
largely on the vague phrase " rights of Englishmen," on
their charters or on natural rights, or simply because
of political or economic advantage. The growth of the

power of the assembly and its resistance to English control is perhaps the outstanding event in colonial constitutional history.

The questions dividing the governor and assemblies were varied and numerous. On the financial side the Nature of assembly sought complete control over Disputes provincial funds; made specific rather than general appropriations; demanded the right to verify expenditures made by governors; voted an annual rather than a fixed and permanent salary; and sought to issue paper money, contrary to general instructions to all the governors to limit or refuse such issues. On the administrative side the assembly wished to share with the governor in the establishment of courts; to restrict his power to call, prorogue, and dissolve assemblies, by fixing by law the time of new elections. Said Andrew Hamilton, the famous lawyer and Speaker of the Assembly of Pennsylvania, 1739: "We sit upon our own adjournment, when we please, and as long as we think necessary; and we are not apt to be sent a packing, in the middle of a debate, and disabled from representing our just grievances . . . which has often been the fate of assemblies in other places." The assemblies also sought to prevent the governor from controlling membership, procedure, and the choice of a speaker.

92. Financial Conflicts

The greatest struggle between the royal governor and assembly occurred over financial issues. Originally Financial the assemblies made general grants of Issues money, to be kept by the treasurer or receiver general, and expended for specific purposes according to the wishes of the governor and council. But these expenditures were not accounted for or checked by the assemblies. Unscrupulous governors sometimes spent the money extravagantly, or even "misapplied" it according to the assemblies. These practices compelled the assemblies to devise ways to limit expenditures. This was accomplished by taking complete control over taxation and by making specific appropriations; that is, by naming the special purpose for which the money was to be expended, and often by naming the individuals to whom the money was to be paid. A clause was often added "for no other intent whatsoever."

Then the councils were excluded from a share in making appropriations, or even in making an amendment to money bills. By refusing to appropriate money for supplies, the assemblies could control military expeditions and expenditures. In many cases the instructions of the governor called for some administrative act which required an appropriation by the assembly before it could be carried out; such as the defense of the frontier, the erection of forts, etc. Governor Belcher of Massachusetts declared in 1739 that "The forts in all the plantation do at this day lye in a sad ruinous condition, especially in all the West India Islands and this is no fault of the Governor, but of the Assemblies who will raise no money to repair and support them." The assembly of Massachusetts wanted to take over the military power of Governor Shute, 1721, after he had declared war against the Indians, by laying out the plans for a campaign before they voted supplies. Likewise it demanded the discharge of certain military officers and declined to pass a law for the punishment of mutiny and desertion.

Another financial conflict was the long struggle over the payment of a salary to the governor. England refused to fix a salary or provide for it from the royal exchequer because they wished the colonies to be self-supporting. The governors brought instructions requiring the assembly to appropriate a fixed and permanent salary. The assemblies however found that they could compel the governor to sign obnoxious bills, even contrary to his instructions, by threatening to lower his salary or refusing to give him any money unless he signed the bills sent to him.

A governor of New York wrote the Lords of Trade in 1741 that the assembly had in effect declared "that if a governor will not blindly consent to their bills, however unreasonable or contrary to instructions, they will starve him into compliance." It was one of the members of the New Jersey assembly who defended this policy with the remark, "Let us keep the dogs poore, and we'll make them do what we please." Such language led the governors to reply in kind. Governor Morris for example said, "Expressions like these may gratify the wicked temper of low minds, unacquainted with common rules of decency, and incapable of anything above the scum of the people."

The assemblies also tried to appoint the treasurer, thus taking this power out of the hands of the governor and council. The treasurer was an important officer, but by 1750 six of the colonial assemblies had gained control of this office, in addition to the two corporate colonies that had always chosen their own treasurer. This was important because under this system money could then be paid out only on the warrant of an officer chosen by and responsible to the assembly.

93. The Victory of the Assemblies

The conflict between the royal governors and assembly included a great variety of issues, varying in the individual colonies. In New Hampshire, for example, the governor, acting for the crown, asserted the

right to regulate representation; that it was a privilege
that might be given to towns or withheld at pleasure.
Other
Disputed
Issues
The assembly held that the towns were entitled to this privilege by law. The purpose of the crown was to have representatives chosen only from a portion of the towns, those
likely to favor the governor.

In Massachusetts a similar contest arose. The early
theory was that every new township had a right to
send members to the General Court. But Governor
Shirley, 1742, refused to approve a bill for three new
townships, and so "to put an end of this way of increasing the number of representatives." This was
deemed by the assembly an encroachment on "ancient
traditional rights" and a step towards dictatorship by
the crown. By 1753, the governor was compelled to sign
a bill erecting three new towns, contrary to his instructions. Governor Belcher of Massachusetts opposed
the formation of "land banks" the purpose of which
was to relieve debtors by issuing paper money to be
loaned on the security of land. This brought out the
old problem of the inflation of the currency and the
consequent losses to merchants and the creditor class
generally. The assembly, on the other hand, was in
favor of large issues of paper money.

In New York much friction arose over the refusal
of the assembly to support the government, in obedience to the instructions of the crown; and particularly
in refusing the council the privilege of amending money
bills. The council claimed that this was a right granted
by the crown. The assembly fell back on "inherent
right" and replied (1711), "'Tis true, the share the
Council have (if any) in the Legislation, (comes) only
from the meer Pleasure of the Prince. . . On the contrary, the *inherent Right* the Assembly have to dispose

of the money of the Freemen of this Colony, does not proceed from any Commission, Letters Patent or other Grant from the Crown, but from the free Choice and Election of the People: who ought not to be divested of their Property (nor justly can) without their consent."

Though this was written in 1711, it has the ring of the protests of 1765, and shows how deep seated was the notion of complete control of internal taxation by the assembly. In fact the very next year Governor Hunter reminded the assembly that his instructions required that no public money " be issued or disposed of otherwise than by a Warrant under (his) Hand, by and with the advice and Consent of the Council."

Conditions in the southern colonies were similar. Quary, vice-admiralty judge, in a memorial (1703), declared that in Virginia " The Assembly conclude themselves entitled to all the rights and privileges of an English Parliament, and begin to Search into the records of the honorable house for precedents to govern themselves by." In South Carolina, Governor Glenn reported to the Board of Trade (1748), that the assembly had drawn to itself most of the powers of government in the province; that officials, such as the treasurer, commissioners, Indian commissioners, powder receiver, controller of duties were chosen by the assembly; and that he was excluded from any share in its legislative sessions. He complained also that the governor was not prayed for in the churches, though the assembly had prayers constantly offered up for itself during sessions.

Thus from about 1715 on, there was a shift in the balance of power, particularly after 1740. Governor Morris of New Jersey complained (1739) that there was a strong " inclination . . . in the meanest of the people (who are the majority and whose votes make

the Assembly) to have the sole direction of all the affairs of the government." Governor Clinton of New
York, in 1745, accused the assembly of
"wresting his Majesty's authority out of
the Hands of the Governor," and of having
"an inordinate thirst of Power" so that "you are become as it were, a dead weight against the other Branches of the Legislature." By 1745 the Privy Council complained that in New York, "The Assembly had taken to themselves not only the management and disposal of the public money, but have also wrested from your Majesty's governor the nomination of all officers of government, the custody and direction of all military stores, the mustering and regulating of troops raised for Your Majesty's service, and in short almost every other executive part of the government."

Shift in Balance of Power

Though encroachment by the assemblies on the power of the governors was general throughout the colonies,
and numerous complaints were made to
the Board of Trade, yet Parliament refused
to grant a salary to the governor out of the royal exchequer, or take measures to protect the crown and Parliament in their rights. It was partly this dilatory and *laissez faire* policy that made possible the great extension of the power of the assemblies in the period from 1689 to 1750. Thus the assemblies became the most important agencies in this period in defending what was believed to be the rights of people, and in increasing the extent of self-government within the colonies. This was a preliminary step leading up to the later movement for complete independence.

Assemblies in 1750

94. Political Conflicts of Coast and Frontier

We have so far considered the structure and workings of the colonial governments mainly in relation to Parlia-

ment, King, and royal officials. The distribution of political power between coast and frontier groups and the
Conflict of Geographic Sections
conflicts arising therefrom constitute another important phase of the constitutional and political history of the colonies. This contest was a struggle for power between geographic sections and classes of the population within individual colonies. The distribution of population and the controlling political ideal characteristic of the seventeenth century had two effects on the distribution of political power.

When the representative assemblies were first organized the bulk of the population was located near
Assemblies and Unequal Representation
the coast and within a small compact area. As a result the assemblies fairly represented the populated area. In Virginia the original counties were made about equal in size, and equality of representation was provided for, two for each county. In South Carolina and Pennsylvania representatives were given to the original counties, roughly according to population. In New England, the early towns were given equal representation. In all the colonies the rights of suffrage and office holding were based on a property or religious qualification.

When, however, population expanded into the interior and out to the frontiers, it was realized by the assemblies that the extension of the privilege of representation to the western counties would disturb the balance of power if the area of each was about that of each coastal county. If given either equal or proportional representation they might eventually outvote the coast counties. The needs of the frontier and the character of the political, religious, and social ideas which developed in the western region, led the assemblies to reject the principle of real equality of representation.

They refused also to reduce the property requirements for the suffrage and for office holding. This was the background of, and reason for, political, economic, religious, and social sectionalism within individual colonies.

Two methods were adopted to prevent equality of representation. One was to erect very large counties in the frontier regions, as was the case in Pennsylvania and South Carolina, with the right of sending only one or two representatives to the assembly. Each of the coast counties, however, though smaller in size, had six, eight, or more. The other method, of which Virginia is an example, was that of having each county send two representatives. But the small number and great size of the western counties and the large number and small size of the eastern counties gave the latter complete control of the assembly. Little or no change was made in representation as the western counties increased in population and relatively few were divided. Thus the distribution of power was undemocratic, and based in reality on the possession of property rather than on the number of people in a given county.

In Pennsylvania for example, the three eastern or "Quaker counties," Philadelphia, Chester, and Bucks, had eight representatives each in the assembly, besides two for the city of Philadelphia, a total of twenty-six. The next county admitted was that of Lancaster (1729) which was allowed four representatives. For twenty years no new county was established; then in 1749 and 1750 York and Cumberland were erected with two members each, and in 1752 Berks and Northampton with one each. No more counties were established till 1771, though numerous petitions were sent to the Assembly complaining of the grievance. Only one additional representative was allowed, one for Berks County in 1769.

Thus at no time in the eighteenth century, to 1771, could the three Quaker counties be outvoted by all the rest of Pennsylvania, since this western section had at most only eleven votes against twenty-six. If representation had been based on the number of taxables even the western counties by 1760 would have had 27 representatives, while the three Quaker counties, with Philadelphia, would have had only 23. Inequality in the franchise was also a characteristic feature of the coast and frontier population. In Pennsylvania the right to vote was based on the possession of fifty acres of land, ten acres being seeded and cleared, or fifty pounds lawful money. The effect of this law was to limit the franchise to one man in ten in the farming communities. Thus poor farmers, squatters, and all with small holdings or incomplete or illegal title to land were disfranchised.

The system of representation enabled the tide water region in all the colonies to determine the character of the legislation enacted; that favoring the interests of the propertied classes, the planters, merchants, exporters, and ship owners; the Byrds, Fairfaxes, Randolphs, and Rutledges; the Van Rensselaers, Schuylers, and Livingstons, the Hutchinsons, Olivers, and Bowdoins. The most significant characteristic of much of the colonial legislation is the fact that it was designed to benefit the men with property, while it limited the privileges and opportunities of the poor men with little or no property — the small farmer, squatter, day laborer and artisan. In colonies where there was a union of church and state, the assemblies resisted the progress of religious toleration and liberty and forced the dissenters

Effects of Inequality on Legislation

to attend and pay taxes towards the support of the established church, in whose doctrines they disbelieved.

The poor man on the frontier was compelled to bear much of the burden of its defense, and in effect acted as a buffer between the Indians and the tidewater population. He not only gave his time and money, but often sacrificed his farm, his family and his own life, because of the character of the cruel Indian warfare. One of the curious effects of this policy was the conflict between the governor and assembly on frontier defense. By his instructions he was obliged to defend this region against the French and Indians. Royal governors frequently complained, however, that the assemblies encroached on their military powers, and refused to appropriate funds for defense, and hence they were unable to carry out their instructions to protect the frontiers against the French and the Indians.

The frontier counties sometimes petitioned the assemblies to provide men and supplies for the defense of the frontier or for division of counties, in order to secure more equitable representation, and more accessible courts of justice; or for improvement of roads and bridges. Such petitions were usually "laid on the table." Laws affecting paper money, banks, debtor and creditor, rate of interest, system of taxation, distribution of land and many other questions were framed primarily in the interests of the coast and propertied class. Before 1750 much of the back-country population, especially in Pennsylvania and the southern colonies, lacked adequate provisions for local government, courts of justice, liberal franchise, and fair representation in the assemblies. The privilege of holding higher office was restricted to those with large land holdings.

Conflicting and inconsistent political theories developed within the tidewater region and the assemblies.

The latter preached and practised the theory of democracy in their relations with King, Parliament, and the royal governor, but were distinctly undemocratic, and
Conflict of
Political
Theories illiberal with respect to their relations to the back-country population and even to the small farmers, and artisans on the seaboard. Thus we have the paradoxical tidewater gentleman who posed both as a leader of democracy and as an aristocrat. At the same moment he was fierce for liberty for himself and his class, but lukewarm and even hostile to liberty for other citizens and classes. Illustrations of the political, economic, religious, and social effects of the sectional conflict within the colonies will be discussed in the chapters that follow.

95. Political Development

The motives for the founding of Georgia varied somewhat from those of other colonies, because of less emphasis on economic and religious factors.
Founding
of Georgia General James Oglethorpe was a prominent military figure, a member of Parliament and chairman of a committee to visit prisons and recommend reforms. Desire to better the lot of poor debtors who had been imprisoned was his main motive in seeking a grant of land and a charter for a colony. The crown and Parliament were also interested in setting up a colony between South Carolina and the Spanish, as a border or buffer state acting as a protection against Spanish Florida. A desire to secure a part of the Indian fur-trade and to make the colony a refuge for persecuted German Protestants is observable.

By the charter granted in 1732, a group of men called the Trustees of Georgia were granted land between the Savannah and Altamaha and then west to the "South Sea." Their proprietors, resident in England, were given the land in perpetuity, with powers of government for 21 years, somewhat curtailed by the crown. The governor, if approved by the King, was obliged to enforce the acts of trade. The King could also appoint officers to collect his revenue. The trustees could found settlements, grant lands, govern settlers, appoint officials, erect courts, etc. Laws, however, must be approved by the crown. There was no provision for an assembly, and negro slavery was prohibited. Georgia was the only American colony to which the British government granted direct financial support, £10,000 in 1732, and other grants from £2500 to £16,000 at various times later. It was expected that these grants would be used for purposes of defense.

The Charter and Government

The early settlers consisted of English debtors, a group of Germans, estimated at 1200 by 1741, mostly Salzburgers and Moravians, and some Scotch Highlanders. Two very noted men, resident in the colony for a while, were John Wesley, founder of Methodism, and George Whitefield, the greatest evangelist of the century. The latter founded the first orphan asylum in the colonies, near Savannah. A real colonial government was not set up, but rather a municipal system. The local government of Savannah and the county, acted for the whole colony; the important officials being three bailiffs and judicial and executive powers.

Progress of the Colony

Many factors limited progress in Georgia. Dissatisfaction arose over the prohibition of slaves and liquor; over the system of primogeniture and entails, and over the lack of an assembly. War broke out between England and Spain in 1739, and much of the energy of the colony was expended in an unsuccessful attack on St. Augustine in 1740 and in successful defense from an attack by the Spaniards in 1742. Some economic relief was obtained when slavery was allowed in 1749. In 1751 an assembly was granted and in 1752 the charter was surrendered, as provided for in 1732 and Georgia was made into a royal colony similar to those farther north.

Though the colonies remained to a large extent quite independent of each other, yet in certain ways they were drawn into political relationships with each other. This was because of joint interest in the problems of coöperation in the French Wars; in their relations with the Indians; in their disputes over boundary and trade questions; and occasionally on other matters. The governors made many complaints of the failure of the assemblies to coöperate in military operations. New York with its greatly exposed frontier was continually seeking aid of other colonies, supported by the King's " Letters Mandatorie " to the several governments to assist New York. Yet Governor Fletcher complained " that Pennsylvania being mostly Quakers will give no men or money for war; " and that young men flee from New York " to the neighboring Government where they are wholly free from Tax or any other contrybution towards the Common Security," thus furnishing an early case of " slackers." On the other hand the colonies on numerous occasions shared in providing troops for defense in war time, as will be narrated later.

Political Relations of the Colonies

Numerous controversies arose over boundaries, such as that between Connecticut and Rhode Island over the Narragansett country. A joint commission was finally appointed by the two colonies which reached an agreement in 1703, though the line was not drawn until 1728. The boundary dispute between Pennsylvania and Maryland was not settled until 1767, when the famous Mason and Dixon line was run. From 1704 Maryland prohibited the importation from Pennsylvania into Maryland of breadstuffs, beer, malt, and horses. The purpose was to stimulate the production of grain in Maryland and an export trade similar to that of Pennsylvania.

Colonial union began in 1643 with the formation of the New England confederation as already narrated.

Colonial
Union
to 1750

After 1684, progress towards union was made first through congresses with delegates from several colonies, called principally to discuss Indian problems and the defense of the frontier against the French and Indians as described in the following chapter. Besides these formal meetings, the assemblies of the various colonies corresponded with each other on numerous topics of common interest, both those respecting which they were in disagreement and those in which they were in agreement.

With the outbreak of the French-English intercolonial wars in 1689, talk of the need of a union for defense became more common. A " Memorial of the State of the Northern Colonies " in 1696, complained of " the number and independency of so many small governments, whereby our strength is not only divided and weakened, but by reason of their severall interests, are become and does in a manner esteem each as foreigners the one unto the other, soe that whatever mischiefs doth happen in one part, the rest by the reason of this disunion remain unconcerned and our strength thereby weakened."

Between 1684 and 1754 several plans of union were drawn up. The best known are those of William Penn

Plans of
Union

in 1696–1697; Daniel Coxe, 1722; and the famous Albany Plan of 1754, drawn up by Benjamin Franklin. The colonists were left largely to their own resources for defense during the early French Wars. External dangers, heavy taxation and loss of men suggested the value and need of union. " We have a common interest and must have a common council — one head and one purse." There was need also of union in order to enact regulations in relation to the collection of debts, currency, weights and measures, boundary disputes, and particularly " to establish an equal liberty of trade in all the plantations on the continent of America (1701)." All this looked towards greater self government.

The crown usually disapproved plans which tended to give the colonies more powers and liberties, while the colonies disapproved plans which tended to strengthen the crown. Thus when in 1725 the assembly of Massachusetts proposed a convention of all the colonies it was dubbed by the Board of Trade as " a mutinous proposal." On the other hand the royal governors were anxious for union, but chiefly as a means of checking popular power, to further the royal prerogative, to secure the advantages of mercantile monopoly, and to obtain revenue, men, and supplies for war with greater ease and dispatch.

In general it may be said that before 1750, the idea of union had been discussed in an academic manner at least, and the need of union was realized to some extent, both by the royal governors and the colonists. But the differences in the objects of union and its character were vital. One party wished to limit still further the assemblies, and enhance the power of King and Parliament, while the other desired a union that would protect privileges and rights already in its possession, and extend them still further.

CHAPTER XII

POPULATION AND IMMIGRATION PROBLEMS
(1689–1750)

96. References

Bibliographies. — J. T. Adams, *Prov. Society*, 332–335 (by racial groups); C. M. Andrews, *Colonial Folkways*, 241–242; Channing, Hart and Turner, *Guide*, §§ 37–39, 42–43, 45–48, 117, 119–121, 123–124, 126, 146, 149, 160–162, 165; E. B. Greene, *Prov. Am.*, 335–336; Grace Griffin, *Writings on Am. Hist.*, 1906–1923; J. N. Larned, *Lit. of Am. Hist.*, 69–76; A. M. Schlesinger, *New Viewpoints in Am. Hist.*, bibl. for ch. ii.

Historical Maps. — Edward Channing, *Hist. U. S.*, II (end); A. B. Faust, *The German Element in U. S.*, I (end); C. A. Hanna, *The Scotch-Irish, etc.*, I (end).

General Accounts. — J. T. Adams, *Prov. Society*, ch. vii; J. D. Butler, "British Convicts Shipped to Am. Colonies," in *Am. Hist. Rev.*, II, 12–33; *A Century of Population Growth* (Census Bureau 1909); A. H. Carpenter, "Naturalization in the Am. Colonies," in *Am. Hist. Rev.*, IX, 288; Edward Channing, *Hist. of U. S.*, II, ch. xiv; J. R. Commons, "Colonial Race Elements," in *Chatauqua Mag.*, XXXVIII–XXXIX, and *Races and Immigrants;* F. B. Dexter, "Estimates of Population in The Am. Colonies," in *Proc. of Am. Ant. Soc.*, V, 1887; also in *A Selection from the Misc. Hist. Papers of F. B. Dexter, etc.;* E. B. Greene, *Prov. Am.*, ch. xiv; H. L. Osgood, *Am. Col. in 18th Cent.*, II, ch. vi; E. E. Proper, "Colonial Immigra. Laws," in *Columb. Studies in Hist.*, XII; A. M. Schlesinger, "Significance of Immigration," in *Am. Journ. of Sociol.*, XXVII, and ch. ii of *New Viewpoints in Am. Hist.;* F. J. Turner, *Frontier in Am. Hist.*, ch. ii; see discussion of racial influences in *Am. Ant. Soc. Proc.*, X, 1–10.

Special Accounts, Races. — (a) GERMANS: L. F. Bittinger, *The Germans in Colonial Times;* S. H. Cobb, *The Story of the Palatines;* A. B. Faust, *The German Element in the U. S.*, I (new ed. in one vol. with additions, 1928); J. T. Hamilton, *Short Hist. of Unitas Fratrum* (Moravians); J. P. Hoskins, "German Influ. on Thought and Culture in the Colonial Period," in *Princeton Theolog. Rev.*, V; C. H. Smith, *The Mennonites.*

(b) IRISH AND SCOTCH-IRISH: C. K. Bolton, *Scotch-Irish Pioneers;* H. J. Ford, *The Scotch-Irish in Am.;* Samuel S. Greene, "The Scotch-Irish in Am.," in *Am. Ant. Soc. Proc.*, X (1895), 32–71; C. K. Hanna, *The Scotch-Irish, etc.;* J. C. Linehan, *The Irish-Scots and the Scotch-Irish;* M. J. O'Brien, *A Hidden Phase of Am. Hist.;* (see review by J. F. Jameson, in *Am. Hist. Rev.*, XXVI, 797). (c) SCOTCH: J. P. McClean, *Hist. Acct. of Settlement of Scotch Highlanders;* Peter Ross, *Scot in America.* (d) SWEDES: Amandus Johnson, *The Swedes on the Delaware.* (e) SWISS: A. B. Faust, "Swiss Emigration to the Am. Colonies in the 18th Cent.," in *Am. Hist. Rev.*, XXII, 21–24. (f) FRENCH: C. W. Baird, *Hist. of Huguenot Emigration to Am.;* L. J. Fosdick, *The French Blood in Am.;* J. F. Rosengarten, *French Colonists and Exiles in U. S.* (g) JEWS: M. L. Peters, *Jews in Am.* (h) NEGROES: U. B. Phillips, *Am. Negro Slavery.*

Sectional Racial Histories. — (a) NEW ENGLAND: (See bibl. in J. T. Adams, *Rev. New Engl.*, ch. iii, and refs. in footnotes pp. 30, 88); E. L. Parker, *Hist. of Londonderry, N. H.* (b) MIDDLE COLONIES. — C. H. Browning, *Welsh Settlements in Pa.;* T. F. Chambers, *Early Germans in New Jersey;* H. T. Colenbrander, "The Dutch Element" in *Am. Hist. Assn. Rpt.* 1909, 193–201; F. R. Diffenderfer, *The German Immigration into Pa., 1700–1775;* T. A. Glenn, *Merion and the Welsh Tract;* Oscar Kuhns, *The German and Swiss Settlements of Colonial Pa.;* A. C. Myers, *Immigration of the Irish Quakers into Pa., 1682–1750;* "Pennsylvania, The German Influence in its Settlement and Development; A Nar. and Crit. Hist.," (various authors), in *Pa. German Society Proc.*, VII–XVII; Ruth Putnam, "The Dutch Element in the U. S.," *Am. Hist. Assn. Rpt.* 1909, 205–218; J. F. Sachse, *The German Pietists of Prov. Pa., 1694–1708*, and *The German Sectarians of Pa., 1708–1800.* (c) SOUTHERN COLONIES. — G. D. Bernheim, *Hist. of German Settlements and Luth. Ch. in North and South Carolina;* A. H. Hirsch, *The Huguenots of Colonial South Carolina;* C. E. Kemper, "Early Westward Movement in Va.," in *Va. Mag. of Hist.*, XII–XIII; H. Schuricht, *History of German Element in Va.;* P. A. Strobel, *The Salzburghers, etc.;* G. P. Voight, "Swiss Notes on South Carolina," in *S. C. Hist. Mag.*, XXI, 93–104, and "German and Swiss Element in S. C.," in *Bull. of Univ. of S. C.*, no. 113; J. W. Wayland, *German Element of the Shenandoah Valley.*

Biography. — See refs. to ch. viii; Martin Brumbaugh, *Life of Christopher Dock;* Henry Harbaugh, *Life of Michael Schlatter;* M. D. Learned, *Life of Francis Daniel Pastorius;* Ann Maury (tr.) Jacques Fontaine, *Memoirs of a Huguenot Family, etc.;* J. S. Walton, *Conrad Weiser and the Indian Policy of Pa.*

Contemporary Accounts. — (a) BIBLIOGRAPHY: Channing, Hart and Turner, *Guide*, §§ 37–39, 42–43, 45–48, 117, 119–121, 123–124, 126, 146, 149, 160–162, 165; W. P. Trent (ed.), *Camb. Hist. of Am. Lit.*, I, 365–380, 385; see bibls. chs. xiii, xv, and J. T. Adams, *Prov. Society*, 332–335. (b) NARRATIVES: Israel Acrelius, "A History of New Sweden," (1759), in *Hist. Soc. Pa. Memoirs*, XI; C. T. Eben (tr.) Gottlieb Mittelberger, *Journey to Pa.* (1756); John Harrower (indentured servant), "Diary " in *Am. Hist. Rev.*, VI, 65–107; T. C. Holm, "A Short Description of the Province of New Sweden, 1702," in *Hist. Soc. Pa. Memoirs*, III; N. D. Mereness, *Travels in the Am. Colonies;* "Moravian Diaries of Travels through Va.," also in *Va. Mag. of Hist.*, XI–XII; Benjamin Rush, "Account of Germans," in *Pa. German Soc. Proc.*, XIX; J. F. Sachse (ed.) Flackner's "Curieus Nachricht," *etc.* (also in *Pa. German Soc. Proc.*, XIV); A. G. Spangenberg, "Diary," in *N. C. Col. Rec.*, V; "Rotterdam to Phil." (1728), in *Pa. German Soc. Proc.*, XVIII; V. H. Todd (ed.) Christopher von Graffenried, "Acct. of Founding of New Bern," in *Publica. N. C. Hist. Com.*, X. (c) DOCUMENTS AND RECORDS: Edith Abbott, *Immigration: Select Docs.*, and *Hist. Aspects of the Immigra. Prob.;* R. A. Brock, "Documents Relating to Huguenot Immigration," in *Va. Hist. So. Coll.*, n. s., V; B. R. Carroll, *Hist. Collec. of S. C.* (documents concerning John Peter Purry and Swiss emigration); A. B. Faust (ed.), "Documents Relating to Swiss Emigra. to Am.," in *Am. Hist. Rev.*, XXII, 98–132; A. L. Fries (ed.) "Recs. of Moravians of North Carolina," I–II (1752–1771); in *Publica. of N. C. Hist. Com.*, XII, XV; A. B. Hart (ed.), *Contemporaries*, II, §§ 29, 40; see numerous reprints and documents in *Pa. German Soc. Proc.*, VII–XIV.

97. Numbers and Races

FROM 1689 to 1754 the white population of the thirteen colonies increased from about 200,000 to 1,000,000 or more. At the latter date there were about 300,000 people in New England, 300,000 in the middle, and 400,000 in the southern colonies. This increase was due partly to natural growth, rapid because of large families, ten or more children being not uncommon. While the great

Population. Number and Distribution

bulk of the settlers in 1689 were of English stock, the situation was very different in 1750. This was due to immigration of non-English races, which came in increasing numbers from 1725 on. The largest group was that of the negroes, some 200,000, nine-tenths of them located in the southern colonies. Next in number were the Scotch-Irish; then the Germans, Irish, Scotch, French Huguenots and several small groups, such as Swiss, Scandinavians, and Hebrews. The ancestors of the Dutch and Swedes had come earlier, and their descendants lived mostly in the middle colonies. A considerable number of Indians were still living east of the Alleghenies. The Iroquois tribes were the most important single group of Indians.

The distribution of these racial groups was very uneven. In New England perhaps nine-tenths of the inhabitants were still of English descent. Due to scarcity of good cheap land, and to religious intolerance, few non-English immigrants settled in this region. In the middle colonies on the contrary, nearly two-thirds of the population by 1750 was made up of Dutch, Scotch-Irish, Germans, Irish, Scotch, Swedes, and French. In the southern colonies, the coast region was still largely occupied by the English, while the western regions were settled mainly by non-English groups, chiefly Scotch-Irish and Germans.

Immigration, westward expansion, the growth of the democratic ideal and sectionalism are among the most

Frontier and Coast important factors which help to explain the condition of the colonies in 1750. The last three were largely a result of the migration to the colonies of some 200,000 or more white immigrants, between 1689 and 1750. They settled principally on the frontier; that is, west of a line drawn about fifty miles from the coast, and therefore in general west of the fall line of the rivers flowing into the Atlantic. To this region have been given various names, such as "Interior," "Back country," "Up country," "Frontier," and "Old West." Likewise the region east of the fall line has been named "Coast," "Seaboard," "Tidewater," and "Low Country." The differences between these two regions in their environment, in the composition of their population, and in their ideals, gave rise to important results, which will be described later.

The various racial groups mentioned were identified with particular religious sects. Thus most of the Eng-

Race and Religious Sects

lish were Anglicans, Puritans, and Quakers; the French were Huguenots; the Scotch-Irish and the Scotch were nearly all Presbyterians; the Irish were Catholics; the main body of the Germans were Lutheran and German Reformed. Of minor German groups, the so-called German Sectarians were Mennonites, Dunkers, Moravians, and others. The Dutch adhered to the Dutch Reformed Church; the Swedes, to the Swedish Lutheran; and the Hebrews, to the Jewish. Geographically, the Anglicans, Puritans, Quakers, Huguenots, and Jews, and most of the Dutch were settled near the coast; while the other church groups were "up country" sects.

It is clear that most of these new immigrants were inhabitants of foreign countries, and hence were without previous allegiance to Great Britain. Two groups, though coming from the British Isles, had been so persecuted, that they started with either lack of full loyalty to England or with a distinctly hostile attitude; these were the Scotch-Irish and Irish. Next we may note that the tendency to settle on the frontier placed these groups in an isolated area, far removed from the immediate control of the King and his royal officials. In the effort of Great Britain to exercise political and economic control over the colonists, it is obvious that this large section of the population was, both through inheritance and environment, difficult to control. Hence British policies that directly affected these groups, such as land grants, quit rents, and religious intolerance, met a particularly hostile reception.

98. Causes, Agencies, and Methods of Immigration

The ideals of the immigrants were in part inherited and in part acquired. The inherited ideas were a product of those influences which induced emigration. After arrival immigrant ideals were influenced by the nature of the environment and the attitude of the crown and colonial governments towards immigrants in general. Various general causes operated over all of western Europe and the British Islands, that help to account for the movement. It may be noted first that the process of migration was largely by individuals and families, for the most part without the aid of, and often contrary to the wishes of, the nation from which the immigrants came. Witness the opposition of Swiss Cantons (1720–1738) to Swiss emigration. Bad conditions — political, economic, religious, and social — were the primary causes of emigration. The European wars of the seventeenth century had impoverished large numbers and brought on heavy taxes. A congestion of population existed in many localities. Political and religious persecution were frequent. Emigration was also stimulated by agents and companies. Many came as indentured servants, voluntarily and involuntarily — the latter largely of the convict and felon class. The poorer classes of Europe and the British Isles were land hungry, and saw an opportunity to better their economic condition by emi-

Old World Causes of Emigration

grating to America. A relatively large degree of political and religious liberty also attracted many people
greatly oppressed in these two respects. Illustrations
of these general causes will be given in connection
with the immediate causes for the migration of particular racial groups.

Besides conditions in the old world, forces operated
within the colonies that influenced immigration. After
Causes the second French war came a compara-
Operating tively long period of peace (1715–1740)
Within the
Colonies during which there was great economic
expansion. This was the period of the rapid extension
of the plantation system in the south, with a great
demand for labor, both negro slave and indentured
servant. The southern colonies also adopted a policy
of westward expansion and encouraged immigration,
besides allowing a large degree of religious toleration.
In the middle colonies this last factor was even more
general. Then the heirs of William Penn, as proprietors,
were anxious to profit from their lands, and sought
immigrants as a means of revenue from quit rents
and sale of lands. Speculators like Lord Fairfax were
also eager for immigrants to enhance the value of their
lands. In both sections the land laws were very loosely
administered. Immigrants soon discovered that land
was often virtually free on the frontier, so that " squatting " became a general method of settlement. Another
factor inducing large immigration was the realization
on the part of the crown and the colonial assemblies
that the best protection against the French and Indians
was a ·large population on the frontier, one that could
be depended on to bear the brunt of the fighting and to
act as a buffer between the French and Indians and
the coast settlements.

Since most of the immigrants were too poor to pay

the cost of their passage, the system of indentured servitude continued to be the main agency which en-
Agencies and Aids to Immigration
abled large numbers to cross the ocean to the promised land. This method of immigration was supplemented by aid given by the English government and the proprietors, by religious bodies and societies, and by the colonial governments. The latter offered generous grants of land, freedom from taxes or quit rents for a period of years, and even more direct aid, such as money, supplies, tools, food, etc. Forced emigration from Africa occurred as a result of the negro slave trade, and from England because the latter continued her policy of sending political prisoners and " jail birds " to the colonies as a punishment for crimes committed at home.

The speculative incentive too, led to great activity by land agents, ship-masters, and others who saw a chance to make a profit, honestly or dishonestly, by inducing people to emigrate by false promises and descriptions which told of the advantages and great ease of life in America. The " newlanders," or " soul sellers," were agents of this type, a heartless crew who preyed on the poor German. Their main purpose was to persuade poor people to sell all that they had and to turn the proceeds over to the agent. These agents then proceeded to fleece the victims so that the last penny was taken for passage and the " soul seller's " pockets. Thus the immigrant who landed in Philadelphia, or some other port, often minus even his baggage, was forced to become an indentured servant for four or five years.

Paid land agents also plied their trade, such as Benjamin Furley, agent of William Penn, who persuaded groups of Germans to purchase tracts of Penn's land for settlement. Another such agent was John Peter

Purry who entered into contracts with the colonial assembly of South Carolina to transport Swiss emigrants. The southern planters employed agents in England to recruit servants for their plantations, and numerous other types of agents managed the problems of emigration for the poor class. Of course there was always a steady non-assisted independent emigration of settlers who could afford to pay their passage and support themselves, pending the time when they could obtain work or income in their new home.

The printing press was also actively set to work. William Penn and Benjamin Furley may be said to have been the first great " realtors " and founders of American advertising. Some fifty or sixty books and pamphlets were published in the English, Dutch, German, and French languages and widely circulated in the Rhine country, giving glowing accounts of Pennsylvania as a veritable Garden of Eden, with a perfect climate, cheap and rich land, high wages, and most of the valuable products of earth and waters. Directions for the voyage over were given. One pamphlet, called " Authentic Tidings " (1702) contained 103 questions and answers relating to supplies, to the voyage over, the Indians, land, animals, and settlements. Pennsylvania was the best advertised province of the thirteen colonies, and it was largely due to printer's ink that the great stream of immigrants entered that colony.

The conditions affecting the immigrants on arrival varied according to whether they came voluntarily or involuntarily; according to the locality where they settled; and according to their occupation. To put it mildly most immigrants were sadly disillusioned. Few general laws were passed for their protection on shipboard and little or no attempt was made to protect or aid them, or even to regulate or

Conditions on Arrival

control them, after their arrival. Such problems as the responsibility of the ship-master for the health or food of passengers, the care of sick persons on arrival and the enforcement of the terms of indenture were the subjects of occasional legislation, but the laws were rarely enforced. The passage over was often a terrible experience. Crowding of vessels, poor and little food, lack of medical attendance and contagious diseases, often resulted in great mortality and sickness. Half of the passengers might die on a single ship. Of those who survived many were compelled to become indentured servants.

99. Immigration and Distribution of the Germans

The first large migration of Germans was to Pennsylvania, encouraged by William Penn and his agents, as already described. Conditions in Germany were ripe for emigration during the eighteenth century, because of religious, economic, and political conditions. By the treaty of Westphalia, which ended the Thirty Years' War in 1648, each reigning prince, lay or clerical, had the right to establish in his territory his own faith as that of all his subjects. Catholic princes persecuted the Mennonites, Waldenses, and in general the various Protestant sects. The wars of the seventeenth century laid waste large parts of Germany and there was terrible economic distress. Famine, exile, and the tyranny of the princes, who levied heavy taxes, reduced many almost to serfdom and beggary. The district known as the Palatinate in southwest Germany, with a population of 500,000, suffered most and became the focus of a large emigration.

The Germans in the Middle Colonies

In 1709, 13,000 Palatines, on the invitation of the English Government and as a result of books and

pamphlets sent to Germany, left their native land for
England. On arrival they were housed in barns, warehouses, and tents, and supported from funds provided
by the Queen. As a result of further aid from the
government and large voluntary contributions taken in
churches, the Palatines emigrated again, mainly to
South Ireland and America. Three thousand were sent
to New York in ten vessels, but 773 died on the voyage
over. Many settled on the Livingston Manor and were
employed in making naval stores. Later, 1712, they
removed to the Schoharie region in the Mohawk Valley.
The colony failed to prosper, for governmental support
was withdrawn and even some of the land acquired
by the Palatines was granted to several wealthy men
who demanded rents. They were known as the " Seven
Partners," among whom were Robert Livingston and
John Schuyler. Some remained and others moved to
Herkimer County. Finally, on the initiative of Governor Keith of Pennsylvania, many of the Palatines
left New York led by Conrad Weiser, and settled in
Pennsylvania during the period from 1723 to 1728.
This event greatly influenced later emigration to this
colony, and caused Governor Cosby of New York to
report to the assembly: " I see with concern that the
neighboring provinces are filled with honest useful
and laborious white people." He complained that New
York was receiving little benefit from such immigrants,
due in part to the bad treatment of the Palatines.

Germans from Switzerland, and others who were
called " Pietists," because of the peculiarities of their
religious beliefs, migrated to Pennsylvania and settled
largely in compact groups. Among these sects there
were the Mennonites, Moravians, Dunkers, and others.
These sects were noted for extreme piety and for their
contributions to social progress such as anti-slavery

and educational ideas, to be discussed later. Among the pietistic religious leaders who came to America and the sects they represented and the locality where they settled, there were the following. Pastorius was the leader of the Mennonites at Germantown. Conrad Beissel headed the Dunkers (German Baptists) who settled at Ephrata, Lancaster County. Count Zinzendorf was the leader of the Moravians at Nazareth and Bethlehem.

The main body of the Germans came to Pennsylvania after 1730. They were Lutherans, and German Reformed, who were followers of Calvin and Zwingli. They held religious doctrines similar to those of the Presbyterians and Dutch Reformed. These sects increased very rapidly, and by 1750 the Lutherans had established forty churches and the German Reformed thirty. The great religious leaders of these two groups were Henry Muhlenberg and Michael Schlatter, the latter sent to America by the Synod of Holland. Most of these later comers settled on the frontiers and in less compact groups than those already mentioned. The total number of Germans who migrated to Pennsylvania is not known. But it is known that 22,000 arrived by ships between 1727 and 1745. These with the 20,000 who had arrived before 1727 make a total of 42,000. It is probable that with other arrivals up to 1750, and the natural increase, a total number of 70,000 Germans were living in this one colony at this date. They were the original source of the so-called "Pennsylvania Dutch" still occupying portions of central Pennsylvania.

Germans also migrated to the southern colonies. As early as 1714–1720 Governor Spotswood founded a colony of Germans at Germana in Virginia for the purpose of developing iron mines. Direct immigration of Palatines to Maryland seaports between 1748 and

1753 amounted to about 2800. Frederick County was largely settled by Germans. Some 600 of the Palatines who fled from Germany in 1709 migrated to North Carolina and founded Newbern. Large numbers settled in the western counties of the southern colonies, who had migrated there from Pennsylvania, a movement to be described later. In South Carolina settlements were made at Purrysburg, Beaufort County, and in Orange County. These were largely the Swiss immigrants from German speaking Cantons. To Georgia came the Salzburgers who founded Ebenezer. Even New England had in 1740 a German settlement, that at Waldoborough, Maine, east of the Kennebec River. It is estimated that the total number of Germans in all the colonies in 1750 was not far from 100,000.

100. Scotch-Irish and Other Racial Groups

Another large emigration movement originated in northern Ireland, known as the Scotch-Irish emigra-
The Scotch-Irish tion. This group was not a mixture of Scotch and Irish, but rather Lowland Scotch Protestants who had originally been given land by James I, in Ulster Province, Ireland, as early as 1610. Their descendants lived in this and in the adjoining counties for several generations. They seldom intermarried with the native Catholic Irish, and generally retained their religious and social beliefs and customs. In fact, they were hated by the Irish whose land they seized.

Even Protestants in Ireland were subject to adverse legislation by England. Statutory restrictions provided for the exclusion of Presbyterians from all offices under the crown, civil and military, and for the payment of tithes by all sects for the support of the Anglican church. Presbyterian ministers could not legally perform the marriage ceremony, under very severe penalty.

The English restrictive commercial policy was applied to Ireland as well as to the colonies. Thus there were laws in the interest of the English farmers to prohibit the exportation into England from Ireland of live stock, salted meats, and dairy products. The Navigation Acts applied to Ireland, and continental goods destined for Ireland must come through England. The Irish woolen industry was also suppressed, and wool could be exported only to England. Moreover after 1718, rents increased to double or treble their former amount, and ejections occurred on a considerable scale. Several times crop failures occurred as in 1718–19 and 1740. Thus political, economic, and religious conditions drove many persons from Ireland most of whom were already haters of England.

The Scotch-Irish immigrants dispersed widely throughout the colonies. Between 1714 and 1720, fifty-four ships carrying emigrants from Ireland entered the port of Boston. In one year (1718), five shiploads came with 750 immigrants. Settlements were made at Worcester, and in western Massachusetts, around Londonderry, New Hampshire, and in Maine. Later, Ulster and Orange Counties, New York, and particularly Western Pennsylvania, received large numbers. As a result of a famine in Ireland, in 1740–1741, for several years some 12,000 emigrated to America each year.

Distribution in the Colonies

The Scotch-Irish emigrated also to the southern colonies. For example Henry McCulloch from Ulster County obtained a grant of 64,000 acres in Dauphin County, North Carolina, and brought over some 3000 to 4000 Scotch-Irish. As in the case of the Germans,

large numbers of Scotch-Irish from Pennsylvania settled in the western counties of the southern colonies.
It has been estimated that 100,000 of this racial group
had migrated to America up to 1750 though this number undoubtedly includes many who were Irish or
Scotch, rather than the so-called Scotch-Irish.

The migration of the French Huguenots was due
principally to the revocation of the Edict of Nantes
The French   in 1685 by the French. The effect of this
Huguenots   act was to deny religious toleration, and
hence it stimulated emigration to the colonies. The
important centers were New York (especially Westchester County), Virginia, and Charles Town, South Carolina. Massachusetts also received some Huguenots. The
French Huguenots did not come in large numbers, but
the immigrants of this race were above the average in
intelligence. In proportion to their numbers they were
a very valuable element in the population, for they
mixed easily with the English. Thus their racial characteristics disappeared rather rapidly.

Other white racial groups included the native Irish,
Scotch, Scandinavians, and Jews, who came in smaller
Other Racial   groups or as individuals. Except in a few
Groups   localities they were scattered, and therefore made no such impress on the political and social
history of the colonies as in the case of the groups
previously described. It must be remembered that the
largest number of newcomers was that of the negroes
from Africa. It is estimated that 260,000 were living
in the colonies in 1754.

101. Problems of Immigration

Many problems were raised by this great wave of
immigration, especially in relation to the occupation
of the frontier region. By 1750 two settled regions ex-

isted, particularly in the middle and southern colonies; two societies unlike in racial composition, and in politi-

Nature of   cal, economic, social, and religious ideals.
Problems   The frontier was a region of democratic tendencies inspired by belief in political equality, free land, and religious liberty. In the coastal area minority rule was defended, as well as monopolistic control of natural resources, and religious intolerance. The contest for the supremacy of such conflicting ideals is the key to an understanding of much of the history of eighteenth century America. Some exceptions to this general statement must be made. For example, in Pennsylvania there was religious toleration, and in New England few racial problems.

In proportion as the two sections amalgamated and became one people with common purposes and ideals, a desire for the development of democratic ideals and for union and independence became possible. In proportion as the desires of the two sections diverged, the forces of sectionalism and particularism were bound to prevail. In nearly every colony there was a struggle between aristocracy, conservatism, and minority rule on the one hand, and democracy, liberalism, and government by the majority on the other. The great problem was to mould these diverse elements of the population into a self-conscious unity in each colony, and then into one nation with common ideals. Many forces were at work, some promoting and some retarding unity.

More in detail, must be emphasized the significance of such problems as assimilation and Americanization; intermarriage and naturalization; political equality, suffrage, representation, and qualifications for office holding; protection of the frontier; equitable distribution of land; a fair system of taxation; widespread means of transportation, roads and bridges; separation of church and state; religious toleration and liberty; establishment of schools, courts, and an equitable administration of justice.

Certain influences always tended towards unity of ideals and purposes. The physical environment, in its Unifying relation to that of England and her policies, Influences usually made for union. Isolation and the effect of environment on political and economic needs and desires tended to unite all groups of the population in their resistance to English policies. Social environment tended to make the newcomers conform to one type. The use of the English language, in oral and written speech, the forms of local government, system of courts, legal ideas, all tended to produce a common type. The general method of settlement, except in parts of Pennsylvania, Virginia, and in a few other places, was by individuals and families rather than by groups. On the frontier intermarriage between racial groups also promoted a common type.

The policy of both England and the colonial assemblies was to favor Americanization though not Natural- completely. Naturalization and the privi-ization leges of citizenship did not necessarily lead to liberal and equal political privileges. Nevertheless the charters of Virginia (1609) and Massachusetts (1629) granted the right to "abide and live" not only to our "loving subjects" but to "any other strangers that will become our loving subjects." From time to time the newcomers were given certain rights as citizens by general naturalization laws enacted by Parliament. This status did not include the right of suffrage, which was under the control of the Assemblies.

A general act was passed by Parliament in 1709 naturalizing the Palatines. The proprietors of the Carolinas and New Jersey gave to the assemblies the right to grant "naturalization unto all strangers as to them shall seem meet." At various times the colonies of New York, Pennsylvania, and Virginia passed acts naturalizing all foreign-born inhabitants, usually requiring that they should take the oath of allegiance. South Carolina passed an act in 1704 to encourage settlement and granted citizenship to aliens allowing them the suffrage under certain conditions. But naturalized aliens were prohibited from taking seats in the assembly. In 1740 Parliament passed an act conferring naturalization, with some restrictions, on all persons who had resided seven years in any of the British colonies in America.

On the other hand many factors retarded immigration, amalgamation and unity. Some colonies opposed the settlement of particular racial and religious groups to which great intolerance was shown. The Quakers, Catholics, and Baptists suffered most. Where immigrants settled in groups, the tendency was to maintain their native language and religion and old world customs and ideals. In such cases groups were likely to oppose marriage with other racial groups and to rely on parochial schools for education so that the language and religion of the parents might be taught. This greatly hindered the progress of Americanization.

Influences Against Union

Pennsylvania was disturbed over the influx of immigrants and the governors expressed fear that it would become a "foreign" colony unless measures were taken to stem the tide. Governor Keith complained in 1717 that "great numbers of foreigners from Germany, strangers to our language and constitutions," had arrived, and pointed out the danger from other "foreigners from any nation whatever, as well enemies as friends, who might throw

Fears of Immigration

themselves on us." James Logan wrote to the Proprietor of Pennsylvania (1727), "You will soon have a German Colony here and perhaps such a one as Britain received from Saxony in the fifth century." Two years earlier (1725) he had written, " It looks as if Ireland is to send all her inhabitants hither . . . if they will continue to come they will make themselves proprietors of the Province."

In the year 1750, 4317 Germans were brought into Pennsylvania besides 1000 British and Irish passengers and servants, and it was suggested that an act of Parliament should be passed to prevent such numbers from entering the province which might " soon degenerate into a foreign colony." Benjamin Franklin, in a famous letter of 1753, commented on the dangers of immigration; he feared disorders because of the failure of the Germans to learn English and because of the influence of the German newspapers. He said, " Unless the stream of importation is turned to other colonies they will outnumber us. We will not be able to preserve our language and our government will be precarious." These fears, however, were not realized. The Germans were not interested in politics. Many were located on the frontier far from centers of political agitation and in general most of them were willing, especially in the second and third generations, to abide by English rule and customs.

Some anti-immigration laws were passed to keep out undesirable servants — convicts and felons — whom Anti-immi- England endeavored to unload on the gration Laws colonies. Restrictive duties were placed on such, but they were usually disallowed by the Privy Council. Pennsylvania tried to prevent importation of convicts in 1722, and again in 1730, with a duty of £5 on each. Maryland attempted to restrict Catholics

(1715) by imposing a fine of 20 shillings on Irish servants ("Papists") imported. Virginia passed an act (1699) imposing a tax of 20 shillings on servants imported "not born in England or Wales."

102. Effects of Immigration

Immigration and racial influences are closely connected with the nature and course of political, economic, and religious sectionalism within individual colonies. The colonial assemblies were almost exclusively English in their racial makeup. From a racial standpoint the English were inclined to look down upon other racial groups as inferior. This was intensified by religious complications, as where Anglicans in the South and New York, Quakers in Pennsylvania, and Puritans in New England, struggled to maintain not only political but racial and religious control. Most of the immigrants of the eighteenth century were naturally democratic in their ideals; because of the causes leading to emigration, of frontier influences, and of the nature of their creeds and church organization. That is, they were practically all opposed to centralized governments, and were upholders of equality of economic opportunity, religious toleration, and liberty.

The democratic nature of the Pietists and their followers is especially significant. Pietism is the name of a religious movement originating in Germany, having as its basis a simple and spiritual form of Christianity, believed to be like that of the primitive Christians. The Mennonites and Moravians belong to this group, as well as the Quakers and the Methodists. They all had one common quality — the belief that religious truth could be obtained by independent, direct insight, or the "inner light" as the Quakers described it. Many of these religious sects migrated to Pennsylvania, such as the Mennonites, Dunkers, and Moravians. They were opposed to a union of church and state, believed in religious liberty, discarded ritual and ceremony, demanded conversion and reform in conduct, encouraged missions and opened their churches to people of all classes, especially the poor. This religious movement then was therefore essentially popular and democratic in its tendencies. The frontier Presbyterians and Baptists were democratic in their ideals because of similar reasons.

The influence of racial characteristics is difficult to evaluate. It is generally agreed that most Germans Racial Con-   were religious-minded, tolerant, peaceful, tributions   industrious, and thrifty. Their contributions were largely religious, social, and economic rather than political in character. The Presbyterian Scotch-Irish, on the other hand, were militant, political-minded, and jealous of their political rights. Their clergy generally were educated, promoters of education and of civil and religious liberty. The value of a racial stock depends principally on its power of assimilation and its ability to pass on to the nation the best elements of its culture, through its important leaders and the race itself.

This Scotch-Irish element, owing to its numbers, its inherited antagonism, and attitude, towards England; because of its religion, settlement on the frontier, militancy, love of liberty, and the character of its clergy, was one of the most important in the colonies. From the Scotch-Irish came some famous political leaders, east and west, such as Patrick Henry and Andrew Jackson. The French Huguenots, though a small group, produced some noted leaders in commercial and political life, such as Gabriel Manigault of South Carolina,

James DeLancey and John Jay of New York, Elias Boudinot of Pennsylvania and Peter Faneuil, Paul Revere, and James Bowdoin of Massachusetts.

The important and immediate influence of immigrants representing non-English racial stocks was their contribution to the defense of the frontier and the help they gave in wresting the interior of the continent from the French. They also promoted democratic ideas in the distribution of land, and religious toleration and liberty. Thus they became important factors in the sectional conflict within the colonies, and later in the struggle to apply the philosophy of the American revolution to all classes and races. During the Revolution unity was hindered somewhat because certain racial and religious groups upheld pacifist doctrines, and in some cases supported the British cause. Many native born Americans, however, were also "loyalists."

Many were the types of immigrants, representing a great variety of races, classes, occupations, and re-
Immigrants and Social and Economic Progress ligious beliefs, with varied moral and mental characteristics. Generally speaking, most of them were poor, many were illiterate, and some were undesirable, especially the hardened convicts. Fortunately, starting life in a new environment tended to improve the opportunity of the immigrant to develop into a good citizen; yet the colonies contended that England was sending far too many "jail birds" to America. During the eighteenth century the home country continued to think of the colonies as a place for "undesirable citizens." Political prisoners were banished, and convicts and felons continued to be transported and sold as indentured servants, a penalty for crimes committed. This practice called forth a famous remark of Dr. Samuel Johnson (1769); referring to the colonists he said,

"Sir, they are a race of convicts and ought to be content with anything we allow them short of hanging." But Benjamin Franklin in reply to the argument that it was necessary to rid England of convicts, asked whether, for the same reason, the Americans would be justified in sending their rattlesnakes to England!

While the bulk of the immigrants settled on the frontier and became farmers, many artisans plied their trade. It must be remembered that the immigrant, often an indentured servant, was the main source of supply for skilled workmen of all sorts; and that many types of craftsmen were represented, as is shown by the following advertisement, found in the Virginia Gazette, of a shipload of servants whose time was to be sold, "Just arrived at Leedstown the Ship Justitia, with about one Hundred Healthy Servants. Men, Women and Boys, among which are many Tradesmen — *viz.*, Blacksmiths, Shoemakers, Tailors, House Carpenters, and Joiners, A Cooper, a Bricklayer and Plaisterer, a Painter, a Watchmaker and Glazier, several Silversmiths, Weavers, a Jeweler, and many others. The sale will commence on Tuesday, the 2d of April, at Leeds Town on Rappahannock River. A Reasonable Credit will be allowed, giving Bond with Approved Security to Thomas Hodge." Nevertheless it must not be forgotten that the mass of the immigrants engaged in agricultural pursuits. The attractive power of free land was in fact one of the great weaknesses of the colonies from one standpoint.

One writer described the colonies about 1763 as follows: "Some few towns excepted we are all tillers of the soil from Nova Scotia to West Florida. We are a people of cultivators, scattered over an immense area." Almost everywhere there was a great shortage of mechanics, artisans, and skilled workmen, because of the fact that few immigrants cared to remain long as day laborers or mechanics working for a daily wage, when fifty acres of land could be had for a few dollars, or gratis, if squatted on.

CHAPTER XIII

THE FRENCH–ENGLISH WARS, FRONTIER POLICIES AND WESTWARD EXPANSION
(1689–1750)

103. References

Bibliographies. — See bibls. to chs. ii, xi and xii; H. D. Bolton and T. M. Marshall, *Coloniza. of North Am.*, 273–274, 328, 383; Channing, Hart and Turner, *Guide*, §§ 30–35, 37–39, 42–43, 45, 48, 91–97, 99, 106, 108–110, 147–149, 161–165; H. U. Faulkner, *Am. Economic Hist.*, 138–139; E. B. Greene, *Prov. Am.*, 327–340, and *Foundations of Am. Nationality*, 386–387; Grace Griffin, *Writ. on Am. Hist.*, 1906–1923; J. N. Larned, *Lit. of Am. Hist.*, 410–421; R. G. Thwaites, *France in Am.*, 296–305; F. J. Turner and Frederick Merk, *List of Refs. on the Hist. of the West*, 13–30, esp. 31–37; Justin Winsor, *Nar. and Crit. Hist. of Am.*, V, 560–611.

Historical Maps. — H. D. Bolton and T. M. Marshall, *Coloniza. of North Am.*, 260, 311, 372; Channing, Hart and Turner, *Guide*, §§ 32–34, 96–97, 162, (bibliography); map no. 4 of this volume; D. R. Fox, *Atlas of Am. Hist.*, 12–16; Ralph Harlow, *Growth of U. S.*, 118 (North Am. in 1713), 123 (1760); A. B. Hart (ed.), *Commonwealth Hist. Mass.*, II, 92–95, 452–454; L. K. Matthews, *Expansion of New Engl.*, p. 70; Justin Winsor, *Nar. and Crit. Hist. of Am.*, maps in V.

General Accounts. — (See refs. to ch. ii); W. C. Abbott, *Expan. of Eu.*, II, chs. xxv-xxx, xxxii; H. E. Bolton and T. M. Marshall, *Coloniza. of North Am.*, chs. xiii, xv, xvii, xx; Edward Channing, *Hist. of U. S.*, II, ch. xviii; F. C. Dietz, *Polit. and Soc. Hist. of England*, 338–348; J. A. Doyle, *Engl. Col. in Am.*, V, 406–426; H. U. Faulkner, *Am. Econom. Hist.*, ch. vi; E. B. Greene, *Prov. Am.*, chs. vii-x and *Foundations etc.*, ch. x; Ralph Harlow, *Growth of U. S.*, chs. xi-xii; C. J. H. Hayes, *Polit. and Soc. Hist. of Mod. Europe*, chs. vi-ix; S. L. Mims, *Colbert's West Indian Policy*; H. E. Osgood, *Am. Colonies in the 18th Cent.*, I, chs. ii-iii, vii, xiii-xiv, xvi, III, ch. xvii; pt. III, ch. iii; J. G. Palfrey, *Hist. of New Engl.*, V, 58–91, ch. xi, IV, 257–287; Francis Parkman, *Count Frontenac and New France* and *Half Century of Conflict;* F. W. Pitman, *Devel. of British West Indies 1700–1763;* C. G. Robertson, *England under the*

Hanoverians; Theodore Roosevelt, *Winning of the West,* I; J. R. Seeley, *Growth of British Policy;* Ellen Semple, *Am. Hist. and its Geog. Conds.,* ch. i-iii; R. G. Thwaites, *France in Am.,* chs. vi-vii, F. J. Turner, *Frontier in Am. Hist.,* chs. i-iii; Justin Winsor, *Nar. and Crit. Hist. of Am.,* V, ch. vii and 483-490, and *Westward Movement,* chs. i-vii.

Special Accounts.—(a) GENERAL: C. M. Andrews, "Anglo-French Commercial Rivalry" (1700-1750), in *Am. Hist. Rev.,* XX, 539-556, 761-780; O. M. Dickerson, *Am. Colonial Govt.,* ch. vi. (b) NORTHERN FRONTIER: J. T. Adams, *Revolutionary New England,* chs. i, v, vi, viii, ix; A. H. Buffington, "New England and the Western Fur Trade," in *Coll. Soc. Mass. Pubs.,* xvii, 160-192; S. A. Drake, *Border Wars of New Engl.;* John Fiske, *New France and New Engl.;* A. B. Hart (ed.), *Commonwealth Hist. Mass.,* II, chs. iii, xiv; L. K. Matthews, *Expansion of New Engl.,* chs. i-v; George Sheldon, *Hist. of Deerfield, Mass. etc. and Indian Wars;* H. M. Sylvester, *Indian Wars of New Engl.* (3 vols.). (c) WESTERN FRONTIER: C. W. Alvord, *Miss. Valley in British Politics,* I; G. A. Cribbs, *Frontier Policy of Pa.;* A. H. Buffington, "The Policy of Albany and Engl. West. Expan.," in *Miss. Val. Hist. Rev.,* viii, 327-366; R. W. Kelsey, *Friends and Indians;* C. H. McIlwain (ed.), Peter Wraxall, *Abridgment of the N. Y. Indian Records* (Introduction). (d) SOUTHERN FRONTIER: H. E. Bolton and Mary Ross, *The Debatable Land, etc.;* V. W. Crane, *The Southern Frontier;* C. C. Jones, *Hist. of Ga.,* I, 314-369; Edward McCrady, *Hist. of South Carolina under Proprietary Govt., 1670-1719,* chs. xvi-xvii; *Hist. of South Carolina under the Royal Govt., 1719-1776,* 187-229.

Biographies.—(See references to ch. xi); Everett Kimball, *Public Life of Joseph Dudley;* W. L. Stone, *Sir William Johnson;* A. T. Volweiler, *George Croghan and the Westward Movement;* J. S. Walton, *Conrad Weiser and the Indian Policy of Colonial Pa.;* G. A. Wood, "Public Life of William Shirley" in *Columb. Stud.,* XCII.

Contemporary Accounts.—(a) BIBLIOGRAPHY: Channing, Hart and Turner, *Guide,* § 162; A. R. Hasse, *Materials for a Bibliog. etc., Hist. Sources in Schs.,* § 75; see references under "Contemporary Accts.," chs. x-xi and xii. (b) NARRATIVES: C. W. Alvord and Lee Bidgood, *First Explorations of the Trans-Allegheny Region by Virginia, 1650-1674;* J. S. Bassett, *Writings of Wm. Byrd, etc.,* Cadwalader Colden, *Hist. of Five Indian Nations* (ed. by G. P. Winship, 1904); Christopher Gist (1751) and Dr. Thomas Walker (1750), Journals of, in *Filson Club*

Publication, no. 13; J. F. Jameson (ed.), *Narratives of Early Am. Hist.*, (C. H. Lincoln, *Narratives of Indian Wars*). (c) DOCU-MENTS AND RECORDS: See Channing, Hart and Turner, *Guide*, p. 322, for "Colonial Laws on Frontier Counties;" for "Land Companies" see *Ibid.*, p. 322; Peter Force, *Tracts, etc.* (4 vols.); Ralph Gabriel (ed.), *Pageant of America;* A. B. Hart (ed.), *Contemporaries*, II, chs. xvii, xviii (Indians), xix (Wars); C. E. Kemper, "Early Westward Movement," in *Va. Mag. Hist.*, XII, XIII; C. H. Lincoln (ed.), William Shirley, *Correspondence;* C. H. McIlwain (ed.), Peter Wraxall, *Abridgment of the N. Y. Indian Records, etc.* (1678–1751); Alex. Spotswood, "Official Letters," in *Va. Hist. Soc. Colls.* I–II; James Sullivan (ed.), *Sir William Johnson Papers* (5 vols.); R. G. Thwaites, *Early Western Travels*, I (journals of Conrad Weiser and George Croghan).

104. The Struggle of France and England for the Interior

THE Wars of France and England for supremacy, from 1689 to 1763 were staged on a world wide arena; Meaning of the International Conflict in Europe, India, Africa, and America. The conflict within North America was accordingly only one aspect of the struggle. In a large sense it was a contest of two civilizations, in which political, religious, and economic ideals were in conflict: absolute versus limited monarchy; a restricted versus an extensive system of local self-government; Catholicism versus Protestantism, and a feudal system of land tenure and monopolistic control of commerce, as compared with a system of free holdings of land and to a large extent free economic development. With these differences must also be connected the rivalry of pioneer explorers and missionaries in the seventeenth century.

During the first half of the eighteenth century the French territory was occupied by a very small population made up largely of traders, soldiers, missionaries, and officials. Thus in time of war, French resources in

men and supplies were meager as compared with the English. On the other hand, the French had more In-
French and English Advantages and Disadvantages
dian allies than the English, a fact which was one of the chief sources of their strength. While the English colonies were relatively strong in population and resources, they were loosely organized, jealous of each other, and indifferent to danger to their neighbors. They could be induced to act together only when actually threatened with attack on their own territory.

The year 1689 marks the outbreak of the three-quarter-century-long French wars and England's long
Expansion of New France
struggle with France for empire and trade, culminating in the peace of 1763. France had been gradually extending her power towards the great lakes and south into the middle west throughout the seventeenth century. France like England was aiming at colonial and commercial supremacy in Europe, Asia, and America. Traders explored the upper Mississippi; and Joliet and Marquette reached the junction of the Arkansas and Mississippi in 1673. French explorers and missionaries were particularly active during the administration of Count Frontenac, governor of Canada from 1672 to 1682. Fort Frontenac was built at the outlet of Lake Ontario in 1673. La Salle reached the mouth of the Mississippi in 1682 and took possession of the whole Mississippi Valley in the name of the King. French missionaries and fur traders followed, military posts and forts were erected, and alliances were formed with the Indians. The result was international rivalry for the profits of the fur trade, both in the north through the Iroquois country and in the south around South Carolina. These events aroused English statesmen to the serious dangers from French expansion, and the growing obstacle to the

expansion of England into the interior of North
America.

In Europe, too, the ambition of France to play the
leading rôle, anxiety over the balance of power, com-
European   mercial rivalry, and the effort of Louis
Influences   XIV to put back on the throne of England James II, Catholic, finally led to the outbreak of
war in 1689. The new King, William III, now headed
the European alliance against Louis XIV. Again
shortly after the Peace of Ryswick (1697) the Union
of the French and Spanish crowns under Louis XIV
and Philip V (1701) challenged England's political and
commercial supremacy, and caused war in several
quarters of the world.

In the first struggle, King William's War (1689–
1697), most of the fighting was on the northern fron-
The First   tier, and the French directed their
Two Wars   attacks against the Iroquois, alienated from
the French since 1609. The Iroquois thus served as a
buffer state, protecting New York and New England
from blows that otherwise might have fallen directly
on the English. The most important success of the
colonists was the capture of Port Royal by Sir William
Phips in 1690. England, for the first time, was faced
with the problem of fighting both France and Spain
on the continent and in the West Indies and also along
the frontier of the colonies. The Peace of Ryswick
(1697) failed to make a real settlement of the problem.

The second war in America was known as Queen
Anne's War (1702–1713). Border warfare, attacks on
the frontier towns of New England and massacres by
the Indians were the characteristic features. It was in
this war that the famous massacre at Deerfield, Mass.
(1704) occurred. The Treaty of Utrecht, 1713, had one
important clause bearing on the control of the interior;
the French acknowledged the suzerainty of the British

over the Iroquois, which amounted to a kind of protectorate. On the strength of this political relation the shadowy claims of the Iroquois to lands south of the Great Lakes were claimed by England. By the "Asiento" British slave traders gained the privilege of supplying slaves to the Spanish colonial possessions. Newfoundland, important for New England fisheries, became a British possession; and Acadia was transformed into the British province of Nova Scotia. Nevertheless the war and the peace left unsolved the great question, that of control of the interior.

Between 1713 and 1740 the two nations strengthened their positions and their plans concerning western Third lands in America. English hunters, traders, French War and explorers were continually penetrating farther west, and thus coming into conflict with the French and Spanish. The settlement of Georgia (1732) brought the English into close contact with the Spaniards and their Indian allies.

England declared war on Spain in 1739, and the offensive was taken on the southern border by an expedition under General Oglethorpe in 1742 against St. Augustine. The war in Europe was known as the War of the Austrian Succession.

French aid to Spain led England into war again. Thus was precipitated the third colonial war, known in America as King George's War, 1744–1748. The capture of Louisburg on Cape Breton Island by a New England military expedition (1745) was the outstanding colonial event. Border warfare and Indian raids again brought distress on the New England frontier. The peace of Aix-la-Chapelle, in 1748, again failed to settle the main issue in America, for both sides retained the territory which they had previously possessed.

Between 1747 and 1753, both sides were active in

extending their power in the Ohio Valley. In 1747
Governor Dinwiddie of Virginia and nineteen other gen-
The Rivals   tlemen organized a land company called the
in the Ohio   Ohio Company. Among the stockholders
Valley,
1747–53   were Augustine and Lawrence Washington,
brothers of George Washington. A grant of 500,000
acres of land in that wilderness was made by the
Council of Virginia, for the purpose of founding frontier settlements. The French also were active, and sent
Céloron de Bienville (or Blainville) down the Allegheny
and Ohio in 1749. He deposited lead plates which set
forth the French claim to this region, and built forts in
the disputed territory. Thus the rival claims of the two
nations indicated that another conflict must soon take
place to settle the great question of the possession
of the interior. This fourth war, treated in the next
volume of this series, is known as the French and
Indian War, 1756–1763, and finally resulted in victory
for the English.

105. Indian Relations in Peace and War

The policy of the Board of Trade towards the Indi-
ans from the year 1696 included three main points:
Indian   first, preservation of the alliance of the
Trade
Policy of   Iroquois and southwestern Indians as a
New York   barrier against the interior tribes and the
and the
French   French; second, the policy of " divide and
rule " — of playing off one tribe against another; third,
development of the fur trade at the expense of the
French. The necessity of holding the support of the
Iroquois stimulated the practice of making presents to
the Indians on a large scale. Conferences were held almost yearly at Albany and the official Indian Commissioners were busy men as the Iroquois influence
extended west to the Mississippi and even to the

Carolinas. They were thus a great obstacle to French territorial aims and, acting as middlemen, seriously interfered with the French fur trade.

The Indian fur trade of New York was extremely important in the eighteenth century, both for its intrinsic value, and because of its relation to the plans of the French. The governmental trade policy was not only economic but political in character. For it was realized that friendly trade relations were one of the best means to secure political control over the Indians in competition with the French. Effort was made to prevent frauds on the Indians, and to concentrate trade, especially at Albany; also by establishing in 1675 a board of commissioners for Indian affairs. Sir William Johnson, resident in the Mohawk Valley, was a member from 1743; and from 1746 he was sole superintendent of Indian Affairs. Peter Kalm, a Swedish traveler, wrote in 1749, " There is not a place in all the British Colonies, the Hudson Bay Settlements excepted, where such quantities of furs and skins are bought of the Indians as at Albany. Most of the merchants in this town send a clerk or agent to Oswego, an English trading town on Lake Ontario, to which the Indians resort with their furs. The merchants from Albany spend the whole summer at Oswego, and trade with many tribes of Indians who come to them with their goods."

The Indian commissioners stationed at Albany were usually themselves traders and anxious for profits. They were able to furnish goods for trade more cheaply than the French, and, besides, made great use of liquor as an article of trade, though the sachems of the Five Nations protested and declared to the Commissioners, " We must think you sell it with no other design than to destroy us." Due to the cheapness of British goods and the Indians' love of liquor, the Iroquois remained true to the British alliance, and thus offset the natural advantage and ability of the French in Indian diplomacy.

The relation between Christianizing the Indians and protecting them was a matter of considerable thought on the part of the governors of New York, who sought to send -missionaries to them. Governor Hunter's instructions (1709) provided that he was to use his endeavors with the assembly to arrange for missionaries to live among the Iroquois " in order to instruct them and also to prevent their being seduced from their allegiance to us by the French priests and Jesuits." Even more explicit is a letter of Sir William Johnson, Indian agent, to Governor Clinton, 1744. He advocated fair business dealings, aid and sympathy when in trouble. " But you can never completely depend on him or overcome the inherent fickleness of his nature until you have made a Christian of him and brought him thereby under that sense of personal responsibility not only to men, but to the Almighty that religion teaches. Either in war or peace, one Christian Indian is always worth two heathen ones."

Both New York and Pennsylvania maintained Indian agents; and on the tact, wisdom, and skill of these men, often depended the peace and safety of the colony. George Croghan and Conrad Weiser were the most noted of these in Pennsylvania and Sir William Johnson in New York. Much of the credit for holding the Iroquois true to the English cause during the French and Indian war must be given to these men.

The Quakers and the Indians

In spite of the friendly attitude and care of the Quakers, Indian disaffection arose because of the encroachment of the squatters on Indian territory. The famous three days' walking purchase of Penn and the Indians (1682) covered only thirty miles in one and a half days. In 1733, however, it was decided to complete the walk; hence three of the fastest walkers in the colony were employed, roads were cleared for them, and horses provided to carry them across rivers. This enabled one of the walkers, Edward Marshall, to cover 86 miles in a day and a half. The Indians asserted that he ran and that they were cheated.

Attempts were made to regulate trade, but many non-resident traders from Maryland, Virginia, and New York refused to be bound by such regulations. Traders were furnished with instructions which prohibited trading with drunken Indians, incensing the Indians against any trader, and providing that goods should be sold at a common price. Traders were also licensed, and after 1710 no one could trade without a license issued by the governor, though the rule was evaded. The Indian agent, Conrad Weiser, was active in informing against unscrupulous traders, and recommended the revocation of their licenses. Rum as an article of exchange was prohibited by several laws, and the heavy fine of £20 provided for violation. Many Indian traders were, however, unscrupulous and dishonest, and violated the laws. Great rivalry among traders within the territory and among those from neighboring colonies existed, one of the causes leading up to the final struggle for the control of the Indian trade of the Ohio Valley.

Some of the colonial assemblies offered bounties for Indian scalps. The Connecticut assembly, for example, Bounties in 1704, enacted that "this court will allow out of the publick treasurie the sume of five pounds for every mans scalp of the enemy killed in this Colonie." And Massachusetts offered bounties for scalps graduated according as scalps offered were those of men, women or youths. The Reverend Solomon Stoddard of Northampton, Massa-

Bounties for Indian Scalps in New England

chusetts, 1703, urged the use of dogs " to hunt Indians as they do Bears." The excuse for this was that the Indians acted " like wolves and are to be dealt with as wolves." One woman took part in this pastime: Hannah Dustin of Haverhill, Mass., received a bounty of £50 for ten Indian scalps, won in her famous rescue of herself and her children. The ferocious attitude of some white men towards the Indians added to the difficulties of maintaining friendly relations between the races.

At the outbreak of war with France in 1689, the more complete knowledge of the plans of the French to occupy the Mississippi valley and to use the Indians against the English caused the Indian problem to become more serious than ever. Along the frontier from Maine to Florida the Indians were a menace in time of peace and especially of war. They were an obstacle to westward expansion and the occupation of the land for agricultural purposes. They were dangerous in the international wars involving Spain, France, England, and the colonies, because nearly all the tribes except the Iroquois were hostile and in alliance with England's enemies. Even the Iroquois were at times almost won over by the French.

Within the English colonies the Indians were the occasion for internal disturbances between the newly arrived immigrants and squatters and the colonial assemblies; and they affected the course of the constitutional struggle between the Crown and royal governors and the assemblies. The problems of protection of military defenses, supplies, control of military forces, taxation and expenditures were all closely related to the Indians. In the colonial wars the Indians occupied a middle region between the English and the French. There they were in close contact with the English colonists through trade, through encroachment on their lands by squatters, through treaties, Indian agents, meetings and congresses; more directly through destruction of villages and houses during the wars, and through the scalping and capturing of the colonists. The frontier, forts, rangers, and militia with garrisons were centers of forest warfare for a century.

106. Frontier Policies of the Colonial Governments

Every frontier colony had to solve two main problems. First was the problem of self-preservation
Problems of through self defense. The second problem
Defense and arose after a colony had become firmly es-
Expansion tablished, with a relatively strong and compact population; for then it might safely extend its borders and encourage the settlement of its western lands. The Indian tribes of New England and the middle colonies had gradually been driven back towards the mountains, but they were still dangerous, especially when allied with the French. For this reason it became desirable to settle and extend the frontier regions, in order that the new settlers might bear the brunt of the border warfare and act as a buffer and protection for the coast population. Up to the eighteenth century the colonies were generally on the defensive, opposed the extension of settlements westward, and restricted intercourse with the Indians.

The frontier policy of New York was conditioned by special factors, partly geographical and partly due to
New York the proximity of the French and Indians.
and Frontier The two great river valleys, the Hudson
Defenses and Mohawk, gave easy access to the West, but the latter was jealously guarded by the Iroquois, who, however, were fortunately friendly to the English.

The presence of the French on or near that border was also of great importance to New York.

The plan of keeping the population concentrated was attempted but without success. The Board of Trade openly stated (1709) that they believed the Palatines would be a good barrier between the English subjects and the French and Indians; and further that "in process of time by intermarrying with the neighboring Indians (as the French do) they may be capable of rendering very great service to her Majesty's subjects there."

The general plan in New York was to keep the important trading posts and carrying places protected by forts; and to establish and train the militia. Albany was essentially a military post in the seventeenth century. Governor Fletcher wrote in 1694, "Albany is in better circumstances than it ever yet was. I have caused it to be new stockaded and furnished with an addition of 20 great guns, there is 200 men in Garrison besides Major Ingolesby's Company of Grenadiers." At Schenectady was also a fort. With the development of western trade a fort was established at Oswego as early as 1727 with a lieutenant and twenty-four men. The French were greatly disturbed over this outlying stronghold and both hated and feared it. These forts were not kept in good repair, due in part to the disputes between the governors and the assembly over the raising of money for their maintenance.

The Militia Law of 1721, in New York, provided for universal military service between 16 and 60, and the plan of scouts, rangers, and night watches was tried out. Sir William Johnson, Indian agent, was made the recipient of money appropriated in 1746 for various expenses incurred in supplying provisions for garrisons. The militia plan often failed, however, because of disagreement of the Governor and Assembly. Governor

Hunter in fact used a part of his own private fortune to keep up the militia when the assembly refused to appropriate funds for its needs. Colonel Quarry wrote the Lords of Trade (1703): "My Lord Cornbury found the Militia of this Province under no regulation at all, having neither arms nor ammunition as they ought, nor were they even so much as drawn out to exercise or view them in all my Lord Bellomont's time, except the Regiment at the foot of New York." Even the militia of Albany county in 1747, "had fallen into a state of sad demoralization."

Though the Quakers held pacifist doctrines and opposed wars, in general they drew a line between external warfare and internal police protection. To put down rebellions and insurrections against the government, even against Indians, was held justifiable. During the French and Indian wars when the King or governor called on the Quaker assembly of Pennsylvania for aid, it generally refused to take any active part in the struggle or to make definite grants for military purposes. Nevertheless the assembly was not opposed to a militia and the defense of the colony by others. Franklin said: "Indeed I have some cause to believe that the defense of the Country was not disagreeable to any of them, provided they were not requested to assist in it." He says also that many Quakers supported defensive warfare.

One Quaker wrote, "We did not see it inconsistent with our principles to give the Queen money, notwithstanding any use she might put it to, that not being our part but hers." A grant in 1745 for provisions "or other grain" was interpreted to mean *powder*, without objection from the assembly, and the money was so expended. Pennsylvania, like New York, appropriated large sums for presents to the Indians, as one means of

Frontier Policies of Pennsylvania

defending the frontier. Unlike other colonies, the Quaker assembly generally refused to build forts, and relied on the settlers to defend the frontier in their own blockhouses. The frontiersmen formed bands of rangers at their own expense and fought with the Indians.

When in 1749 Céloron made his voyage down the Allegheny he claimed the land for the French, warned out the English traders and tried to win the Indians away from the English alliance. Yet as late as 1754, the Quaker assembly refused to take action with a view to protecting the headwaters of the Ohio.

The defensive frontier policy of Massachusetts was determined by many of the factors which operated in other colonies; where, for example, danger was feared from Indians on the French border and those coming from other colonies. The Indian problem was so serious during King Philip's War, 1675–1677, that it was proposed that a fence eight feet high be built from the Charles River to the Concord and Merrimac rivers to keep the Indians out. In 1694 certain frontier towns were warned that the inhabitants were forbidden to desert, even in time of war, thus placing the burden of defense on the settlers. Connecticut also named certain frontier towns in 1704 which were "not to be deserted" under any circumstances.

Massachusetts and the Frontier Towns

Some thirty acts were passed by the General Court of Massachusetts between 1695 and 1715 forbidding inhabitants to leave frontier towns named on penalty of forfeiting their estate or a heavy fine. In 1722 the General Court ordered that certain houses in frontier towns, designated by military officers, should be fortified at the expense of the inhabitants of the town. They were to be places of refuge in time of attack. The colony also relied on the local militia and sent garrisons at the public expense. Rangers were employed to patrol from fort to fort.

Many appeals came to the General Court from the frontier towns for help. Wells (Maine), for example, requested (1689), "eight good brisk men that may be serviceable as a guard to us whilest we get in our Harvest of Hay and Corn (we being unable to Defend ourselves and to do our work, and also to Pursue and destroy the enemy as occasion may require." They asked that these men be completely furnished with arms, ammunition, and provisions "and that upon the Country's account, it being a Generall War." Dunstable, Lancaster, and Deerfield made similar requests between 1675 and 1689. Thus by the opening of the eighteenth century a military cordon consisting of forts with garrisons, mounted rangers, and militia, stretched from New England to the Carolinas. Besides, every individual frontiersman was his own protector.

107. Westward Expansion and Settlement of the Back Country

From the opening of the eighteenth century some of the colonies commenced to bid for settlers by grants of land on the frontier, with the idea of using the settlers for frontier defense. New lands were needed also because of pressure of population, due to natural increase and to immigration. Moreover, the better lands near the coast had risen in price and little good unoccupied land was available. This condition led many to purchase the cheaper lands farther west. If settlers did not have the money to purchase land they often took up land illegally as squatters.

Causes of Westward Expansion

As early as 1701, Virginia adopted the plan of placing the responsibility for defense on settlers, by granting land to companies in return for the promise to maintain armed men. Later in 1727 the local militia was made responsible as " the most ready defense " against invasion and insurrection. Governor Spotswood made his notable exploring expedition across the Blue Ridge into the Shenandoah region, as early as 1716, with the object of extending the frontier line and checking the French, preparatory to filling the western region with settlers. Large grants were made and privileges given to induce settlement on the frontier, always with the proviso for defensive measures. In 1735 William Byrd II was granted 100,000 acres on the south branch of the Roanoke River on condition that he settle there a family of Protestant immigrants for each 1000 acres.

Plans of Southern Colonies for Attracting Settlers

Quit rents were often remitted for a term of years; settlers were exempted from public and county levies; and some money was appropriated out of the public treasury for arming the inhabitants. With liberal naturalization laws, virtual religious toleration, and land bounties, there was great inducement to immigrants to migrate to the southern colonies. In South Carolina the assembly appropriated (1731) £5000 currency to make surveys of land and to provide tools, provisions and live stock for prospective settlers. In 1735 the expense of settling 200 Palatines in the interior was borne by the assembly. Land was granted and provisions were supplied for a year.

The policy of entering into relations with an immigration agent was also tried out. John Peter Purry, for example, entered into a contract with the assembly of South Carolina in 1731, and agreed that for every one hundred able bodied men

Immigration Agents

he might bring from Switzerland he should receive
£400. Colonel Purry in 1734 petitioned the assembly
for £200 due him for bringing over a greater number
than he had engaged for; and asked that provisions
be supplied for 260 persons. The assembly granted his
petition.

The effort of Georgia to place settlers on the frontier is shown in an advertisement in the *Virginia Gazette* of September 3d, 1736, when an agent promised to those who would emigrate, money for six
months, 50 acres of land, a year's provisions, "tools,
and household stuff of all Sorts; necessary Arms of
all Sorts, Iron-Work, and Nails sufficient for building
a House 24 by 16 Feet, a Cow and Calf, a Breeding
Mare and a Breeding Sow; with several other advantages." These promises were perhaps seldom fulfilled,
but the offer shows the anxiety of the authorities to
draw people to Georgia.

The immigration movement to the southern colonies
was influenced somewhat by the effort of Pennsyl-
Indentured vania to limit immigration by placing a
Servants and duty on servants. South Carolina in fact
Frontier Set-
tlement passed acts forcing planters to use indentured servants bearing a certain proportion to negro
slaves. Thus in 1727 and 1751 every owner of a plantation or "cowpen," was obliged by law to have one
white servant to every ten slaves. Indentured servants
were granted land free and bounty money was promised
at the end of their term of service. Though Virginia
and Maryland sold land outright in the eighteenth century, yet servants continued to come in and were given
land on the frontier as a part of their freedom dues.

Many Germans left their homes in Pennsylvania
after 1730 and moved south into western Maryland, and
on to the Shenandoah valley, the Piedmont region of

Virginia, and western North Carolina. The northern
half of the "Valley" was almost wholly German.
Migrations
from North
to South
Some of the frontier counties of North
Carolina were settled by Germans. Thus
the Moravians founded an important settlement at Wachovia, now Winston-Salem. These
migrations were largely due to the efforts of the
southern colonies to attract immigrants by low-priced
lands, for the purpose of protecting the frontier;
and they explain, in part, the nature of the frontier elements of the population, so different in character, religion, and purposes from that of the tidewater area. Lord Baltimore in 1732 offered 200 acres
of land to any person having a family, with a rental
of four shillings per hundred acres, who would settle
between the rivers Potomac and Susquehanna. Single
persons were allowed 100 acres, with a rental of one
penny per acre; but exempted for three years. At the
same time the heirs of William Penn were demanding
over £15 per hundred acres with a quit rent of one
penny per acre. The price of Maryland lands at this
time was about £5 per hundred acres. Frederick and
Washington Counties were largely settled by Germans.
Robert Beverley, Lord Fairfax, and other large land
holders in Virginia sold land cheaper, by from £6 to £7
per hundred acres, than the Penn proprietors.

The Virginia council commenced about 1730 to grant
land on the frontier in large tracts to individuals who
would bring settlers there. Some Germans were
granted tracts of 25,000 acres on condition that
they would settle twenty-five families. Hanover
and Augusta Counties in Virginia were centers
of the Scotch-Irish who had come from Pennsylvania;
and the central counties of North Carolina around
Mecklenburg, where the Regulator movement occurred,

were also settled largely by Scotch-Irish. The same is true of northwestern South Carolina. The rapidity of settlement in the southern colonies is remarkable. In 1746 hardly 100 men could be found in Orange County, western North Carolina; by 1753 there were 3000, besides 1000 Scotch in Cumberland County.

By 1715, after the period of forced concentration of the population, Massachusetts was in a position to ex- Expansion in pand the frontier in Maine, and to the New England west and north. Border warfare ceased, peace was made with the French, and a treaty was agreed on with the " Eastern Indians." It is significant of the conditions during the thirty years previous that not a single new town had been founded in Maine from 1675 to 1715; nor had there been appreciable extension of settlement in western Massachusetts and New Hampshire. As population became congested the price of the old lands rose rapidly and the time for expansion of the frontiers had arrived.

A remarkable change in the land and immigration policy followed from that pursued in the seventeenth century. As we have seen, Massachusetts was not opposed to immigration of the Scotch-Irish or Irish since fifty-four shiploads of immigrants from Ireland arrived in Boston between 1714 and 1720. Massachusetts even encouraged a settlement of Germans at Waldoborough, Maine, 1740; and by 1749 the General Court was voting to encourage the settlement of four townships by " foreign Protestants."

108. Controversies with Squatters

William Penn's original expansion policy was to keep a broad strip of land between the frontier and the Indian territory, though his successors were not so careful. Squatters on Indian lands thus became a great frontier

problem. In 1683 purchases of land from the Indians by
private parties were forbidden, without leave of the gov-
Squatters in
Pennsylvania ernor and proprietor; but the practice still
continued as late as 1729. Penn also had in
mind a concentrated population, less as bearing on the
problem of defense than for ease in collecting quit rents.
With the coming of immigrants in large numbers (1720-
1750) vacant lands were " squatted " on irrespective of
the rights either of the proprietor or of the Indians.
James Logan referred to these settlers as bold and
indigent strangers who possessed themselves of land
" in an audacious manner." As early as 1726 it is estimated that 100,000 squatters were illegally settled in
Pennsylvania.

In 1727 Logan wrote John Penn: " We have many
thousand of foreigners, mostly Palatines, so called,
already in the countrey of whom 1500 came in this last
summer; many of them a surly people, divers Papists
of Ireland, great number yearly, 8 or 9 ships last fall
discharged at Newcastle. Both these sort sitt frequently
down on any spot of vacant land they can find without
asking questions." He adds that one applied in the
name of four hundred as to where they should settle.
" They say the Proprietor wanted people to come and
settle his county; they came for that end, and must live.
Both they and the Palatines pretend that they will buy,
but not one in twenty has anything to pay with. The
Irish settle generally towards the Maryland line, where
no lands can honestly be sold till the dispute with Lord
Baltimore is decided."

He adds in another letter (1730), " I must own, from
my experience in the land office, that the settlement of
five families from Ireland gives me more trouble than
fifty of any other people." In a letter of 1729, " Vast
numbers of poor but presumptuous people without any

License have entered your lands." In still another, 1730, he complained of the Scotch-Irish who in an " audacious and disorderly manner" took all of Conestoga Manor, fifteen thousand acres of the best land in the county, reserved by the Penns for themselves, alleging " it was against the laws of God and Nature, that so much land should be idle, while so many Christians wanted it to labor on and to raise their bread, etc." Writing in 1743 he said that the people " crowded in so thick to settle, and knowing that they were equally Trespassers, encroached upon the first settlers, sate down where they pleased, every man according to his forces, by himself or friends, thereby occasioned great Quarling and disorders."

Proclamations were issued ordering squatters to vacate, and sheriffs were ordered to evict them and destroy their cabins. Richard Peters reports finding five cabins or log houses on the Indian hunting grounds on the Big Juniata and ordered "some of the meanest of those cabbins to be set on fire." In attempting to repel squatters on Marsh Creek, 1743, he was met by about seventy armed men who forbade him to proceed, broke his chain, and compelled him to retire. They held their ground until the sheriff retired defeated. Peters describes the cabins: " It may be proper to add that the Cabbins or Log Houses which were burnt were of no considerable value, being such as the country people erect in a day or two."

Even in New England squatting occurred, particularly in Maine. East of the Kennebec, settlers were cutting timber from trees designated as masts to be sent to England. Governor Hutchinson remarked that the King was thus obliged to pay bounties on his own timber. He wanted to declare all such timber forfeited, but found that it

New England and Southern Squatters

would take away the means of support from one thousand to fifteen hundred families.

Squatting was a great problem in the southern colonies. It is estimated that very few of the German settlers who occupied the Shenandoah valley had acquired any legal title to the land they occupied; in fact, of 670,000 acres occupied from 1732 to 1740, 400,000 were occupied without grants. When George Washington at a later date went to Augusta County to examine land to which he had acquired legal title, he found numerous families of squatters already occupying it.

In North Carolina (1724), the lower house addressed the governor and council to the effect that many had settled on vacant lands without payment, rent, or title. But the council ordered that the squatters might continue to occupy the land if they would agree to pay a quit rent, for thus the revenue of the proprietors would be increased. In 1735, however, Governor Johnson issued a proclamation to the effect that unless the great numbers of people who had settled on lands without having taken out warrants for surveys should supply that defect, they would lose " the benefit of their cultivation, and the said lands will be deemed vacant lands, and few for any other person to take up."

An act passed by Georgia in 1764 stated that many persons in the back settlements of the province had taken up land without authority, by building huts, planting crops, etc., and later sold the land to other settlers and then had taken up land farther west. Such persons were to be warned to vacate and on refusal the governor was to have their cabins burned.

The colonial governments were naturally opposed to squatting, for a variety of reasons. On the method of settlement depended the security of the settlers

and the safety of the colony. Again, indiscriminate settlement led to confusion of land titles and many disputes arose between settlers and the colonial governments. Further, the latter were contin-
Colonial Governments and ually in trouble with the Indians because Squatters squatters encroached on Indian lands. Then those colonies and a quit rent system were deprived of a large revenue because the squatters paid little or no rent.

On the other hand, the poor immigrant or pioneer not only had no money but he could not afford to wait for the long delay involved in making accurate surveys, purchasing lands from the Indians, or making treaties with them. He was willing to take the risk of defending himself, considered that the Indian had no rights, and even adopted the idea that the pioneer had a " natural right " to land, similar to his right to life and liberty. He felt that in a way he paid for the land by risking his life, by blazing a path through the forests, by fighting the Indians, and by protecting the coast population in war time.

109. Frontier Society and Grievances

The region east of the Appalachians was divided into a coast and interior, or " back country " region,
Geographical the dividing line being roughly the falls of Basis the rivers. It should be noted that the river valleys were occupied first and frontier conditions might exist comparatively near the coast at some points, while tidewater conditions might penetrate far inland — following the river valleys. The general name given to the region between the fall line and the Appalachian Mountains, disregarding the boundaries of the colonies, is " The Old West." It extends from the northern into

the middle colonies and south into Georgia. This region geographically is the Piedmont plain, a long, narrow oval, which has a geographic unity of its own. Throughout one finds similarity of the soil, lack of accessibility, similar occupations, and frontier conditions. Particularly in contrast with the tidewater the "Old West" lacked contact with the ocean and hence was cut off from the opportunities of maritime life. Because of soil and climatic conditions, some of the staple crops such as tobacco, rice, and indigo, were unsuited to this region.

From the standpoint of cultural advance, education, literature, religion, etc., it is clear that the back-country of the South was at a great disadvantage. Diversification of industry, division of labor, the raising of a surplus for export, ease of transportation, opportunity for rapid increase of wealth, contact with the outer world of thought, and institutional life — all these were made easier by geographical influences in the tidewater region, and were retarded by those prevailing in the backcountry.

The structure of society in the frontier regions was very simple. Indeed there was little, and could be little, of that division into classes so common in Structure of the coast towns, based on wealth, family, Frontier and occupations. The population was not Society yet segregated into classes; family prestige counted for little; and practically all the people were following the same calling, viz., agriculture and closely allied industries. The frontiersman, often a squatter, as we have seen, seized and settled on some piece of land that fitted his immediate needs, caring little to whom it belonged — whether Indians, proprietors, the crown, or settlers. In such a frontier society one class predominated — independent farmers working tracts of land from 50 to 200 acres, purchased or squatted on.

The frontiersman was largely self-sufficing and produced primarily for home needs. In a few localities
Agriculture and Industries
produce was finding its way from the up-country to the region along the coast. As early as 1750, stockraising had developed in the back country of the southern colonies. Thus the herder succeeded the hunter and Indian trader. This industry developed to a point where herds of cattle were driven to Baltimore for market from distant points in the Carolinas. Thus arose a thriving industry in beef and pork packing, mainly for export to the West Indies. Roads and bridges, however, were poor and few in number so that there was comparatively little intercourse between frontier and coast. This isolation of the population is important, for it accentuated differences in political, social, and economic ideals between the two regions.

The general attitude of the frontier population towards life in all of its aspects was democratic. The
Frontier Ideals
frontiersman however wished to apply democratic ideas directly to his own needs in a way that made the coast population and their representatives in the colonial assemblies fearful of the results. It is true that the democratic idea made progress in the assemblies, in their struggles both against the royal governors and against the English political economic and commercial policy. The assemblies, as we have seen, fought the efforts to limit their power and to restrict colonial trade and manufactures. Besides the general grievances of both the coast and frontier towards absentee proprietors and the home government, the frontier population nursed special grievances against the colonial assemblies. These bodies were active from 1763 on, in formulating stirring assertions of liberty which, however, they applied to England only. Such

were: "No taxation without representation"; "Government rests on the consent of the governed"; and "All men are created free and equal." On the frontier, however, these phrases had a double meaning. They were not only battle cries that aroused the frontiersmen to resist England, but often they also expressed the frontier feeling towards the colonial governments. For the latter frequently resisted the application of such principles when changes were demanded by the frontier groups. Paradoxical as it seems, the colonial assemblies often turned a deaf ear to frontier petitions and demands calling for equality of representation, equitable taxation, equal benefits from taxes paid, local self-government based on choice of officers by the people, fair administration of justice, availability of land, courts of justice, churches and schools, and religious toleration and liberty. Such an application of democratic ideas was anything but pleasing to most of the assemblies, which represented chiefly the more important property owners along the seaboard. For the most part they refused to pass legislation which would make possible such reforms. Here was the basis for internal sectionalism, political, economic, and religious, West against East.

110. Racial Religious and Economic Sectionalism

The problem of sectionalism (see § 94) may be illustrated by conditions in Pennsylvania, where the situation was complicated. The eastern counties were settled largely by English Quakers, who controlled the assembly. The northeastern counties were largely German, and the southwestern and far western largely Scotch-Irish. Other racial stocks also contributed to the confusion. Provost William Smith of the University of Pennsylvania declared in 1755: "We are a people drawn together from

Races and Sectionalism in Pennsylvania

various quarters of the world, differing in all things, language, manners, and sentiments." By 1750 the Germans outnumbered the Quakers, and in the northeastern counties were conservative. They wished to be let alone and were especially anxious to escape military service. They were willing to work with the Quaker minority in attacking the proprietors, not so much for political as for economic reasons. It would enable them to avoid payment of quit rents.

On the other hand the Germans in the counties farther west on the frontier were more radical and militant, for their danger was not so much from the proprietors as from the French and Indians. The Quaker assembly was opposed to providing adequate military defense, and usually left these Germans to defend themselves, and act as a buffer for the eastern Germans and Quakers. Thus the western Germans were early engaged in an unremitting struggle with the English Quaker minority. These differences were taken advantage of by the politically minded, militant, liberty-loving, Presbyterian, Scotch-Irish element in the southwestern and western counties, which was naturally distrustful of government by the English Quaker element.

By 1750 the Scotch-Irish element of the population was equal to that of the Quakers. The western Germans and Scotch-Irish were thus drawn together by community of interests. Both desired protection against the Indians and French, increased representation, better transportation facilities and more equitable taxation. Because the Germans had little or no political experience and lacked leadership, they complacently accepted that of the Scotch-Irish, who ably led both groups. This is the background, in part, of the conservatism of the Quaker eastern counties in the later revolutionary movement. For independence from Great Britain would inevitably bring a new system of representation and new ideals into Pennsylvania. It might in fact establish the principle of majority rule and the overthrow of the Quaker minority.

Another phase of sectionalism arose because of the church establishments. In the five southern colonies Religious the Anglican Church was established by Sectionalism law. In three of the New England colonies the Congregational was the established church. On the other hand, the frontier regions of the middle and southern colonies contained multitudes of dissenters. Thus arose the demand for religious toleration and liberty. The history of this momentous struggle belongs to a later period; but the beginnings of it are evident before 1750. It is a part of that larger struggle for democracy which includes not only political but also economic and social phases. The privileged classes in control of the assemblies feared that a grant of religious toleration and liberty would weaken their powers, much as James I in England feared to permit freedom of worship to the Puritans.

The general rule in those colonies having an established church was to require dissenters to support it by paying tithes or taxes, and also to attend the official church services under penalty. They were also frequently required to submit to various tests or oaths, and to subscribe to the creeds and catechism of the established church. Sometimes the right to settle in a colony, or the privilege of naturalization, or citizenship, or the right to vote and hold office, depended on submission to religious tests. Moreover, opposition arose to the building of dissenting churches and to the preaching of doctrines contrary to those of the established church. In this respect the Quakers, Catholics, and Jews were the greatest sufferers; but Presbyterians and Baptists also suffered because of intolerance in various colonies.

Owing particularly to the migration of Scotch-Irish to the backcountry of Virginia, and the great increase of their itinerant or traveling preachers, the problem became acute in that colony even before 1750. In general there was an effort on the part of the governor and council of Virginia to restrict religious opportunities; to limit preaching by requiring a license for a minister, which authorized him to preach only to one or a few congregations located entirely in one county, as was the case with the famous Presbyterian clergyman, Samuel Davies. In Massachusetts much friction arose over taxation of the Baptists for the support of the Congregational or established church. Thus the sectional conflict was made more acute wherever there was an attempt to interfere with the religious views, the preaching, or the setting up of churches by dissenters.

Other grievances caused sectional conflict besides those related to political and religious matters. Complaints abounded concerning economic problems, unequal or unjust taxation, failures of the assemblies to provide for roads and bridges, or courts of justice and, as we have seen, for protection from the French and Indians. The pre-revolutionary discussion of all these questions coincides with the rise in the backcountry of democratic ideals, important in their influence on the Revolution. It was fortunate that in the movement for union and independence these frontier grievances were identified to a greater or less extent with England's political and economic policies; so that in spite of sectional conflict between coast and frontier the backwoodsman was usually willing to join in the common movement to

[margin note: Economic Grievances and Sectionalism]

resist England. For the frontier groups expected, with reason, that if the Revolution were successful more equal privileges and opportunities would be granted them by their own independent governments.

CHAPTER XIV

ECONOMIC DEVELOPMENT (1689–1750)

111. References

Bibliographies. — (See refs. under "bibliographies," for chs. iv, vii, x, xii); J. T. Adams, *Prov. Society*, 324–356, and *Revolutionary New Engl.* (esp. footnotes to chs. vi-viii); C. M. Andrews, *Colonial Folkways*, 239–243; Channing, Hart and Turner, *Guide*, §§ 36–39, 42–43, 45, 47–48, 117, 120, 121, 126, 146, 149, 161–165; H. U. Faulkner, *Am. Econom. Hist.*, 76–77, 100–101, 115–116; E. B. Greene, *Provincial Am.*, 331–340, and *Foundations of Am. Nationality*, 256, 279–280, 336–337, 355–356; Grace Griffin, *Writings on Am. Hist. 1906–1923;* J. N. Larned, *Lit. of Am. Hist.*, 69–76.

Historical Maps. — See chs. iv, vii, ix.

General Accounts. — (See refs. under "General Accounts" for chs. iv, vii, ix-x, xii); J. T. Adams, *Prov. Society*, chs. ii, viii-ix; C. M. Andrews, *Colonial Period*, ch. iv, and *Colonial Background of Am. Rev.*, ch. ii, and in *Cambridge Hist. of British Empire*, volume I; Chas. and Mary Beard, *Rise of Am. Civilization*, I, chs. ii-iii; G. L. Beer, "Com. Pol. of Engl. towards the Am. Cols.," in *Columb. Stud.*, III; Edward Channing, *Hist. of U. S.*, II, chs. xiii, xvii; V. S. Clark, *Hist. of Manufacs., in U. S. 1607–1860*, chs. iii-x; D. R. Dewey, *Financial Hist. of U. S.*, ch. i; J. A. Doyle, *Engl. Cols. in Am.*, V, ch. iii; H. U. Faulkner, *Am. Econom. Hist.*, chs. ii-v; E. B. Greene, *Prov. Am.*, chs. xvi-xvii; Ralph Harlow, *Growth of U. S.*, ch. x; E. R. Johnson, *Hist. of Domes. and Foreign Commerce of U. S.*, I; H. L. Osgood, *Am. Col. in 18th Cent.*, I, ch. v; II, pt. II, ch. i; III, ch. xvi, 346–359; IV, chs. v-viii; A. M. Schlesinger, *Colonial Merchants and the Am. Revolution, 1763–1776*, ch. i; R. M. Tryon, *Hist. of Household Mfgs. in U. S.*, chs. i-iii.

Special Accounts. — (See refs. under "Special Economic by Topics," chs. iv, vii, ix and "Special Accounts," ch. x.) (a) ENGLISH BACKGROUND: See "Gen. Accts.," ch. x; W. J. Ashley, "Com. Legisla. of Engl. and the Am. Col. 1660–1760," in *Quar. Journ. of Economics*, XIV, 1–29; Edward Channing, "Naviga. Acts," in *Proc. Am. Ant. Soc.*, n. s. VI, 160–179;

M. P. Clarke, "Board of Trade at Work," in *Am. Hist. Rev.*, XVII, 17–43; O. M. Dickerson, *Am. Colonial Govt.*, esp. chs. i, vi; J. W. Horrocks, *Short History of Mercantilism;* D. O. McGovney, "Naviga. Acts and European Trade," in *Am. Hist. Rev.*, IX, 725–734; W. T. Root, *Relations of Pa. with Brit. Govt.*, *1696–1765;* Gustav Schmoller, *The Mercantile System.* (b) WEST INDIES: Violet Barbour, "Piracy in W. I.," in *Am. Hist. Rev.*, XVI, 529–566; Herbert Bell, "W. I. Trade Before the Rev.," in *Am. Hist. Rev.*, LXII; V. T. Harlow, *Hist. of Barbados;* S. L. Mims, Colbert's, *W. I. Policy;* F. W. Pitman, *Devel. of Brit. W. I.*, 1700–1763. (c) LAND AND LABOR: (See references under "Special Economic by Topics," ch. iv, and "Land and Labor," chs. vii and ix); J. T. Adams, *Rev. New Engl.*, chs. vi-viii; R. G. Akagi, *Town Proprietors of New Engl.;* R. G. Albion, "Forests and Sea Power," 1652–1862 (*Harvard Stud.*, XXIX); J. S. Bassett, "Introduction to Southern Econom. Hist. — The Land System," in *Am. Hist. Assoc. Rpt.*, 1897, 101–129; P. W. Bidwell and J. I. Falconer, *Hist. of Agricul. in North'n U. S. before 1860;* B. W. Bond, Jr., *Quit-Rent System in Am. Cols.;* Edward Channing, "Narragansett Planters," in *J. H. Stud.*, ser. IV; E. M. Coulter, "Granville Lands," in *James Sprunt Hist. Monographs*, XIII, no. i; A. O. Craven, "Soil Exhaustion as a Factor in the Agricult. Hist. of Va. and Md.," in *Univ. of Ill. Studies*, XIII; Melville Egleston, "Land System of New Engl. Colonies," in *J. H. Stud.*, ser. IV; C. P. Gould, "Land System of Md.," 1720–1765, in *J. H. Stud.*, ser. XXXI; A. B. Hart (ed.), *Commonwealth Hist. of Mass.*, II, ch. xiii; L. K. Matthews, *Expan. of New Engl.;* U. B. Phillips, *Am. Negro Slavery*, and Introduc. to *Plantation and Frontier Documents;* R. F. Seybolt, *Apprenticeship in Colonial New York and New Engl.* (d) INDUSTRIES AND OCCUPATIONS: (See refs. under "General and Special Econom. by Topics," ch. iv and "Industries and Occupations," ch. vii); Edith Abbott, *Women in Industry;* J. L. Bishop, *Hist. of Am. Manufactures;* P. A. Bruce, *Econom. Hist. of Va. in the 17th Cent.;* V. S. Clark, *Hist. of Mfgs. in U. S.*, *1607–1860;* Elizabeth Dexter, *Colonial Women of Affairs;* A. B. Hart (ed.), *Common Hist. of Mass.*, ch. xiv ("Colonial Business and Transportation"); M. W. Jernegan, "Slavery and the Begins. of Industrialism in the Am. Cols.," in *Am. Hist. Rev.*, XXV, 220–240; Eleanor Lord, "Indust. Experiments in the Brit. Cols.," in *J. H. Stud.*, extra vol. XVII; R. M. Tryon, *Hist. of Household Mfgs. in U. S.;* W. B. Weeden, *Econom. and Soc. Hist. of New Engl.*, I, ch. viii; II, chs. xiii, xvii.

(e) TRADE AND COMMERCE: (See refs. under "General Economic by Topics," ch. iv; and "Trade and Commerce," chs. vii and ix; and "Gen. Accts." and "Special Accts.," ch. x); C. M. Andrews, "Colonial Commerce," in *Am. Hist. Rev.*, XX, 40–64, and "Anglo-French Commer. Rivalry," in *Ibid.*, 391, 761; J. S. Bassett, "Relas. Between Va. Planter and London Merchant," in *Am. Hist. Assn. Rept.*, 1901, I, 559–573; H. M. Chapin, *Privateer Ships and Sailors*, 1625–1725; W. E. B. Du Bois, "Suppression of the African Slave Trade" (*Harvard Stud.*, I); Edward Eggleston, "Colonial Commerce," in *Century Mag.*, VI, 234–256; W. C. Fisher, "Am. Trade Regulations before 1789," in *Papers of Am. Hist. Assn.*, III (1888), 223–249; A. A. Giesecke, *Am. Com. Legislation before 1789;* M. A. Hanna, *Trade of Delaware District before the Rev.;* William Hill, "Colonial Tariffs," in *Quar. Jour. of Econom.*, VII, 78–100; S. E. Morison, *Maritime Hist. of Mass.*, ch. i; M. S. Morriss, "Colonial Trade of Md., 1689–1715," in *J. H. Stud.*, ser. XXXII; Ugo Rabbeno, *The Am. Commercial Policy;* W. F. Rich, "Hist. of U. S. Post Office," chs. i–iii (*Harv. Econom. Studies*, XXVII); St. G. L. Sioussat, "Va. and Engl. Commer. System," in *Am. Hist. Assn. Rept.*, 1905, I, 71–97, and "Economics and Politics in Md., 1720–1750," in *J. H. Stud.*, ser. XXI; W. B. Weeden, *Econom. and Soc. Hist. of New Engl.*, I, ch. ix; II, chs. xii–xvi, and "Early African Slave Trade to New Engl.," in *Am. Ant. Soc. Proc.*, V, and "Early Commerce of Providence," in *Am. Ant. Soc. Proc.*, n. s. XIX, 420–429. (f) PIRACY AND SMUGGLING: W. J. Ashley, *Surveys Historic and Economic* (Smuggling, 309–335); G. F. Dow and J. H. Edwards, *Pirates of the New Engl. Coast*, 1630–1730; S. C. Hughson, "Carolina Pirates and Commerce," in *J. H. Stud.*, ser. XII; W. S. McClellan, *Smuggling in the Am. Cols., etc.;* R. D. Paine, *Book of Buried Treasure.* (g) FINANCE: (See refs. in ch. vii, "Special Economic," and footnote J. F. Adams, *Rev. New Engl.*, p. 159); K. L. Behrens, "Paper Money in Md., 1727–1789," in *J. H. Stud.*, ser. XLI; Henry Bronson, "Hist. Acct. of Conn. Currency," in *New Haven Hist., Soc. Paps.* I; C. J. Bullock, *Essays in the Monetary Hist. of U. S.*, ch. iv; A. McF. Davis, "Currency and Banking in the Province of Mass. Bay," in *Am. Econom. Assoc.*, 3d ser. i–ii; J. B. Felt, *Hist. Acct. of Mass. Currency;* C. P. Gould, "Money and Transportation in Md., 1720–1765," in *J. H. Stud.*, ser. XXIII; Henry Phillips, Jr., *Hist. Sketches of Paper Currency in Am. Cols.*, ser. I.

Biographies. — (See refs. under Biographies, chs. x–xiii, xv); D. R. Fox, *Caleb Heathcote, etc.*, 1692–1721; L. H. Gipson,

Jared Ingersoll; St. G. L. Sioussat, "Economics and Politics in Md., 1720–1750" (for Daniel Dulany the Elder), in *J. H. Stud.,* ser. XXI.

Contemporary Accounts. — (a) BIBLIOGRAPHY: Channing, Hart and Turner, *Guide,* §§ 38 (Travel), 43 (Colonial, State, and Local Recs.), 47–48, 117, 120, 121, 126, 146, 149, 161–162, 165; A. R. Hasse, *Materials for a Bibliog., etc.; Hist. Sources in Schools,* § 74; W. P. Trent (ed.), *Camb. Hist. of Am. Lit.,* I, 365–380; for list of titles of travelers' accts., *etc.,* see ch. xv, under "General Travels," and "Diaries, Journals, Letters, and Contemp. Hist." (b) BRITISH DOCUMENTS: *Acts of Privy Council Colonial; Cal. of St. Papers Colonial and W. I.; Journal of Board of Trade;* L. F. Stock (ed.), *Proc. and Debates of the Brit. Parl., etc.* (c) COL-LECTIONS: E. L. Bogart and C. M. Thompson (eds.), *Readings in the Econom. Hist. of U. S.,* chs. ii–v; A. M. Davis, "Colonial Currency Reprints, 1682–1751 " (4 vols.), in *Prince Society Pubs.,* XXXII–XXXV; Ralph Gabriel (ed.), *Pageant of America;* A. B. Hart (ed.), *Contemporaries,* II, chs. xiii (Commerce and Cur-rency), xi (Slavery and Servitude); J. F. Jameson (ed.), *Privateers and Piracy in the Colonial Period.* (d) AGRICULTURE: (bibl. in L. B. Schmidt, *Top. Stud. and Refs. of the Econ. Hist. of Am. Agricult.*); Anon., *American Husbandry* (2 vols., 1776); Jared Eliot, *Essays on Field Husbandry;* reprinted in *Mass. Society for Promoting Agricult., Papers,* 1911; U. B. Phillips, *Plantation and Frontier Documents.*

112. Underlying Conditions and Tendencies

THE eighteenth century witnessed the development of numerous and important economic problems and Economic tendencies. (1) Large tracts of land were Tendencies engrossed by wealthy men, partly for speculative purposes. Such was the vast estate of Wil-liam Byrd II and, after 1750, that of George Wash-ington, both of Virginia. (2) A growing scarcity of good unoccupied land in the tidewater region caused a rapid rise in land values. (3) Wide-spread soil deple-tion, due to unscientific methods of agriculture led to a reduction of the yield per acre at increased cost. (4) These three tendencies stimulated a westward move-ment of population to the frontiers; the occupation of cheaper and poorer lands. largely by immigrants, freed servants, the poorer small farmers and squatters, all more or less antagonistic towards the tidewater groups. (5) A rapid and large increase occurred in the importation of negro slaves in the South and of indentured servants in the middle colonies. (6) Increasing distress was felt among the tobacco planters due to low prices and over-production. (7) A consequent tendency was diversification of agriculture; to produce more corn and wheat and other crops than tobacco. (8) A larger utilization of natural resources enabled the colonists to profit from their forests, mineral deposits (iron), and the back-lands, especially for grazing. In consequence developed the naval-stores industries, the raising of livestock — hogs, cattle, and sheep — the production of hides and wool, and the packing of pork and beef. (9) A large increase of manufactures took place, particularly shipbuilding, textiles, and iron products. (10) A rapid expansion of trade with other regions than England developed; especially with the West Indies and Africa. This consisted largely of exports of provisions, lumber, and fish, and imports of slaves, molasses, and manufactured goods.

The first four of this list of tendencies affected the relations of frontier and coast and tended to stimulate antagonisms, especially those having to do with land and taxation. The last six enumerations affected the relations of the colonies with England and in part represent efforts to escape from the objectionable features of the commercial policy of the mother country.

These tendencies stimulated the growth of powerful economic groups, especially the great planters of the

Rise of the Great Planters and Merchants

South and the merchants of the North. The possession of lands and slaves enabled the great planters, though a minority, to dominate the political, economic, and social policies of the South. The merchants controlled the agencies of dis-

tribution, the ships, warehouses and shops; and through
their acquisition of wealth exercised more and more influence on legislation.

Both groups, planters and merchants, tried to evade
their just share of colonial taxes, and to place an unfair
Unequal   proportion on the small farmers. For this
Taxation and   and other reasons, economic class-con-
Class Con-
flicts   flicts arose. The great proprietors — such
as the Penns and Baltimores, the Fairfaxes of Virginia,
the Granvilles of North Carolina; the Livingstons and
Van Rensselaers of New York, and the absentee town-
proprietors of New England — all were agreed on
low taxes for themselves; as well as on the policy of
acquiring and then withholding from settlement large
tracts of the best lands with a view to future profits.
The small farmers on the frontier were the victims of
these policies. Such practices were among the principal
causes of economic and political sectionalism (p. 289)
already well developed at the close of our period, and a
great factor in the revolutionary movement.

113. Land and Labor Problems

The land systems of the colonies were greatly modified in the eighteenth century. Though the head-right
Changes in   system continued in Virginia and Mary-
the Land   land, the principal method of acquiring
Systems.
Southern   land was by purchase. Maryland in 1683
Colonies   sold fifty acres of land for 100 pounds of
tobacco with an annual quit rent of four shillings per
hundred acres. In Virginia an act of the assembly in
1705 provided for the sale of fifty acres of land for
five shillings. This opportunity to purchase land outright
enabled the planters to acquire even larger tracts than
before, against future years when land would be needed
and cost more. By 1730 practically no good unoccupied

land located near the coast or on a navigable river, was left vacant, either in Virginia or South Carolina. Edward Randolph reported as early as 1696 that "colonists are forced to go to the utmost bounds of the colony for land; exposed to danger and often occasion war with the Indians," [because the planters] "hold twenty or thirty thousand acres of land apiece very largely surveyed without paying one penny for quit rent for it." Moreover, little of this land was in actual use. William Byrd II, "King" Robert Carter, and Governor Spotswood held huge uncultivated tracts. As early as 1705, many inhabitants of Virginia were leaving the colony "for the want of land to plant and cultivate." The act of 1705 however made it easier for the poor man, freed servant, and immigrant to acquire land on the frontier. Then too, the less successful planters and farmers of the coast region tended to move to the frontier, thus creating a class of small landholders and non-slave holders.

In New York most of the best land, especially along the Hudson River, was held during this period by a class of large landholders (see p. 220). In Pennsylvania the proprietors and the squatters held the bulk of the land, as already shown. In New England, with the gradual disappearance of the common lands in the older towns, many were forced to settle on the frontier. Here friction arose because of absentee landlords, and their demands for low taxes on untilled land. Wealthy men commenced to accumulate enormous tracts and to profit by the rise in the value of the land, as population and settlements increased. After 1735 Massachusetts and Connecticut commenced to sell whole townships to speculators, who resold as the land increased in value. For this reason poor settlers were often obliged to pay

Land Problems of the Middle and New England Colonies

higher prices for land, one reason for antagonism between frontier and coast, from Maine to Georgia.

The southern colonies, after 1700, showed a tendency to rely mainly on slave labor. The 3000 or more slaves Labor in Virginia in 1689 increased to 23,000 in Problems 1715; by 1756 there were 120,000; the white population at this date being 173,000. This rapid increase was due to several causes. Slaves were servants for life and their children were slaves. They cost less, were easier to manage, feed, and clothe, and could endure the hard labor and climate better than the white laborers.

The southern colonies developed elaborate slave codes in the eighteenth century in order to establish Economic complete control over the negro and to Control of prevent dangers which might arise from Negro Slaves too lenient treatment. He could be bred, worked, neglected, punished, marked or branded, bought and sold. He could be taken for debt, inventoried, taxed, and inherited. He could not absent himself from the plantation without a certificate from his master or overseer; nor could he assemble with other negroes, because of danger of plots and insurrections. If a slave were "casually" killed as a result of necessary or moderate correction, it was not a felony. Slaves were denied a jury trial, were not allowed to appear as witnesses against white men, and were denied the right to hold property.

In practice, however, the slave codes represented a theory rather than the practice. One of the ends desired was profit from the slavery system. Therefore, privileges which might decrease profits were generally withheld. On the other hand profitable practices, though forbidden by law, were continued. Thus trusted slaves were often allowed to hold personal property — hogs or poultry — for such a privilege reduced the cost of supporting the slave. It is true of course that some planters had a real affection for their slaves, and a sense of responsibility for their welfare, particularly in Virginia, where the slavery system existed in a milder form than farther south.

Three groups of negro slaves were important: the field hands, house servants, and craftsmen. The first, Classes of the "Guinea" negroes, newly imported Slaves from Africa, were savages, difficult to control and often with low moral standards. They usually became "field hands" and performed the rough, hard labor on the tobacco and other plantations. The second group, the "country born" negroes, were more intelligent and hence more valuable; many of these became house servants. Third, the mulatto slaves, possessing more or less white blood, were the most valuable: many of the more intelligent of this class were trained for plantation industries. Lacking a sufficient number of free artisans or indentured servants skilled in the trades, planters had the more intelligent slaves taught various trades. This process, begun in the seventeenth century, became important after 1725. Governor Glen of South Carolina estimated (1751) that some "New Negroes" were worth £20 sterling per head; that many others had been made "useful mechanicks, as Coopers, Carpenters, Masons, Smiths, Wheelwrights, and other Trades . . . expert at the different kinds of Labor in which they are employed. . . I know a Gentleman who refused five hundred Guineas ($2500) for three of his slaves."

Generally, indentured servants, apprentices and free craftsmen, the latter arising largely from these last two classes, performed the skilled work in the northern colonies. Indentured servants were advertised in the

New York Gazette (1728) thus: " On Wednesday last arrived here the ship George, Jonh Anthony Adamson, Commander, from Ireland, who has on board several Irish men, women and Boys, Servants, among whome there is several Trades Men as Carpenters, Weavers, Taylors, Blacksmiths, etc." Their " time " was offered for sale and " They will take either Flower or Wheat as pay." In New England the story is much the same, except that there were more apprentices and free skilled laborers because of the expansion of town life, the division of labor and the tendency to produce some manufactures for export. More free common laborers existed in New England than in other colonies because of the relatively small number of slaves and indentured servants. Franklin remarked that the labor of the colonies was "performed chiefly by indentured servants brought from Great Britain, Ireland, and Germany, because the high price it bears cannot be performed in any other way."

Labor Problems in the Middle and New England Colonies

The indentured white servant was a semi-slave. In general there was no limitation on the amount or severity of the labor which might be demanded, or on the character of the food and clothing supplied. A servant could not marry without his master's consent. Runaway indentured servants were punished, if caught, by adding a year or more to their term of service. On the other hand the indenture and the laws called for good treatment, care in case of sickness, and the right to bring a case into the courts for breach of the indenture. The lot of the servant, however, was generally a hard one, and his social status low. This was particularly true where he was forced to work in the fields with the negro slave and to associate with the negro in other ways.

Control of Indentured Servants

114. Industries and Occupations in the Southern Colonies

In the tobacco colonies, Maryland and Virginia, over-production, low price and heavy import duties levied in England, brought the planters into debt. Agriculture and the Tobacco Problem In 1724 Hugh Jones, author of *The Present State of Virginia,* complained that "planters who have had a great dependence upon their year's crop of tobacco for the support of themselves and families have instead of clearing anything, been brought into debt by it." The planters, however, failed to solve one of their most serious problems — depletion of the soil, due to inefficient methods of cultivation. With the price of land rising and old lands wearing out, the eighteenth century witnessed a serious drop in the number of hogsheads of tobacco produced per acre. The one crop system doomed the planter to the raising of tobacco at a continually increased cost with diminishing profits. In fact, contrary to common belief, many if not most of the tobacco planters of Maryland and Virginia had great difficulty in making their plantations pay.

By 1732 debts were so numerous that English merchants sought parliamentary legislation. The planters Planters' Debts stated their side in a famous pamphlet, *The Case of the Planters of Tobacco in Virginia.* The principal grievances presented were overcharges by the merchants, excessive duties levied by England on imported tobacco (six pence per pound); and the high cost of marketing the tobacco, including freight charges, commissions, brokerage, cartage, warehouse rent, etc. The Virginia planter could not export direct to the continent, though about four-fifths of the tobacco that reached England was re-exported by the English merchants.

After 1732 it may be said that the normal condition of many Virginia planters was that of debtors. "Factors" or agents in Virginia warned the English merchants against granting too "loose" credit. Robert Plumstead, a Quaker and a London merchant, wrote Sam Burge, a Virginia planter in 1756 as follows:

"Have yours of 25th, 10th month, and continue to admire at the excuses thou makes. . . As to remittances thou may think that out of the question, however for forms sake I enclose thy account current balance still due £74 6s. 5d; to be out of temper with thee is not worth while . . . however, perhaps, an honest fit may take thee and if it should, pray remember thy old friend."

While the English government and merchant were in large part to blame for the troubles of the tobacco planter, yet the planter himself was not free from responsibility. He was often guilty of excessive importation of negro slaves purchased on credit; of extravagant living, and of purchasing goods, far in excess of his needs. The planters declared that, without close application annual debt was inevitable, since negroes must be fed and clothed, "crop failure or no."

The English commercial system, the scarcity of rich, fresh tobacco lands, and the decline in the natural fertility of the old lands forced diversification Diversification of Industries of industries and greater utilization of natural resources. Hence other industries than raising tobacco developed in the South, particularly the production of forest-products and the raising of live stock. England established bounties in 1705 for the production of indigo, tar, pitch, hemp, turpentine, and masts. Between 1729 and 1774, £1,028,584 were paid in such bounties. Most of this sum was received by the southern planters for the production of those articles.

Lumber was in great demand for domestic use and for export to the West Indies for buildings, ships, staves, hoops, and " headings." These last were made into hogsheads, barrels, and tierces, mostly by slave labor, as containers for tobacco, molasses, rum, rice, and other products. Sawed lumber was one of the major industries in North Carolina, her mills sawing annually some 8,000,000 feet of lumber. In 1768 fifty sawmills were in operation in that colony which ranked second of all the colonies in trans-Atlantic trade in sawed lumber.

The beginning of the live-stock industry is seen in a description of South Carolina in 1731, which notes " a prodigious number of swine, which multiply infinitely and are kept with very little charge, because they find almost all the year acorns, walnuts, chestnuts, herbs, roots, in the woods, so that you give them ever so little at home and they become fat, after which you may salt and send great quantities to the Isles of Barbados, St. Christophers, Jamaica, etc., which produce very good return in money or merchandise."

In general, industries in the southern colonies were much more diversified than is commonly believed. Maryland and Virginia produced tobacco, cereals — corn, wheat, flour, live stock — cattle, sheep, and hogs, and packing products — beef and pork, and lumber products. In South Carolina, the two great crops were rice and indigo, the former introduced in 1693 and the latter in 1742, both becoming very important articles of export. The other chief product for export was naval stores. South Carolina produced more pitch and tar than all the other colonies combined. She exported 52,000 barrels of pitch, tar, and turpentine as early as 1724.

As for Georgia, Governor Wright reported:

" Our whole time is employed in planting rice, indigo,

corn and peas, and a small quantity of wheat and rye, and in making pitch and tar, turpentine, shingles, and staves, and sawing lumber and scantling, and boards of every kind, and raising stocks of cattle, mules, horses, hogs and next year, I hope some essays will be made towards planting and making hemp."

Another form of diversification was the development of meadow lands, producing grass for cattle, and ex-
Diversified Agriculture tensive growing of cereals. As the center of population moved westward, the new land was better suited to cereals than to tobacco. The great increase in the negro slave population called for a larger supply of food, especially corn and pork. Since the practice of allowing the herds to roam in the woods proved costly, a tendency appeared to feed cattle with corn. Governor Dinwiddie reported (1755) the export from Virginia of 200,000 bushels of corn valued at £12,500 and 40,000 bushels of wheat. The increased production of cereals was due in part to the fact that land unfit for further production of tobacco might produce profitable crops of corn and wheat.

The diversification of crops and the utilization of natural resources laid the foundation for the growth of
Plantation Manufactures other industries such as flour milling, beef and pork packing, tanning, leather manufactures, shoe making, textile industries, the weaving of cloth from flax, wool, and cotton. Governor Spotswood wrote, as early as 1710, that the disappointing returns from tobacco caused many to attempt cloth making; "this is now become so universal that even in one of the best counties for tobacco, I am creditably informed that there has been made this last year about forty thousand yards of diverse sorts of woolen, cotton, and linen cloth." William Nelson of Virginia remarked, " we can do very well without many other things that we

used to indulge in. I now wear a good suit of cloth of my son's wool, manufactured, as well as my shirts, in Albemarle, my shoes, hose, buckles, wig, hat, etc. of our own country, and in these we improve every year in quantity and quality."

Because of these new industries the number of artisans and skilled workmen increased. The supply came principally from the indentured servants, apprentices, and negro slave artisans. The southern colonial assemblies passed numerous apprenticeship acts in order to stimulate and increase the supply of artisans, through the binding out of poor boys and girls to learn trades. Thus as the eighteenth century advanced we find mention of millers, brewers, weavers, butchers, tanners, curriers, shoemakers, blacksmiths, sawyers, carpenters, shipwrights, brickmakers, masons, plasterers, and other artisans.

The plantation then tended to become a more or less self-sufficing unit, with varied life and industries. The purpose was not merely simple agriculture, the production of crops by wholly unintelligent slave labor, but rather the utilization of land and forests, the employment of laborers and fieldhands in the tobacco field, and artisans as coopers, blacksmiths, shoemakers, carpenters, and weavers. The planter, more and more, utilized his slaves to make, fashion, build, or repair the buildings, tools, shoes, clothes, and utensils needed on the plantation.

115. Industries and Occupations in the Middle Colonies

In the middle, or " Bread Colonies," agriculture predominated. The settled regions around Philadelphia, including Delaware, and Western New Jersey, were primarily agricultural, and wheat flour and bread were their most important products. Gristmills increased in number. Franklin, for example, reported to the House of Commons in 1760 that there were eighty-three in Pennsylvania. New York was also a bread colony, and many mills were set up, the average having a capacity of 100 bushels of wheat a day. Since much of the flour was put into barrels and exported, the cooper's shop was placed near the mill or bolting plant. In fact the windmill and flour barrel were on New York's seal as emblems of its major industry.

The Middle Colonies: Agriculture

More and more attention was given to woolen manufactures, Germantown being a center of this industry, Burnaby, the British traveler, reported in 1758 that 60,000 pairs of "Germantown stockings," were made there in one year. He also remarks that "The Irish settlers make very good linents" and estimated that the farmers of Pennsylvania made nine-tenths of all their wearing apparel. Household clothmaking was a widespread industry in New York in the eighteenth century. A report of 1708 declared that three-fourths of the linens and woolens worn by the people were of their own make. Governor Moore reported (1767); "The custom of making these coarse Cloths (Linsey Woolseys) in private families prevails throughout the whole province, and almost in every house a sufficient quantity is manufactured for the use of the family, without the least design of sending any of it to market . . . everywhere swarms of children are set to work as soon as they are able to spin and card, and as every family is furnished with a loom, the itinerant weavers put the finishing hand to the Work."

Textiles

Next to the flour and textile industries, lumber products were of greatest importance. Many sawmills were erected along the rivers, and staves, barrels and hogsheads were manufactured in large quantities and sent to Ireland for packing their butter and salt provi-

Lumber Products

sions, and to the West Indies for sugar and molasses. Franklin stated (1760) that there were about forty sawmills in Pennsylvania with an average capacity of 1500 feet daily. This colony had much white oak timber, the most suitable for making staves; and in the year 1765, 3,912,000 staves, besides heads, shingles, hoops, and boards, were exported from Philadelphia.

Manufacture of lumber products was carried on by men who devoted their whole lives to the work, and also by "farmer coopers." Lacking a sawmill, the "sawpit" was the factory. Two men with a saw, one standing over the logs and the other underneath in a pit, turned out a great quantity of sawed lumber. Shingles and staves were hewn out by hand labor. A man could make 15,000 clapboards or pipe-staves in a year, worth £4 a thousand in the colony or £20 a thousand in the Canary Islands. Farmer-coopers, like farmer-nail-makers in New England, added to their income, by using their spare time in making barrels and casks which were sent "knocked down" to the West Indies and exchanged for sugar, molasses or money. Ship-building was another industry well developed in Phila-delphia and New York by 1750.

Another significant industry in Pennsylvania and New York was the manufacture of iron. At first most

Iron Manu-factures

of the pig iron was exported, but by 1750 so much was kept in the colony for manu-facturing that England passed an iron act to prevent further establishment of iron mills. Acrelius the Swedish traveler in 1750, described the iron works of Lancaster county, Pennsylvania, thus: "There is a furnace which makes twenty-five tons of iron a week and keeps six forges regularly at work." At Warwick the iron works were managed by Robert Grace, a friend of Franklin. In his Autobiography the latter wrote: "I made a present of the model (the Franklin stove) to Mr. Robert Grace, one of my early friends, who, having an iron furnace, found the casting of the plates for these stoves a profitable thing as they were in growing demand." John Taylor owned the Sarum Iron Works, on Chester Creek, which included a rolling and slitting mill. It is said that he manufactured nails and nail-rods cheaper than they could be purchased in England.

The iron industry in the colonies advanced so far by 1737 that a hearing was given in the House of Commons and testimony taken as to colonial competition and its effects. Mr. Edward Knight testified to a decrease of one-third in the output of bar iron in England, since 1718. He also said that the iron mongers reported almost no demand for nails, because a sufficient supply was available in America. He declared also that since 1722 no axes had been shipped to New England, New York, or Pennsylvania, and very few to Carolina; that there were sundry forges in New Jersey for the manufacture of bar iron; that andirons were being manufactured in Rhode Island, and garden spades, carpenters' axes and nails in Pennsylvania.

116. Industries and Occupations in New England

The general condition of agriculture in New England was unsatisfactory during most of this period. The natural fertility of the soil had been exhausted by unscientific methods and lack of fertilization. As a result, New England was obliged to import quantities of food supplies, especially the cereals, obtained principally from the bread colonies, New York and Pennsylvania. In fact, wheat almost

New England Colonies

passed out of cultivation in New England by 1715; but Indian corn continued to be the chief cereal crop. Next to agriculture the principal industries in the New England colonies were as follows: fishing, shipbuilding, cloth-making, lumber products, distilling of rum, the African slave trade, and the import and export of goods for themselves and for other colonies.

The fishing industry, particularly cod-fishing, was given a great stimulus by the treaty of Utrecht (1713) by which France surrendered Acadia, bet-
Fishing
ter known as Nova Scotia. From 1721 on the New England fishermen frequented this coast to dry their fish. About half of the catch was made up of "refuse" codfish, which were exchanged in the West Indies for sugar and molasses, out of which rum was made. The remainder, the better grades, was sold in the Catholic regions of southern Europe for specie or manufactured goods. Without a free exchange of the poorer fish for sugar and molasses the trade to Europe would have been unprofitable. By the middle of the eighteenth century, some 400 vessels from Massachusetts alone were engaged in the fisheries, employing 6000 men, the total value of the catch being around three-quarters of a million dollars annually. Whaling also commenced to be an important industry by 1750.

Shipbuilding was in its hey-day in the second quarter of the eighteenth century. Indeed by 1724 sixteen master ship carpenters, of London, complained
Shipbuilding
to the King that their trade was injured and their workmen were emigrating on account of New England competition. The "schooner" was invented, and the "strangely rigged craft" was launched at Gloucester, Massachusetts, in 1713. It gradually displaced the ship and brig for short voyages. The business of shipbuilding maintained some thirty other types of

tradesmen and artificers, such as sail makers, ship
carpenters, rope makers, etc., an interesting illustration
of the division of labor.

One of the great features of the lumber industry in
northern New England (New Hampshire and Maine)
Lumber   was the supply of masts to the royal navy.
Products   This industry was stimulated because the
British government paid a premium of one pound per
ton on masts, yards, and bowsprits. The industry involved many problems closely related to the political
and economic regulation and evolution of the New
England colonies. The King's rights in the forests interfered with the practices of the squatters; with poach-
ing, evasion of taxes, violation of the law, and conflicts
with the King's officers.

Massachusetts set up the peculiar claim in 1720 that
though the great trees marked by a broad arrow by
the King's surveyor of woods for masts for the royal
navy belonged to the King, yet, once felled, the timber
became the possession of the land owner. The lawless
element, squatters and "loggers," looked on the King's
surveyors much as the southern squatters looked on
the proprietary and royal quit rent collectors. In fact
the doctrine of individualism and natural rights was
greatly stimulated in these regions by the mast industry.

An observer of conditions in New England in 1689
says there were some manufactures, but not "one
Textile   twentieth of their need or consumption."
Manufactures   But by 1708, however, a letter from Boston to the Board of Trade complained that "country
people and planters are entered so far into making their
own woollens, that not one in forty but wears his own
carding, spinning, etc. If the growing trade of woollens
be no way prevented in its growth, England must loose
the woollen export to all this part of America." From

this date to 1750, woven fabrics of woolen and linens increased in importance. The large immigration of the Scotch-Irish around 1720 stimulated the linen industry, particularly in Londonderry, New Hampshire. In 1747 was founded the Boston Society for promoting Industry and Frugality. On its fourth anniversary, 300 " young female spinnsters " spun at their wheels on Boston Common. This was known as the " Spinning Craze," and indicates a popular instinct and desire for home production.

It is clear why England was disturbed over the development of the textile industry. While not competing directly with English products in foreign markets, the colonists were making much of their own cloth by 1750. This development, in connection with smuggling, seriously checked English woolen manufactures. This in turn affected the English merchants and was in part the background for the significant change of policy in 1763, when it was decided to enforce the navigation acts.

One of the important industries in this period was the distilling of rum. In Massachusetts and Rhode Island, especially at Boston, Medford, and Newport, many distilleries sprang up. By 1750 many of the smaller coast towns of New England had set up one or more. Newport, R. I., was a large center of this industry, and by 1762 contained 22 distilleries. " Long Wharf," says one observer, " was alive with molasses coming in and rum going out." No less than 1,500,000 gallons were made in Massachusetts alone by 1750. The economic and social consequences of this industry will be considered later (p. 412).

In New England many small industries were in operation, too numerous to mention. Lynn, Massachusetts, for example, began to export shoes, and Boston set up ropewalks. In other towns, such industries were started as glass making and paper mills. Indeed industrial activity and the division of labor were increasing very rapidly by the mid-century. It was a prelude to, and a necessary foundation for, the movement towards economic independence which paralleled the religious and political movement for independence from 1763 to 1783.

117. Trade Relations with the West Indies

While there was an undoubted tendency towards diversification of industries in the southern colonies, agri-

Basis of Trade in Southern Colonies

culture was the principal occupation throughout this period. The main effort was to produce a surplus for export to England and the West Indies: especially tobacco, naval stores, lumber products, provisions, rice, and indigo. By far the larger portion of the export trade was with England: first because of legal requirements, and then because of the advantages of this market, which provided agents, ships, and personal relationships. Moreover the Virginian and Maryland trade with England centered around tobacco, a problem which became more and more unsatisfactory. This bulky, low-priced product brought too small a return to pay for the relatively expensive imported manufactured goods, such as housefurnishings, tools for agriculture, woolens, cottons, silks, linens, furniture and luxuries.

The West Indian trade was based on the problem of finding a market for products not salable in England,

West Indian Trade

and to obtain specie to pay debts contracted to English merchants. The main products of the South — tobacco, rice, beef, pork, and lumber — were traded for negroes, rum, molasses, and sugar. Other products imported from the West Indies were coffee, mahogany, spices, and salt, the latter being a very important article. It was reported in 1706 that vessels usually take on salt from the Bahamas, especially Tortuga, which is carried to " New England, Virginia, Pennsylvania, New York and other places," to be used mainly for salting beef and pork. An example of the trade is the order of William Byrd II, one of the great planters of Virginia. He ordered from Barbados four negroes, 1200 gallons of rum, 3000 pounds of Muscovado sugar, one barrel of white sugar, three of molasses, one cask of lime juice, and some ginger.

The middle colonies, like New England, sold little to Great Britain. They depended largely on the profits Trade of the of their West Indian trade to pay the bal-
Middle ances due English merchants. Two brief
Colonies contemporary descriptions of the trade of the middle colonies in the early eighteenth century will illustrate its character. In 1705 it was reported that " New York exports to our sugar-islands great quantities of flour, peas, bisket, bacon, butter, pork, etc. and receives in return sugar, molasses, rum, cotton, ginger, pimento, etc. and also Spanish money, which pays Great Britain for all the various necessaries they receive from thence." A similar report stated that Pennsylvania exported " corn, peas, flour, bisket, beef, pork, fish, staves, poultry, lumber, horses, etc. . . They get silver also by their clandestine trade with the Spanish main; and their trade in logwood, which they import into England, helps to pay for what they bring."

The particular advantages of the West Indian trade to New England were as follows. First, it was in the Trade of the West Indies that her surplus of fish was
New England sold, especially those of poor quality. An-
Colonies other advantage was the great opportunity to obtain specie. Since New England sold little to England direct, but bought heavily of manufactured goods

it was necessary to obtain specie to settle their adverse balance of trade. A report concerning Connecticut trade (1763) declared that this colony owned 79 vessels. "Those vessels that go to the French and Dutch plantations (in the West Indies) carry horses, cattle, sheep, hogs, provisions, and lumber, for which are received molasses, cocoa, cotton, and some sugar, and from the Dutch plantation, bills of exchange; the most of which importation and bills goes to New York and Boston to pay for British goods this government received from those places." The third advantage was the molasses trade. This was the basis of the great distilling industry, the manufacture of rum, which in turn was the basis of the slave trade. After 1700, vessels from Boston and Newport were regularly engaged in the slave trade, carrying New England rum to the African "Gold Coast." The slaves bought with this and other commodities were sold in the West Indies in exchange for molasses and sugar; and in South Carolina and Virginia for rice and tobacco. By 1750 Newport alone had 120 vessels engaged in the West Indian, African, and European trade. Governor Stephen Hopkins declared that "for more than thirty years prior to 1764 Rhode Island sent to the Guinea coast annually eighteen vessels carrying 1800 hhds of rum;" and that this commerce in rum and slaves was worth about £40,000 per annum "for remittance from Rhode Island to Great Britain."

Fish, lumber, and provisions were the articles most needed by the West Indian planters, articles they did not or could not produce themselves. Since the West Indies lacked ships, slaves must be brought in principally by English or New England ships. This interdependence of trade is the central feature of the growth of New England's commerce in this period. The foreign West Indies, especially the French Islands, Martinique and Guadeloupe, took New England's surplus fish in large quantities, paying in molasses produced and sold more cheaply than in the English West Indies. The French were also free of the four and one half per cent export duties levied in the English islands. New England carried on a large part of her trade with these foreign islands, whence she obtained much of her specie.

Although all the British continental colonies had a share in the West Indian trade, the New England merchants and captains had another great advantage. They were the chief carriers for the other colonies, because of their ability to build ships more cheaply. In 1769 New England had 13,435 tonnage, while all the other continental colonies together had but 6567. The New England ship masters also cruised about and traded among the islands and so became carriers for the " Carribees." This will appear more clearly if we consider the instructions to the captain of the " Charming Polly " of Newport, R. I. Captain Penmure was to take a cargo of goods to St. Vincent's (Danish) there " to dispose of the cargoe if he can. If not to proceed to Dominico (Spanish) and there sell what he can and proceed from thence to St. Eustatius (Dutch) and dispose of any part of the cargoe he may have left, and also what goods he may be obliged to take in pay for his cargoe at St. Vincents or Dominico, and when the whole is converted into money to proceed with all possible dispatch of the island of Hispaniola (Spanish) without any goods whatsoever, and there invest the neat (net) proceeds of his cargoe in good molasses, best muscovado sugars and Indigoe."

The British planters in Barbados and Jamaica complained that when the New Englanders did sell their produce to them, they demanded money and would not take molasses in exchange. This tended to draw

off specie from the British islands. With this money
they purchased the same kind of merchandise (molasses
and sugar) from the French islands, that the British
planters had offered. To stop this practice and other
practices the Molasses Act of 1733 and the similar
Sugar Act of 1764 were passed. Their enforcement
would have been disastrous to New England. This is the
reason why John Adams said that molasses was an important " ingredient of the American Revolution."

Two main routes of trade used by New England ships
were known as the triangular trade routes. One was
from New England to the West Indies;
Trade Routes   thence to England or the continent of Europe; and back to New England, often via the West
Indies. The second was from New England, perhaps via
the West Indies, to Africa; back to the West Indies; and
thence to England or via southern ports or direct to New
England. In the trade in which England or the continent was one corner of the triangle, New England
produce was sold in the West Indies for money or
salable goods, molasses and sugar; and exchanged in
England for woolens and other English or European
manufactured goods. In the second route, New England
fish were taken to the West Indies and rum to Africa,
and the latter was exchanged for slaves, which were sold
in the West Indies or southern colonies for cash or for
sugar, molasses, tobacco, and provisions. The molasses
was converted into rum to buy more slaves.

118. Piracy and Smuggling

A pressing problem connected with the development
of commerce was that of piracy. In 1699 Parliament
passed an act for the suppression of pi-
Piracy   rates. These sea robbers committed many
thefts and acts of violence ruinous to trade and were a

source of demoralization. They were frequently tried and executed. Lord Bellomont had instructions to put down pirates that infested the coast of New England, particularly Rhode Island, a colony that was growing rich by its trade with pirates. He captured the famous Captain Kidd and sent him to England for trial whence he was found guilty, justly or unjustly, and hanged.

Smuggling was a common practice in England before colonization was attempted. So along with other customs the art of, and the tendency towards smuggling may be said to have been inherited.

Smuggling

Geographic factors were favorable — the indented coast line with numerous bays, harbors, and creeks. Note also the non-enforcement of the navigation acts; the belief that they were unjust; anger over the establishment of admiralty courts; and the small number of officials and their willingness to accept bribes, this being a practice even of some of the royal governors. One collector of the port of New York was suspended for " countenancing illegal trade." Another factor was the long distances between ports of entry, the inadequacy of the naval patrol, and the failure of colonial juries to convict offenders.

After the passage of the trade act of 1696, one main purpose of which was to remedy the evils of smuggling by providing for trial of cases in vice-admiralty courts, greater effort was made to enforce the laws. The sufferings of one John Townsend, a customs house officer at Oyster Bay, New York, in 1699, illustrate the difficulty of preventing smuggling. The law allowed him a salary of £30 and a third of the seizures of smuggled goods, a position he undertook " cheerfully." Within a month he begged the governor that he might resign from his job, because " though most of that towne were his near relations and several of them of his name, yet he was threatened by them to be knocked on the head, and he already suffered many abuses, insomuch as he was in fear of his life."

The Board of Trade complained (1733–1750), that the practice was for vessels to clear from Rhode Island for Jamaica, but to proceed to another settlement, sell their produce for specie, "refusing rum and molasses and have then gone to some foreign settlement and bought a cargo of Rum and Molasses with that specie, and sometimes Linnens, Silks, East India Goods, and other prohibited merchandise," that is, goods which by the navigation laws they should have purchased only in England. In fact the purchase of European goods at St. Eustatius (Dutch) and St. Lucia and St. Thomas, so-called neutral ports, to be smuggled into New England ports, was a great worry to the British merchants. One report of 1736 reads, "These practices [illicit trading] will never be put an End to till Rhode Island is reduced to the subjection of the British Empire; of which at present it is no more a part than the Bahama Islands were when they were invaded by the Bucanneers."

After 1725 colonial commerce expanded very rapidly. During Walpole's premiership the colonial administration was in the hands of the Duke of Newcastle, who was later accused by Walpole of being incompetent and of treating the colonies with "salutary neglect." Thus the colonists had a wonderful opportunity to smuggle, especially from the foreign West Indies. The extent of smuggling will never be known exactly, for obvious reasons. That there was a large amount is certain. Governor Clinton declared in 1752 that while the consumption of tea had increased annually, the exportation of tea to the colonies from London had decreased, because of smuggling.

The chief methods of smuggling were as follows. (1) Loading and unloading vessels at night in out-of-the-way places where there were no officials. (2) Transferring goods at sea from one ship to another. (3) Use of false ship papers and manifests of cargoes. (4) Mislabelling barrels of goods, "provisions" instead of "tobacco." Thus: "Several Scotch merchants in Pennsylvania drive a continual trade into their country, and from thence carry the tobacco of Maryland and Virginia to Surinam and Curaçao in bread casks covered with flour at each end. Care is therefore to be taken to stop the illegal trade carried on in Pennsylvania when it is now as irregular as it ever was practiced at Boston." (5) Non-enumerated goods were shipped to Holland, but tea and silks were brought back without entering British ports. (6) Goods loaded on vessels in the foreign West Indies, molasses, for example, were entered in North America as having come from the British West Indies.

Robert Quary, Surveyor General of Customs in 1707, visited Connecticut and found many dishonest practices. The collector, he says, was a "Pillar of their Church but a great rogue." He accused him of giving false certificates to vessels that had brought in tobacco illegally from Virginia, so that they might ship this tobacco to other plantations. Col. William Byrd II wrote Lord Egmont concerning New England smugglers: ". . . tho with respect to Rum, the Saints of New England will, I fear, find out some trick to evade your acts of Parliament, [e.g., Molasses Act of 1733.] They have a great dexterity at palliating a perjury as well as to leave no taste of it in their mouth, nor can any people like them slip through a penal statute. They will give some other name to their Rum, which they may safely do, because it goes by that of "Kill-Devil" in this country from its baneful qualities. A watchful eye must be kept on these foul traders, or all the precaution of the trustees will be in vain."

Robert Snead of Philadelphia, however, thought as little of the Quakers as Byrd did of the Puritans. He wrote: " as long as the government is in the hands of Quakers, as it is, it must be expected that pirates and unlawful traders will still be encouraged." The basic cause of illegal trade was of course the desire for large profits. But the English commercial system so disregarded some of the important and natural economic needs and interests of the colonists, by restricting profits and raising the price of imported goods, that smuggling was almost inevitable.

The importance of smuggling was not so much in the amount of goods brought in, as in its effect on the relations of England with the colonies. Illegal trade was one of the chief irritants in this relation. It will be remembered that John Adams said of the speech of James Otis in 1761 against the Writs of Assistance, on that day " the Child Independence was born." Conflict of authority, corruption and bribery, quarrels, opposition to the vice-admiralty courts — all grew out of smuggling. It helped, in the formation of the colonial mind, to bring about an attitude of self-sufficiency, and a desire for economic independence, both revealed in the American Revolution.

119. Balance of Trade

Officially the balance of trade of the middle and New England colonies was almost always adverse. The Balance of Trade Thus in 1698–99 the value of the exports of England to Pennsylvania and New York was £59,843, but these same colonies returned goods to the value of only £21,358. So in 1727, while Pennsylvania imported goods from England to the value of £26,397 she exported only £6,882. The conditions were much the same in New England (see p. 375). In the case of the southern colonies, it is more difficult to know the facts. Governor Seymour of Maryland declared in 1705 that it was "impossible for all the officers in the world to know what is shipt or unshipt," because of smuggling. As we have seen, the southern colonies sold most of their surplus products to England, while the New England and middle colonies sold most of theirs to the West Indies.

While it is often stated that the balance of trade was in favor of the southern colonies, two items are usually omitted in this estimate: (1) the actual net return to the planter of goods sold after charges and the net cost to him of goods purchased, (2) the cost of slaves brought in largely by English ships and purchased of English slave dealers. If these items are taken into consideration, the South probably bought goods of more value than she sold. The fact that Virginia was in debt to English merchants some $10,000,000 at the opening of the Revolution is further evidence of an adverse balance of trade.

CHAPTER XV

SOCIAL DEVELOPMENT (1689–1750)

120. References

Bibliography. — (See under "Bibliographies," chs. iv, vii, ix, xii, xiv); J. T. Adams, *Prov. Society*, 338–349; C. M. Andrews, *Colonial Folkways*, 239–243; Channing, Hart and Turner, *Guide*, §§ 36–39, 42–43, 45, 47, 48, 117, 120, 121, 126, 146, 149, 162–165; E. B. Greene, *Prov. America*, 325–340, and *Foundations of Am. Nationality*, 256, 279–280, 336–337, 355–356; Grace Griffin, *Writs. on Am. Hist.*, 1906–1923; J. N. Larned, *Lit. of Am. Hist.*, 331–359; T. J. Wertenbaker, *First Americans*, 317–338.

Historical Maps. — (See references to chs. v, ix, xii); Edward Channing, *Hist. of U. S.*, II, 604 (cols. in 1760; extent of settlement).

General Accounts. — See refs. under "General Social" and "Special Social," chs. iv (esp. Calhoun), vii, ix, xii; J. T. Adams, *Prov. Society*, chs. v, vi, x (colonial culture); C. M. Andrews, *Colonial Folkways*, and "Am. Revolution — An Interpretation," in *Am. Hist Rev.*, Jan. 1926 (for English social background); Chas. and Mary Beard, *Rise of Am. Civilization*, I, chs. iii–iv; Edward Channing, *Hist. of U. S.*, II, chs. xiv, xv; J. A. Doyle, *Engl. Col. in Am.*, V, chs. i, iv–v; A. M. Earle, *Colonial Dames and Goodwives*, and *Home Life in Colonial Days;* S. G. Fisher, *Men, Women and Manners in Colonial Times;* E. B. Greene, *Prov. America*, chs. v, xii, xiii, xviii; Earl Holiday, *Women's Life in Colonial Days;* M. S. Locke, *Anti-Slavery in Am.*, 1619–1808; H. L. Osgood, *Am. Cols. in 18th Cent.*, II, ch. xviii; III, chs. i–iii; F. J. Turner, *Frontier in Am. Hist.*, chs. i–ii; Anne Wharton, *Colonial Days and Dames.*

Special Accounts. — (a) SECTIONS AND COLONIES: (See ch. viii, "Special Accts.," and ch. ix; for titles on slavery and servitude see chs. iv, vii, ix, xii.). (1) New England: J. T. Adams, *Revolutionary New Engl.*, ch. iii; Sam Briggs, *The Essays, Humor, and Poems of Nath. Ames, Father and Son, etc.* (1726–1775); F. B. Dexter, "Social Distinctions at Harvard and Yale before the Rev.," in *Am. Ant. Soc. Proc.* n. s. IX; A. B. Hart (ed.), *Commonwealth Hist. Mass.*, II, chs. x (literature), xi (C. Mather), xii (women); J. G. Palfrey, *Hist. of New*

Engl., IV, 312–376; V, bk. VI, ch. viii; W. B. Weeden, *Econom. and Soc. Hist. of New Engl.*, I, ch. x; II, chs. xiii, xv, xvii; and *Early Rhode Island, etc.*, and "Ideal Newport in the 18th Cent.," in *Proc. Am. Ant. Soc.* n. s. XVIII; Justin Winsor, *Memorial Hist. of Boston*, II, chs. ix (influ. of Mather family), xvi, xviii. (2) Middle and Southern Colonies: Tom Peete Cross, "Witchcraft in North Carolina," in *Studies in Philology*, XVI; J. O. Knauss, *Social Conditions among the Pa. Germans;* Edward McCrady, *Hist. of South Carolina Under the Royal Govt., 1719–1776;* C. L. Raper, "Social Life in Colonial North Carolina," (in *North Carolina Booklet*, III); H. H. Ravenel, *Charleston, the Place and the People;* Esther Singleton, *Social New York under the Georges, 1714–1776.* (b) RELIGION AND MORALS: (Bibliogs. in Adams, *Prov. Society*, 339–341; Peter Mode, *Source Book and Bibliogr. Guide for Am. Ch. Hist.;* T. J. Wertenbaker, *First Americans*, 325–328. See refs. under "General Social" and "Special Social," chs. iv, v, titles under "Puritans," and ch. vii, under "Religion and Morals," and ch. ix); C. F. Adams, "Some Phases of Sexual Morality and Church Discipline in Colo. New Engl.," in *Mass. Hist. Soc. Proc.*, 2nd ser., VI; Isaac Backus, *Hist. of New Engl. with Partic. Ref. to Baptists* (ed. 1871); A. L. Cross, *The Anglican Episcopate and the Am. Colonies;* F. M. Davenport, *Primitive Traits in Relig. Revivals;* E. B. Greene, "Anglican Outlook on the Am. Cols.," in *Am. Hist. Rev.*, XX, 64–85; Ernest Hawkins, *Missions of Ch. of England in Am. Colonies;* Rufus Jones, *Quakers in the Am. Cols.;* C. H. Maxson, *The Great Awakening in the Middle Colonies;* Susan Reed, "Church and State in Mass., 1691–1740," in *Univ. of Ill. Studies*, III; H. R. Stiles, *Bundling, Its Origin, Progress and Decline in America;* Joseph Tracy, *The Great Awakening.* (c) GENERAL INTELLECTUAL CONDITIONS: (See bibliogs. in J. T. Adams, *Prov. Society*, 341, 343–348, and T. J. Wertenbaker, *First Americans*, 329–330; see refs. under "Gen. Social" and "Special Social," ch. iv; and under "Intellectual Conditions," chs. vii, ix; see also "Biographies" below, and works by M. C. Tyler, W. P. Trent (ed.) and V. L. Parrington listed in ch. iv); P. E. Aldrich, "John Locke and the Influ. of his Works on Am. Thought," *etc.*, in *Am. Ant. Soc. Proc.*, 1879, 22–39; H. D. Foster, "International Calvinism through Locke and the Revolu. of 1688," in *Am. Hist. Rev.*, XXXII, 475–499; C. E. Merriam, *History of Am. Polit. Theory*, ch. i; Phillips, "Early Proceed. of Am. Phil. Soc.," in *Am. Phil. Soc. Proc.*, XXII, pt. II, 1884; and "Hist. Acct. of Am. Phil. Soc.," in *ibid.*, 1914; I. W. Riley, *American Thought;* E. C. Smith,

"The New Philosophy," in *Am. Ant. Soc. Proc.*, n. s. xi.
(d) LIBRARIES AND BOOKS: F. B. Dexter, "Early Private Libraries in New Engl.," in *Am. Ant. Soc. Proc.*, n. s. XVIII, 135–147; D. C. Gilman, "Bishop Berkeley's Gift to Yale College," in *New Haven Hist. Soc. Paps.* I; A. B. Keep, *The Library in Colonial N. Y.* (1698–1776); E. V. Lamberton, "Colonial Libraries of Pa.," in *Pa. Mag. of Hist.*, XLII; B. C. Steiner, "Thos. Bray and His Libraries," in *Am. Hist. Rev.*, II, 59–75; J. H. Tuttle, "The Libraries of the Mathers," in *Am. Ant. Soc. Proc.*, n. s. XX, 269–356; S. B. Weeks, "Libraries and Literature in North Carolina in 18th Cent.," in *Am. Hist. Assn. Rpt.*, 1895, 171–266. (e) LITERATURE, PRINTING AND NEWSPAPERS: (For bibliogs. see Brigham, "Bibl. of Am. Newspapers," in *Am. Ant. Soc. Proc.*, n. s., XXIII–XXXV; Isaiah Thomas, "History of Printing in Am.," in *Am. Ant. Soc. Trans. and Collecs.*, v, vi; G. T. Watkins, *Bibliog. of Printing in U. S.;* W. P. Trent (ed.), *Camb. Hist. Am. Lit.*, I, 452–462); see also "Biographies," below, Hugh Gaine. E. C. Cooke, *Literary Influences in Colonial Newspapers, 1704–1750;* C. A. Duniway, *Development of Freedom of Press in Mass.;* A. B. Hart (ed.), *Commonwl. Hist. Mass.*, II, ch. x; Charles Hildeburn, *Sketches of Printers and Printing in Colonial New York;* E. P. Oberholtzer, *Literary Hist. of Philadelphia;* R. F. Roden, *The Cambridge Press*, 1638–1692; L. A. Rutherford, *John Peter Zenger, His Press, Trial, etc.;* L. R. Schuyler, *Liberty of the Press in the Am. Colonies* (with ref. to New York); Justin Winsor, *Memo. Hist. of Boston*, II, ch. xv; T. G. Wright, *Literary Culture in Early New Engl.;* L. C. Wroth, *Hist. of Print. in Colo. Md., 1686–1776.* (f) PROFESSIONS: Alice M. Baldwin, *New Engl. Clergy and the Am. Rev.;* J. M. Toner, *Contribu. to the Annals of Med. Prog. in U. S.;* Charles Warren, *Hist. of the Am. Bar.* (g) CULTURAL HIST. AND FINE ARTS: (Bibliog. in J. T. Adams, *Prov. Society*, 345–348; C. M. Andrews, *Colonial Folkways*, 242, and W. P. Trent (ed.), *Camb. Hist. of Am. Lit.*, I, 490–493); William Dunlap, *Hist. of Rise and Prog. of Arts and Design in U. S.;* H. D. Eberlein, *Architecture of Colonial America;* Ralph Gabriel (ed.), *Pageant of America*, XI–XIII; A. H. Quinn, *A Hist. of the Am. Drama, etc.;* J. T. Wertenbaker, *First Americans*, 329–331; O. G. Sonneck, *Early Concert Life in Am., 1731–1800.* (h) EDUCATION: (Bibliogs. under "Intellectual Life," ch. vii, and "Intellectual Conditions," above, and J. T. Adams, *Prov. Society*, 341–342); H. B. Adams, *The Coll. of Wm. and Mary;* E. E. Brown, *Making of our Middle Schools;* E. P. Cubberley, *Public Education in U. S.;* M. W. Jernegan, articles in *School*

Review, XXVI–XXVIII; W. W. Kemp, *Support of Schools in Colonial N. Y. by Soc. for Prop. of the Gospel, etc.;* Edward McCrady, "Educa. in South Carolina Prior to and During the Rev.," in *S. C. Hist. Coll.*, IV; John Maclean, *History of the College of New Jersey;* T. H. Montgomery, *Hist. of Univ. of Pa.;* C. L. Raper, *Church and Private Schs. in North Carolina;* W. H. Small, *Early New England Schools;* L. F. Snow, *Hist. of College Curriculum.* (i) MEDICINE AND SCIENCE: (Bibliog. in Wertenbaker, *First Americans*, 334–335; see also under "Biography" below, Bartram, Colden, Franklin, Mitchell); J. T. Adams, *Prov. Society*, ch. x (bibl. 342–343); G. L. Kittredge, "Cotton Mather's Election into the Royal Society," in *Colo. Soc. Mass. Pub.*, XIV, 81–114, 285–292; and "Scientific Communications to the Royal Society," in *Am. Ant. Soc. Proc.* n. s. XXVI, 18–57; *Records of Celebration of 200th Anniversary of Birthday of Franklin* (Phil., 1906); F. R. Packard, *The Hist. of Medicine in U. S.;* W. T. Sedgwick and H. W. Tyler, *A Short Hist. of Science.*

Biography. — (Bibl. in Channing, Hart and Turner, *Guide*, §§ 39, 46, 47; J. T. Adams, *Prov. Society*, 330–331; W. P. Trent (ed.), *Camb. Hist. Am. Lit.*, I, 424–425, 432, 440–441, 449); see refs. under chs. ii (Blair); vi (Sibley, I. Mather, C. Mather, Sewall, and Dudley); viii (Penn); ix (Pastorius); x (Franklin); xii (Harbaugh); A. V. G. Allen, *Jonathan Edwards;* Allen Bradford, *Jonathan Mayhew;* E. E. Beardsley, *Life of Samuel Johnson* (1696–1772); Martin Brumbaugh, *Life of Cristopher Dock;* Lyman Carrier, "Dr. John Mitchell," in *Am. Hist. Assn. Rpt.*, 1918, I, 201–219; William Darlington, *Memorials of John Bartram and Humphrey Marshall;* Elizabeth Dexter, *Colonial Women of Affairs;* F. B. Dexter, *Biog. Sketches of the Graduates of Yale College*, I–III; Jonathan Edwards, *Life of David Brainerd;* S. G. Fisher, *True Benjamin Franklin;* P. L. Ford, *Many Sided Franklin;* F. L. Humphreys, *Life and Times of David Humphreys;* A. M. Keyes, *Cadwalader Colden;* Ann Maury (tr.) Jacques Fontaine, *Memoirs of a Huguenot Family;* H. H. Ravenel, *Eliza. Pinckney;* H. W. Smith, *Life and Correspondence of William Smith;* W. S. Sprague, *Annals of the Am. Pulpit* (8 vols. by denominations); Luke Tyerman, *Life of George Whitefield;* Williston Walker, *Ten New England Leaders;* F. J. E. Woodbridge, "Jonathan Edwards," in *Philosoph. Rev.*, XIII.

Contemporary Accounts. — (a) BIBLIOGRAPHY: See refs. to chs. iv, vi, vii-viii, ix, xii, under "Contemporary Accounts." J. T. Adams, *Prov. Society*, 326–328 (documents); Channing,

388   *Social Development*

Hart and Turner, *Guide*, §§ 43 (colonial state and local records),
47–48, 117, 120, 121, 126, 146, 149, 161–162, 165; A. R. Hasse,
Materials for a Bibliog., etc.; Hist. Sources in Schools', § 74 (Colo.
Society); see A. P. C. Griffin, "Bibliog. of Am. Hist. Societies,"
in *Am. Hist. Assoc. Rept.*, 1905, II, for lists of documents,
inventories, court records, *etc.;* Milton Waldman, *Americana,
etc.*, chs. ix-xi.   (b) GENERAL COLLECTIONS: See references under "Contemporary Accts.," chs. iv, vii, ix, xii, xiv; compare
newspaper extracts in New Jersey Archives, XI–XII, 1704–
1750; A. B. Hart (ed.), *Contemporaries*, II, chs. xii, xiv (In-
tellectual Life), xv (Relig. Life), xvi (Slavery and Servitude);
E. C. Stedman and E. M. Hutchinson, *Library of Am. Lit.*,
I–II. (c) GENERAL TRAVELS: (Bibliography: J. T. Adams, *Prov.
Society*, 354–356; C. M. Andrews, *Colonial Folkways*, 239–245;
Channing, Hart and Turner, *Guide*, § 38; W. P. Trent (ed.),
Camb. Hist. Am. Lit., I, 365–380; Justin Winsor, *Nar. and
Crit. Hist. of Am.*, VIII, 489–494); John Birket, *Some Cursory
Remarks* (1750–1751); H. L. Bourdin and others (eds.), St. John
de Crèvecœur, *Sketches of 18th Cent. Am.;* William Douglass,
Summary, Historical and Political (ed. 1760); A. B. Hart (ed.),
Alex. Hamilton, *Itinerarium* (1744), ed., 1907); A. H. Hoyt,
Extracts from Capt. Goelet's Journal, 1746–1750 (ed. 1870); see
also *N. Engl. Hist. and Gen. Reg.*, XXIV, 50–63; Peter Kalm,
Travels in North Am., 1748–1751; also in *Pinkerton's Voyages*,
XIV; N. D. Mareness (ed.), *Travels in the Am. Colonies;*
G. P. Winship (ed.), *The Journal of Madam Knight* (1704), ed.,
1920; (Journey, Boston to N. Y. 1704). (d) DIARIES, JOUR-
NALS, LETTERS, AND CONTEMPORARY HISTORIES: (Bibliography in
J. T. Adams, *Prov. Soc.*, 327, 330–331; Channing, Hart and
Turner, *Guide*, § 37, 38, 45, 47; Harriet Forbes, *Bibl. of New
Engl. Diaries;* W. P. Trent (ed.), *Camb. Hist. Am. Lit.*, I,
384–467); see under "Contemp. Accts.," ch. iv (Phillips); ch.
vii, (Mather, Sewall), ch. xii (Harrower, Mittelberger, Flackner,
Holm, Acrelius, and Carroll; latter contains Hewatt's S. C. and
Ga., 1779). (e) NEW ENGLAND: (See refs. under "Contemp.
Accts.," ch. vii); G. F. Dow, (ed.), *The Holyoke Diaries*, 1709–
1856; Jonathan Edwards, *Works*, esp. III (Revival in New
Engl.); J. Hemstead, *Diary in Colls. New London Hist. Soc.*,
I (1901); James MacSparran, *A Letter Book and Abstract of
Services, 1743–1751;* K. B. Murdock, *Selections from Cotton
Mather*, 1926; M. Van Doren, *Samuel Sewall's Diary* (Selections)
1927. (f) MIDDLE COLONIES: Cadwalader Colden, "Papers,"
in *N. Y. Hist. Soc. Colls.*, 1917, III–VII; Benjamin Franklin,

"Autobiography" in *Works*, ed. by Smythe, I; William Logan, *Journal* (1745), in *Pa. Mag. of Hist.*, XXXVI, 1–16, 162–186; Samuel Smith, *Hist. of the Col. of Nova Cesaria, of New Jersey*, 1765 (reprint 1877); William Smith, "History of the Late Province of N. Y., etc. to 1762," in *N. Y. Hist. Soc. Coll.*, 1st ser. IV, V; J. G. Whittier (ed.), John Woolman, *Journal*. (g) SOUTHERN COLONIES: J. S. Bassett, *Writings of Col. William Byrd of Westover;* Robert Beverley, *Hist. of Va., etc.* (1702 and 1722); W. K. Boyd (ed.), "Some 18th Century Tracts Concerning North Carolina" (1740–1791), in *Pub. of N. Carolina Hist. Com.*, XVIII; John Brickell, *Natural Hist. of North Carolina* (1737), reprint 1911; Philip Fithian, *Journal and Letters;* J. C. Fitzpatrick (ed.), *Diaries of George Washington*, 1748–1799; Henry Hartwell, James Blair, and Edward Chilton, (Virginia in 1696), in *Cal. State Pa. Colonial and W. I.*, 1696–1697, no. 1396; H. P. Holbrook, *Journal and Letters of Eliza. Lucas;* D. Jarrett, *Life of Devereaux Jarrett, etc.;* Hugh Jones, *Present State of Va.* (1724), ed. 1865; "New Voyage to Ga." (1733–1734), in *Ga. Hist. Soc. Colls.*, II; John Lawson, *History of North Carolina* (1714), reprint, 1903; Josiah Quincy, "Southern Journal," in *Proc. Mass. Hist. Soc.*, XLIX (1916). (h) RELIGION AND MORALS: (Bibliog. in Peter Mode, *Source-Book and Bibliog. Guide to Am. Ch. Hist.*), see "Contemp. Accts.," ch. iv (Perry), ch. vii (Walker), ch. ix (Hastings) and ch. xii, E. Slafter (ed.), "John Checkley or Evolu. of Relig. Toleration in Mass. Bay" (1719–1774), in *Prince. Soc. Pubs.*, 23–24; J. T. Thornton, *The Pulpit of the Am. Revolution* (for Jonathan Mayhew's sermon on Unlimited Submission, 1750); W. P. Trent (ed.), *Camb. Hist. Am. Lit.*, I, 398–424 (Mathers), 426–438 (Edwards); Philosophers and Divines, Mayhew, Whitefield, Woolman, (438–442); Franklin (442–449). (i) INTELLECTUAL CONDITIONS: (See "Contemp. Accts.," ch. iv, Stedman and Hutchinson and Clews; ch. vii, Evans, Littlefield, W. C. Ford, and Wright); F. B. Dexter (ed.), *Documentary History of Yale University*, 1701–1745, and *Literary Diary of Ezra Stiles* (3 vols.), 1727–95; P. L. Ford (ed.), *Journals of Hugh Gaine, Printer;* A. B. Hart (ed.), *Contemporaries*, II, nos. 90 (Yale Coll. 1744); 95 (Diary of Coll. Life at Harv. (1758); "Harvard College Records, 1638–1750," in *Pub. Colonial Soc. Mass.*, XV, XVI; "Journal of the Meetings of the President and Masters of William and Mary College, 1729–1784," in *Wm. and Mary Coll. Qr.*, I–V, XIII–XV; Isaiah Thomas, "Hist. of Printing in Am.," in *Am. Ant. Soc. Trans.*, V–VI (1874).

121. The Basis of the Social Order

THE colonial social order in the eighteenth century was determined by numerous influences, some of which The Material have already been discussed. First comes Basis the material foundation of the type of society developed which included exploitation of natural resources — land and forests, rivers and oceans, and the distribution of products through trade and commerce — the two chief pathways to wealth. The distribution of wealth among the various classes of society largely determined the social order. It fixed the social status of the planter, merchant, shipowner, farmer, sailor, artisan, unskilled laborer, servant, and slave. Class divisions followed in the main the English tradition of gentry, merchants, yeomen, tenants, artisans, and servants. Several important elements were missing, however, such as a titled nobility, a clerical hierarchy, and the peasant class. Corresponding somewhat to these old world class divisions arose in the colonies a landed aristocracy, a merchant class, a privileged clergy, principally Anglican and Puritan; and at the other end the poor farmer, often a squatter without any title to land, the laborers, and the bondmen.

The chief forms of visible wealth were in land, livestock, slaves, ships, and merchandise. The distribution of The Landed land was perhaps the most important factor Aristocracy in determining the social order and the degree of social power and prestige possessed by the super-aristocrat on the one hand and the poorest yeoman on the other. In the southern colonies the social leaders were the great proprietors and planters, the owners of the manors and baronies, and the speculators in western lands. In the middle colonies they were the manorial lords of the Hudson valley, and the great proprietors further south in Pennsylvania and the Jerseys. Even in New England huge estates were developing, especially those owned by speculators in the wilderness lands of Maine and in the western townships of Connecticut and Massachusetts. Another wealthy class was the proprietors of the common lands, still largely undivided in the western regions. The gentlemen who owned all these lands, the landed aristocracy, acquired them partly because of the favor of the King, or the colonial councils, or by inheritance, or by lucky speculation. In any case ownership of land gave political and economic power and hence social prestige.

Besides the landed aristocracy there were the merchants. These gentlemen advanced rapidly in the latter part of the seventeenth century.

The Merchant Princes Randolph reported in 1676, that in Massachusetts there were thirty merchants with from ten to twenty thousand pounds. Planters and speculators looked to the land for the source of their wealth. The merchants looked largely to the ocean. The merchant princes lived in the commercial seaport towns of the northern colonies, sometimes in houses as pretentious as those of the great planters. The merchants and the growth of the seaport towns greatly affected the structure of eighteenth century society. The eight leading towns in 1750 were Boston, Salem, Providence, New-port, New London, New Haven, New York, and Philadelphia. The only considerable commercial town in the South was Charles Town, South Carolina. To these towns came ships which brought merchandise from many ports located on the seven seas.

By 1750, some 300 vessels of over 60 tons burden hailed from Newport, Rhode Island, alone. They smelled of molasses, rum and distilleries, Africa, tobacco, and spices. To these seaport towns came also privateers and pirates to spend their ill-gotten gains. Some of the merchants and royal officials, " the higher ups," were in league with these scourges of the sea and shared some of the spoils and profits arising from the loot of these colonial " bootleggers." Similar methods were also applied to the fine art of smuggling, another important source of the wealth of some of the " first families " of merchants. But from whatever sources or by whatever means the merchant class acquired their wealth, most of it, perhaps, fairly and honestly in legitimate trade, it strengthened their political and economic, and hence their social, power and prestige.

The landed aristocracy and the merchants wielded a power out of proportion to their numbers. Each group The Small was a relatively small one. On the other Farmers hand the great central backbone of American society was the small farmer who tilled the soil from Maine to Georgia. This class was made up of farmers who ordinarily cultivated from 10 to 100 acres or more of land. The farmer might be independent, owning his land outright; a renter, one who paid quit rents or other fees for the use of the land; a tenant; or a squatter. The engrossing of a large part of the best lands by a relatively small group of landholders made it harder for the small farmer to acquire good land at a low price. Thus the land problem widened the social gulf between these groups.

Many lesser personalities depended on the favor of the aristocrats. They were attached to the household The Common or business, as overseers, servants, and Man slaves; as traders and agents, as captains, sailors and fishermen, shopkeepers and peddlers. In the seaport towns emerged several groups and classes that later became important in the American Revolution such as the artisans. The social gulf between the merchant princes on the one hand and the laborers and artisans on the other was similar to that which existed between the landed aristocracy and the poor farmer and squatter. Socially these groups were of little importance. For the most part they were disfranchised, unorganized, largely ignorant, and illiterate.

Ownership of so large a part of the great national resources and control of the agencies of distribution Symbols of gave the landowners and merchants their Social Prestige high position in the social order. The privileges and perquisites were made known by the symbols commonly adopted to mark off the "upper crust" of society — stately homes, like that of the famous Byrds at Westover, Virginia, and that of Benning Wentworth of New Hampshire. The latter lived in a palatial mansion having fifty-two rooms. In such homes would be found the fine mahogany, the "lowboys" and "highboys," now the prizes of the colonial antique hunter. These were evidences and badges of wealth and leisure, necessary passports to an entrance into "high society," and to the perpetuation of this class through family marriages. Planters, landowners, and merchants often improved their social standing by occupying important offices in the colonial government, especially as members of the council of the royal governor. This officer was himself an important center of social influence.

Other elements can be traced in the social order besides those arising out of the economic background. Spiritual, Here we enter the realm of the spiritual, Intellectual, and Cultural intellectual, and cultural side of colonial Basis life. The status of religion, humanitarianism, education, philosophy, literature, and science, and the learned professions, was determined in part by the material factors already discussed. An increasing number of able and influential clergymen, educators, physicians, political leaders, and even a few social reformers, essayists, scientists, and artistic enthusiasts were included in the small vanguard that preceded the great army that now represents the cultural life of America. These elements were in one sense of the greatest importance, because, though small in number, they largely determined the nature and course of colonial ideas and thought.

122. Eighteenth Century Colonial Leaders

The chief leaders and agencies for the interchange of ideas were located in the larger seaport towns and in the lower tidewater region of the South.
The New Leaders — Here was centered the wealth that gave leisure to the able and fortunate, and freedom and opportunity to join voluntary clubs of a social, literary, and scientific nature. Here were located those institutions which survive largely as a result of leisure and wealth — the colleges, bookshops, newspapers, and libraries; and here resided the cream of the *intelligentsia*. This new social order then was based in part on the transmitted influences from the Old World and in part on the adaptation of ideas and institutions to the new environment. It was a social order differing in many important respects from that in England.

For we now begin to see the emergence of an American society. This new society called for new leaders in each and every field. The increase of wealth, the growth of towns, and the spread of agencies for the transfer of knowledge, provided opportunities for the higher education of leaders, some of whom were men of great intellectual power. The colonial assemblies were a laboratory for political leaders to acquire political experience and skill, and to practice the useful art of resistance to authority. So also religious movements gave opportunity for religious leaders to organize a portion of the inarticulate masses into new churches, in opposition to ecclesiastical authority, particularly that of the Anglican church. The French wars developed a few military leaders, and the rank and file had some practice in intercolonial coöperation and some knowledge of the ideals and institutions of people living in different colonies.

This is the place to mention a few of the family names associated with the landed aristocracy, the great planters, proprietors, and land barons; with the business leaders, the merchant princes and shipowners; with the spiritual and intellectual interests, the clerical giants, and the literary and scientific leaders. Among the landed gentry we may note in the southern colonies the Byrds, Fairfaxes, Randolphs, and Washingtons, of Virginia; the Calverts, Dulanys, and Carrolls, of Maryland; and the Rutledges and Pinckneys, of South Carolina. In the middle colonies were the Van Rensselaers, Schuylers, Livingstons, and Penns. In New England the Wentworths, one of whom acquired a hundred thousand acres of land. Samuel Waldo was one of the great land barons in Maine. "Big business" was represented by such names as the Faneuils, Bowdoins, Browns and the Morrisses. The old spiritual order was represented by Cotton Mather and Jonathan Edwards; the new by John Wise, Gilbert Tennent, Samuel Davies, George Whitefield, and Jonathan Mayhew.

The intellectuals were led by Benjamin Franklin, an incomparable genius, eight men in one — a publisher, editor, author and educator, scientist and philosopher, statesman and diplomatist. Little that was worthwhile escaped the attention of this greatest of the new colonial leaders. Of lesser importance were such men as Cadwallader Colden of New York and Jared Eliot of Massachusetts; the former an embryo scientist and the latter the first to consider seriously the problem of scientific agriculture. Some of these men became also political leaders. The greatest political leaders, however, belong to the next two decades. They were born towards the end of our period and were educated as lawyers. Among them were James Otis and John Adams, Daniel Dulany and John Dickinson, Patrick Henry and Thomas Jefferson.

In general it may be said that most of the important leaders were conservatives. That is to say, in 1750 men of wealth, the great planters, landholders, and merchants, were little influenced by the democratic movement which had been in progress for two generations. While some of them were hostile to England and desired a greater degree of self-government, they were in no hurry to share their wealth, power, or social position with other and lesser people. The really liberal leaders, those who worked for a revision of the social order, in order that the common man might have more liberty and opportunity, came from the ranks of the clergy or the middle class. Important clerical leaders were John Wise and Jonathan Mayhew. Middle-class leaders were Benjamin Franklin, the son of a tallow chandler, and Andrew Hamilton, speaker of the house of representatives of Pennsylvania and defender of John Peter Zenger of New York in his fight for freedom of the press.

The structure of colonial society was complex. Besides the various groups already described, this society The Structure may be analyzed from other standpoints. of Society Politically some of the people were free, but might be enfranchised or unenfranchised, depending on the amount of their real or personal estate. Generally the suffrage depended on the possession of about fifty acres of land or a personal estate of £40 or £50. A very large number were thus automatically disfranchised — the squatters, artisans, laborers, servants, fishermen. shopkeepers, and clerks. Similar requirements limited the office-holding class to an even smaller number. A large number were debarred from any political privileges, such as negro slaves, free negroes, Indians, indentured servants, and women. Among voters and non-voters there were many inequalities in land distribution, in taxation, and in freedom of religion. The beginnings of protest and dissent from the disfranchised, and from the renters, squatters, and dissenters, can be traced before 1750, but tidewater colonial society was still essentially aristocratic in its structure, from a political, economic, religious, and social standpoint.

123. Social Problems and Conditions

The development of numerous and important social tendencies and problems in the eighteenth century
Social   should be analyzed more in detail. (1) A
Problems   relative increase in non-English racial
groups occurred, the result of forced or voluntary immigration; on the one hand Negroes, and on the other Irish
and German indentured servants. A great variety of free
persons also immigrated. (2) The population became
more complex because of the additional races represented, and because of intermarriage between races. (3)
Humanitarian and philanthropic impulses increased;
such as sympathy for the down-trodden and unfortunate
classes, and gifts for education and charities. (4) Religion was affected by an expansion of missionary efforts, a growth of the idea of religious toleration, a
decline in the influence of the clergy and also in general religious interest; shown especially in the out-

break of "The Great Awakening," a series of religious revivals commencing in 1734. (5) The cultural aspect of life received more attention and there was an expansion of the agencies for the transfer of knowledge — schools and colleges, newspapers, printing-presses, books, and libraries. (6) Of great importance was the rise of a scientific attitude of mind, and the acquisition of knowledge by direct observation and experiment; and in consequence, a decline in reliance on conventions, dogma, faith, and precedent. (7) Old World ideas were more rapidly transferred and there was a more careful study of the writings of the great thinkers in every department of human knowledge — political theory, religious doctrines and ideals, philosophy, economic theory and practice, and literature, etc. (8) Underlying all these social tendencies was the expansion of the democratic idea — opposition to aristocratic government and to the special privileges claimed by the minority; and demands for greater equality, privileges, and opportunities for the common man.

The composition, increase, and distribution of the population has already been discussed in Chapter XII. In the South extremes met. The planter Population aristocracy became more powerful and dominated political, economic, and social policies. The South not only received the bulk of the newly imported negroes, but also many of those indentured servants, classed as "felons and convicts," greatly complained of by the assemblies. Important social effects followed from these changes in the population, such as miscegenation, particularly in the case of indentured servants and negro slaves, resulting in the large increase of the mulatto class, from whom came many of the free negroes. The immigration into the middle colonies of so many different racial stocks made this geographical section the home of a variety of customs, habits, institutions, and social tendencies, and that was a great aid to receptivity of new ideas. The lack of a large migration of non-English stocks to New England helps to account for the slow progress of religious toleration there, and the hostility of the Puritan leaders to ideas in conflict with Puritanism.

Social relations were still largely determined by inherited notions of social superiority and inferiority, en-
Social Superi- couraged in the South by the great dis-
ority and In- parity in wealth as between the great
feriority planter and the poor farmer, and between the free and unfree. While it is true that the small planter and farmer had benefited by the democratic movement, yet the traditions of the seventeenth century respecting the place of the " gentleman " in society still continued. A Virginia back-country Church of England clergyman, Devereaux Jarrett, with Methodist leanings, remarked, " We were accustomed to look upon what were called gentlefolks as being of a superior order." Social progress in this respect came largely from the opportunity for any free white person to pass from a lower into a higher social class. Thus native ability and economic success were socially rewarded. Moreover, frontier society was organized on the principle of substantial social equality.

In the middle and New England colonies a tendency is visible for the common man to increase in power and influence. This is noticeably true in New England, and is illustrated by the success of the " non-commoners " in bringing about a more equitable distribution of the common lands; the abolition of the sumptuary laws, and the decline of the practice of seating in the church according to social prestige. On the other hand, the custom persisted of classifying student at college in a manner to indicate the relative social position of their family. The names of students, as printed in the catalogue, were arranged by classes, Yale to 1767 and Harvard to 1772, not in alphabetical order but rather in a manner to indicate the social standing of their fathers or families. Ancestral qualifications, family estate, official position, or professional standing, were taken into account. The common man gained through the increase in the artisan class in the seaport towns of the northern colonies. It was from the caulkers, carpenters, masons, and craftsmen, called by Thomas Hutchinson the "rabble," that the Sons of Liberty were largely recruited in 1765; the organization that so successfully registered the emotions of the masses by means of riots, parades, and demonstrations.

Among the social problems which confronted the colonies in this period, one of the most serious was to Class find methods of settling class conflicts; as, Conflicts for example, those arising out of the relations of coast and frontier, religious antagonisms, and economic inequalities. Equally difficult were conflicts between proprietors, and tenants and squatters; between planters and merchants and the small farmers; between contenders for and the opponents of freedom of speech and the press and privileges of education for the poor. Some of these class conflicts have already been described (p. 359). The struggle over the problem of the freedom of the press is illustrated by the argument of Andrew Hamilton in the famous case of John Peter Zenger, a German, in New York in 1734. He printed "Several Seditious libels," according to the governor and council, but won his contention that he might in his newspaper, *The New York Gazette*, criticize the government. This is an important landmark in the progress of the assault on authority and indirectly contributed towards the loosening of the bonds between the English Government and the colonies.

In religion The Reverend John Wise of Ipswich, Massachusetts, argued against an ecclesiastical aristocracy.

Social Democracy in Religion and Education

His *Vindication of the Government of the New England Churches* (1717) was an argument for a Congregational system of authority centered in the individual churches, rather than in a central body composed of delegates from the churches, as advocated by Increase and Cotton Mather. John Wise was one of the first in the colonies to insist that " power is originally in the people," and that men are " all naturally free and equal." In New England the expansion of the population within towns led to a demand for a more democratic distribution of schools. The district system (p. 417) was the answer, for it widened educational opportunity for the middle and poorer classes. An increasing tendency to support schools by general taxation, rather than by tuition fees, proved of great advantage to the poor.

The second quarter of the eighteenth century witnessed a decided advance in sympathy for the downtrodden and unfortunate classes of society.

Humanitarian and Philanthropic Efforts

First in importance was the growth of anti-slavery sentiment. George Fox and William Penn, the two great leaders of the Friends, were both opposed to slavery. The first distinctly anti-slavery document in all the colonies was the protest made in 1688 by a Mennonite group of Quakers in Germantown, Pennsylvania, including the memorable words, " Here is liberty of conscience which is right and reasonable. Here ought also to be liberty of the body." The Quakers, after 1730, were represented by three men, Ralph Sandiford, Benjamin Lay, and the famous John Woolman, who portrayed in burning words the evils of the slavery system (p. 414). The Puritans tolerated slavery, though such men as John Eliot and Cotton Mather argued for kind treatment; and Samuel Sewall, in a famous pamphlet, *The Selling of Joseph* (1701), argued particularly against the slave trade.

Another evidence of interest in the less fortunate classes of society was the effort of philanthropic persons to provide free schools for the poor, and the work of the great Anglican missionary society, *The Society for the Propagation of the Gospel in Foreign Parts,* chartered in 1701, in sending schoolmasters to the colonies to teach poor children (see p. 418). Some sympathy was even felt for the hard lot of the indentured servants. Owing to abuses which had arisen, the Pennsylvania assembly passed a series of laws in 1749–1750, one of which aimed to check the overcrowding of ships. Captains were subject to a penalty of £10 for each passenger that did not have the legal amount of space provided for in the act. Such laws, however, were inadequately enforced.

Each of the three geographical sections of the colonies had a type of manners of its own, due in part to
Domestic Manners   the surrounding environment, the character of the people and the nature of their social system. In New England, the Puritan background, the necessity of working hard for a living, and the influence of town government, produced an industrious, serious, and sober people. Strict and repressive laws regulated rather minutely the religious, moral, and social life of the individual. The lighter side of life was often frowned on in sermons and by regulatory legislation. Strict laws were enacted on keeping the Sabbath and attending church service.

On the other hand, the common picture of New England colonial life is probably too somber. In spite of Puritan tradition and the thunderings of the preachers against fun, levity, and amusements, even of the harmless variety, the youth at least often ignored these warnings (p. 404). The lighter side of Puritan character is illustrated by the drinking habits of the times (p. 412). Card playing and dancing, even dancing schools, were not unknown in Boston before 1750.

In the southern colonies, the physical environment, the desire to acquire wealth, and the ease of living, bred a society that was less interested in the hereafter than the present. Hence, that section lacked the somberness of the Puritan colonies and their restraints on pleasures. Here was the region of cockfights, horse races, and fox hunts, dinners, dances, and music — the popular pastimes of the typical southern planter. The last three forms of amusement called for fine clothes, silver buckles, powdered wigs, coats of arms, and coaches, by those who could afford such symbols of leisure.

In the middle colonies the cosmopolitan character of the population and religious toleration made this region, particularly around Philadelphia, receptive to new ideas and new habits of life. Here Benjamin Franklin fired the imagination of his generation by introducing European ideas, in literature, education, science, and civic improvements. The Germans brought from their home land many habits and ideals which continued to characterize this racial group in their new homes.

124. Religion and Morals

The period from 1689 to 1750 was one of great importance in the religious history of the colonies. It is

marked by four principal tendencies and movements.
(1) The first was a general decline in religion up to

Four Re-
ligious Ten-
dencies and
Movements

1734. The second and third generation
of colonists were not influenced by such
striking events as those that provoked the
intense religious interest of the first generation, for example, the persecution of the dissenters under James I
and Charles I. On the contrary, the major interest of
these later generations was in economic rather than
in religious problems. (2) A secondary tendency in religion was the effort of the Church of England to expand its influence and to make the Church a powerful
force in the colonies. This force was exerted first
through missionaries, and second through the unsuccessful effort to appoint colonial bishops. (3) Of great
significance was the large immigration of dissenters
and their demands for religious toleration. (4) The
Great Awakening, a series of religious revivals beginning in 1734, began in part as a protest against a general
decline in religion and morals and was more or less
widespread throughout the colonies. These tendencies
may be understood by a more detailed account of the
conditions in the three geographical sections of the
colonies.

From 1660 on there had been a gradual decline of
religion in New England. According to Jonathan Ed-

Decline of
Religion in
New England

wards, in 1734, such a condition had continued. At that time he declared that the
greater part of the people in the neighborhood of his parish of Northampton, Massachusetts, were
" very insensible of the things of religion, and engaged
in other cares and pursuits. . . . Licentiousness for
some years greatly prevailed among the youth of the
town; they were, many of them very much addicted to
night walking, and frequenting the tavern, and lewd

practices, wherein some by their example exceedingly corrupted others. It was their manner very frequently to get together in conventions of both sexes, for mirth and jolity, which they called frolicks; and they would often spend the greater part of the night in them, without any regard to order in the families they belonged to."

Alongside the decline of interest in religious faith and practice, arose a growing opposition to the preaching and the theology of the orthodox clergymen. Religion had become cold, formal, and conventional, with great emphasis on doctrine. Moreover, the orthodox New England theologians condemned most people to eternal punishment, for only those "elected" by God could be saved. Such teachings turned many from the churches. Again material advance — the acquisition of wealth — was of greater interest to most New Englanders than the saving of their souls.

In the middle colonies much the same conditions existed as those just described for New England. For example, take Benjamin Franklin's comment on the preaching of a Presbyterian clergyman, "His discourses were chiefly either polemic arguments or explications of the peculiar doctrines of our sect, and were all to me very dry, uninteresting, and unedifying, since not a single moral principle was inculcated or enforc'd, their aim seeming rather to make us Presbyterians than good citizens." However, a much larger degree of religious toleration existed in the middle colonies than in New England, and no established church existed in that section except in a part of New York.

The Middle Colonies

In the southern colonies the power and influence of the Anglican Church gradually declined. The passage of the English toleration act of 1689, and that of Vir-

ginia in 1699, opened the way for the growth of dissenting sects in this colony. Moreover the governments

The South-
ern Colonies
of the southern colonies were more interested in settling the frontier, for the purpose of economic development and for protection,
than in insisting on religious conformity. Therefore
the dissenters migrated in large numbers to the southern backcountry. Some friction arose because of the
number of these dissenters, their demand for complete toleration, and for the opportunity to establish
churches with freedom from the obligation to help
support the Anglican church.

The established church neither met the needs of
the newcomers, nor did it seek to convert them to the
Anglican faith. Many of the Anglican clergy were
men of inferior ability and were generally accused of
lacking those spiritual and moral qualifications expected
of clergymen. The fact that the royal governors were
themselves Anglicans widened the breach between the
two religious groups.

The Church of England nevertheless made notable
progress in establishing missions throughout the col-

The Church
of England
onies. *The Society for the Propagation of
the Gospel* sent out numerous mission-
aries who founded new churches especially in the middle
and New England colonies. Another important proposition was that of introducing Anglican bishops in the
colonies. This had been suggested on several occasions.
Thomas Sherlock, Bishop of London, again proposed
(1748) that one or more colonial bishops should be
appointed. These efforts brought a reply from one of
the great men of this period, the Reverend Jonathan
Mayhew, in a famous sermon delivered in Boston
(1750). It was a blast against high authority and political and ecclesiastical domination, in both State and

Church. Mayhew declared that ecclesiastical tyrants, bishops, love to "lord it over God's heritage." When they were fairly mounted he said "their beasts the laity, may prance and flounce about to no purpose and they will at length be so jaded and hacked by their reverend jockeys, that they will not even have spirits enough to complain that their backs are galled, or like Balaam's ass, to rebuke the madness of the prophet."

In New England some measure of religious toleration was granted to such sects as the Quakers, Baptists, and Anglicans. This stimulated demands for freedom from taxes for the support of the established Congregational church. In Massachusetts, by the acts of 1728 and 1734, Baptists and Quakers were exempted from ministerial taxes, provided they regularly attended the meeting of their own society. Anglicans were also exempted from taxation for building and repairing Congregational churches.

In the southern colonies, particularly in Virginia, the movement for religious toleration was greatly stimulated by the activities of Samuel Davies, a "newlight" Presbyterian preacher, who demanded free opportunity to preach and establish churches where he liked, in opposition to the governor and council who tried to limit him by requiring a license to preach in only a few specified places in a county (see p. 410).

125. The Great Awakening

The Great Awakening, that series of religious revivals commencing in 1734, was in part the outcome of the conditions described. It was not only an inter-colonial movement but an international evangelical revival. In Germany it was preceded by the Pietistic movement and in England by the

Methodist movement. Underlying all these religious movements was the fundamental idea that personal piety and reformation of conduct were more important than correctness of belief; emphasis was placed on emotional religious experience rather than on formal creeds and doctrines and the observance of outward forms and ceremonies.

In New England the first great revivalist to attempt to arrest the decline of religious interest was the famous Jonathan Edwards, pastor of the Con-

Jonathan Edwards and George Whitefield gregational church at Northampton, Massachusetts. His object was to turn the people back to the old Puritan faith and doctrines. His sermons were filled with threats of the sufferings of hell fire for those unsaved and the joys of heaven for the saved. Edwards' chief appeal was one of terror. He described the Almighty, for example, as holding the souls of the unsaved " over the pit of hell much as one holds a spider or some loathesome insect over the fire." Edwards combined the severe piety and doctrines of the early Puritans with the fervor of the revivalists.

George Whitefield, having adopted the rules of Methodism, came from England to Georgia for his first American trip in 1738. In 1739 he made a second trip, preaching in Philadelphia and New York and all the way down to Georgia, and later made a tour of New England. Whitefield was more responsible than any other person for the continuation of the revivals. His preaching was condemned by the conservative orthodox ministers because of his emotional appeals. His main topics were sin, regeneration, and new birth. He made several more journeys to the colonies, one in 1744, another in 1751, and at later dates. Benjamin Franklin said of Whitefield's preaching " From being thoughtless or indifferent about religion, it seemed as if all the world were growing religious, so that one could not walk thro' the town in an evening without hearing psalms sung in different families of every street."

Evangelists of the type of Whitefield appealed to the emotions and feelings of the people more than to Phenomena of their reason. This purpose was both de-
Revivals fended and criticized. The effects produced on the audience by powerful preachers were amazing and are now attributed in part to hypnotic and mesmeric influence. The more common reactions were groaning, crying out, fainting, falling down, praying, exhorting, singing, laughing, jumping up and down, etc. One report reads, "Some had Fits, some fainted . . . (some) seeing others distressed, fell into deep Distress under a Conviction of Sin and Sense of the Divine Wrath due to them." Opponents of this emotional appeal complained that in many cases it had only a temporary effect. The Reverend Thomas Prince of Boston remarked, "And though this terrible preaching may strongly work on the animal passions and frighten the hearers, rouse the Soul, and prepare the way for terrible Convictions; yet these mere animal terrors and these Convictions are quite different things."

Opposition to the Great Awakening was widespread. Harvard and Yale both protested against Whitefield's
Opposition to excesses. The Congregationalists and Pres-
the Great byterians were divided in their attitude
Awakening towards the revival, while the Anglican clergy were almost unanimous in opposition. "Old Lights" and "New Lights," "Old Side" and "New Side," "Regular" and "Separate," were some of the names indicating the divisions and parties representing the conservative and liberal elements.

The New Light Presbyterians formed a separate synod in 1745 and did not reunite with the old synod until

1758. Connecticut passed an act in 1743 against itinerant preachers and the "Separatists," and the next year
repealed an act of 1708, which had granted some degree
of religious toleration. In Virginia, Governor Gooch
charged the Grand Jury (1745) to search out and
indict "false teachers that are lately crept into this
government professing themselves ministers under the
pretended influence of *new light, extraordinary impulse* and such like fanatical enthusiastical knowledge
(who) lead the innocent and ignorant people into
all kinds of delusion."

The most important effect of the Great Awakening,
after all, was not so much religious reform as the

Religious,
Political, and
Social Effects
of the Great
Awakening impetus that it gave to various political
and social ideas and movements. For ex-
ample, there was (1) the principle of self-
determination, which is comparable to the
right of revolution; or the right of a minority to break
away from established authority, for sufficient cause.
(2) The principle of local democratic church government, based on the majority vote of members, replaced
a government directed by councils composed of the
clergy. The opposition to centralized authority and to
the theory of uniformity was a great blow to church
establishments. (3) The rise of evangelism is of great
importance. The evangelist, the itinerant preacher or
circuit rider, met the people more on a level, in houses,
barns, and open fields, rather than in the pulpit of a
church — the "preacher's throne." The strict Puritan
preacher spoke with authority. The evangelical clergy
relied more on persuasion. The circuit rider brought the
church to the people and not only gave religious instruction but enlightened the people in other fields of knowledge. (4) The Great Awakening stimulated sympathy for
the common man, and helped to mitigate the evils of the

indentured servant and slavery systems. (5) New impetus was given to the founding of colleges, Princeton being a direct outcome of the movement, and to "new-light" classical schools which arose in the middle and southern colonies. (6) One of the greatest influences of the Great Awakening was the stimulation of the emotions and feelings of the people. Undoubtedly it helped prepare the way for the emotional aspects of the American Revolution. (7) The "Popular Churches," especially Presbyterian, Baptist, and Methodist, became liberal in politics, while the Anglican remained conservative. This became important when the Revolution took on a religious aspect by attacks on the Anglican Church, particularly in opposition to the threatened appointment of an American bishop. (8) Nevertheless the Great Awakening failed to improve, to the degree expected, the religious and moral conditions of the people, and complaints of spiritual and moral decline soon reappeared. This was due partly to the fact that sudden conversion was often of short duration.

So much of the Great Awakening is associated with the name of George Whitefield that his special contributions should be noted, since his ideas had great political and social influences. Whitefield taught that divine law recorded in the Scriptures was superior to any man-made law; that no earthly political power could lawfully violate that law. This was a close approach to the identification of the law of nature or natural rights with divine law. Whitefield also preached salvation for all, rich and poor, wise and ignorant; those having the "new birth" were equal as before God. One effect of this idea was to consider simple uneducated men as equal in value, as leaders of the people, to those educated and trained especially for the purpose. Toleration was also one of Whitefield's beliefs. " I am of a

Catholic spirit, and if I see a man who loves the Lord Jesus in sincerity, I am not very solicitous to what outward communion he belongs."

126. Moral Problems

The chief moral problems of this period were much the same as those of the earlier period already described. Rum, Morals, The major moral problems of New Eng- and Religion in New land, as reported by Jonathan Edwards in England 1734, have been mentioned. One may be commented on in more detail, namely, the problem of spirituous liquors and intemperance. Far-reaching social consequences came from the liquor traffic. As population increased people resorted to taverns more and more for a variety of reasons — drink, marketing, auctions, military drills, dancing, and parties. John Adams wrote of the taverns, "If you call, you will find dirt enough, very miserable accommodations of provisions and lodgings for yourself and your horse. Yet if you sit the evening, you will find the house full of people drinking drams, flip, toddy, carousing, swearing; but especially plotting with the landlord to get him at the next town meeting an election for selectman or representative."

At ordinations of the clergy, at weddings and funerals, huge quantities of liquor were often consumed; the rich served expensive wines and the poor cheap rum. Even paupers were buried with libations of rum. A charge allowed by the selectmen of the town of Woburn, Massachusetts, at the death of George Wilkinson, a pauper, was one for three quarts of rum to be "drunk at his funeral;" while the selectmen allowed the next year a charge of two pounds nine shillings, for fourteen gallons of wine "to be drunk at Reverend Thomas Carter's funeral." Common soldiers were allowed their

" drams " in regular rations, and the farm laborer received his ration, especially during haying season, cornhuskings, and hog-killing time. With rum the principal ingredient of "toddy, sling and grog," with " blackstrap, stonewall and sling " not to mention wine, cider, brandy, and a host of other drinks, the New Englander had ample opportunity to choose from a tempting variety of liquors.

Increase Mather, President of Harvard, and John Adams both in their times bewailed the effects of strong Prohibition   drink. Said the former, in a sermon Sentiment   preached to a criminal awaiting execution, 1686, " It is an unhappy thing that in later years a kind of strong drink called Rum has been common amongst us, which the poorer sort of people, both in town and country, can make themselves drunk with. They that are poor and wicked too, can for a penny or two pence make themselves drunk. I wish to the Lord some remedy may be thought of for the prevention of this evil." John Adams describes his efforts to reform his erring countrymen: " I was fired with a zeal, amounting to enthusiasm, against ardent spirits, the multiplication of taverns, retailers, and dram shops, and tippling houses. Grieved to the heart to see the number of idlers, thieves, sots, and physicians, in those infamous seminaries, I applied to the Court of Sessions, procured a Committee of Inspection and Inquiry to reduce the number of licensed houses, etc. But I only acquired the reputation of a hypocrite and an ambitious demagogue for it."

If intemperance and its effects on morals was one of the chief worries of New England reformers, so the effects of negro slavery in the southern colonies was one of the great moral problems to be solved in that section. John Woolman, the Quaker missionary, who journeyed through Maryland and Virginia in 1746, writes in his journal of slavery and the slave trade as follows: "I saw in these southern prov-

Slavery and Morals in the South

inces so many vices and corruptions, increased by this trade and this way of life, that it appeared to me as a dark gloominess hanging over the land; and though now many willingly run into it, yet in future the consequences will be grievous to posterity." A long series of laws designed to prevent intermarriage of whites and negroes and unlawful intercourse, particularly as between indentured servants and negroes, is evidence of the serious character of this problem. Almost all travelers who observed the baneful effects of the slavery system on morals passed adverse criticism. Later Thomas Jefferson penned a scathing denunciation of this evil in Virginia, after forty years' observation of the system.

127. Intellectual Conditions

The intellectual development of the colonists in this period may be measured and evaluated from several

Aspects of Intellectual Development

standpoints; the temper of their literary productions; the facilities for and ideals of education; the agencies for the expansion and transfer of knowledge; the extent of their acquaintance with the works of the important English and European writers in every department of knowledge; their scientific and cultural attainments, and their main currents of thought.

While most of the publications of the colonists in the seventeenth century were religious in character,

Character of Literary Output

in this later period we do find an increasing number of historical, educational, social, and even scientific writings. Cotton Mather (1663–1728), himself interested in other subjects than religion, nevertheless endeavored, in his more than four hundred publications, to excite sympathy for the old Puritan theology, notably in his *Magnalia*, etc. (1702), or Ecclesiastical History of New England. He praised the beliefs and way of life of the first generation. He appealed to divine interposition and judgments in daily life, indicated his belief in signs, omens, and portents, in the depravity and badness of man, in an angry rather than a merciful God and in the doctrine that few were "elected" to be saved. His *Wonders of the Invisible World* (1684) was answered by Robert Calef in 1700, in a book called *More Wonders of the Invisible World*. The least satisfactory portion of the literary output of the colonists was their poetry, if such it can be called. Most New Englanders were still satisfied with Michael Wigglesworth's *Day of Doom or a Poetical Description of the Great and Last Judgment*, published in 1662. He it was who defended damnation of infants and made the Lord consign " such sinners " (the unsaved) to eternal punishment in the oft quoted words,

> "A crime it is, therefore in bliss
> You may not hope to dwell;
> But unto you I shall allow
> The easiest room in Hell."

The literature of many of the religious sects in the middle colonies, like that of the Quakers, exhibits a different note; a merciful God, man not essentially bad and all persons having the opportunity to be saved who voluntarily made the effort. No layman better illustrates the changed attitude towards life than Benjamin Franklin. He represents the other side of New England character — its sagacity, thrift, and common sense. His writings have an earthy odor utterly unlike those of Cotton Mather. Franklin's attitude, typical of an increasing number of his own generation, was to let the people attend to the things on earth, and to leave to God those that concerned heaven and hell. This was the philosophy outlined in *Poor Richard's Almanac*. Honesty might get one to heaven, but the important thing was to be honest because it brings success in this world. Franklin wished to improve conditions and society, not as a preparation for the next world, but because it would bring about more happiness in this world.

The other outstanding colonial writer of the period, Jonathan Edwards, works from the other end. He explored deductively the mysteries of theology and philosophy. Franklin explored inductively the mysteries of nature and the art of living together. Edwards represents the conservative and conventional, while Franklin represents the radical and experimental attitude towards knowledge.

128. Education

The facilities for education and the ideals governing educational thought show a marked change in this

Education in New England

period. In New England the public school systems were expanded, with more specific general laws compelling towns to establish elementary and grammar schools. It was still optional in Massachusetts, whether a town would support a school by general taxation, or depend on tuition fees. Public sentiment was lukewarm towards the Latin Grammar Schools, and even towards the elementary schools in the frontier towns. The general court in 1718 complained that "by sad experience it is found that many towns that not only are obliged by law, but are very able to support a grammar school, yet choose rather to incur and pay the fine or penalty than maintain a school." A large number of the poorer frontier towns failed to establish or support elementary schools according to law, and were "presented" and fined for delinquency.

Another feature of the educational systems of New England was the rise of the "district school." From 1689 to 1750 there was a rapid expansion of the population to the frontier and to the outer sections of the towns. Thus many families were deprived of the opportunity of attending church or of sending their children to the one town school at the village center, a particular hardship in the winter months. Notwithstanding this fact in many towns all were taxed for the support of the town school. Because of the growing influence of democratic ideas in this period — political, economic, and religious — small groups of families in the outer sections of a township, the frontier of the town, complained of the burden of taxes from which they received little or no benefit. Accordingly many petitions were sent in to the governments of Massachusetts, Connecticut, and New Hampshire requesting a division of the town into districts. The control of taxes collected within the district was demanded for the support of a school in that district.

The general effect of the New England educational systems was to bring pressure to bear on towns to support schools, and to enlarge the facilities for education for many children. In this respect the democratic movement in education paralleled that in the political and religious world. One adverse effect, however, may be noted. The district system tended to cut a town up into smaller and smaller school units. The result was often a very short school term, because of inability to

raise funds, perhaps only a month. The quality of the
teacher and teaching, school equipment, etc., was also
correspondingly poor.

In the middle colonies, where various religious groups
established churches, there was a tendency to set up
The Middle   parochial or denominational elementary
Colonies   schools connected with the church. Pennsylvania and Delaware so far recognized the church
as a proper agency to further schools that acts were
passed, legalizing this practice. Pennsylvania in 1715
empowered "religious societies or assemblies and Congregations of Protestants" to purchase and hold lands
for erecting schools by trustees or otherwise. Though
this act was disallowed by the Privy Council in 1719
it was reënacted in 1730, with the information that
sundry religious societies had at their own cost purchased small pieces of land and erected churches,
schoolhouses, etc. Delaware passed a similar act in
1743. Under this system the Church of England
through its missionary society, sent schoolmasters to
establish their church schools. The Quakers of Pennsylvania and New Jersey, the Lutherans, German Reformed, Dutch Reformed, and other denominations
established many such schools in the middle colonies,
primarily to perpetuate their own faith.

In the southern colonies more reliance was placed
on private agencies for the establishment and support
Southern   of schools. This was natural, because of
Colonies   the sharper class distinctions and the notion that a free school was a charity or "pauper"
school. Public schools were socially undesirable for the
children of those who could afford to pay tuition fees.
Beverley's statement made in 1705 well describes the
situation (p. 106). Parish schools, often endowed by
some wealthy planter for the poor, a few partially state-

supported secondary schools, as at Annapolis, Maryland, and Charles Town, South Carolina, privately established pay schools for the middle class, and private tutors for the wealthy planters, were the principal agencies in this section. The total number of schools, however, was comparatively few in proportion to the population, and located largely in the tidewater region. Even in this region they were very unevenly distributed.

The general character of the elementary curriculum remained much the same, reading, writing, and arithmetic, but the curriculum of the public secondary and private schools, outside of the Latin grammar schools of New England, changed materially. This was due to the demand for a more practical education, one more closely related to the economic life of the period. The introduction of mathematics and its applications, higher arithmetic, algebra, geometry, and trigonometry, with bookkeeping or "merchants accounts," mensuration, surveying, and navigation, are the most striking new subjects. The study of modern languages is observable in the more pretentious private schools, English grammar, composition, rhetoric, etc. In the Philadelphia Academy, which Franklin established in 1743, and in his *Proposals Relating to the Education of Youth* (1749) he emphasized history, geography, oratory, mathematics and its applications, and introduced apparatus for performing experiments. All these subjects were almost unknown in seventeenth-century schools. The changed political, economic, and social conditions were thus reflected in the types of schools and curriculum. The general tendency was first to extend the opportunity and privilege of education; secondly, to enlarge the range of knowledge to be taught; and third, to make education more liberal, practical, and vocational.

Higher education is marked also by changing tendencies. Yale was founded in 1701. Harvard offered a
Higher
Education
more liberal curriculum by 1750 than at the opening of the century. The middle colonies followed New England and Virginia by founding the College of New Jersey (Princeton), 1746, the University of Pennsylvania, 1749, and King's College (Columbia), 1754. These colleges, especially the University of Pennsylvania, set up a more liberal course of study than that of the older colleges. Due largely to the influence of Franklin, emphasis was placed on mathematics and its applications, history, and modern languages. Another phase of higher education was the tendency in the middle and southern colonies to send boys abroad to be educated in the English public schools, as, for example, the two elder brothers of George Washington. The Universities of Oxford and Cambridge and particularly the Inns of Court, the great law schools in London, received a number of Americans, particularly from the southern colonies, who later became prominent in the Revolution.

129. Cultural Development

The opening of the eighteenth century witnessed the publication (1704) of the first successful newspaper,
Agencies for
the Expansion
and Transfer
of Knowledge
The Boston Weekly News Letter. Before 1756 newspapers had been established in all of the colonies excepting New Jersey, Delaware, and Georgia. These papers printed more foreign than domestic news, and hence helped bring the colonists into closer touch with England and Europe. One important influence was the advertisements of the booksellers, offering the "latest" books from abroad on a great variety of topics, as well as domestic

publications. There was some extension of the postal service, so that by 1711 Massachusetts, New Hampshire, New York, and Pennsylvania, and, in 1732, Virginia, had entered the postal system.

The impetus to the founding of libraries came from a number of sources. Thomas Bray, commissary of the Church of England, in Maryland, was instrumental in founding a number of parish libraries particularly in the southern colonies about 1700. Franklin started the Philadelphia Subscription Library in 1731, the first important semi-public circulating library in the colonies. By 1750 a number of semi-public collections existed in the larger towns, such as that owned by the Charles Town Library Society in South Carolina and the Redwood Library in Newport, besides the various college libraries. In 1723 Harvard had some 3200 volumes. An increasing number of private libraries approached fairly large collections, like those of Cotton Mather, the largest, with some four thousand volumes. Franklin had a large collection, and likewise a number of wealthy planters in the southern colonies, especially William Byrd II, who had four thousand volumes.

Lacking outstanding and original leaders of thought, as is usual in new countries, the colonists were largely dependent for their intellectual progress on the new discoveries and ideas set forth by English and European thinkers and writers. During the seventeenth century the colonists were little interested in the progress of philosophy, literature, and science. By the second quarter of the eighteenth century, the activities of the booksellers and their advertisements in the colonial press helped create such interest. The college libraries also expanded rapidly and the subscription libraries like that at

Importation of English and European Ideas

Philadelphia, were active in purchasing the works of the leading writers in every field of knowledge.

One of the most important tendencies in the latter part of our period was the emphasis placed on the study Political of the writings of the great political Philosophy theorists of the old world by the rising young intellectuals in the colonies. Before 1750 the works of the political philosophers like Hooker, Harrington, Hobbes and Locke were read by many of the intellectual leaders in the colonies, lay and clerical. Hooker wrote that law must be obeyed unless " the law of reason or of God doth enjoin the contrary." Locke taught that the only true foundation of government was the consent of the people. The writings on the law of nature or natural rights, by such men as Pufendorf and by the radical French thinkers, like those of Montesquieu, Voltaire, and Rousseau, were all advertised in colonial newspapers between 1747–1752. Thus there was repeated, on a small scale, that great European rationalizing movement, the intellectual revolution that shook England and Europe in the eighteenth century.

The great advance in science in England and Europe for a hundred years and more, beginning about 1620, Scientific made little impression on the colonists be-Progress fore 1720, though in 1714 Cotton Mather had been won over to belief in the Copernican system. Original research and the discovery of knowledge by observation and experiment was the message of such English thinkers and writers as Francis Bacon and Sir Isaac Newton. Paralleling these men were those who pleaded for freedom of thought and the substitution of reason for authority and dogma, men like John Locke, Descartes, and Voltaire.

These currents of thought came to a focus in the

person of Benjamin Franklin, the outstanding figure in the colonial scientific world. Franklin instructed his gen-
Benjamin   eration in a method of attaining knowl-
Franklin   edge, not from the Bible, like the Mathers,
but through experiment and patient observation of natural phenomena. He formed a society in 1743 " For Promoting Useful Knowledge Among the British Plantations in America." It was to meet once a month and its members were to communicate observations, experiments, and discoveries and "everything tending to increase the power of man over matter, and multiply the conveniences of life." Its membership included a physician, botanist, mathematician, chemist, mechanician, geographer, and a general natural philosopher.

In his own scientific work Franklin was guided by three ideas: first, the conservation of energy; second, greater accomplishments, through original research and inventions, with less energy; and third, the utilization and socialization of scientific knowledge for the good of mankind. His researches in electricity commencing in 1746 and his proposals and experiments made in 1749 and 1750 resulted in the identification of lightning and electricity and in the invention of the lightning rod, both landmarks in the history of American science.

The fine arts made slow progress in this period, as might be expected in a new country so much under the
Cultural   influence of frontier conditions. There
Development   were, it is true, some artists, and many
of their portraits have survived. But the quality leaves much to be desired. The same may be said of the few attempts at sculpture. More interest was shown in music, often taught in private schools.

Plays were given, however, in Williamsburg, New York, and Charles Town from 1716 to 1735 and interest in the drama increased rapidly just at the close of our period. A professional company from England arrived in 1750 and some of Shakespeare's plays were given. His works were advertised in the *New England Courant* (Boston), as early as 1722, and soon after, copies were acquired by Harvard and Yale. As a whole, however, the frontier environment was not conducive to artistic expression and the absence of really notable poets, musicians, novelists, painters, sculptors, and architects is undeniable. Material problems, not those of the spirit, most occupied and interested the colonists.

While there were important leaders among the clergy already mentioned, there were few great leaders repre-

The Pro-senting the medical and legal professions.
fessions   Medicine was in its infancy, and very few native physicians rose to prominence before 1750. There were a few important and learned lawyers; notably Charles Pinckney the Elder, Daniel Dulany the Elder, and Andrew Hamilton.

130. Accomplishments and Problems of the Colonists in 1750

Between 1689 and 1750 the colonists made great progress along political, economic, religious, and social

Territorial   lines. Territorially Georgia was added, the
Unity   grant of land extending from " sea to sea." Through coöperation for frontier defence, in congresses and wars, the colonists were made more familiar with the " oneness " of the thirteen colonies, and to some extent with the desirability of considering them as a whole. Franklin's famous snake (1754), cut into thirteen parts with the legend " Unite or Die " is evidence of this idea.

The assemblies had grown so powerful that in some cases they almost completely overshadowed the execu-

tive. The general drift in this period was from proprietary to royal colonies, seen in the case of New Jersey,

Political
Progress

the Carolinas, and Georgia. Disrespect for
both the prerogative of the King and acts
of Parliament, at least in the case of navigation, trade,
and manufacturing acts, is observable. The doctrine of
natural rights, also looms up in the latter part of the
period.

In the economic life, the tendency towards the growth
of large estates is noticeable. But this was in part

Economic
Development

counteracted by the occupation of the
interior by freed servants, immigrants,
and squatters, all of whom acquired small tracts. The
proprietary common lands of New England also passed
largely into the hands of individuals each holding a small
acreage. Transportation facilities were greatly improved
and the post office extended. Agriculture and manufactures were diversified, the fisheries extended, and shipbuilding, trade, and commerce, especially the West
Indian and African slave trade, were greatly extended;
so also were the naval stores, stock raising, and packing industries. Negro slaves were brought in so rapidly
that efforts were made to check their importation. This
diversified economic life enabled the colonists to greatly
increase their wealth, partly because of the stimulation
of industries by England, partly by evading the restrictive features of her commercial policy, and partly because of the richness of their natural resources and their
own industry.

One of the significant gains was the large increase
in population, and even more important was the ex-

Population
and Racial
Progress

pansion to the frontier. Thus a buffer population was established between the French
and Indians, and the tidewater groups.
This made for the greater security of this region.

From the standpoint of opposition to England, the composition of the population was more favorable to the colonists than in the earlier period. A large number of the immigrants were either naturally hostile to England, the Irish and Scotch-Irish, or they lacked any background of loyalty, the French and Germans.

From a religious standpoint the greatest gain was in the movement for religious toleration and the weakening of the state-church idea of government — the overthrow of theocratic government. Religion also exerted greater influence on social progress, over a wider area, as a result of the Great Awakening.

Religion

The greatest relative advance, however, in this period is in the intellectual and cultural aspects of colonial life. By 1750 the number of learned men had so increased that the new currents of thought and new books were soon known in the colonies. This, with the extension of colleges, libraries, bookshops, and newspapers, and publishing facilities, greatly influenced the rapid extension of knowledge.

Intelligence and Culture

Many important problems, however, remained unsolved in 1750. Their solution will be discussed in later volumes of this series. It is sufficient here barely to mention some of the more important. From an English standpoint the question of most importance was whether France or England should control the great interior of America. This was decided in the fourth French-English War, ending in 1763. The problem of whether the colonists should continue to develop tendencies towards a greater degree of self-government or be brought more closely under England's control remained unsolved from several standpoints — political, economic, commercial, and religious. What should be the exact relations of

England, France, and the Colonies

King, Parliament, and the colonial assemblies? What was the solution of the increase of colonial manufactures, of the demand for more free trade, of the practice of smuggling, and of the opposition to the extension of the power of the Anglican Church through colonial bishops?

Internally the colonists were working out several pressing problems, particularly those having to do with Internal the relations of coast and frontier; that is, Problems the extent to which the rapidly increasing population of the interior and back-country regions should have political power in the colonial governments. This involved the nature and extent of suffrage and representation, a fair system of land distribution and taxation, adequate transportation facilities, and the degree of religious toleration and liberty. In brief the great question was whether the democratic ideal should carry on to its logical conclusion. Another problem was that of obtaining some degree of unity, so necessary for protection and development, in spite of varied and often conflicting ideals in the various sections — political, economic, social, and religious. The greatest problem in 1750 was the tendency of the colonists to diverge in their ideals from those of England. If the process continued, the thirteen colonies would most likely become an independent national state.

INDEX

tion, 366; increase of, 425. *See*
Artisans, Board of Trade,
Bounties, Commerce, Distilling, Indentured Servants,
Iron, Linen, Lumber Products,
Naval Stores, Plantation,
Slaves, Smuggling, Spinning,
Trade, Woolen, West Indies,
and colonies by name.
Markets, *see* Commerce, Trade.
Martha's Vineyard, 116, 203.
Maryland, settled, 65–67; land
policy of, 66, 86, 358; government of, 68–69; and proprietors, 70–71; and English revolution, 71; land problem in,
86; manufactures in, 93; toleration act, 103; religious conditions in, 103–104; a royal
province, 104; education in,
107–108, 419; Germans in, 310;
industries in, 365; and immigration, 340; libraries, 421.
See Catholics, Calvert, Immigration, Plantation, Slaves,
South, Tobacco.
Marquette, Jacques, 325.
Marshall, Edward, 331.
Mary of England, 18.
Mason, Captain John, proprietor of New Hampshire, 137–
138.
Mason and Dixon's line, 209,
276.
Massachusetts, origin and charter, 125–126; transfer of charter, 127; leaders, 127–128;
settlement of, 128–129; an
oligarchy, 129; taxation in,
129–130, 148; representative
government, 131; intolerance
in, 131–134; absorbs New
Hampshire, 138; aggressiveness
of, 145, 147, 153; in New England Confederation, 147, 296;
expansion of, 148; liberal
elements in, 148; relations
with England, 152–154; and
royal commission, 155; charges
against, 154; and Charles II,
156–158; loss of charter, 158;
and Dominion of New Eng-
land, 159; new charter of
(1691), 160; population, 165;
land problems, 169, 359; labor
problems, 170, 361–62; fisheries, 172, 327, 371; ship-

building in, 173; trade of,
174–177; 375–377; Body of
Liberties, 182; and Quakers,
185; social conditions in, 177–
191; religion and morals, 180–
185; 404–407; witchcraft delusion, 185–187; intellectual
life, 188; education, 190–191;
416–417; and parliament, 271;
and independence, 282; and
immigration, 301, 310–312,
341, 359, 397, 399; in French-
English wars, 326–328; frontier
policy of, 336–337, 341; and
Indians, 152, 331–332; and
toleration, 351; and industries,
370–373; merchants in, 391.
See Great Awakening, General Court, Governor, Indians,
Maine, Navigation Acts, New
Hampshire, New England,
Physical Environment, Plym-
outh, Puritanism, Trade
Smuggling, West Indies.
Massasoit, and Pilgrims, 120.
Mast Industry, 175, 226, 372. *See*
Naval Stores.
Mathematics, 419–420.
Mather, Cotton, 401, 402, 420;
and science, 422; writings of,
444–445. *See* John Wise,
Witchcraft.
Mather, Increase, and Witch-
craft, 186; on liquor, 413.
Mathews, Captain Samuel, of
Virginia, plantation of, 93.
Matthews, John, governor of Vir-
ginia, 61.
Maverick, Samuel, 148, 154.
Mayflower, 119.
Mayflower Compact, 120.
Mayhew, Jonathan, 406–407.
Mechanics, *see* Artisans.
Medicine, 241, 424.
Mediterranean, trade in, 5, 14,
17.
Menendez, in Florida, 37.
Mennonites, in Pennsylvania,
308; and democracy, 317; so-
cial ideals of, 229–232, and
slavery, 401.
Mercantile system, 17, 62, 257–
259.
Merchants, English, 22; in-
crease of colonial, 357–358;
number and importance of,
391–392.
Merrimac River, 138.

NORTH AMERICA
1750
Showing claims arising out of
exploration and occupancy

English —————— French
Spanish